Dissimilar Similitudes

In this devotional image from the cloister of Wienhausen (Andachtsbild, Inv. Nr. Wie Kc 020), we find the so-called "Doubting Thomas" putting his finger into Christ's wound paired with an image of Christ's Ascension (Acts 1:9–12), in which only the vanishing feet are visible above and the gaze of those left behind seems to focus on the footprints. The image thus explores contact with salvation in two different ways. On the left, a follower literally touches Christ, although the gospel account (John 20:24–29) does not tell us that Thomas acted thus, only that Christ told him he could. On the right, the tangible evidence of Christ's grace is the trace left on the Mount of Olives in the prints of his feet. In the later Middle Ages, devotional images and objects focused the attention of worshippers on tactile ways of making contact with God.

Dissimilar Similitudes

Devotional Objects in Late Medieval Europe

Caroline Walker Bynum

ZONE BOOKS · NEW YORK

2020

ZONE BOOKS
633 Vanderbilt Street
Brooklyn, NY 11218

First paperback edition 2022
ISBN 978-1-942130-71-0

Printed in the United States of America.

Distributed by Princeton University Press,
Princeton, New Jersey, and Woodstock, United Kingdom

Library of Congress Cataloging-in-Publication Data
Names: Bynum, Caroline Walker, author.
Title: Dissimilar similitudes : devotional objects in late Medieval Europe / by Caroline Walker Bynum.
Description: Brooklyn, NY : Zone Books, 2020. | Includes bibliographical references and index.
Identifiers: LCCN 2019055435 (print) | LCCN 2019055436 (ebook) | ISBN 9781942130376 (hardcover) | ISBN 9781942130383 (ebook) | ISBN 9781942130390 (ebook)
Subjects: LCSH: Devotional objects — Europe. | Material culture — Religious aspects — Christianity. | Material culture — Europe. | Civilization, Medieval. | Resemblance (Philosophy) | History — Methodology.
Classification: LCC NK1652.2 S96 2020 (print) | LCC NK1652.2 (ebook) | DDC 704.9/4820940902 — dc23
LC record available at https://lccn.loc.gov/2019055435
LC ebook record available at https://lccn.loc.gov/2019055436

In Memoriam

Nora Bartlett

1949 – 2016

Contents

Dissimilar Similitudes

Preface

The essays in this volume first appeared in whole or in part as follows: "Holy Beds: Gender and Encounter in Devotional Objects from Fifteenth-Century Europe," in a very short form as "Encounter: Holy Beds," in *Gesta* 55.2 (Fall 2016), pp. 129–31; "'Crowned with Many Crowns': Nuns and Their Statues in Late Medieval Wienhausen," in *The Catholic Historical Review* 101.1 (2015), pp. 18–40 (reprinted by permission of the Catholic University of America Press); "The Sacrality of Things: An Inquiry into Divine Materiality in the Christian Middle Ages," in *Irish Theological Quarterly* 78.1 (2013), pp. 3–18 (reprinted by permission of Sage Publishing); "The Presence of Objects: Medieval Anti-Judaism in Modern Germany," in *Common Knowledge* 10.1 (Winter 2004), pp. 1–32 (reprinted by permission of Duke University Press); and "Avoiding the Tyranny of Morphology, or Why Compare?" in *History of Religions* 53 (May 2014), pp. 341–68 (reprinted by permission of the University of Chicago Press). A number of paragraphs in the final chapter appeared under the same title but in different form in "Footprints: The Xenophilia of a European Medievalist," in *Common Knowledge* 24.2 (2018), pp. 291–311.

These chapters were not all written at the same time or for the same audience. One (chapter 4, "The Presence of Objects") dates back to 2005. Two (the first, "Holy Beds," and the last, "Footprints") were in large part written for this volume. Each of the others (chapters 2, 3, 4, and 5) retains the original framing of the question it addresses. Hence, I intend that each can be read as a stand-alone piece. Taken together, however, the chapters ask similar questions about religion in the European Middle Ages. These are questions that they can in no way fully answer, for each is only a single example or a fragment of a much larger interrogation. Moreover, they focus on continental northern Europe (especially the areas of present-day Germany and the Low Countries), and one must always be careful about extrapolating specific practices from north to south. Nonetheless, each chapter is intended as a methodological challenge to current ways of asking questions about medieval religion, and each tries to provide an example of what a new answer might look like.

I have attempted to replace overlapping documentation with cross-references and to eliminate repetition. Nonetheless, both because each essay retains its original focus and because I rely here partly on some of my earlier work that is still debated and debatable, I have sometimes felt it wise to repeat a bit of evidence or explain a previous insight. I have illustrated and strengthened my arguments by adding many images, and I am grateful to Zone Books for facilitating this.

Any scholar who writes after a career of more than forty years has incurred debts too vast to be acknowledged in a mere list of names. I hope that those whom I have thanked in other books and articles or in the notes here will feel themselves recognized and appreciated. In this current project, however, I must single out for thanks my editor at Zone Books, Ramona Naddaff, always my best critic and interlocutor; Meighan Gale and Kyra Simone, also of Zone, for assistance with many different aspects of production, including gaining permissions for reproducing images; Susan Kramer for perceptive, often inspired, editing, help with image acquisition, and assistance with the index; and Alena Jones for unusually careful proofreading. I also thank Jeffrey Hamburger, Cynthia Hahn, and Yve-Alain Bois for dozens of pieces of art historical advice over many years, not only about the topics treated in this book but also more broadly; and my former student Eleanor Goerss, whose lively curiosity and capacious learning gave me several crucial tips as I was attempting to sort out the topics treated here. I am also extremely grateful to the three scholars who read the manuscript for Zone Books. Although their recommendations sometimes canceled each other out, I have learned from the seriousness with which they have taken my scholarly questions, and in several cases they have impelled me to far greater precision in argument and formulation. In the late spring of 2019, while I worked on this book, my husband Guenther Roth, always a supporter of my work, died after a long illness. I am glad to think that he knew, from other books I have dedicated to him and from our many years of help to each other in our scholarly endeavors, how much his love for me and pride in my work sustained me over all the years of our marriage.

I dedicate this collection to the memory of my friend Nora Bartlett, whose vibrant, wise, and often funny emails brightened every day of our long, transatlantic friendship. Without Nora, I find it hard to know what to read and indeed, once I decide what to read, what to think about it. Remembering her leads me to think with profound gratitude of the contributions to my intellectual life made by other colleagues I have lost over the past decades: Ethel Cardwell Higonnet, John Eastburn Boswell, Donald J. Wilcox, Charles T. Wood, Claudia Rattazzi Papka, Ann Freeman Meyvaert, Paul Jeffrey Meyvaert, Thomas F. Head, Olivia Remie Constable, Anne Middleton, and Astrid Witschi-Bernz. I have been blessed in my scholarly friends. None is forgotten.

Recent work in history, art history, and the history of religions has underlined, with striking urgency, the questions I address here: the agency of objects, the nature of good and bad comparison, the philosophical problems of representation and similitude. It therefore seems useful to preface these essays with a general introduction that situates them in recent and wide-ranging scholarly discussion. That discussion has been predicated on the glaring fact, too little commented on perhaps because it is so obvious, that the later Middle Ages is characterized by a growing abundance of holy things in an abundance of venues and discourses. All religions use objects to mirror, approach, propitiate, defend against, and interrogate an Other toward which they reach. Hence for all religions, objects raise the philosophical question of similitude: How can the earthly and the now mirror, reveal, intimate, or in some way point toward the ineffability, the dissimilitude, the non- or more-than-being, of the Power that some religions denominate the "divine"? But for the European Middle Ages, from about 1100 to 1500, the rapid proliferation of religious objects and of astonishing claims for them posed a special kind of challenge and opportunity.

I hope that my introduction, which is intended for the nonspecialist, will situate the questions I ask in the broader context of this medieval enthusiasm. The heart of the book lies, however, in the examples considered in the individual chapters. They are meant to suggest new ways of thinking not so much about discourses concerning objects as about religious objects themselves.

Figure I.1. Antependium of Rosary Altar from Church of Dominicans in Frankfurt, c. 1484. 78 × 185 cm (detail). Now in Heidelberg, Kurpfälzisches Museum, Inv. Nr. G 493. In an example of the literalism of late medieval devotion, roses plucked from the mouth of a praying friar depict the prayers he offers to the Virgin Mary, which she then weaves into a rosary. In an image such as this, the rose is not a metaphor or symbol of a devotion offered but rather an object that literalizes, embodies, and in some real sense *is* the fact of offering prayer.

INTRODUCTION

Holy Things and the Problem of Likeness

When a medieval nun spoke of the dangers of soiling her garment of chastity or of the duty of weaving a garland of roses for Mary the Virgin by saying the rosary, what was the meaning of the dress or the flower? Did the praying nun, clothed herself in the veil of a virgin, really think chastity was an intact garment ripped or dirtied by impure thoughts or bodily acts? Did she think she emitted a rose from her mouth while praying, as some preachers and some panel paintings might suggest? (See figure I.1.)[1] When craftsmen in Tuscany in the fourteenth or fifteenth century fashioned a crystal container that nestles in curling golden vine tendrils for the tooth of Mary Magdalen, did they or those who commissioned it think the fragment was Mary present behind the crystal? (See figure I.2.)[2] When, in 1383, a priest at Wilsnack in northern Germany discovered three Eucharistic hosts, intact yet bleeding after a fire, did he and his parishioners really hold, as they claimed, that the wafers were the visible flesh of Christ—and that this was so even if the hosts had not been consecrated?[3] What can it mean for chastity to be a garment, for a prayer to be a rose, for a tooth to be a person, for a bit of bread to be the body of God? And are these objects, which modern commentators tend to differentiate sharply as literary metaphor (garment of chastity), work of art (reliquary or panel painting), sacrament (consecrated Eucharistic host), or physical body part (tooth of a saint), presences in the same way? They have usually been discussed by theorists in isolation from each other. Yet the striking fact that confronts even casual readers or observers about the later Middle Ages is this ever-increasing plethora of holy objects. Is anything at all to be gained by considering them together as "things"?

Figure I.2. Reliquary of Mary Magdalen, fourteenth or fifteenth century. Made in Tuscany, Italy. Gilded copper, gilded silver, rock crystal, and gilded glass. 55.9 × 23.8 × 20.2 cm. The object revered in the central container is allegedly Mary Magdalen's tooth. Preserved behind crystal, which suggests the hardening of eternity, the tooth is also presented within curling vines, which suggest that it is still living and unfolding. The Metropolitan Museum of Art. Accession number 17.190.504. Gift of J. Pierpont Morgan, 1917.

A Plethora of Things

Objects proliferated in all religious texts and venues in the later Middle Ages. Liturgy and devotional writings are filled with references to them; theological treatises analyzed their meaning and value. Churches were crowded with them. Containers called reliquaries (themselves of an immense variety of shapes, sizes, and appearances) held all sorts of bones and body parts, bits of natural materials, fragments of cloth, and so forth.[4] (See figures I.3a–d and I.4.) Referred to by different names (*reliquiae*, remains, or *pignora*, pledges, or sometimes simply *res sanctae*, holy things) and not yet organized into the categories of first-, second-, and third-class relic familiar in modern canon law, relics included not only bits of bodies but also objects that had touched holy people or holy sites or that were understood to transfer the power of the holy by some sort of resemblance to or contact with it. They were inserted (sometimes visibly and sometimes hidden under the surfaces of paint or wood) into crucifixes, frescoes, wall paintings, and sculptures, displayed on altars, even worn by the faithful as a kind of jewelry or talisman.[5]

Ordinary domestic objects were also infused with religious power.[6] They acted. Oats blessed on New Year's Eve were understood to protect a farmer's cattle from disease; holy water restored health (spiritual and physical). Even unconsecrated objects were understood to act both up close and at a distance.[7] Amulets bearing religious or magical incantations warded off misfortune and made one lucky in love. A girdle depicting the wound in Christ's side might open the womb of a laboring woman and grant her a safe delivery.[8] As far as the power of objects is concerned, the line between holy and ordinary or domestic was porous indeed; almost anything might acquire the charge or spark of sacrality. According to what cultural anthropologists and folklorists call the principle of *similia similibus*—the conviction found in many cultures that like affects or effects like—objects could act to empower or protect against characteristics they in some sense resembled. Something red, for example, might stop or induce bleeding.[9]

In paintings and sculpture, a stunning array of objects was depicted. These objects (for example, swords, chalices, towers, dragons, lions, keys, griddles, and so forth) were sometimes understood as attributes—that is, as a kind of code for the saint in question and often for the form of his or her martyrdom as well. St. Jerome could, for example, be identified by his faithful lion, St. Peter by the keys he

Figures I.3a–d. Containers called reliquaries held all sorts of material (bones and body parts, fragments of cloth, earth, stones, and so forth) and were of an immense variety of shapes, sizes, and appearances, some of which reveal and some of which obscure the nature of the holy matter within.

a. Reliquary of St. Stephen, French, c. 1200. Princeton Art Museum, accession no. y1943–91. The little casket is shaped like a church, which suggests the gathering together of the saint's body parts and the communion of all the saints in heaven.

b. Arm reliquary of St. Nicholas of Myra, showing a mummified finger within, from Halberstadt Cathedral. Made shortly after 1225.

c. Reliquary of St. Thekla. Late fifteenth–early sixteenth century. German. Princeton Art Museum, accession no. y1954–127. The column and lion are attributes, representing some of the various forms of attempted martyrdom to which the saint was subjected. The relic (which has now disappeared, as is usual for reliquaries in museums) was probably in a crystal in the breast.

d. Reliquary pendant, Spanish, from 1550–1600, 5.4 × 4.13 cm, gold, *basse-taille* enamel, and glass. Walters Art Gallery, 46.10, acquired by Henry Walters. By the later Middle Ages, relics could be worn by laypeople as a kind of jewelry. This pendant has a relic inside; the mount is later.

Figure I.4. Reliquary box with stones and wood fragments from the Holy Land. Sixth to seventh century. 24 × 18.4 × 3 cm. From the Sancta Sanctorum treasure, Rome, Vatican, Museo Sacro, Inv. Nr. 61883.

carried, St. Margaret of Antioch by the dragon from whose belly she escaped, St. Lawrence by the griddle used to roast him, and so forth. (See figure I.5.) On altarpieces and panel paintings, things — often quite ordinary things — served as symbols or allegories that could both be enjoyed for what they were and also decoded as doctrinal statements. For example, a lily in the bedroom of the Virgin of the Annunciation signaled her purity; an oven or a fire behind a fire screen could suggest her bearing of Christ within her belly and also the Eucharistic bread that became him in the mass. A coral necklace worn by the Christ Child visually associated him with both the ancient tradition of coral amulets as protection from disease and the redness of Christ's blood, shed for humankind's redemption. (See figures I.6 – I.8.) Christ himself was depicted in various sorts of physical or mechanical apparatuses: as a wafer ground out by a host mill, a pool or fountain of blood squeezed out by a wine press, a figure whose hands and feet are pierced by vines and sheaves of wheat so that he almost becomes a garden plot. (See figure I.9.)[10]

In the liturgy chanted by clergy and heard by parishioners, in the private prayers of monks, nuns, and laypeople, and in the theological speculation the liturgy often inspired and impregnated, things proliferated. Although certain writers theorized God as "unknown" or "hidden," as obscurity itself, the writings of contemplatives and visionaries were ever more enthusiastically populated with figures and objects — the sights, sounds, smells, and tastes of glory. For example, the thirteenth-century beguine become nun Mechtild of Magdeburg described the souls of the blessed in heaven as darting about like fish in the sea but also as clear crystal containers (that is, reliquaries) through which their virtues gleamed like light.[11]

As Rachel Fulton Brown has shown with wonderful learning, the Virgin Mary became in the high Middle Ages the "container of the uncontainable." Mary's unbroken virginity stood in for the whole creation, which God entered without destroying, like light shining through a jewel.[12] An anonymous early thirteenth-century author of a series of sermons on the antiphon *Salve regina* exclaimed:

> Not only heaven and earth but also other names and words of things (*rerum vocabulis*) fittingly designate the Lady. She is the tabernacle of God, the temple, the house, the entry-hall, the bedchamber, the bridal-bed, the bride, the daughter, the ark of the flood, the ark of the covenant, the golden urn, the

Figure I.5. The saints were often identified by objects they carried, known as attributes, which served as a kind of code for the saint. This rood screen from St. Helen's Church, Ranworth, Norfolk, England—recognized as one of the finest examples of the genre—was probably painted in the fifteenth century and has figures of male and female saints. In this portion, devoted to the twelve apostles (of which we see four here), the saints depicted are Bartholomew (with the attributes of knife and book), James the Major (associated with one of the greatest pilgrimages of the Middle Ages and identified by the pilgrim staff), Andrew (identified here by the diagonal cross on which he was crucified), and Peter (with his attribute of the keys of heaven, given to him by Christ).

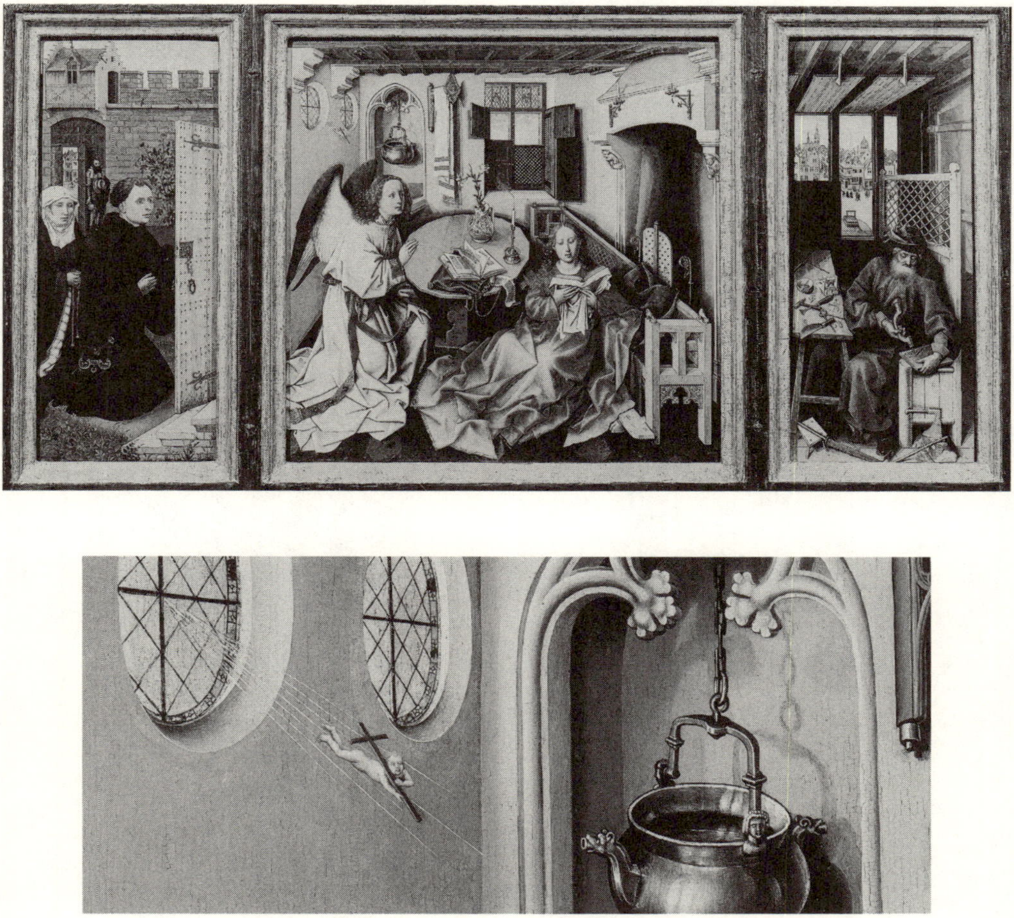

Figure I.6. Annunciation Triptych (known as the Merode altarpiece). Netherlandish. Workshop of Robert Campin, 1427–32. In the right-hand panel, the mousetrap that Joseph, Jesus's foster father, has just made is an example of the theological loading ordinary objects could have in late medieval images, for Christ himself is a trap to catch the devil. But the altarpiece is also a sophisticated exploration of levels of seeing and reality. The patrons looking through the open doorway, Mary receiving the angel, and the tiny baby sliding down the beam of light toward her womb are not all on the same ontological, visible, and physical level. The Metropolitan Museum of Art, the Cloisters Collection, 1956; accession no. 56.70a–c.

Figure I.7. The Virgin Mary and Christ before a fire screen. Follower of Robert Campin, early fifteenth century. The National Gallery, London. NG2609. The oven or fire behind a fire screen suggests Mary's bearing of Christ within her belly as well as the Eucharistic bread that becomes him in the mass. The large wicker fire screen behind the Virgin frames her as if it were a halo.

Figure I.8. Madonna and Child with Angels. Giovanni dal Ponte, 1410s. Florence, Italy. Tempera and tooled gold leaf on wood panel. Blanton Museum of Art, University of Texas at Austin; bequest of Jack G. Taylor, 1991, accession no. 1991.101. The child Jesus looks out at the viewer and raises his right hand in a gesture of blessing. In his left hand he holds a finch, a foreshadowing of the Crucifixion that refers to a legend that this bird removed a thorn from Jesus's crown and was marked by a drop of blood. Around his neck he wears a piece of coral, which both associates him with the ancient tradition of coral amulets as protection from disease and foreshadows the redness of the blood Christ will later shed for humankind's redemption.

Figure I.9. Host mill on a Swabian retable of about 1470, open state. Oil on wood. From the Old Master Collection, Ulm Museum Inv. Nr. AV 2150. Mary, with the assistance of the four Evangelists, provides the stuff of salvation by pouring grain into the funnel. The saints turn the mill. The prelates assembled below receive wafers that seem to become the baby Christ. The offer of grace in the Eucharist is here imagined as the product of mechanical apparatus and Christ comes to humankind as wafers of bread.

> manna, the rod of Aaron, the fleece of Gideon, the gate of Ezekiel, the city of God, the heaven, the earth, the sun, the moon, the morning star, the dawn, the lamp, the trumpet, the mountain, the fountain of the garden and the lily of the valley, the desert, the land of promise flowing with milk and honey, the star of the sea, the ship, the way in the sea, the fishing net, the vine, the field, the ark, the granary, the stable, the manger of the beast of burden, the store-room, the court, the tower, the castle, the battle-line, the people, the kingdom, the priesthood.[13]

Making a theological and/or devotional point, these references stress not just containing ("ark," "urn," "net," "manger") but the containing of fertility ("bridal-bed," "dawn," "vine," and so forth). Even the "desert" is paired with a land "flowing with milk and honey."

For a medieval worshipper, to use things in their specific materiality to talk about that which is clearly other or beyond or unfamiliar is not, as is sometimes thought, either an arbitrary or simply a traditional move. The anonymous commentator on the *Salve regina* glosses "names" as "words" that refer to "things," not to abstractions or concepts. Moreover, they refer "fittingly." And "fittingly" means both appropriately in theological terms and powerfully. As the modern critic James Wood has said: "independent, generative life . . . comes from likening something to something else. . . . As soon as you liken x to y, x has changed, and is now x + y, which has its own parallel life."[14] The medieval writer clearly understands that if you liken Mary the mother of God to a trumpet or a fishing net, a manger or a storeroom, it changes your perception of and access to Mary. It may also change your perception of trumpets and mangers, so that, forever after, encountering the objects may remind you of a specific Other in heaven. The reference calls up, or to, a physical reality—a concrete content—that is more than evocative or elegant, more than simply rooted in, or echoing, its scriptural or liturgical source. It asserts something basic about the relationship of an Other to creation, underlining the Other as an engendering or a flowing out.

Ritual on earth mirrored heaven not only in the language of analogy but also physically. Nuns not only sang praises to a Christ crowned in glory; they also received cloth crowns of their own at their investiture in hope of future crowning. Dukes and merchants who wanted support in war or business commissioned real crowns for statues of Christ and his mother in churches.[15] When people gave to the Virgin or the saints or to God those objects we call

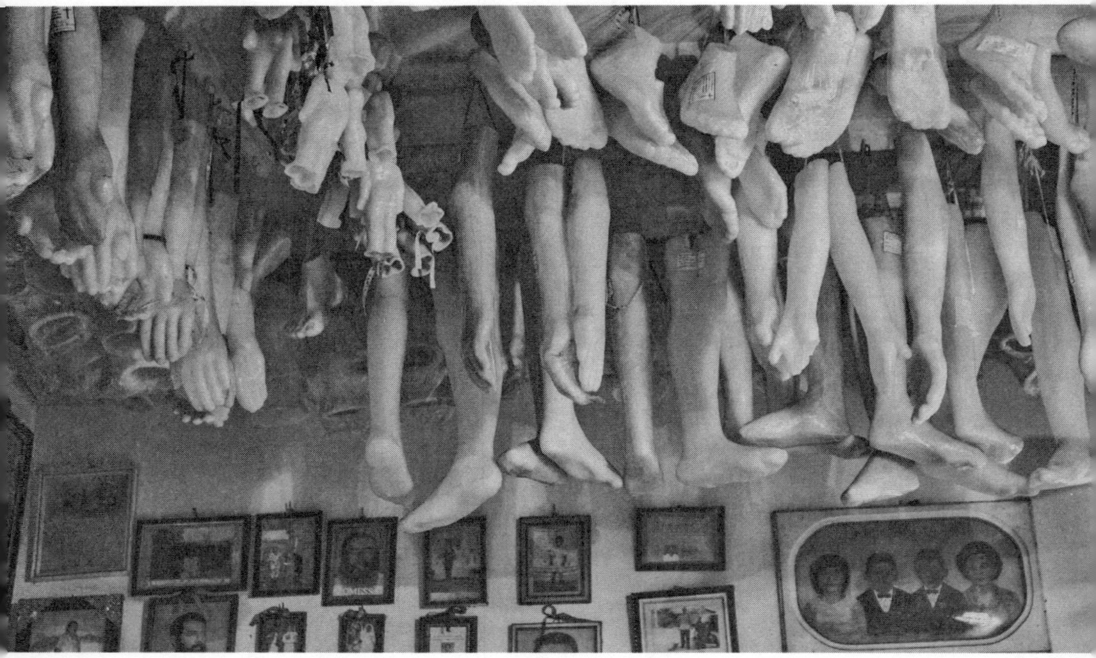

Figure I.10. In the room of miracles in the church of Nosso Senhor do Bonfim, in Salvador da Bahia, Brazil, dozens of wax images of body parts hang from the ceiling. These models of healed body parts are objects called *ex-votos*, from the vow made by the petitioner or penitent to give back to God the physical reality God is understood to have healed or saved, a gift given in return for a gift.

ex-votos—objects such as models of healed arms and legs, the shoes of babies saved from death, crutches thrown away, and so forth—they were giving back to God the physical reality he was understood to have healed, a gift given in return for a gift.[16] (See figure I.10.) Measures of the length of Christ's body or body parts brought back by pilgrims from the Holy Land were understood to transport the presence of Christ. Leather or linen strings that measured Christ's footprints or Mary's, and even measures of relics (such as thorns from the crown of thorns or the body parts or clothing of saints), carried not so much memory or a proof of travel to holy places as the presence of the holy itself. (See figure 6.8.) Even the power of statues could be transported by their "lengths" or measures.[17] Hence, objects could carry presence, power, or even identity by mathematical rather than visual similarity. In the later Middle Ages, worshippers sometimes gave to a church or its saint an amount of wick or candle wax calibrated to their own height or weight, as if they were in some sense giving themselves by offering their measures.[18]

Increasingly in the thirteenth to fifteenth centuries, religious experience was literalized into encounter with objects. A twelfth-century monastic author could speak of nails in the hand as a metaphor of cloistered obedience, but by the thirteenth century religious writers claimed that the nails of the crucified appeared physically in the body of Francis of Assisi as stigmata (wounds) with clearly visible and tactile black nailheads inside the wounds. Crusaders and pilgrims wore iron or cloth crosses on their garments; but some went further and claimed to see crosses miraculously incised on bodies themselves.[19] As veneration of the physical crucifix increased, claims that it spoke or moved increased also. Depictions of Francis of Assisi receiving the stigmata show him marked not by Christ but by an object—a crucifix—bearing the carved or painted figure of Christ.[20] (See figure I.11.) By the fifteenth century, we find the sophisticated Franciscan theologian Johannes Bremer grouping under the rubric *reliquiae* what modern analysts see as relics of the Crucifixion proper (both things in contact with Christ's body, such as the holy lance or a thorn from the crown of thorns, and bits of Christ's body itself, such as Christ's foreskin or blood) and the Eucharist (invisibly Christ's body but visibly bread and wine). In such analysis, the Eucharist is an object among objects, albeit a religiously superior one.[21]

Living as we do in a hyperacquisitive and image-saturated world,

Figure I.11. Hand-colored woodcut made by one Caspar (active in Regensburg about 1470–80) and later pasted into a book from the Franciscan house of Ingolstadt. Munich, Bayerische Staatsbibliothek, Rar.327–1/4#1. On this little prayer card, the wounds in Francis's body seem to be made not so much directly by Christ as by a devotional object, the crucifix.

ever bombarded by visual and auditory stimuli, we are inclined to see late medieval religious experience as similarly saturated, as if the gaudily painted late medieval church (and churches *were* gaudily colored) was a kind of Times Square, shrieking and blinking with light and sound. Inured perhaps to stimuli because we experience so many of them, we forget how image-poor much medieval experience was. We need to imagine the power of a medieval prayer card or an altarpiece or relic, or the impact of a chant, in a world where such an object or sound might be all we had to conjure up — to relate us to — an unknown realm of power. In such a world we might have to return again and again to a single depiction or prayer, object or sound, to find in it ever new, even radically new, meaning.

A glance at one of the many representations of the so-called "arms of Christ" (*arma Christi*) makes this clear.[22] (See figure I.12.) Such depictions of Christ surrounded by objects of torture are not narratives of the events of the Crucifixion. Judas's kiss in betraying Christ, the bag of silver he received, and his subsequent hanging are often telescoped into one image; objects such as the knife of Christ's circumcision (as a baby) are included to evoke and link the many bloodsheddings of his life. The devotee would move around such a picture in meditation, choosing whatever thing seemed most appropriate to the religious need he or she felt at that particular moment of prayer.[23] In the so-called Sunday Christ (also known as "Christ crucified by the sins of the world") such depictions were used to associate various occupations (such as carpentry, plowing, and so forth) with sinning against the Sabbath or against God. (See figure I.13.) Even here the occupations and the sins committed are represented not by human figures but by things — the tools of the workers or, occasionally, by a kind of partial figure that serves as shorthand for the act (spitting, gossiping, and the like).[24] The meditating person travels around the image, identifying Christ's suffering and human responsibility for it in object after object, accessed through ever new and varied sensual and intellectual paths. Or, to give a parallel example: if we study the depiction of one of the Seven Sorrows of Mary in the extremely popular devotional book *The Mirror of Human Salvation*, we find that, in some variants, not only are the *arma Christi* arranged around Mary but a little image of a green hump with footprints on it serves almost as an attribute signaling the Ascension (which left Mary behind and therefore sorrowing). A geographical location becomes an object among other objects.[25] Indeed, moving around images of objects is what the anonymous commentator on the *Salve regina* is doing when he lays dozens of comparisons over the greeting to Mary that will itself be repeated in ritual after ritual. If Mary is like the whole of creation, a single reference in a single liturgical text becomes the entire universe, changing the way the hearer understands both Mary and the world and making both a place of almost infinite devotional creativity.

In this aspect of response, praying before a medieval altarpiece or prayer card, hearing a chant, viewing a reliquary, even listening to a saint's story, was probably more like clicking on a site on the worldwide web and connecting to whatever comes up than like standing passively in Times Square bombarded by sound and movement. Indeed modern historians have drawn an analogy between the internet and the medieval gloss, which, even as it presents itself on the manuscript page, looks something like a modern hypertext. (See figure I.14.) But the interactivity, so to speak, of medieval devotion would have taken more effort and required more knowledge by the viewer or hearer than our own hyperconnected world requires. And the individual object would have been far more central to religious experience because accompanied by, and cluttered by, far fewer other objects of power. Thus, while it is helpful to draw an analogy between some contemporary ways of experiencing and the nonlinearity with which a medieval person moved around a text or object, we must not forget that the objects which a medieval nun or monk, layperson or schoolchild, encountered and used devotionally had their power in part because they were few as well as valuable.[26] It is true that the extremely wealthy attempted to amass vast collections of relics, and rich churches commissioned ever more images of the

Figure I.12. This image of the *Schmerzensmann* (Man of Suffering) with the *arma Christi* (arms of Christ) is a colored woodcut from about 1470–85, now in the Germanisches Nationalmuseum, Nuremberg. The Christ figure is surrounded by the instruments used to torture him, but many moments of his life are pictured simultaneously here, for the instruments include the knife of his circumcision as a baby, Judas's kiss of betrayal in the garden, and the column of the flagellation as well as the nails of the Crucifixion. Such depictions are not so much narratives of the gospel story as objects the devotee might use in meditation, moving around the image as spiritual needs seemed to demand. It is striking that most of the abuses of Christ are pictured here as committed by things.

Wer dis gebet sprichet mit andacht der het als mengen tag aplas als menig wonden unser herr
ihs xps het enphangen durch unsern willen. Herre ihu xpe Ich ermanen dich dines gottlichen

Figure I.13. The figure known as the "Sunday Christ" or "Christ crucified by the sins of the world" was found on parish churches to warn the laity against violating the Sabbath or other days of obligatory church attendance by working or engaging in frivolous activities such as games or gossiping. These sins were depicted as the worker's instruments (ploughs, hammers, and so forth) that attack Christ, the suffering servant, and draw from his wounds fresh streams of blood. The motif of the Sunday Christ is found especially in southern England and Wales and on the continent in Alpine regions. This monumental example is from St. Breage's Church, Cornwall, England.

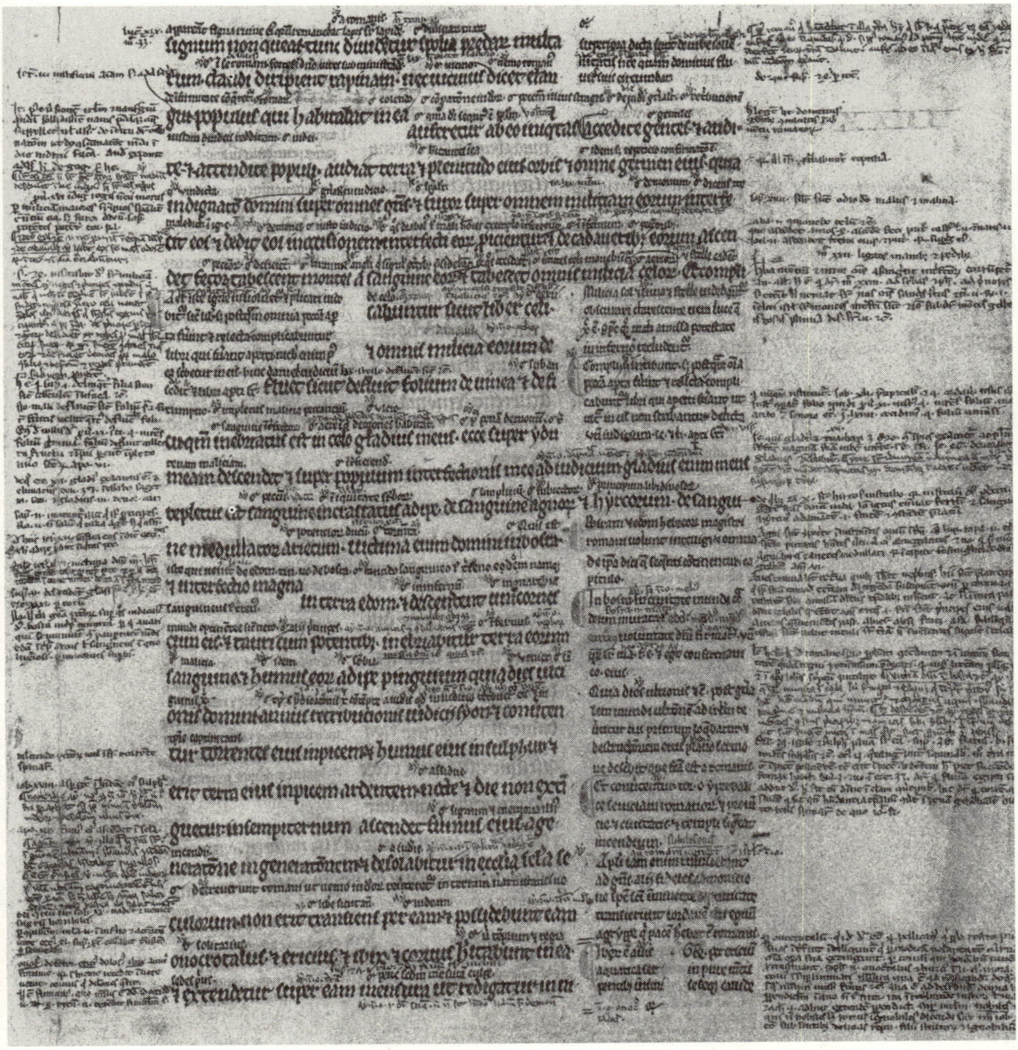

Figure I.14. Bible with commentary from the *Glossa Ordinaria*, text material from c. 850–1499. Department of Special Collections, Stanford University Libraries, M0389, Medieval Manuscript fragments, box 1, folder 9. Around the biblical text are added glosses (commentaries) from the famous medieval "Ordinary Gloss." The image shows clearly the way in which medieval glossing made what was almost a hypertext of a central manuscript, so that the student or reader could go back and forth between main text and information about and interpretations of it.

saints, but this amassing was not because of any loss of significance by individual objects. More was better exactly because each object had power. Even that precursor to the museum — the early modern "cabinet of wonders" — was initially a collection of powerful (not merely valuable) things; that is why they were denominated marvels or "wonders."[27]

People in the Middle Ages encountered ordinary buckets and milking stools, cows, birds, and babies, of course. But almost anything could become charged with special power — holy, magical, or simply unusual (nor, as I explained earlier, were types of power always sharply differentiated).[28] Even a part of a bone or the inner organ of a holy person could transmit his or her entire presence, *pars pro toto*.[29] A column in an Italian church that looked like a column in Jerusalem might come to be treated as what Anthony Cutler denominates a "visual contact relic" and Nadine Mai calls (with greater precision) a "similarity relic" — that is, an object that has the same effect as the holy place or object it exactly resembles and evokes.[30] In such cases, the likeness of an object (that is, its visible or optical likeness) itself confers power and agency, even without contact to the original.[31]

Indeed, in considering the efficacy of objects, we need to expand the category of "visual contact relic" or "similarity relic" to include parallels of dimensionality as well as of shape and appearance. The column of the flagellation in Bologna, studied by Nadine Mai, acquires holiness from its exact duplication of dimensions, not just its appearance, and documents explicitly refer to this likeness as *similitudo*.[32] (See figure I.15.) "Similarity" could be mathematical — that is, a sameness of length or breadth as well as of appearance. As I discussed earlier, exact measures of Christ's body or Mary's, or even of statues and relics, carried the holy. The Bayerisches Nationalmuseum in Munich possesses measures of a statue of a pope, of a thorn from the crown of thorns, of the statues of Mary and the Christ Child at Loreto, and of St. Sebastian's footprints in Rome, which were considered useful to induce pregnancy, cure illness, and protect from enemies, fire, and flood.[33] Color itself, without similarity of shape or other aspects of appearance, could carry likeness and hence power. The birthing girdle that was thought to reduce birth pangs and to open the laboring womb was understood to be effective because it reproduces, as a parallel structure and shape, the vagina-shaped

Figure I.15. Here we see a pillar in Bologna, known as the "column of the flagellation," that acquires its holiness from its exact duplication of both the dimensions and the appearance of the column of the flagellation in Jerusalem. Documents explicitly refer to this as *similitudo*, so that likeness here almost acquires a power to act on its own.

wound in Christ's side from which he gave birth to the salvation of humankind.[34] The Christ Child wears coral in a number of paintings not just because medieval babies did sometimes wear coral as an amulet against bleeding and injury but also because its redness evokes Christ's blood as a talisman against destruction and damnation. (See figure I.8.) In wearing a red amulet or tying around the wrist a red string, a medieval devotee might "put on" Christ's blood for physical and spiritual healing, just as the baby held by his mother in this painting puts on, proleptically, his own accomplishment of salvation.

Such objects were understood not only as protective but also as dangerous in the variety of their potentialities. The fear of images, of relics, and of realist interpretations of the Eucharist, found already in the fifteenth century not only among Lollards and other dissident groups but also in much orthodox preaching and advising of the laity and the cloistered, grew at least initially from a sense that objects were perilously powerful—and powerful especially in their similitude to the holy Other—not from any mere disdain for them. Long before Calvinist iconoclasm, theologians and preachers warned against making holy objects into "idols."[35] The Dominican Bartholomew of Florence, for example, attacked the wooden tablets carved with Jesus's holy name whose popularity was rapidly spread by San Bernardino in the fifteenth century. However much Bernardino maintained that the tablets were only triggers of devotion, opponents attacked them as idols, arguing that no manmade circle but only the Eucharist could "represent" God.[36] In this case, even the circular shape of the devotional object, mimicking the shape of the Eucharistic wafer, was opposed by some theologians as a threat to God's singular power. Often aware of the potential contradiction in their discussions, theologians and spiritual directors supported the education of both the literate and the illiterate by objects and images yet tried to uphold "imageless contemplation" as a higher form of access to God.[37]

The objects I study in each of these chapters are all holy objects, freighted with such power and such contradiction. That is, they are things or stuff used by worshippers to lift their earthly experiences and beliefs toward an Other that is beyond or outside the here and now, or to bring that beyond (sometimes literally, as in the case of stigmata, animated wall paintings, or Eucharistic miracles) into a time and space that is here. The issue at stake in my discussion is not, however, the nature of their materiality. Materiality has been keenly discussed for the past ten years by anthropologists, art historians, literary critics, philosophers, and historians of religion.[38] But that is not my topic here.

Nor is my topic the relationship of such objects to Eucharistic theology, especially the doctrine of transubstantiation, although in considering the problem of likeness I do consider the Eucharist at some length in the articles collected here. A number of scholars, chief among them Peter Browe and Gavin Langmuir, have argued that the doctrine of transubstantiation led to an increase in Eucharistic miracles because literalist Eucharistic theology stimulated skepticism and hence miracles that refuted such skepticism or assuaged the guilt it caused.[39] Building in part on such reasoning, some recent historians have not so much argued as assumed that the metaphysics of transubstantiation became the basic way of thinking about change and representation in Christianity in the late Middle Ages and Reformation.[40] Yet the fundamental aspect of medieval Christianity that distinguished it from its sister religions, Judaism and Islam, and would come to distinguish it from early modern Protestantism was not Eucharistic theology per se but the proliferation of increasingly tactile and insistent things—winged altarpieces, moveable statues, prayer cards with raised, Braille-like images and text, oozing wall paintings, bodies and body parts of saints—that to the horror of some and the delight of others hovered on the brink of animation, sometimes tipping over into life.[41] Given the late medieval enthusiasm for enactments of transformation generally (in, for example, stories of werewolves and other shape-changers, in the proliferation of claims of miraculous bodily changes such as stigmata or mystical pregnancy, and in increasing philosophical and scientific acceptance of efforts at species transformation such as alchemy), it seems wrong to privilege transubstantiation and Eucharistic theology as the ontology underlying assumptions about the world rather than to understand the increasing realism of Eucharistic theory as one manifestation of a more wide-ranging and general attitude.[42]

My concern here, however, is neither the understanding of materiality that underlay the power of objects nor the theories of transformation that were sometimes used to explain it. My concern is the question of "likeness."[43] That is, assuming as they did that heaven exists and access to it is possible, how did medieval Christian worshippers understand earthly stuff (down to the lowliest rock or worm) to mediate between earth and heaven, representing or communicating each to the other? For to medieval Christians, God is Other. "No man hath seen God at any time" (John 1:18).[44] Moreover, as Exodus 20:4 enjoined: human beings should make and worship no graven images nor "the *likeness* of any thing that is in heaven above, or in the earth beneath, [or] in the waters under the earth." *Similitude* itself is a problem. Nothing "like" earth in any sense should be understood or revered as representing God. Yet God is also creator, and as creator, he is the author of everything here below. Human beings are made in his image (*imago*) and likeness (*similitudo*) (Genesis 1:27) just as Christ is his image in a special sense; and nature is God's book, containing traces of himself.[45] The concept of *imago*, used in many senses by theologians, conveyed an idea of mimesis (not necessarily identity) and was therefore a way of thinking about how things relate or refer to God.[46] Moreover, theologians from the early church to that opponent of images John Calvin maintained that God's signatures, traces, and footprints, are in the world so that humankind should be able to argue from them to him.[47] But how can objects be "like" something that is Other — something that cannot, and should not, be represented, named, or imaged? The essays collected here consider then not medieval theories of matter and change but rather how, in the Middle Ages, particular things were understood to point to, look like, refer to, even convey the un-representable. The kind of holy objects I treat here raise questions about "representation" and "likeness" much debated recently by art historians, semioticians, and students of religion, as well as questions concerning the agency of objects and access to them discussed by anthropologists and cognitive scientists.

Approaches to the Power of Things: Historical, Art Historical, and Anthropological

Any study of how medieval things refer or make present must begin with the brilliant and often misunderstood work of Johan Huizinga, *The Autumn of the Middle Ages* (first Dutch edition 1919), published in a flowing but not literal English translation, shortened and lacking most of its documentation, in 1923.[48] Historians must still ask, as Huizinga asked long ago: Why was there such a proliferation of things, which Huizinga calls a search for "concrete expression," at the heart of late medieval religious experience? What did such expression enable? Was it in danger of becoming petrified, mechanical, or overly familiar? In an example he made famous, Huizinga describes the fourteenth-century saint Henry Suso dividing each apple he eats into four parts, three for the Trinity and one for the love with which the Virgin Mary offers an apple to her young son. Suso leaves the fourth piece unpeeled because little boys do not like their apples peeled.[49] Huizinga views such behavior, which seems as odd to modern readers as it did to some medieval theologians and to the early Protestants who reacted against it, not as unholy or superstitious but as a "sanctification of all aspects of life"—a sanctification that, however, "overloads belief."[50] Although himself critical of such fusing of what modern thinkers consider to be separate worldly and religious spheres, Huizinga treated the increased materiality and literalism of late medieval practice with profound understanding of how it made faith stable and immediate to worshippers. He also argued that it threatened to tip devotion into ordinary day-to-day experiences that can be ignored or even ridiculed. Huizinga's work—one of the dozen great treatments of the Middle Ages written in the twentieth century—thus raises the question of the power and the danger of likeness. If that which gestures toward the eternal, the divine, the "other," is too close to earth, too literally like the ordinary, can it lift the worshipper to heaven? How can cutting an apple be "like" approaching or loving God?

The past century has seen a number of major theorizings of medieval objects that have focused on only a part of the range Huizinga considered. The great Erwin Panofsky, drawing on Aby Warburg's enthusiasm for objects, especially folk material and other items and motifs not usually considered by art historians, expanded older ideas of iconography from the identification of painter, subject, venue, and so forth to an iconological theory of how one might decode the objects (such as, for example, the ovens and coral necklaces mentioned above) in medieval painting using theology, exegesis, or devotional writing. Much art historical writing in the mid-twentieth century followed Panofsky's lead.[51] Art historians have also attempted, using C. S. Peirce's semiotic theory, to describe objects such as relics and religious images with his threefold categories of index (a sign that denotes its object by virtue of an actual connection), icon (also called "likeness" or "semblance"—a sign that denotes its object by virtue of a quality that is shared by them, that is, that "imitates" or "resembles" its object), and symbol (a sign that points to another entity or concept because it is assigned in a system of signifiers to do so).[52] Hence, a painting or statue is an icon, because it "looks like" or "depicts" a holy figure; a relic is an index, because it comes from (that is, has a "real relation" to) what it stands for; an image such as a lily in the liturgy or on an altarpiece is a symbol, because it designates its referent (purity) only in a known system of signs.

Even a glance at a few of the kind of objects I enumerated earlier makes clear how much such analyses, though advances over many earlier treatments, leave out. For example, one may learn a great deal about the splendid triptych of the Annunciation known as the Merode altarpiece (workshop of Robert Campin) by placing the mousetrap that Joseph, Jesus's foster father, has just made against the background of discussion, going back to the patristic period, of Christ on the cross as trap for the devil.[53] (See figure I.6.) The lily in the Virgin's bedroom is also clearly a reference to her purity. But such iconological analysis leaves unexplored the way in which viewpoints or even, we might say, ontological levels are explored. How would a medieval viewer actually view or pray before such a religious object; how would he or she, identifying with the patrons on our left for whom the door is open, actually see the event not only of the angel appearing to Mary but also of the tiny baby sliding down a sunbeam into the space of both bedroom and womb? Are patron, Mary, angel, and descending baby all on the same level of see-ability and physical, earthly existence? Moreover, what does the placing, on the far right, of a completed mousetrap on the window ledge toward the town square suggest about how any sinful viewer, perhaps himself or herself part of the townspeople, might be freed by a trapping Christ?

Or, if we turn to another example, the Mary Magdalen reliquary, it seems that Peirce's distinctions fail to indicate what is really at stake. (See figure I.2.) The tooth, for example, is an index (because physically connected to the holy body from which it comes) and yet also has iconic elements. Although it is probably not a human tooth, it looks like the body fragment it signifies and therefore by a kind of resemblance signifies body.[54] It is clearly more than a symbol. Not merely signified or pointed to by the tooth, the saint is fully present behind the crystal in soul and body, just as she is also present in heaven. Not only is she not the part she looks like; the part is also not really a tooth since it is presented by golden vines and rock crystal both as something living and growing and yet also as something frozen into the gem-like permanence of eternity. The power of the object lies, I would suggest, not so much in indexicality as in the paradox of what we might call "dissimilar similitude"—that is, both in the dissimilarity of tooth, body, hardened gem, and unfolding vine to each other and in the wholeness of heaven they, taken together, present and re-present.[55] If the analytical categories of index, icon, and symbol do not work very well fully to describe the relic in its reliquary, they seem even less helpful for the garment of chastity I discuss above. Clearly not index or icon, it is much more literally what it refers to than we usually think a symbol is.[56]

Such considerations have led historians, art historians, and students of religion to raise questions concerning the agency of objects and access to them recently discussed by anthropologists and cognitive scientists. Some have had recourse to the theories of psychologists to suggest that certain shapes, colors, and so forth, have an impact on the human brain independent of the particular cultures that produce them or the understandings in those cultures of what the objects signify.[57] With greater sophistication, some art historians have employed the theories of Alfred Gell or Bruno Latour to argue that images are "living pictures" or agents, not symbols or signs pointing to an other but themselves presences. To such scholars, religious objects are less representations of particular moments in a sacred story that need decoding (although there may be elements of this) than participations in the immediate and palpable power of the holy.[58] Or, following the MET (Material Engagement Theory) of Lambros Malafouris and Colin Renfrew, some scholars propose that we abandon the current mind/object dichotomy entirely and concentrate instead on networks of engagement (sensual, affective, and spiritual as well as cognitive) between people and things.[59] Hence in the words of Byzantine historian Glenn Peers, separation of object and presence is an illusion: "a reading of late antique animism would view all objects as potentially communicative subjects. This . . . is a relational position: that is, all human and material things relate in transformative and productive ways, and they do so . . . as equal participants."[60]

The chapters that follow provide many examples that can be

understood as such objective agency or presence. Chapter 6, on the footprints of Christ supposedly left behind on the Mount of Olives outside Jerusalem when he ascended into heaven, underlines how devotees employed physical traces left by the gone-away Jesus to convey his power from Palestine to Europe. Christ's actual presence traveled not only in depictions or outlines of the prints but also in particles or bits of them (both sand and stone) and in aniconic measurements of their length. The crowns and veils I discuss in the chapter on Wienhausen themselves formed the girl child into a nun. The Judensau, an apotropaic and anti-Semitic image that I discuss in "The Presence of Objects," was understood by Christian contemporaries not only to depict Jewish activities but also to itself act. Placed on the gables of inns, on bridges, and on city gates to ward off Jewish presence, this disgusting object showed Jews suckling from the teats and anus of a pig. It was understood not merely to announce that Jews were unwelcome but to actually repel them, insuring that, if expelled, they would not return.[61]

As the case of the Judensau or the nun's garment of chastity suggests, some applications of cognitive theory to images and artifacts seem reductive, hence misleading. The anti-Semitic image of the Judensau is dependent on long-standing cultural assumptions in Christian Europe about the relationship of Jews to money and money to excrement, and it echoes far more than human reactions to the smell of pigs. The depiction of virginity as an intact garment rests not so much on bodily fears of penetration as on medieval assumptions about women's work and about clothing as constituting, not merely reflecting status. Nonetheless, despite some reductive misuse, the recent interest in objects and how exactly they act has been not just productive but positively liberating for medievalists. The understanding of things as agents or presences, especially in the sophisticated analysis given by Alfred Gell to non-Western as well as Western examples, has done much to induce medieval art historians to consider a wider range of objects than the altarpieces, sculptures, and manuscript illuminations that used to be taken as the extent of "medieval art," and to re-embed the things they study in the contexts of liturgical performance, private meditation, and daily life, where they clearly belong. I cite here, as an example of such new attention to the agency of objects, a charming study by Aden Kumler, who analyzes a manuscript in which the movements and positions in a

Christian ritual seem to be depicted not so much by the movement in space of the officiants as by the vessels used.[62] (See figure I.16.) In such depictions, we the readers see the ritual enactment of the mass as if it is performed by the chalices, patens, candles, and other objects themselves. Those who perform the ritual appear only as circles that look like wreaths, which are their tonsures seen from above.

For all the recent stress on what objects do, it is, however, difficult to move completely beyond attention to what a devotional image or a devotional object depicts, represents, or presents itself as being. And questions of "representation" have been much debated recently by art historians. Although a Renaissance portrait may be like the sitter, is a Picasso or Braque portrait "like" its object in the same way? How does it "represent" the sitter? Suppose it has only one eye or breast?[63] Moreover, can a portrait of the Virgin Mary look like the Virgin Mary? We have no record of what she looked like. But the absence of any earlier image is almost beside the point. The question is rather: Can the now and here refer to a realm beyond the earthly, and if so how? Can any object "represent" the queen of heaven (or *a fortiori* Christ the God-man or God himself)? This is in fact the question of iconoclasm or iconophilia, debated repeatedly in the Christian tradition and solved for the Middle Ages in somewhat different ways for the Eastern and Western churches. I do not intend to engage that issue directly here, in part because it has been extensively discussed by others (a discussion I summarize in chapter 3) and in part because I want to return the question of "image" to the question of "thing."[64] My topic is not that discussed by Christian theologians of East and West in the eighth to ninth centuries: Can one depict or image holy persons in the material stuff of paint and gold leaf or in three-dimensional statues of wood or marble? My concern is rather to reinsert physical images, sculptures, and icons where I think they belong—that is, in a conversation about how all holy things refer (including blessed water and oats, bits of saintly bones, and liturgical references to gems and flowers). How did people in the late medieval West think devotional things meant? Does—*can*—a nun's crown (a simple cloth circlet) represent the golden crown of martyrdom the nun hopes to attain in heaven? If so, how? Suppose her earthly crown does not look like a crown at all? Can it be "like"—can it "represent"—the crown of the heavenly Jerusalem?

Thus my question is: What does it mean for something (whether

Figure I.16. London, British Library, Add. MS 57534, fol. 62v. In this explanation and graphic illustration of the exact moves to be made in the ritual of the mass, the ceremony seems almost to be performed by the vessels used. The officiants are represented by the little circles at the bottom and in the middle, which are their tonsures seen from above.

crown or garment, icon or sculpture, miraculous occurrence or poetic image) to be "like" something else religiously? In this query, it will be clarifying to explore a little further the concept of "representation." For to "represent" can mean more than simply to "show"; it can mean to re-present or present anew or stand in for. An elected delegate can, for example, represent Denmark or the state of New York without "looking like" these entities. Some relationship or function or identity of interest (if not of appearance) is, however, assumed between a representative and what he or she represents.[65] Recent art historical writing sometimes rejects the idea of art as representing anything in the sense of looking like or standing in for something else. What does a Barnett Newman line or a Mark Rothko square "represent," one might ask. Yet the line raises the question of its material and perhaps even, one might suggest, of the nature of "line-ness." It is hard to see how one can move completely "beyond representation," as the title of a conference in 2012 suggests.[66] Beyond a certain type of decoding, yes; beyond all representing or re-presenting, no.

To deny that medieval objects or images are "like" the Other they evoke and yearn toward removes many of the most interesting questions about them. To a medieval devotee, things are agents and representations; but they are more. They are likenesses ontologically (that is, as what they are). Incense is really like the rising up of a prayer; gold is really like heavenly light or power in more than an arbitrary or simply attributed sense. The veil and crown of a nun do not merely symbolize her virginity; they *are* her intactness. The flesh of Francis of Assisi is not only nail-like; it has literally become Crucifixion nails, even if Francis, despite being known as the *alter Christus*, does not become Christ.[67] Although the stigmata of Francis, the bloody wafer of a host-desecration miracle, the tooth of a saint presented in crystal, the nun's habit, and the gold of a statue's crown are not "like" the Other of heaven and of God in the same way, they are not simply symbols, icons, or indexes. All are "like" the holy ontologically—that is, in more than an assigned or arbitrary, literal or purely visual sense. Hence, in the chapters that follow, I agree with recent emphases on the agency of objects and recent efforts to extend understandings of representation beyond visual "looking like." But I go further to consider the problem of likeness or similitude by focusing on objects themselves.

What These Case Studies Suggest

The chapters that follow explore likeness by studying in detail particular things: crowns and dresses, beds and dolls, relics and bleeding hosts, the footprints of gods and humans. They consider what people saw and did in acts of devotion in addition to what theologians wrote. As Gertrude the Great of Helfta said, supposedly quoting Hugh of St. Victor: We need things. If the heavenly Jerusalem has no gems of the sort we find on earth, there is nonetheless in it "nothing lacking." "For if no such things are there in outward appearance [*per speciem*], they are all there in likeness [*per similitudinem*]."[68] Or as that theorist so important for the entire Middle Ages, the figure known to us as pseudo-Dionysius, said: "dissimilar similitudes" or "figures without resemblance" elevate our minds better than resemblances because they do not mislead us into taking images literally—for example, into thinking that heavenly beings are actually made of gold.[69] As both Gertrude and pseudo-Dionysius make clear, to affirm "dissimilar similitude" is not to reject representation or deny likeness nor is it to understand either in a strictly literal or visual sense. To Gertrude, "likeness" is not "outward appearance" but a deeper similarity. To pseudo-Dionysius, "similitudes" are "without resemblance" but they are still specific "figures" that elevate our minds in specific ways toward heaven.

Philosophers and theologians from Augustine to the fifteenth century discussed the nature of "likeness" as a question of both ontology and predication.[70] For example, Thomas Aquinas's *Summa contra Gentiles* explains (bk I, ch. 32): "It is . . . evident that nothing can be predicated univocally of God and other things. An effect that does not receive a form specifically the same as that through which the agent acts cannot receive according to a univocal predication the name arising from that form." In other words, Thomas explains, we cannot say that the heat of the sun and the heat of sunshine can be called hot univocally (that is, by a term having only one sense), nor can the forms of things created by God ever be "that which is found in Him in a simple and universal way."[71] So we can speak of God only analogically (that is, in terms used in a related but not the same sense). Yet Thomas also points out (bk I, ch. 29) that creatures are like God:

> Effects that fall short of their causes do not agree with them in name and nature. Yet, some likeness must be found between them, since it belongs to

> the nature of action that an agent produce its like. . . . Hence it is that Sacred Scripture recalls the likeness between God and creatures, as when it is said in Genesis (1:26): "Let us make man to our image and likeness." At times the likeness is denied, as in the text of Isaias (40:18): "To whom then have you likened God?" . . . Dionysius is in agreement with this argument when he says (*Divine Names*, bk IX, ch. 7): "The same things are both like and unlike to God. They are like according as they imitate as much as they can Him Who is not perfectly imitable; they are unlike according as effects are lesser than their causes." In the light of this likeness, nevertheless, it is more fitting to say that a creature is like God rather than the converse. For that is called *like* something which possesses a quality or form of that thing. Since, then, that which is found in God perfectly is found in other things according to a certain diminished participation, the basis on which the likeness is observed belongs to God absolutely, but not to the creature. Thus, the creature has what belongs to God and, consequently, is rightly said to be like God.[72]

It is not my purpose in this book to explore the complexity of such theories of analogical predication. I merely remind my readers that the nature of likeness and how one refers to it was at the heart of much medieval philosophical exploration for a thousand years.[73] Such discussion makes "representation" the enabling of and encounter with presence. It affirms likeness as ontological (that is, as lodged in what things *are* as created, or empowered, or especially designated by God) rather than visual or morphological (how they may appear to us on initial encounter). To such medieval theorists, a thing of earth is "like" heaven not because it is made of heaven's matter or because it mirrors a heavenly appearance morphologically but because it can be a specific link to or a specific instantiation of the Other that is the realm of God.[74]

The point of this volume, however, is to go beyond using medieval theological discussion to understand medieval (or indeed modern) viewing. I am not suggesting that Augustine, pseudo-Dionysius, Gertrude, Hugh of St. Victor, or Thomas Aquinas should be our key to understanding medieval worship. Such a link between theory and object is helpful but ultimately too tenuous. It does not seem to me that a few theoretical statements by theologians or visionaries can explain the experiences of medieval worshippers with the glorious or horrifying things they encountered—those concrete expressions of devotion to which Huizinga pointed so long ago. In such encounters, what things mirrored, re-presented, or evoked in the worshipper often constituted what they were.[75] What I have found myself noticing, therefore, is *what things themselves tell us*. That is what all the chapters begin, in various ways and to various degrees, to explore.

I argue that the objects I analyze themselves depict and induce how the devout should react to them, use them, and worship with them. Just as the Merode triptych of the Annunciation suggests how we as human viewers might look toward the Virgin by how it positions patrons before a partially open door, so the crowns of Wienhausen and the cradles of Low Country beguinages suggest by what they *are*—their structure, materials, and dimensionality—how they are to be viewed and handled, valued, and worshipped with. Hence in my approach, recognition of the agency and the tactility of medieval objects—the way in which they call out for and thematize touch (as Jacqueline Jung has so brilliantly shown us)—is not separated from issues of representation.[76] I suggest that, at least for medieval art and worship, we need to go not "beyond representation" but further with it. We need to let objects themselves—for example, the shape of crowns, cradles, or footprints, the redness of coral and blood—form our encounter with them and point us into the deeper reality they conjure up.

The way in which such objects "speak" or induce reactions cannot of course be understood apart from historical and geographical context.[77] Each of the objects I consider, including those from non-Western cultures—the penile form of the Shiva linga, for example, or the cosmos with earth, seas, sun, and stars seen by Yaśodā in Krishna's mouth—is studied, as it must be, in the context of other objects and experiences from its culture, place, and period.[78] In the case of the Wienhausen statues, for instance, the context is the general significance of crowns and crowning in medieval culture and the importance of the nun's crown in the entry ceremonies, liturgy, and daily life of north German convents. In my exploration of the empty cradle and occupied manger found in the Burgundian crèche, I consider the very different chronologies with which the cradle as a meditational image and the manger as a furnishing in a concrete Nativity scene developed. In the case of the processions of goddesses compared in chapter 4, the context that differentiates the two cases decisively is the attitude toward the organic world displayed in the cultures that revere the goddesses Mary and Durga. Durga can be understood only against a background of other goddesses who grow and return. The anti-Jewish libels treated in "The Presence of Objects" are understood against the background of social change and growing anti-Semitism; the specific religious context includes late medieval ambivalence about and obsession with sacrifice, the increasing realism of medieval Eucharistic theology, and basic assumptions about materiality. Each chapter is a historical study. Most concentrate on holy objects from northern Europe; extrapolation from their specific characteristics to a southern European context must be made with caution.

In this book, however, I underline two general, theoretical claims about the objects I explore as dissimilar similitudes. First: I emphasize the way in which each object itself not only stresses its tactility (its thingness, so to speak) but also, in doing so, gives contradictory visual signals simultaneously. The beguine cradle presents itself as both bed and church — both a place to lay a Jesus doll and a sanctuary within which the Eucharistic Christ comes. Like the well-known Escher Waterfall or the so-called rabbit-duck illusion, the cradle forces the viewer to flip from one view to the other, while retaining the understanding that it is "the same" object, however differently it has to be perceived.[79] The Burgundian crèche shows an occupied manger, whose attendant angels, shepherds, and beasts explicitly thematize the senses with which a devotee should grasp the astonishing event of Jesus's birth. Yet before the waiting mother is a second, empty bed — a cradle — that seems to conjure up the waiting heart with which she (and those who view her) should pray. As the beguine cradle is both church and bed, the cradle in the Burgundian crèche is both an empty bed and a concrete expression of the mother's expectant heart as she gazes upward, rapt, toward fullness. Similarly, the crowns of the Wienhausen sisters and their statues refer both to glory achieved and to unfulfilled desire. The golden hoops of the convent's Madonna statues thrust their spires upward, yet the crowns the nuns themselves wear, however proleptically they signal a sister's place in heaven, are cloth caps that fit snugly; their bands point downward. Hence, each object is, as a thing encountered visually, both what it is and what it is not. The nun's crown is a crown and yet, as only a cap, it is visually not a crown. The object itself tells us that it is full and empty, glorious yet lacking, achieved yet waiting.

The relics I treat in several chapters give similarly contradictory signals. As Anthony Cutler and Cynthia Hahn have explained (and recent scholarship needs to pay more attention to the point), the dissimilarity between relics themselves—the tiny, friable, decayed pieces of body or bits of soil, wood splinters, and so forth—and the figures they re-present through golden frames or vials of crystal is intrinsic to their capacity to make the holy not only present but also active and powerful.[80] The final objects I consider at length, the footprints of Christ, are likewise paradoxical. Footprints are by definition absence and presence, for the print or trace both images that which is gone and yet cannot exist without the gone-away matrix that leaves its presence behind in shape, measurement, and material. One cannot see a footprint without seeing what is not there and what is there. Indeed the "likeness" of an object to the holy or to heaven may not be any sort of visually discernible similitude at all. The footprints medieval pilgrims carried home from Jerusalem sometimes did not look like feet; they were "similar" only in bearing the same length or measurement as the object they imaged and in some sense transported.[81] Even the host miracles I treat in "The Presence of Objects"—for all their vivid redness—have something of this dissimilar and contradictory quality, for they manifest both the moment of their violation and of Christ's Crucifixion (that is, the drastic change of destruction) and also, in the claim that they last unchanged in their monstrances for decades or centuries, the permanence of the salvation won by that Crucifixion. Similar in evidencing violation, they are dissimilar in permanence.

Second: the objects and the devotions that accrue around them both collapse and maintain the distinction between earth and heaven. Thus, as used liturgically and devotionally, the objects do what Huizinga suggests: they erase any clear distinction between now and eternity, the daily and the heavenly. But (and here I depart from Huizinga) they retain distance too. Hence, they are truly a coincidence of opposites.[82] The liturgy and the prayers, like the objects, maintain simultaneously an unlikeness as well as a likeness, both presence and absence. Hearts are full and empty; beds are full and empty too. Crowns point toward heaven and toward earth. Footprints are both empty (of the presence that formed them) and yet full (of similitude to the figure who has left them behind when departing to heaven). Hence I suggest that those who commissioned, made, found, copied, or worshipped with these objects behaved as if the similitude to heaven they encountered, created, and sought was also always dissimilar. In the devotional objects they crafted and handled, as in the prayers, hymns, and devotions they voiced, there is a sense — sometimes implicit, sometimes explicit — of "not yet," "not here."

This is not to imply that every viewer is positioned similarly by religious objects, either in the past or now. A schoolchild singing a rocking carol at Christmas and a nun meditating in ecstasy are not experiencing the devotional cradles I describe in chapter 1 in the same way, even if both children and nuns confront a baby's bed. Bishops responsible for deciding whether red marks on a piece of bread or wood display the visible blood of Christ may differ not only about the fact of what they see but even about whether such a thing is theologically possible.[83] As I suggest in "The Presence of Objects," ordinary folk who discovered such objects, Jews against whom such things provided a pretext for attack, and prelates and princes who hoped to raise money by displays of miracles differed radically in what they saw.

Moreover, the anti-Semitic objects I consider in chapter 4 also raise issues concerning response and audience for modern viewers. Images of supposedly desecrated hosts or of the footprints of a Jewish woman accused of attacking Christian objects invited Christian viewers in the Middle Ages to use them, and participate in the miasma and horror they created, in ways modern viewers will, I hope, want to resist. Hence this chapter, which directly addresses modern political response, is something of an outlier to the others in this volume. Nonetheless a number of the anti-Semitic objects in question were considered holy and/or miraculous by medieval contemporaries; as such they raise similar issues about representation to those raised by golden crowns and the dresses of statues. They also pose more acutely than the other objects I treat questions about display that all modern historians need to bear in mind.

Considering what such anti-Semitic objects represent in many senses of the word "represent" makes clear the problems both with simply arguing for their removal and with naively suggesting that placing them in historical context is enough to neutralize their power. If one argues that retaining them is to retain the insolence, prejudice, and barbarism of those who made and viewed them and therefore to accuse makers and users, one must also consider how such things may activate further barbarism today exactly because objects do have agency. Anti-Semitic objects and slogans are still used for evil. But if such things remain on view, their very agency may be useful morally in frightening modern viewers at the guilt of Christian European culture in doing and condoning what such objects represent. Jews whose ancestors and relatives have been targeted by such objects may feel, however, that such considerations are obfuscating and that the objects should simply be removed.[84]

For many of my readers, deciding how to understand such anti-Jewish objects or even supporting their removal will be easier than taking seriously the crowns that a nun of Medingen or Wienhausen wore on earth in expectation of attaining crowns of glory in heaven. Dismissing or contextualizing objects that appear to be impregnated with evil may be easier than analyzing wherein lies the power of objects and images that will seem to many modern viewers merely peculiar rather than dangerous. If, however, we probe rather than dismiss exactly the peculiarity of the "dissimilar similitude" of medieval devotional objects, whether bleeding hosts or jeweled cradles, a deeper question arises about likeness itself.

Encounters with and questions about the power of objects lead one to ask what sort of ontological or methodological significance ostensible similarity has. Should one hold that likeness is located in some substance or physiological reaction behind appearance—that light or gold, for example, indicates in some more than arbitrary sense aspiration or glory or being lifted up?[85] Or should one maintain that behind certain appearances—for example, the bread of the Eucharist or water from a holy spring—there may be a dissimilar presence unseen but really there (that is, God's body or spiritual cleansing)? And if one recognizes that, within religions, "likeness" takes on such complex valences—so that likes are often unlike, if understood in context, and unlikes can be like—what are the implications of this recognition for the comparisons that historians or students of religion so often and so blithely make between cultures?

In the last two chapters, I move to consider some methodological implications of the notion of likeness by raising the question of comparison. Although I suggest no final structural or functional or ontological place where we scholars should necessarily seek comparables, I do warn against assuming that what I call "look-alikes" are a good place to start. Considering morphology (shapes or appearances that seem parallel or similar) can distract us from deeper and better questions. I make this argument explicitly only in chapters 5 and 6, but it is implicit in the other chapters as well. For example, chapter 1 argues that, if we assume that what looks like a bed is simply a bed to be compared to other beds, we may not even "see" the object (which is simultaneously crib, church, and altar) at all.

The last chapter, which was originally commissioned by the journal *Common Knowledge* for a symposium on "xenophilia" (love of the other), combines treatment of a single object with consideration of the nature of comparison.[86] Scrutinizing the footprint Christ allegedly left on the Mount of Olives not only as a relic found in the Holy Land and transported to Europe but also as the subject of a large number of illustrations in medieval miniatures and blockbooks, I take the footprint as understood in the Middle Ages (and the "as understood in the Middle Ages" is crucial to the argument) as a summary of what I wish to say about medieval things and modern theorizing.[87] For the footprint in medieval Christian devotion is both like and unlike that which it instantiates. In a way particular to medieval understandings of devotional objects, it images and *is* presence and absence. That is, it is itself a trace of something gone away or beyond, and yet it is in itself active and full of power. Models of it were understood actually to convey what it is in Jerusalem to Christians in northern Europe. The print is not the foot nor the Christ who left it behind, yet it is like (at least incompletely or partially like) the foot. It images the foot. And not only does it bring with it the presence of the Christ who made it; even copies of it carry him and his power through space and across time.

I suggest that the medieval devotional objects I study in these chapters have power just as such footprints do: they are themselves *as themselves* powerful exactly because they are a presence that holds absence within itself, a dissimilitude that is, *as what it is*, similar to what it represents. Even to modern scholars, who can never view as medieval viewers did (nor, as I comment above, did all medieval viewers see the same thing in the objects they encountered), devotional objects such as cradles, garments, relics, wafers, footprints, and crowns may engender more complex and fruitful reactions if we take the time to see in them the paradoxes of dissimilarity and similitude they body forth.

The final image I consider—that of the ascending Christ leaving his footprints behind—compels our gaze to the space *between* trace and departure. (See figure I.17.) At the very focal point of the

Figure I.17. Prayer book attributed to the scribe Cornelia van Wulfschkercke (d. 1540) from a Carmelite convent in Bruges. Princeton University Library, Garrett MS 63, chapter 1. Christ ascends into heaven leaving his grieving mother Mary and his disciples behind. They see only his departing feet and the footprints he has left on the Mount of Olives. We, the viewers, like the watchers in the image, gaze into the space *between* trace and departure. Thus, at the very focal point of the miniature, an empty but tantalizing space hovers between heaven and earth, known and unknown, present and beyond.

woodcut or miniature, an empty space hovers between heaven and earth.[88] It thus images for us something of what we historians experience when we look at medieval objects. Our efforts at interpretation lie in the space between what the objects seem to be and what they gesture toward. But just as the footprint clearly makes present the foot it is not (and in substance and appearance is not really "like"), so medieval objects tell us about that to which they are like and unlike, similar and dissimilar. Like medieval viewers and worshippers, we as historians gaze into the gap between the object and the referent that object strives to make truly present. For us as for them, the gap is always there. But we can also know from the specificity of the trace something about the glory or the horror that those who encountered it experienced here on earth, and feared or longed for in the life beyond.

Figure 1.1. Crib of the infant Jesus from the Grand Béguinage of Louvain, made in Brabant, southern Netherlands, fifteenth century, wood, polychromy, lead, silver-gilt, painted parchment, silk embroidery with seed pearls, gold thread, translucent enamels, 35.4 × 28.9 × 18.4 cm. The Metropolitan Museum of Art, acquisition number 1974.121a–d; gift of Ruth Blumka in memory of Leopold Blumka, 1974. Often called "the beguine cradle," this little bed, into which a Christ doll was laid in liturgical performance or private devotion, is carved to look like a church. It is thus the place where God appears, both as a baby in a cradle and as the redeemer on the altar.

CHAPTER ONE

Holy Beds: Gender and Encounter in Devotional Objects from Fifteenth-Century Europe[1]

In 1960, an exhibit titled *Flanders in the Fifteenth Century: Art and Civilization* opened at the Detroit Institute of Arts. One of the objects included was the so-called beguine cradle, or crib, given to the Metropolitan Museum of Art in New York City in 1974 by Ruth Blumka and now on display there.[2] (See figure 1.1.) The difference between the treatment of this little object in Detroit so many decades ago and the questions it raises today are instructive and tell us much about how the field of art history has changed over the past half-century.

The catalogue for the Detroit exhibit was organized, like the exhibit itself, according to medium, or some sort of understanding of medium as genre or type, with "paintings" the largest group by far.[3] Next came "sculpture," which seems to have meant carvings in wood, for the categories "metalwork" and "goldsmith's work" included figures we would today call sculpture. Reliquaries were in several different groups, categorized by what they were made of, with no regard to their supposed sacred content. The beguine cradle was located in "furniture" along with a prayer stool, a small lectern, and a door. It is striking to read, from the distance of more than half a century, the catalogue description.[4] It begins:

> These miniature cradles reproduced in small size the types of larger cradles actually used for babies in the Netherlands in the fifteenth century, of which the most famous example (close in date though of a different type) is the

so-called Cradle of Charles V in the Musées Royaux d'Art et d'Histoire in Brussels, which bears the arms of the Duchy of Burgundy and may well have been used for Philip the Handsome (b. 1478), his sister, Margaret of Austria (b. 1480), and Philip's son, Charles V (b. 1500).

Although the Grand Béguinage in Louvain is mentioned as provenance and the crib is called an "object of devotion," there is no explanation of who the owners of the cradle were.[5] The only specific reference to women is the note that such cribs were "sometimes given to nuns at the time they took their vows." Except for the passing remark that such objects were exhibited at religious festivals, especially Christmas, the question of the cradle's use or impact is not raised, nor is there any suggestion that the rich and complicated details of the carving and embroidery might need decoding or that the presence of such a miniature in a devotional setting might be a mystery that needs explaining. It has not occurred to the catalogers to query: Why give a nun or beguine a miniature bed and one hung with large bells? Indeed, whether or not the analogy to secular cradles is useful or even apropos, a reader might well wonder: Why call this object a cradle at all, since it does not rock?[6]

The Detroit catalogue copy takes us back to the days before the history of women's art that Christiane Klapisch-Zuber, Ulinka Rublack, Eva Schlotheuber, and Jeffrey Hamburger have done so much to create and foster.[7] Nor, despite the fact that the Detroit exhibit was organized by material (gold, wood, and so forth) as well as genre (painting, furniture, sculpture, and the like) do we find there any hint of the recent "material turn," with its stress on the agency of objects, elaborated by theorists such as Alfred Gell, Bill Brown, or Bruno Latour.[8]

Much has happened since the 1960s. No one today would see such objects simply as furniture. In 1998, Peter Keller, building on the work of Rudolf Berliner in the 1940s and 1950s, catalogued twenty-seven little cradles and five miniature beds and ferreted out a number of textual references to them.[9] But for all Keller's exhaustive research, a mystery remains. And that mystery is only deepened when we consider another fifteenth-century devotional object displayed today in the Metropolitan Museum close by the beguine cradle: a little-studied limestone and polychromed carving probably from the 1460s given to the museum by J. P. Morgan.[10] (See figure 1.2.) This Burgundian crèche—alone among the large number of crèches

Figure 1.2. Nativity, attributed to circle of Antoine Le Moiturier. Made in or near Burgundy, c. 1465–70. Limestone with later paint and gilding, 45.1 × 65.7 × 18.4 cm. The Metropolitan Museum of Art, acquisition number 16.32.158; gift of J. Pierpont Morgan, 1916. Mary prays before an empty cradle while Joseph warms the Christ Child's clothes. The baby floats above in a wattle bed or manger attended by angels, shepherds, and the beasts of the stable.

or Nativity scenes known to art historians — has two beds: an empty cradle below and the Christ Child in a crib of wattle suspended above it.[11] What did these beds mean? That is, how were they used devotionally; what do they tell us about the world that created them; what sort of "agency" (to use the current jargon) did they have; what more might we learn about them by simply looking at them, handling them, or turning them over?[12]

Scholarly Approaches: Praesepe *versus* Cunabulum

Although much work has been done on such objects since the 1940s, certain scholarly obsessions have hindered as much as helped consideration of the beds themselves. Research in the past two decades has focused on a sharp distinction between Latin *praesepe* (German *Krippe*; English *crib* or *manger*; French *mangeoir*) and Latin *cunabulum* (German *Wiege*; English *cradle*; French *berceau*) and the various objects to which such terms refer.[13] For example, Peter Keller has differentiated sharply between, on the one hand, the late medieval practice of having little beds in churches on altars, which he asserts to be especially characteristic of women's devotion, and on the other hand, veneration of the manger in Christmas scenes, which both he and Rudolf Berliner see as a Counter-Reformation practice promoted by the Jesuits. (Berliner dates the first full Nativity scene to 1562 in Prague.) Devotion to Mary preparing the cradle for her baby and laying him in it is thus associated with other late medieval devotions and devotional objects that focus on the childhood of Jesus, a subject promoted by the wide circulation of the Apocryphal Gospels. In contrast, the emergence of the Christmas crèche, once incorrectly attributed to Francis of Assisi, is in such analysis connected to the development of the sort of pageants or panoramas of the life of Christ that are familiar to scholars from liturgical drama and the stations of the cross.[14] Stress on the philological distinction between crib or manger (*praesepe*) and cradle (*cunabulum*) has led to a tendency to differentiate sharply between the objects, and even the prayers or devotions in which the terms occur. Hence cribs are seen as a medieval, mostly cloistered devotional emphasis, and crèches are understood to be early modern objects with attendant practices, often found in parish churches and even households.[15] If we were to follow such a philological distinction and relate devotional objects to it, we could simply conclude that the Burgundian crèche conflates the two traditions of manger and cradle and leave it at that. Even this would, however, ignore the fact that the Burgundian sculpture (from circa 1462) is about a century earlier than what scholars usually consider to be the first crèches, nor would it engage with the question of the devotional purpose and effect of either the beguine crib or the Burgundian crèche.[16]

There are many problems with drawing a sharp distinction either in terminology or in historical development between manger and cradle devotions. The distinction does nothing to explain the iconography and architecture of the beds and crèches, or to help us understand the empty bed in the Burgundian crèche. Indeed, the objects themselves conflate traditions that scholars have striven to keep separate. A small ivory bed from about 1600, for example, has Mary and Joseph at the head as standing figures, carved in the round, and the three wise men stand at the foot, bringing their gifts. (See figure 1.3.) The Metropolitan Museum's beguine cradle itself combines Nativity themes with cradle devotion, for on the outside ends, carved in relief, are the birth of Christ in Bethlehem, at the head, and at the foot, the Magi bringing their gifts.

Moreover, even the textual evidence does not really support the idea that medieval devotees distinguished between *praesepe* and *cunabulum* as terms or as objects. Our earliest references to the well-known relic in Santa Maria Maggiore in Rome (placed there in 440 by Pope Sixtus III) refer to it as both manger and cradle; in the minds of pilgrims to it, it seems to have been understood as both.[17] Patristic texts, like early Muslim ones, add to the confusion by revering Jerusalem as the "cradle of Christianity," so what it means to revere "the cradle" in such texts is unclear. And late medieval devotional texts, especially those in the vernacular, like many Christmas carols still sung today (such as the fourteenth-century "Joseph dearest, Joseph mine") use all sorts of words for crib, manger, cradle, and so forth without any clear distinction.[18]

Finally, although crèches or full, freestanding Nativity scenes do seem to have emerged later than cradle devotions, we have very little direct evidence for the use of either before the early modern period.[19] There is a twelfth-century reference to a devotional bed in the writings of Gerhoh of Reichersberg, who disapproved of lay brothers using such a "devotional toy," especially when it enabled them to identify themselves with the Virgin Mary.[20] Gerhoh called the bed

Figure 1.3. Rheinisches Landesmuseum Trier; ME.1992.73/1. Crib from about 1600 that combines crèche (Nativity) and cradle devotions. Ivory with remains of gilding and color. Mary and Joseph stand at the head; the three Magi bearing gifts stand at the foot. John the Baptist and St. Barbara are on one side.

praesepe (manger), not cradle (*cunabulum*). In 1162, there is a mention of a cradle in a play of Herod in Augsburg, and the Synod of Worms in 1316 refers to placing a crib on the altar before Epiphany "according to traditional usage."[21] The doll of the Bavarian nun Margaret Ebner, which she acquired on December 26, 1344, nursed at her breast in a vision, and laid in a miniature cradle, has been much discussed by historians. The doll is still today preserved and venerated by the local populace as a kind of contact relic of Margaret herself. But beds do not really figure in Margaret's elaborate visions of the baby Jesus. Sebastian Franck remarks in his *Weltbuch* in 1534 that at Christmastime people "in many places" set cradles (*Wiegen*) for a little wooden child or tiny God-man in the church. The first Italian references to Nativity scenes with figures in the round come from the 1380s, but the practice of setting up crèches in private homes became widespread there only in the sixteenth century.[22]

Inventories from the southern Netherlands in the late Middle Ages show that cribs were owned by the elite and used in private households. They seem to have stood on sideboards in grand houses, often flanked by candlesticks, and may have taken on the appearance of domestic altars.[23] Down into the twentieth century, Catholic household devotions have survived in which children are urged to place a straw representing their good deeds into the cradle each day during Advent. In such cases, the cradle is usually part of or intended for a Nativity scene.[24] There are also surviving early modern examples of cribs or cradles placed on altars on top of or in place of Eucharistic tabernacles. Such placement underlines the symbolic significance of cradles as a kind of altar—a place where the coming of Christ into consecrated bread parallels the birth of the baby at Christmas and makes present to the devotee the intersection of earth and heaven.[25]

Most of our evidence concerning the active use of cribs or cradles comes from the sixteenth century—either Protestant attacks or Catholic defenses—and concerns practices in parishes. A few fifteenth- and sixteenth-century accounts (both laudatory and hostile) describe cradles placed on the altar in parish churches between Christmas and Candlemas (February 2). Luther called the practice a "silliness," and a seventeenth-century minister referred to the Christ doll as an idol but reported that his congregation was still singing to the cradle. Evidence from the sixteenth century shows that children were involved in crib devotion. Bartholomäus of Middelburg tells of giving little clay cradles to young nuns. And accounts survive of schoolchildren coming to the altar in Amsterdam at the Christmas mass with small clay cradles and bells to "rock the baby." The children shook the bells and sang a carol to the Christ Child when the priest set a cradle on the altar rocking. We have a similar eighteenth-century reference. A large number of these clay cradles, which are fairly crudely made, survive. (See figure 1.4.) They are very small, and historians debate whether each child would have possessed one. The elegant surviving altar cradles, on the other hand, are quite fragile and would, as art historians note, have been quickly damaged by repeated motion.[26] (See figures 1.5a–b for two examples of cradles.) Thus, it seems questionable how often such delicately made beds were present in or actively manipulated in parish liturgies.

The enigmas surrounding the provenance and use of the surviving beds and the few texts that refer directly to them raise a burning question that is as old as the work of Johan Huizinga. It is a question historians of literature as well as of art have been skirting around for a generation: How literally should we take late medieval devotion?[27] Although little beds unquestionably existed, what does it mean when a text refers to a medieval devotee as, for example, "rocking the cradle" or taking the Jesus baby into "the cradle of her heart"?[28] I propose that we can come a little further toward understanding both these two specific objects, the beguine cradle and the Burgundian crèche, and the larger theoretical questions they raise by looking at the objects themselves. I begin with the beguine crib.

The Beguine Cradle: Gender and the Tactility of Devotion

The first aspect of the object we should note is provenance, for the crib comes from a women's religious house, as do many of the surviving cradles or beds whose provenance is known.[29] One of the most studied examples is a little silver crib known as a *Jésuau* that comes from the Cistercian convent of Marche-les-Dames near Namur and was probably made in the early fifteenth century in Liège. About a third the size of the beguine cradle, it is exceptional in being constructed of silver not wood, and exceptional also in that the Christ doll, who is crowned and holds a globe of the world, has been preserved. (See figure 1.6.) A touching account of its history tells us that it was auctioned off by the church of Friedberg near Frankfurt, which had acquired it after the dissolution of the convent of

Figure 1.4. Small clay cradles for the Christ Child from the Rhineland, 1470–1510. Schoolchildren rang bells, sang carols, and rocked little cradles like these in their hands at the Christmas mass. The collection is now in the Hetjens-Museum, Düsseldorf, Inv. Nr. LR 1933, LR 1936, LR 1931, LR 1932, LR 1934, LR 1935, and E 92 (detail).

Figures 1.5a–b. Two examples of the kind of small cradles from the Rhineland or the Low Countries used for private and liturgical devotion. Both are from convents.

a. From northern Brabant. Museum Catharijneconvent, Utrecht, Inv. Nr. ABM varia no. 25. Gilded oak. About 1500. 62.6 cm high.

b. From Antwerp. Museum Mayer van den Bergh, Antwerp, Inv. MMB.0402.1–2. Gilded oak. Second half of the fifteenth century. 39.7 × 31.6 × 19.7 cm.

Figure 1.6. Small silver crib, known as the *Jésuau* or the *Repos de Jésus*, with its Christ doll (partially gilded), from the Cistercian convent of Marche-les-Dames near Namur. Made in the early fifteenth century in Liège, the crib is 12.5 × 11.5 × 8 cm. This little bed is rare in being so small, in being made of a precious metal, and in having its accompanying Christ Child preserved. Namur, TreM.a-Musée des Arts Anciens, Coll. Fondation Société archeologique de Namur, Inv. Nr. B0054.

Marche-les-Dames in the French Revolution, and was purchased around 1822 by the last surviving nun of the convent, who used it in her devotions for another thirty years and presented it to the bishop of Namur a little before she died in 1856.[30] Although in most cases dolls and beds have become separated, there is no question that most cribs had dolls. Moreover, these little beds were manipulatable and interactive. The babies were to be put in and taken out. There were coverlets and pillows that could be removed. Whether or not they were regularly set rocking, most of the surviving beds could be rocked, as we see in a delicate example, made of gilded oak circa 1500 and now in the Museum of the Catherine Convent in Utrecht, and in the restored cradle from the Rhineland, circa 1349–50, now in the Schnütgen Museum.[31] (See figure 1.5a; see also figure 1.8.)

Although Keller and Berliner have not done so, considering the gender dimension of these cribs or cradles is not new. Since the 1980s, historians of women's art have explored such devotional objects, sometimes placing them and the visions they often induced in the context of deprivation theory, sometimes raising sophisticated questions about piety and performance. Did monastic women have recourse to dolls because of unfulfilled erotic and maternal yearnings?[32] Did handling such things as dolls and cribs bring the holy closer to earth, perhaps in ways that would later evoke Reformation doubts about images? Or, in contrast, did such objects make the holy more mysterious and heavenly, raising the nun or beguine herself toward Mary the virgin mother and the Otherness of heaven?[33]

The fifteenth century, when the beguine crib was made (although we are not sure of the precise date), was the period in which figures of Christ as a baby—of many different sizes, dressed and undressed, anatomically correct and not—proliferated in Europe. The most famous is Margaret Ebner's doll, which I mentioned earlier. As Christiane Klapisch-Zuber and Ulinka Rublack showed almost three decades ago, such objects can be associated particularly with cloistered women.[34] One can even argue that cribs and dolls functioned as aids in creating female monastic identity. Male religious orders in the late Middle Ages moved to emphasize personal choice in vocation and rejected child oblation (that is, the gift of children to monasteries). In canon law, the vow of profession of a male novice constituted the monk. But female monasticism continued to recruit primarily young girls (often as young as three or four years old). Whereas paying to enter a male monastic house was condemned as the sin of simony (that is, of buying holy things), the families of girls were expected to pay a large dowry upon their entry into monastic life. How else could the cloistered woman be supported? Hence, although a vow of profession was in law required of female candidates too, it was often the vow of relatives *for* the child that established her status as a nun; the habit and veil she wore, sometimes from toddlerhood, in fact created her feelings of cloistered identity.[35] The little figures of the baby Jesus and his cradle given to the girl when she entered, or when she was first dressed in habit and veil, identified her with Mary, Jesus's mother, just as the crown she received from the bishop at profession identified her with the queen of heaven. Possessing a Jesus doll, dressing it and putting it to bed, underlined for the nun or beguine the special association with the virgin mother of God that *was* her religious identity.[36]

Hence, cribs and cradles, Jesus dolls and their clothing, can be especially associated with women. But it is less clear whether Christiane Klapisch-Zuber and David Herlihy were right to argue that dolls and cradles were compensations for deprivation of erotic and maternal experience.[37] Even today the reasons why children play with dolls are complicated. We should note that identifying herself with God's mother and the queen of heaven might have increased a young girl's sense of religious empowerment rather than compensating for missed secular experience. (It might, of course, have done both.) Moreover, the gendered visions that Margaret Ebner and many other religious women—especially in the Rhineland in the fourteenth century—are known to have experienced were not limited to women. Jeffrey Hamburger has made all of us familiar with Henry Suso's effusive and clearly erotic love of the Virgin, in which Suso sometimes sees himself as a woman.[38] Moreover, anyone who has visited the Bayerisches Nationalmuseum in Munich, where there is a stunning collection of Nativity scenes from Bavaria and the Tyrol made by the wealthy philanthropist Max Schmederer, will readily understand that collecting miniatures is by no means only a female activity.[39] Nonetheless the gender dimension of crib devotion and its role in shaping female monastic and beguinal identity are clear.

Encounter with the Metropolitan Museum's beguine crib also raises questions very different from those stimulated by gender history—questions that have been almost totally neglected in current scholarship. What strikes us, however, if we simply contemplate the crib without preconceptions or even knowledge of its historical setting, is its visual ambiguity and its intense tactility, its insistence on performance.

When we look at the object, the first thing we note is that it is a bed. Perhaps the Detroit catalogue from 1960 is not totally wrong to list it as furniture. As a bed, with pillow, coverlet, and so forth, it clearly indicates that something is to be placed in it. And the multiple bells do suggest toys to amuse a baby or (as they were understood in the Middle Ages) to serve as apotropaic objects, protecting a child from evil.[40] So as furniture, the little crib itself indicates that it is to be handled, and that something is to be placed in it and taken out. Although it does not move, most of the surviving examples, as I indicated earlier, rock. Thus, the bed *is* a bed.

But, as soon as one really looks at it, one sees that the bed—like almost all the other surviving examples—is also a church. It has Gothic windows along the sides, ogival arches on each end through which one looks, as if at an altarpiece or through a window, and Gothic towers at the four corners. The angel musicians are perched on the spires of a roof. On the richly embroidered bed-covering is a tree of Jesse, and the pillow is embroidered with the Lamb of God, surrounded by the symbols for the four Evangelists. Under the bed is an opening that probably contained a relic. (See figure 1.7.) Thus, the object would have been made holy, as an altar is, by the presence of a holy particle within. The bed is both image and reliquary, both representation and presence.[41] It is hard not to think of the pillow and coverlet as altar cloths, given their themes, and surely the Jesus doll that was in former times placed in the bed echoes the coming of Christ into the sacrament at the consecration as well as his birth on Christmas morning. The bells that hang between the bedposts/spires evoke not only the playthings of a baby but also the bells rung at the Eucharist.

Although almost every surviving cradle/crib/bed evokes church and altar as strongly as does the beguine cradle, this aspect has been ignored in the scholarship. For example, if we consider the recently restored cradle now in the Schnütgen Museum in Cologne, we see little heads looking out from the side arches as if from the windows of a Gothic church or from the arches in an altarpiece. The heads are reminiscent of the reliquary busts that look out from the famous

Figure 1.7. Underside of the beguine cradle (see figure 1.1 above) showing an opening that probably contained a relic.

reliquary altar, also in Cologne, that is exactly contemporary. (See figures 1.8 and 1.9.) Scholars have strained to give the cradle a Christmas connection by speculating that the figures in the windows are the ancestors of Christ, which is certainly a plausible interpretation. But such analysis ignores the obvious visual resonances of the bed with altar, reliquary, and church.[42]

Nor has the evident tactility of such objects been sufficiently considered. The beguine crib appeals to several senses. It rings with sound, enriches the sight with red brocade and pearls, and seems, in its multiple textures and surfaces, to ask to be touched. Complexly decorated on all sides, it demands that we move around it, view it from multiple perspectives, even play with it. And it changes form, function, and meaning as we move, almost like an optical illusion such as the well-known duck-rabbit illusion or the Transformer, a child's toy popular some years back that metamorphosed from action figure into machine and back to another action figure.[43]

The Burgundian Crèche: Why Two Beds?

Understanding the seductive materiality of the beguine cradle leads me to a second bed, displayed in the Metropolitan Museum close to it: the Burgundian crèche. Nothing is known for certain about its provenance before the nineteenth century.[44] William Forsyth has argued that it reflects Burgundian themes and sculptural techniques and comes from the workshop of Antoine le Moiturier, active in Dijon after 1462. (Indeed, it is under le Moiturier's name that you must look if you try to access it online.) We have no idea whether it was displayed in Advent, between Christmas and Candlemas, or permanently. It was clearly made to be set against a wall (the back is not carved for viewing), but where? In a parish church? a beguine's or a nun's cell? an aristocratic bedroom or dining room? a private chapel? The size and weight suggest a permanent installation, perhaps on a side altar, since (at 45.1 by 65.7 by 18.4 cm) it is a bit large for a cell or bedroom. But in a church on a side altar, it might have nonetheless been the focus of private more than public devotion.

This second crib scene thematizes both gender and sensuality at least as pointedly as the beguine cradle. It displays two beds: an empty cradle before which Mary prays, and a manger of wattle containing the Christ Child, which floats diagonally above the empty cradle, with an angel and the stable animals in attendance.

Figure 1.8. Christ Child cradle from the Rhineland, c. 1349–50. Oak, stucco, and parchment. 31 cm. high. Restored. Schnütgen Museum, Cologne. Inv. Nr. A 799.

Figure 1.9. Retable from the Cloister of St. Clare in Cologne, second opening. About 1360. Today in the North Side Nave, Hohe Domkirche, Cologne. On the side of the Christ Child cradle now in the Schnütgen Museum (figure 1.8), the faces of saints or holy ancestors look out from the windows carved there in a striking echo of this famous reliquary altar from St. Clare's in Cologne. The altar is exactly contemporary with the little cradle.

(See figure 1.2.) Angels watch from a wall on one side, shepherds from the other. Only Joseph, who airs clothes for the child before a leaping fire, has his back to the baby. Mary waits in rapture for her child to descend, her quiet ecstasy perhaps suggesting the birthing without pain celebrated in many contemporary devotional texts and scenes.

As is the case with the beguine bed, the little scene insistently raises gender issues. The cult of St. Joseph as the elderly protector of the Christ Child and his mother was created and promoted in the fifteenth century by powerful preachers such as Jean Gerson, Pierre d'Ailly, and San Bernardino of Siena.[45] Pope Sixtus IV authorized his feast as part of the church's calendar in 1479. The well-known Merode altarpiece—also owned by the Metropolitan Museum—illustrates the new fifteenth-century attention to Joseph the carpenter. As a number of art historians have noted, the mousetrap he has made and placed on the windowsill refers to the saving work of Christ—trapping the devil—and thus associates Joseph closely with his foster son.[46] (See figure I.6.) Contemporaries would have seen in the Burgundian crèche a suggestion that the elegant cradle prepared for the baby has been made by Joseph, his carpenter-father. By the sixteenth century, Joseph had become the patron saint of the Spanish conquest of Mexico, and in the nineteenth century he was much emphasized as the patron of workers and as a role model for a masculine domesticity. Down into the twenty-first century in Catholic areas, Nativity scenes and panoramas of the childhood of Jesus have strained to give Joseph a prominent position, depicting him bathing the Christ Child or teaching him to walk. (See figure 1.10 for two contemporary examples from the St. Kolumba Church in Cologne.)[47] Moreover, in the later Middle Ages and early modern period, at least two churches claimed to have relics of Jesus's swaddling clothes or diapers, and a legend circulated that Mary had swaddled her baby with Joseph's stockings. Such stories seem to lie behind the depiction of Joseph preparing the baby's clothes while Mary, in ecstasy, contemplates a baby in a manger while awaiting his descent into the empty cradle before her.[48]

In the preaching of Gerson and San Bernardino, the cult of Joseph was a complex response to the increasingly matriarchal themes of the Holy Kinships and Threefold Annas (known as Anna-Selbdritts) that proliferated in the fourteenth and fifteenth centuries.[49] Although exploring the prominence of Jesus's maternal lineage in late medieval

Figure 1.10. Scenes from Christmas crèches at the St. Kolumba Church, Cologne, 2014–15, that illustrate recent efforts to make Jesus's foster father, Joseph, more prominent in Catholic devotion. Joseph and Mary bathe the Christ Child, and Jesus takes his first steps.

art is a fascinating topic and one that has been recently studied, considering it in detail would take me too far afield.[50] I illustrate it here with only a single example: the family group in which the Threefold Anna (Anna-Selbdritt) has become fourfold—an Anna-Selbviert. (See figures 1.11 and 1.12.) In this grouping, Jesus's great-grandmother Emerentia (an entirely apocryphal figure who does not appear in texts until fairly late in the fifteenth century) has been added to the group of Jesus, Mary, and Mary's mother, Anne.[51] Although St. Anne was a popular intercessor in the late Middle Ages, she was mostly glossed by theologians (when she gained theological attention at all) as a reference to the doctrine of the Immaculate Conception. Mary's mother, Anne, was important as the container, the receptacle of Mary, because Mary herself was sinless, either without original sin at the moment of conception because of the foreseen merits of her son (the Franciscan position) or granted this purity a moment after her conception (the Dominican position).[52] The fact that male theologians quarreled about this meant that the issue was important and edgy, causing a good deal of theological anxiety, in the fifteenth century. (It was not settled until 1854.) Nonetheless, however much the preachers associated such figures with the doctrine of the Immaculate Conception, not only Anne but also Emerentia must have seemed familiar in a world where grandmothers frequently raised small children of both sexes and taught them their letters, while mothers worked in the fields or as alewives, weavers, embroiderers, goldsmiths, and so forth in towns.[53] It is hard to imagine that those who prayed to Emerentia for healing and saw the branch she carried as a symbol of fertility were responding primarily to her as the grandmother of a woman characterized by the abstruse doctrine of the Immaculate Conception.[54]

Moreover, although we have learned to avoid the large generalizations of the scholarship of fifty years ago about the rise of patrilinearity in late medieval Europe, we know that inheritance patterns were changing to favor male succession and primogeniture. The simultaneous rise of images of female lineage was both a complement to and a critique of such concepts. The cult of Joseph, promulgated by male theologians in the fifteenth century, is thus a complex response to the fact of female social, psychological, and religious significance—a significance that was itself a response to social roles and circumstances.

Hence the Burgundian crèche, in which a mother contemplates in ecstasy while the male parent prepares for clothing the child, can be understood against the complex background of fifteenth-century gender roles and anxieties.[55] But like the beguine cradle, the crèche not only puzzles and intrigues its viewers with its gender dynamics; it also, even in its fairly poorly preserved condition, elicits a sensual response. For this little object quite explicitly evokes, even depicts, the responses it effects in us the viewers.[56] Sightlines make it clear that the angels gaze at the baby. A shepherd cups his ear to hear the angelic message. An ox licks (tastes) the Christ Child's feet (or blanket), while the baby himself touches (and is touched by) the mouth of the ass for warmth.[57] Thus, four of the senses are themselves pictured, and if smelling is not depicted literally, it is clearly evoked by the fire and the damp swaddling clothes held before it.

As Jacqueline Jung has demonstrated, there is no standard iconography of what we call the five senses in the later Middle Ages. But the sensual quality of much of the sculpture is obvious.[58] Moreover, devotional literature repeatedly speaks of and emphasizes sight, and recent scholarship has stressed the ways in which later medieval liturgy and architecture directed the pious to look and look beyond.[59] The other senses were explored and thematized in medieval devotional objects as well. There was much emphasis on touch as both dangerous and necessary. Depictions of Doubting Thomas putting his finger into Christ's side (John 20:24–29) were often paired with the *Noli me tangere* to explore and problematize, but not to reject, tactile devotion.[60] (See the frontispiece and figures 6.6–6.7.) Hagiography and the vision collections known as nuns' books include a number of miracle accounts in which visionaries receive a host that suddenly tastes like flesh or sweetest honey, rings like a bell, or smells of cloves or incense. The experiences clearly reflect, and are sometimes occasioned by, such Eucharistic antiphons as "O taste and see that the Lord is sweet" from Psalm 33:9. It is thus hard to imagine that some devotees, praying before this little Nativity, would not have seen their own reactions mirrored in the scene before them.

Beds in Medieval Devotion

Beds became important in late medieval piety as objects and as images (both artistic and literary). Devotional literature is filled with references to Christ himself resting or suffering on "the bed of the

Figure 1.11. Anna-Selbdritt. Belgian, c. 1500–25. The Metropolitan Museum of Art, acquisition number 41.100.151. Gift of George Blumenthal, 1941. This is the so-called Threefold Anna or Anna-Selbdritt, an image of Jesus's maternal family line that was popular in the late Middle Ages and reflected both the theological doctrine of the Immaculate Conception and the social prominence of women in caring for and educating young children. It was to such images that St. Emerentia (see figure 1.12, facing) was added, extending the prominence of female relatives even further.

Figure 1.12. Virgin and Child with St. Anne and St. Emerentia. Probably from the area of Hildesheim, Lower Saxony, Germany, c. 1515–30. The Metropolitan Museum of Art, acquisition number 16.32.208. Gift of J. Pierpont Morgan, 1916. The later Middle Ages saw a great increase in devotion to St. Anne, Jesus's grandmother, and to St. Emerentia, Jesus's great-grandmother, a figure who does not appear in medieval devotion until the fifteenth century.

cross" or coming into the "little bed of the heart." Such references resonate with evocations of sexual delight, quiet repose, or the agony of childbirth. The mystic Marguerite of Oingt, for example, spoke of Jesus giving birth on the bed of the cross:

> when the time approached for you to be delivered, your labor pains were so great that your holy sweat was like great drops of blood. . . . Ah! Sweet Lord Jesus, who ever saw a mother suffer such a birth! For when the hour of your delivery came you were placed on the hard bed of the cross . . . and your nerves and all your veins were broken.[61]

The flowery bed of Song of Songs 1:15—"Behold, thou art fair, my beloved, and comely: our bed is flowering"—found echoes in both Christmas and Easter devotions. Confessors and preachers advised the pious, and especially nuns, to make in their hearts palaces within which they prepared a "flowery bed" on which to consummate their love with Christ.[62] One letter of spiritual advice titled *Mea carissima* (My Most Beloved), sent probably by a pastor to the community of nuns and recently studied by Jeffrey Hamburger, exhorted:

> There where the maid's child [that is, Christ] may rest
> You must have a bed
> That should stand in this house,
> That is, strong faith . . .
> Then you'll be able to speak in this way:
> *Lentulus noster floridus* [Song of Songs 1:15],
> Our little bed is decked with flowers.
> Now come sweet Lord Christ
> And lay yourself down in my heart,
> And let me gently be with you,
> And never leave me again.[63]

In another text Hamburger has studied, the biographer of a thirteenth-century Premonstratensian nun writes that she saw a vision of Christ "standing in front of the altar in a cradle and it was blanketed with a cover of roses."[64] Particularly popular in convents were little figures of Mary in childbed, which allowed the meditating nun to identify herself with Mary cuddling or even giving birth to the baby Christ.[65] (See figure 1.13.)

Nor was bed devotion solely female. Friedrich Sunder (d. 1328), an adviser to nuns, described the wedding of his soul with the infant

Figure 1.13. Mary in Childbed. Wooden figure from the Cistercian convent of Heggbach, Baden-Württemberg, about 1340–50; now in Munich, Bayerisches Nationalmusuem, Inv. Nr. MA 1088.

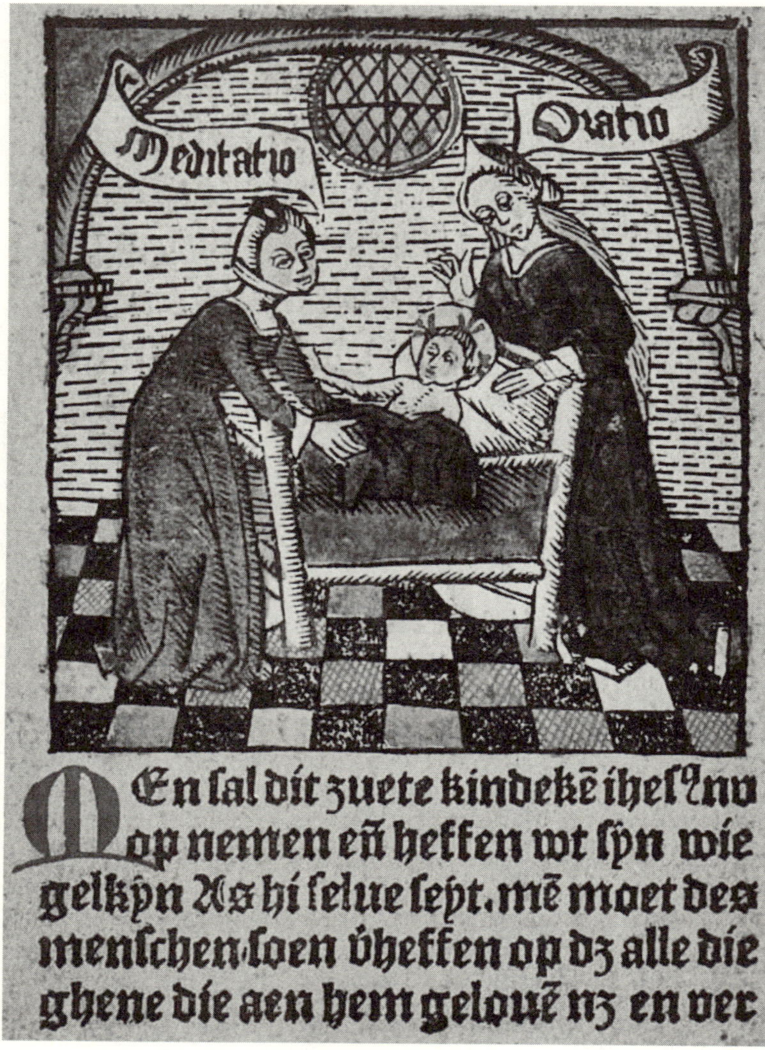

Figure 1.14. The two allegorical figures of *Meditatio* and *Oratio* put the child Jesus to bed in his crib. From a devotional blockbook used by beguines, printed in Antwerp, 1488. Catalogued as BMH il4, Utrecht, Rijksmuseum Het Catharijneconvent. Image from fol. 23v.

Jesus as occurring in a bed of flowers: "Then Jesus advanced to the little bed, and Mary . . . joined the holy soul [that is, Sunder himself] with the little Jesus. And they had . . . loving joy and pleasure with one another of embraces and kisses, with laughter and all divine pleasures."[66] In this image, the baby is not only child but also lover and bride; Mary becomes not only mother but also a kind of priest (or holy Pandarus), joining the one meditating to Christ. The anonymous author of the commentary on the *Salve regina* discussed in the introduction above saw Mary herself as a "manger," a "stable," and a "storeroom," the bed and container of Christ.[67]

A blockbook printed in Antwerp in 1488 that we know was used by beguines is titled "On the Spiritual Childhood of Jesus" and describes spiritual exercises to prepare for the birth of Christ in the soul of the adherent. Meditations in the text follow the life cycle of Christ, and the early meditations especially emphasize the meditating heart as a crib.[68] (See figure 1.14.) Folio 23v shows two female figures representing *Meditatio* and *Oratio* who explain, "One now gathers up this sweet little child Jesus and lifts him from his crib [*wiegelkyn*]. As He Himself said: one must lift up the Son of Man so that all those who believe in Him do not perish, but may have eternal life."[69]

In another, more graphic meditation that does not distinguish crib (*crebbeken*) and cradle (*wyeghelken*), the figures *Justicia* and *Veritas* lay the baby in his bed. The author advises:

> One shall rock the sweet small child as he lies in his crib [*crebbeken*]. The devout soul leads him and teaches him to walk and protects him like the light of her eyes. In the shrine of her heart, [she] has placed Jesus's cradle [*wyeghelken*], which she can rock and rock well [*wel wieghen ende wackelen can*]. . . . So Jesus's cradle is locked in her heart.

And the child says: "I wish to be here eternally and always."[70]

Earlier in the text, the child laid in the crib of the heart is initially seen as "not covered with golden sheets or studded with costly stones. But wrapped in lowly clothes. They found this child in his little crib. He does not sit exalted on a kingly throne but in a crib. He does not reign in an imperial palace but he is miserable in a cold shed."[71]

And yet the meditating beguine knows that the baby she cuddles must eventually grow up and enter his heavenly kingdom. How then can she hold locked in her heart a baby Christ that she must eventually surrender to the adulthood of heaven? The answer is clearly that she can do so not only if the baby is priest and king but also if she can eventually become herself throne and church as well as lowly bed. As if to graphically depict and indeed to embody the paradox of the physical cradles that were placed on sideboards or altars or in monastic cells and in their structure and decoration echoed altars, the text soars to lift the meditating woman to heaven.

> O, were my body the heavenly throne and adorned with choirs of angels and all things in there as they belong, and if my heart were a palace, thou would live eternally in the middle of that palace. And it would be you my Lord and I your servant. And also if my legs would be golden pillars attached to a chair, you would sit upon me.[72]

Just as the crib in the Metropolitan is both bed and church and the cradle in the Schnütgen Museum is both cradle and altar, so here the worshipper *is*, at least proleptically, high as well as low, containing the poverty and suffering of the newborn baby and yet releasing him and herself to the glory of heaven. As Christ is both baby and king, so the beguine is herself a crib of lowly clothes and yet a throne that stands on golden legs in heaven.

Scholars have puzzled about why there are two beds in the Burgundian Nativity and why the bed below is empty. On a straightforward level, one could argue that Mary and Joseph are sculpted here as parents who have temporarily lodged their baby in a manger and are now preparing for him swaddling clothes and a bed. The work of historians such as Keller and Berliner might then suggest that one could explain the doubling of beds as the coming together of two distinct traditions—the earlier cradle devotion of the Middle Ages and the later appearance of enactments of the birth at Bethlehem. Traditions of Mary with the waiting cradle (*cunabulum*) and Christmas scenes of the birth in a manger (*praesepe*) would be understood as conflated here in a way that is somewhat unusual for the Middle Ages.

But a consideration of its context in poetry, devotion, and devotional objects makes the Burgundian crèche much more complex. Although the direction of her gaze is a bit hard to discern, because the figure is abraded, Mary is clearly looking beyond the cradle and upward. She is waiting, still and silent, before an empty place, a receptacle or vessel, and angels accompany her gaze. For all that the receptacle in front of her is empty, she and the angels see the manger above where workmen and animals participate with their senses in the joy of the baby God's arrival. As William Forsyth has suggested, there is a vertical division between the spiritual (which, paradoxically, is anticipation) and the earthly, in which the offered God is already physically present.[73] Yet even the angels (on our left) respond with their senses, and, if the right-hand side of the scene represents the physical, it is there that God has already arrived. As in the Eucharist, the God-man is both physically present and yet hidden, received and yet-to-be-revealed.

Hence, as the plethora of textual images I have explored suggests, beds—empty and waiting—are not just the imaginings of nuns, beguines, and male mystics, yearning for a baby or a God-man to fill arms or wombs. They can be, for lay Christians too, images of the soul waiting to respond with all five senses to the offer of a God who has come and will come to earth. The empty cradle is the waiting soul into which the Christ Child (or the sacrament) will descend. But the child is also already offered and present. The bed of wattle filled with the baby of delight is the moment of hope or even salvation and resurrection for those who dare to adore the child by seeing, touching, even tasting him. As the Metropolitan Museum's beguine cradle bodies forth the paradox of lowly bed and glorious cathedral and the meditation "On the Spiritual Childhood of Jesus" places him within the worshipper's heart and yet expresses the hope of rising to join him on the throne of heaven, so the two beds of the Burgundian crèche depict, in a different yet similarly paradoxical way, the presence and absence of the hoped-for savior.

Theologians and devotional writers such as the famed fourth-century preacher John Chrysostom and the twelfth-century Cistercian Guerric of Igny explicitly compared manger to altar and the incarnation to transubstantiation. Physical cribs or beds like the beguine cradle into which clergy, nuns, or laypeople placed dolls thus echoed in the action of bodies what theology taught minds and prayer enacted in hearts. The fact that cradles were sometimes put on altars in the place of Eucharistic tabernacles or even used to hold the relics of saints only echoes the conviction that the coming of hope, even of salvation, was understood in a profound sense as an event that occurred in the bed (which was also the cathedral and the throne) of the human heart.[74]

Thus the two beds in the Metropolitan Museum raise for us

questions that are very different from those raised by the Detroit exhibit of half a century ago. They impel us to ask not just about royal furniture and Burgundian aristocratic culture but also about the wider social context and the gendering of images: of whom, by whom, and for whom they were made. What sort of society do they reflect, evoke, and critique? They raise questions about response as well. I have argued that the little beguine cradle transforms before our eyes from bed to church to altar, so that it compels us to understand viewing as an act *we* perform. It compels us to telescope the historical moment of Jesus's birth at Christmas into the reception of the host on the altar in every mass and the fervor of every meditating heart. I have suggested that the little Burgundian crèche draws the viewer to move around in it, seeing each of the five senses evoked, as he or she responds to the birth of the Christ Child in a manger and to his hoped-for arrival in the waiting heart of the one who prays.

Some historians of the Reformation have seen in such evokings and responses a foreshadowing of Protestant rejection of images. Amy Powell, for example, building on some of Joseph Koerner's ideas, has argued that making holy figures tactile and manipulatable demotes them — that is, that acts of dressing Mary and Jesus statues, rolling them around in churches, pulling them up into church rafters, or positioning them in or in front of mangers make them so familiar as to desacralize them. A doll that can be manipulated declares itself not alive. It becomes a mere thing.[75] In such an interpretation, late medieval devotional art would itself lead to the Lollard idea that images are "mere sticks and stones," to Lutheran preference (at least in some new chapels) for white walls, to Puritan smashing of altars and stained glass in seventeenth-century England, and even to the Council of Trent's injunction that Catholics should have in their churches no "disorderly" or "unusual" images.[76]

Most medievalists have, however, seen the dressing of dolls to rock in cradles or parade through the streets of towns as an enhancement (not a demotion) of the power and mystery of the image. (See figures 1.15 – 1.17 for an example of a Christ doll and the kind of clothes made for it.) In Hamburger's and Rublack's interpretations, for example, the dressing and undressing of the figure deepens the devotee's sense of an inner secret as he or she handles it and prays with and through it. The way in which the materiality of the object invites encounter is an aspect of its power.[77]

Figure 1.15. Christ Child, from the convent of Heiligkreuz in Rostock, about 1500. Now in Güstrow. The clothing is medieval. Such original clothing survives infrequently, but Christ dolls were often elaborately dressed and used in both liturgical performances and private devotion by nuns and beguines. The belt on this little figure states that the statue contains a relic of the true cross. Thus, like the beguine cradle, the statue is both image and reliquary.

Figures 1.16a–b. Scepter and crown for a statue. Museum August Kestner, Hannover, object numbers: WM XX 30 and WM XX 29. Probably late medieval.

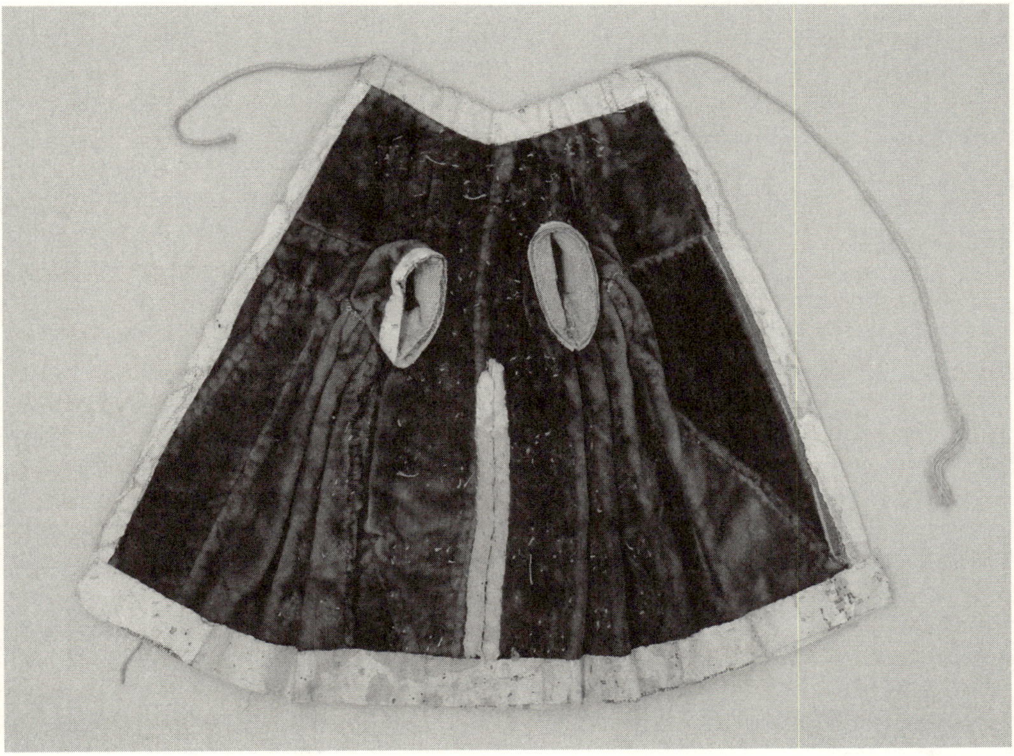

Figure 1.17. Dress for a Christ Child, from Wienhausen, after 1469. Figurenornat (Wie Hb 053): Klosterkammer Hannover, Textilwerkstatt. The dress was probably made for a figure of the baby Jesus seated on his mother's knee and may have been changed with the liturgical seasons. The practice of clothing statues with dresses, jewelry, and crowns continued in some female religious houses in northern Germany, despite Protestant opposition, until the eighteenth century.

Both lines of interpretation, whether they see the performativity of late medieval devotional objects as deposing or as enhancing their sacrality, raise the question of the literalism of devotion that the work of Johan Huizinga suggested long ago. Recent scholarship, such as that of Thomas Lentes, raises similar questions. Lentes has brilliantly demonstrated that some text and images from the later Middle Ages depict such literalizations.[78] The *Nuns' Book of Töss*, for example, tells us that the sisters wove a garment for Mary with their devotions but needed to say fifty additional prayers in order to complete its sleeves. In devotional literature, as we have seen, beguines and nuns were advised to build a cradle in their hearts, before mass or before Christmas, with the straw of good deeds and thoughts.

Like and Unlike Heaven

But what do we make of all this? Does such devotion merely reify spiritual things or collapse the spiritual into an object? When the author of the fifteenth-century beguine devotional book I quoted earlier describes her heart as a palace, her body as a chair with golden legs on which Christ sits, her neck as a candelabrum, does she really mean she is furniture?

Nor should we raise such questions only about the rarified atmosphere of the cloister or beguinage. As both Peter Keller and Rudolf Berliner have pointed out, even in parish devotions or household practices that survive into the modern period, it is not clear whether "rocking the baby" meant singing a Christmas carol or actually handling a devotional cradle or part of a manger scene.

In the late Middle Ages, many of those who wrote about heavenly and earthly roses and cribs, babies and garments, drew sophisticated distinctions. It was common for spiritual advisors to exhort those who prayed to transcend what Augustine had theorized as the two lower levels of corporeal sight (in which the eye sees) and spiritual sight (in which the intellect processes images seen by the eye) in order to reach the third level of vision (seeing beyond or without images). Yes, pictures were understood as useful for teaching; biblical texts had a literal sense. But it was better to rise beyond image to textless truth, to find a layer of spiritual meaning behind the literal words of the Bible.[79]

The biographer of the Premonstratensian nun who saw the Christ Child standing on the altar in a cradle covered with roses, wrote explicitly: "They were not earthly roses, they were heavenly."[80] The anonymous commentator on the *Salve regina* whose text spills forth a cornucopia of images glosses them as "names" or "words of [or from] things," aware that they are analogies although convinced that they also refer "fittingly"—that is, that they evoke some real quality of the Virgin so described.[81] The crib meditation I quote extensively above seems to use exactly the pictorial quality of the meditations to evoke paradox, suggesting that the one meditating can retain within herself both presence and absence, both a literal place for a baby God and the promise of a heaven that lies beyond imagining. In such texts, we find a sophisticated sense of both the salience and the limitations of images.

And yet . . . vision accounts, liturgical antiphons, and simple devotions make it clear that prayers *did* fashion garments to clothe Mary, that good deeds did fill Christ's manger with straw, that hearts *were* beds that received the Christ Child. However carefully preachers and visionaries often spoke of a difference between spiritual and earthly things, I do not think we can assume that every devotee who stood before a baby Jesus doll or crèche—even took that doll to her or his breast—was cradling a symbol or an allegory. Nor can we assume that everyone who "rocked" a cradle was merely singing a Christmas hymn. For every text that sees Christ as beyond humankind's full understanding or even as inconceivable, there is another in which encounter is entirely erotic, corporeal, and experiential. It matters that authors often do not bother to tell us whether an encounter is literal, or metaphorical, or both. To medieval worshippers, the things of heaven are both similar and dissimilar to the things of earth.[82]

As I explain in the introduction, what I am trying to do in studying the beguine cradle and the Burgundian crèche is to turn what we can call the Huizinga question from a consideration of texts to a consideration of objects. Literary scholars have argued about symbols and images, sometimes castigating Huizinga for seeing them as freezing and literalizing piety. In analyzing these two small devotional objects from the Metropolitan Museum, I argue that the things themselves ask the viewer to respond both literally and by analogy. The two beds I have talked about suggest that heaven will and will not be a bed of roses, that prayer does and does not occur in a surround of hearing and smelling and tasting God. The objects themselves impel an attentive viewer to see *and* to see beyond.

Late medieval theology vacillated between an emphasis on the resurrection of the body and the immortality of the soul. Late medieval piety vacillated between an ever-swelling flood of images and anxious rejection of them. Hence, both piety and theology were bound to be inconsistent, even paradoxical. But many devotional objects seem themselves to heighten such paradoxical quality.[83] They insist on being seen and used in more than one way. Indeed, we do not need texts to see that they are paradoxical (although texts can help). The beguine cradle, because it is both a church and a bed, like the Burgundian crèche, because it depicts both sensual encounter with the God-manchild and the emptiness of waiting for him, are objects that themselves are and are not what they depict. They force us to see what they are and that they are other than what they are, to be Mary waiting for fulfillment to descend and the shepherds already seeing their savior as a baby on straw. As objects, they keep us the viewers from completely literalizing or completely spiritualizing pious encounters.

We have come a long way from the Detroit catalogue of 1960 that saw such beds simply as furniture.

CHAPTER TWO

"Crowned with Many Crowns": Nuns and Their Statues in Late Medieval Wienhausen[1]

In the Lüneburg Heath in Lower Saxony lie the foundations of Ebstorf, Isenhagen, Lüne, Medingen, Walsrode, and Wienhausen, six Protestant female communities in the area of the former duchy of Braunschweig-Lüneburg now under the supervision of the Klosterkammer Hannover, a state authority.[2] For art historians, the most important of these is Wienhausen.[3] A backwater in the twenty-first century, Wienhausen was anything but in the medieval period. Altcelle, close by, was the ducal seat in the thirteenth century, and Wienhausen was the ducal house cloister. Founded as a monastery for nuns in the 1220s, affiliated with but not incorporated into the Cistercians, Wienhausen was reformed in 1469 by Johannes Busch according to the Observant reform emanating from Windesheim, a first reformation that ushered in a cultural flowering. But Wienhausen's buildings and properties were partly destroyed in the mid-sixteenth century by the efforts of Duke Ernst the Confessor to impose the Lutheran Reformation. Like other women's houses in the area, Wienhausen survived, changing only slowly over the course of the next two centuries. The nuns resisted communion in two kinds and avoided the required suppression of the *Salve regina* until the late 1530s.[4] Catholic abbesses were elected until 1587. The Cistercian habit was put off only in 1616; the Latin Hours ended only in 1620; as late as 1722, we find the Prince Elector of Hannover still trying to put a stop to the adorning of images with jewels and clothing.[5] Today the women's houses of the Lüneburg Heath, securely Protestant in commitment, work to preserve the cultural heritage of the area, a sense of vocation that emerged only in the twentieth century, fostered especially by the success of the 1928 exhibit of tapestries and embroideries made by the nuns of Wienhausen and Lüne. What is astonishing to the Anglophone world, used as it is to the results of the iconoclasm of the British Isles, is that Protestant Germany—and more than any other single place Wienhausen, with its collection of statues, the remarkable "Find" under the choirstalls in 1953 of small devotional objects, and the vibrant paintings of the nuns' choir itself—is the place where historians, the devout, and the curious public can best still see the art of the Middle Ages, undamaged and sometimes even in situ.[6]

The reasons why Catholic art survives best in Protestant Germany, and especially in women's cloisters, are complicated. German taste was always, as Jeffrey Hamburger has pointed out, conservative. In the sixteenth- and seventeenth-century south, however, where the Counter-Reformation redirected Catholic piety, baroque revivals removed or plastered over out-of-fashion medieval art. But in the north, the lack of political centralization meant that reform efforts were hard to enforce over large areas, nor was there money for redecorating projects; in Lower Saxony, a number of communities went back and forth between Protestantism and Catholicism. After the peasant depredations in Wittenberg, Luther made it clear that images are *adiaphora* (indifferent things), dangerous if revered but harmless if used by the faithful to focus their worship on the God beyond, who is the only font of salvation. Hence, medieval statues, liturgical vestments, chalices, and so forth survived, sometimes simply overlooked in treasuries, sometimes reused in all their original splendor.[7]

The Lüneburg convents survived because it was in the economic and dynastic interests of the aristocracy and the patriciate to provide for supernumerary women, and some sort of monastic commitment protected the family inheritance from further demands for dowries or upkeep once daughters or widows were placed. (Even if Protestant ladies could leave the cloister to marry, very few did so.)[8] Probably, as Hamburger has also suggested, more survives of women's monastic art in German areas because, given the extraordinary flowering of women's monasticism, there was more there to begin with. Although the munificence of the dukes and others to the convents gradually fell away in the early modern period, the art survived, protected by lack of funds from damaging restoration or renewal. In the twentieth century, at the demand of the sisters and in keeping with their new historicist vocation, some of the pieces that had been removed to museums were returned.[9]

The Madonnas at Wienhausen

In this chapter, I discuss two Wienhausen statues of the Virgin Mary, especially the colorful history of her crowns. Wienhausen is an ideal test case for what we can learn from objects, because we do not have, for the north of Germany, the mystical writing and books of revelations by women that flowered, especially in the Rhineland, in the fourteenth century—works that have been used with such skill by a number of historians, preeminent among them Ulinka Rublack, to gloss the spiritual meaning of the adorning of statues in liturgical performance and private devotion.[10] From the Lüneburg cloisters, we do not have the words of impassioned devotion lavished by a Margaret Ebner on the Christ Child or the piling up of remarkable visions in nuns' books such as those of Unterlinden or Töss, although we must also note that similar works had died out even in the south by the fifteenth century under the pressure and skepticism of theologians and Observant reformers.[11] From Wienhausen and her sister houses, we have archival documents, prayer books in Latin and the vernacular, visitation reports of reformers, diaries (*Tagebücher*) and letters, a number of small devotional pictures (sometimes glossed) made by the nuns themselves, and several chronicles, among them one from Wienhausen, written in the seventeenth century but drawn from a much earlier account.[12] Nonetheless, objects are the best place to start in exploring the nature of the nuns' devotion.

I begin with an 89-centimeter high Madonna and child, often called the enthroned Madonna, made in the late thirteenth century at the same time as several other important devotional figures at Wienhausen. (See figure 2.1.) Much of the original color survives, although the throne has been partly pried open, perhaps to remove relics; the right hand, which probably held a scepter, has disappeared; and most of the sixty-six golden eagles that once decorated her blue mantle have been ripped off. Part of a dress that was made for her by the nuns still survives, and the groove that runs around her head shows that she was from the beginning intended to carry a removable crown.[13]

Figure 2.1. Wienhausen, Enthroned Madonna, Inv. Nr. Wie Ac 002. Late thirteenth century. 89 cm high. Much of the original paint survives. This figure once had a removable crown, perhaps of the sort seen in figure 1.16b, above. Wear on the statue's head suggests that the crown may have been changed several times during the year.

Indeed, wear on the head suggests that several crowns may have been alternated during the liturgical year.

We know from the survival of at least twenty garments made for the Wienhausen images that the nuns clung to the practice of adorning their statues.[14] The large number of needles, thimbles, and sewing materials such as thread and pearls found under the steps of the choir in 1953 suggests that the sisters did needlework there; inventories down into the eighteenth century list dresses, crowns, and jewelry for the statues; and repairs to the garments themselves suggest that they were in use well into the seventeenth century, although some of their decorations, especially the gold bangles, were cut off and sold. The memorial book of Wienhausen gives evidence (unfortunately undated) of garments and jewelry donated specifically to statues.[15]

A crown and scepter of the sort with which the enthroned Madonna might have been adorned survive in the August Kestner Museum in Hannover; a similar crown, woven of wire with artificial flowers, survives for the Christ Child from Heiligkreuz in Rostock, now in Güstrow.[16] (See figures 1.15 and 1.16a–b.) *Corona* in the Middle Ages meant both crown and wreath, although German texts distinguish *Kranz* (wreath) and *Krone* (crown). A few reliquary busts survive with woven wreaths, which evoke the bridal garlands bride and bridegroom had exchanged since antiquity as symbols of fertility and affection; more such busts and statues possess golden and jeweled crowns of the *Bügel-* (hoop) or *Reifen-* (ring) shape, evoking royalty and power.[17] (See figures 2.2a–b for examples of wreath and ring crowns; the processional Madonna in figure 2.4 below is an example of a *Bügel* crown.) Although the church fathers, distancing themselves from pagan ceremonial, refused any language that implied human bestowal of crowns (only God crowns the martyrs), by the Middle Ages human beings regularly granted crowns to the saints.[18] Even royal crowns were sometimes donated to statues: for example, the crown made for the baby Otto III was given to the Golden Madonna at Essen and later reduced in size to fit her head.[19] (See figure 2.3.)

Yet the fourteenth- and fifteenth-century crowns of Wienhausen's enthroned Madonna do not survive. And we know why. The Chronicle tells us that in the 1469 reform,

> the Duke and the Reformers came once more into the cloister and when all were assembled in the choir, the abbot of St. Michael's commanded every

Figures 2.2a–b.

a. Bust of a Holy Virgin from the monastery of Adelhausen, Freiburg im Breisgau, Germany; early fourteenth century. As her crown, the virgin wears a wreath made of some kind of paste or plaster with glass stones as jewels.

b. Reliquary bust of St. Paulina from the monastery of Marienstern, Panschwitz-Kuckau, Germany; second half of the fourteenth century. The saint wears a ring-crown made of gilded silver with precious stones.

Figure 2.3. Crown made for the three-year-old emperor Otto III (980–1002) and later given to his cousin and godmother, Abbess Mathilda (971/973–1011), under whom the Essen monastery reached its finest flowering, to serve as a crown for the Golden Madonna. The form is a ring crown with four golden lilies rising up around it, the whole decorated with gold filigree, gems, and pearls. The crown had to be made smaller to fit the head of the statue of the Madonna. Late tenth century; later somewhat restored. Domschatz Essen, Inv. Nr. 12.

> sister . . . to surrender all money and dishes and other things they possessed before. . . . And they agreed and brought . . . from the summer refectory pots, kettles, jars, and other . . . vessels and also the best veils they were accustomed to use on feast days and other valuable things for God's service, which they had made with much work. And the abbess of Derneburg took these and similar things as a thief would and through her nuns and friends in Braunschweig and elsewhere sold them for a small price, among them silver spoons, golden rings, and two golden crowns worked artfully from the best gold. And also several gold crowns for the images of Mary, Alexander and other saints, and a gold chain set with pearls and precious gems on which were images of the saints . . . and decorations and valuable things from the choir — all of these were taken from the cloister. . . . They were promised to be returned but they were never seen again. . . . The images of the saints and their adornments were held in low esteem, and many good customs were abolished and declared to be foolishness, and from these [acts] many a soul that was at peace before was cast into anguish and sadness.[20]

We know from other sources that the Observant reformers were attacking both the proliferation of private devotional objects and what they saw as ostentatious display (for example, those "best veils") in the cloister.[21] We also know both that the nuns of the Lüneburg cloisters struggled to restore the wealth of their chapels and their properties, despite repeated confiscations, and that private devotion, including the use of small prayer cards and devotional objects in private cells, as well as radical differences among the sisters in habit and food, continued. As Robert Suckale has explained, houses of aristocratic canonesses in Germany never practiced poverty of life, and Wienhausen — despite its affiliation with the Cistercians — was in many ways more like a house of canonesses.[22] When in 1499, a widow of the ducal house was lodged at Wienhausen, her aristocratic attire was accepted: "Her habit was outwardly worldly but her modesty was religious and pious."[23] If the community initially opposed her entry, it was not because of her wealthy accoutrements but because they feared (as turned out to be the case) that the income promised to support her would not be forthcoming.[24]

The nature and process of the fifteenth-century reform, about which others have written, are not what concern me here, however. What interests me is that we have in these lines one of the very few expressions in the entire Wienhausen Chronicle of spiritual concerns. (Most of the Chronicle deals with convent possessions, and abbesses described as "good mothers" are those who retain and even increase the monastery's possessions.) The loss of the saints and their adornments, including those "artfully worked" golden crowns, caused spiritual as well as economic anguish. Indeed, so upsetting was this event to the nuns that they were afflicted just afterward — the only time such things are recounted in the Chronicle — with sightings of ghosts and demons.

Although the miracle-working figure of the resurrected Christ was given a new silver crown after the confiscations, we do not have clear evidence that Mary's removable crowns were restored during the reigns of the next two Wienhausen abbesses.[25] But a new Mary figure, made around 1480, the so-called processional Mary, who was provided with iron hand-grips so she could be carried, had a very elaborate crown and scepter made of wood; her regalia were, so to speak, built in. (See figure 2.4.) The apocalyptic Mary placed on the high altar made for the nuns' choir in 1519 also has an elaborate wooden crown.[26] (See figure 2.5.) Thus, whatever happened — and we know that opposition to the practice of clothing and crowning statues increased during efforts to impose the Lutheran Reformation — the new processional Mary and the Mary of the high altar of 1519 could not lose their crowns again. Crowns mattered. Why?

A number of historians, among them Richard Trexler, Ulinka Rublack, Jeffrey Hamburger, and Amy Powell, have explored the religious practice of adorning statues that was formerly ridiculed as the craving of deprived or frustrated women for erotic experience or motherhood.[27] Powell has argued that dressing statues, and constructing them with movable arms or legs to facilitate dressing, causes distance and becomes a prelude to the demotion of the image into an object that presages Reformation iconoclasm. In contrast, a number of historians stress that clothing a statue gives it value and presence; changing its clothes makes the body underneath both more mysterious and more alive. Despite these differences of emphasis, what is clear in both interpretations is that adorning an image is a reciprocal and processual gesture; it gives agency to both the one doing the clothing and the one clothed; it is an experience extended over time, not a mere moment of encounter. In the complex religious act that is sometimes denominated *do ut des* but also involves "the distinctive devotional logic of presence" in which part is whole, the worshipper gives to Mary the crown she wears in heaven, just as

Figure 2.4. Wienhausen, Processional Madonna, c. 1480. Inv. Nr. Wie Ac 009. Note that the form of the wooden crown that is built into the statue is what experts call a *Bügel* crown—that is, one with upward-pointing hoops. The naked Christ baby may have been dressed in a robe like that pictured in figure 1.17 above. These garments may also have been changed with the liturgical seasons. The statue is fitted with hand grips so that it can be carried.

Figure 2.5. Altar in the Nuns' Choir, Wienhausen. This apocalyptic and reigning Madonna with child was placed on the high altar made for the nuns' choir in 1519. She has an elaborate wooden crown of the ring variety built in.

she will give, or has given, grace and love, comfort and presence, to the worshipper.[28] Indeed, as Thomas Lentes has brilliantly demonstrated, what he calls fictive crowns are reciprocal, too.[29] The nuns of Töss who wove a garment for Mary with their devotions but needed to say fifty additional prayers in order to complete its sleeves; the sisters in Strasbourg who made for St. Ursula through prayer "a golden crown . . . befitting . . . a queen"; the roses depicted in a late fifteenth-century painting as plucked from the mouth of a Dominican and woven into a rosary wreath by Mary—all are part of reciprocal gift-giving. (See figure I.1.) Intimate and vibrant, the exchange is also proleptic; it occurs both on earth and in heaven, both now and in the life to come.[30] In the temporal process of praying and in the realm outside of earthly time, the worshipper gives and receives, lifted into glory by a gift that is the giver herself.

Another story in the Wienhausen chronicle refers explicitly to the enthroned Madonna. It tells of a goldsmith, who was unjustly thrown into prison, where he had little hope of freedom until an angel appeared and advised him that he should make a golden crown for "the Mary image in the chapel in the middle of the cloister at Wienhausen." When he promised to do this, the angel freed him; he then went to Wienhausen to measure Mary's head and made a crown for her with his own hands. Although in this case reward preceded gift, the reciprocity of the gifting is clear.[31]

I cite a third story from the Chronicle that demonstrates the way in which clothing and crown were not only part of a complex gift-exchange but also markers, indeed creators, of identity.[32] In 1529, after the onset of the second or Lutheran Reformation, the wife of a burgher of Braunschweig came to the convent and attempted to force her daughter to flee. Although the abbess hid the girl, the mother threatened to denounce the cloister to the duke, so the abbess permitted the girl to go home, supposedly for three days only. But the girl's parents then pressured her to renounce the cloistered life "and when she did not want to conform to their will, they took away from her the cloister-wreath and habit [*Kloster-Krantz und Habiet*]" and forced her to take other clothes. The girl, however, arising very early while her parents slept, managed to escape, and fled to Wienhausen. When she arrived, she found the doors locked. So she waded through the Aller River, came to the cloister on the other side, and hurried into the choir where the sisters were singing and praying. Shocked by the appearance of a wet and bedraggled figure in worldly clothes, the nuns feared that a catastrophe, such as enemy attack or fire, had occurred. (They obviously thought a secular person had breached the bounds of the cloister.) When finally the girl was recognized, thanks were given, and in the presence of all the sisters, the abbess robed her again in "spiritual clothes." Although this was not (alas for the nuns and for the girl) quite the end of the story, it makes clear that both for the parents, who insisted on removing crown and habit, and for the sisters, who did not recognize the girl in her worldly attire, clothing constituted identity.

Crowns in the Devotion and Formation of Northern German Nuns

This story, with its singling out of the *Kloster-Krantz* as a sign of the nun's identity, suggests that the crowns of statues, whether removable or not, may need to be viewed in a wider context. For the nun's crown was especially important in the liturgy and the life of northern German convents and, as we shall see, stood in a special relationship to Mary's heavenly crown. In order to understand this, it is important to note that the role of clothing in constituting the nun has not, until the recent work of Eva Schlotheuber, been very well understood.[33]

From the days of the early church, the significance of clothes had been debated. Pope Celestine I in 428 had said: "We distinguish ourselves from others by *doctrina* not *vesta*."[34] Lothar of Segni, in his work on the misery of the human condition, told with disapproval the conventional story of a philosopher valued for his dress rather than his virtues; as Pope Innocent III, he ruled that "it is not the habit that makes the monk but profession of the rule."[35] Monastic clothing was a witness, just as the reliquary witnessed the holiness of the relic it contained or the king's garments bodied forth his power; the habit could even be understood as a sign that conduced into being what it signified. But in the northern German area, the monastic habit was not itself consecrated, and the male novitiate was a real probationary period, at the end of which the novice made a choice.[36] In the wake of the emphasis on personal intentionality that characterized piety from the twelfth century on (an emphasis that led to the rejection of male child oblation and to an understanding of monastic entrance fees as simony), vow not garb — that is, the making of profession, freely and as an adult, not the habit — was understood to constitute the monk. In large part because late medieval reformers and canon lawyers attempted to insist that this should be so for nuns, historians have sometimes assumed the same for convents.

As Eva Schlotheuber has shown, however, the rituals of female monasteries—especially those of northern Germany—had somewhat different implications.[37] Although for women also, vow was necessary to create the nun's legal status, clothing and being clothed was crucial in forming identity. The practice of oblation—the giving of very young girls to the cloister by their relatives or guardians—continued throughout the Middle Ages and was performed with the clear understanding that they were to become nuns.[38] In oblation, relatives made a vow for the child that she could, in theory, later reject. But we know of no cases in northern Germany in which this happened. Although technically still not monastic in status, the girl thus offered put aside her worldly clothes and received an unconsecrated habit and an unconsecrated nun's crown, constructed of two strips of fairly narrow white cloth that crisscrossed over the head and joined a band that went around the forehead. Not yet bound to the monastic vocation, the child nonetheless looked like a nun and was socialized as such. At Wienhausen, the offered child (sometimes barely beyond babyhood) was placed physically on the altar, as a kind of visible sacrifice—a practice to which the fifteenth-century reformers objected as a violation of the prohibition against women inhabiting sacred space. So important was the ceremony to the convent, however, in part because it mirrored the presentation of the Virgin Mary in the temple when she was three years old, that the abbess Katharina Remstede in the opening decade of the sixteenth century commissioned a theological treatise to defend the practice.

At Lüne, the abbey about which we have the fullest information, the next stage in the fashioning of the young nun was her investiture (*Einkleidung*). At least three years after entry but often much longer, the girl was invested with a consecrated habit, girdle, and head covering in a ceremony that took place in the nuns' choir and was the only occasion on which parents were permitted to enter the cloisters' inner walls. It was followed by a great feast, with dance and song, hosted by relatives, which paralleled a bridal feast, and was probably for the young woman the high point of the socialization process. The girl also received gifts from her family, which might include little statues of the saints, Jesus dolls with their clothes and cradles, or even (despite the efforts of reformers) fine veils for the girl herself. On this occasion, the crown she had worn before was taken away to be appliquéd at the five intersections with red crosses symbolizing the wounds of Christ. The consecrated crown was supposedly returned to the woman only when the bishop arrived to place it on her head and hear her profession, but that might not happen for many months or even years — not in fact until someone had died and made available a cell for the new nun. Both *oblatio* (which involved the parents' vow on behalf of the child) and investiture with the habit were understood in canon law to constitute over time a *tacita professio* — that is, simply by wearing the nun's garb without articulated objection, the young woman promised a life of virginity. So unimportant did the act of profession become that, as Schlotheuber has observed, the sources seldom speak of either a novitiate or of *professio*.[39] Hence, for the nun, clothes made the person in a sense not quite true for the monk, or the priest, or even the male aristocrat (although his clothes were increasingly determined — and privileged — by sumptuary legislation).[40] In constituting the nun, the veil was legally the key, but it was the *corona* that made manifest the nun's hidden spiritual status as the *sponsa* of Christ.

To many medieval theorists, the person's head was the locus of her or his greatest likeness to Christ.[41] Moreover, head covering is in many cultures the major sign of female status — both marital status and social class — and German nuns themselves provide evidence that the crown was particularly important in their self-definition.[42] A *Tagebuch* from the Braunschweig Kreuzkloster makes it clear that the nuns wore their crowns even to bed.[43] As Julie Hotchin has pointed out, bishops found the threat to remove crowns an effective way of enforcing discipline, and in Saxony, convents fought hard against Lutheran reformers who wished to forbid crowns.[44]

We have some evidence, visual and textual, of what the crowns actually looked like. In the twelfth century, Peter Abelard mentions nuns' crowns with red crosses, and Tengswich of Andernach's letter to Hildegard of Bingen, criticizing her for dressing her nuns in bridal array with embroidered crowns, is well known to medievalists.[45] The real veils and crowns described in Tengswich's letter are identical to those illustrated in Hildegard's own vision, supposedly drawn according to her instructions, in *Scivias* 2.5. (See figure 2.6.) In the fifteenth century, the reformer Johannes Busch criticized canonesses for wearing crowns decorated with gold.[46] We have textual evidence from Lüne of crowns with red silk crosses and Henrike Lähnemann has pointed to several illuminations in Medingen manuscripts, showing nuns with red crosses over their veils, including a miniature (Hamburg Staats- und Universitätsbibliothek Cod. in scrin 149 [HH8] fol. 10r) where a nun's head has been cut out and replaced with a new drawing when the style of the convent's headgear changed.[47] One of the little prayer cards discovered under the choirstalls at Wienhausen shows a nun with her red crosses, and there is a painting on the vault of the nuns' choir that shows an abbess in her crown. (See figure 2.10b.)[48] In colonial Mexico, certain orders of nuns wore elaborate wreaths or crowns of flowers and jewels, whereas Bridgettine nuns today wear metal crowns with red crosses or circles, and other orders wear simple circlets of myrtle or thorns.[49] (See figures 2.7 and 2.8.) This evidence suggests that there may be two somewhat different traditions of crowning, one which emphasizes assimilation of the virgin nun to Christ's bride through suffering, the other more a foreshadowing of her glory in heaven.[50] The fact that the "Find" under the Wienhausen choirstalls included three manuscripts of meditation on the crown of thorns (*Dornenkrone*) suggests that references to crowns at Wienhausen had many valences, including both passion and triumph.[51]

Eva Schlotheuber has argued convincingly that the crowns of the Lüneburg cloisters not only symbolized the commitment to virginity but also, by assimilating the new nun to the bride of the Song of Songs, elevated a life of virginity far beyond the "lay" status to which nuns were relegated by canon law. She quotes from the second reform report from Ebstorf, where a nun spells out this spiritual significance: "On the crown are four red crosses . . . which mean the five wounds of our crucified husband, which we bear as the signs of the wounded Christ on our heads . . . as it says in the Song: 'You have wounded my heart, my sister, my bride,' that is, through love."[52] In the first reform report, an Ebstorf sister went further, claiming a status that in some ways mirrors Mary's Immaculate Conception: "To this noble and worthy condition, God foresaw us and pre-elected us before we were received in our mother's body."[53]

To my knowledge, there is only one surviving nun's crown from the Middle Ages. Now in the possession of the Abegg-Stiftung in Riggisberg, Switzerland, it came on the art market in 2000 and is of

Figure 2.6. In Hildegard of Bingen's vision of a beautiful woman of gold and silver, representing the Church and holding holy virgins in her bosom, the veils and crowns of the virgins are identical to those described in a letter from Tengswich of Andernach to Hildegard, criticizing her for dressing her nuns in bridal array with embroidered crowns. Although of gold, the crowns seem to fit down over the head rather like the surviving nun's crown from Riggisberg. (See figure 2.9 below.) From Hildegard's *Scivias*, part 2, vision 5, plate 14, Corpus christianorum: continuatio mediaevalis, vol. XLIII.

Figure 2.7. As this painting of a nun at the Chapultepec National Museum of History in Mexico City shows, nuns of many orders in colonial Mexico wore elaborate wreaths or crowns of flowers and jewels.

Figure 2.8. Bridgettine nuns today wear white metal crowns with red crosses or circles at the joining. These Bridgettine nuns are at the 2009 March for Life in Washington, DC.

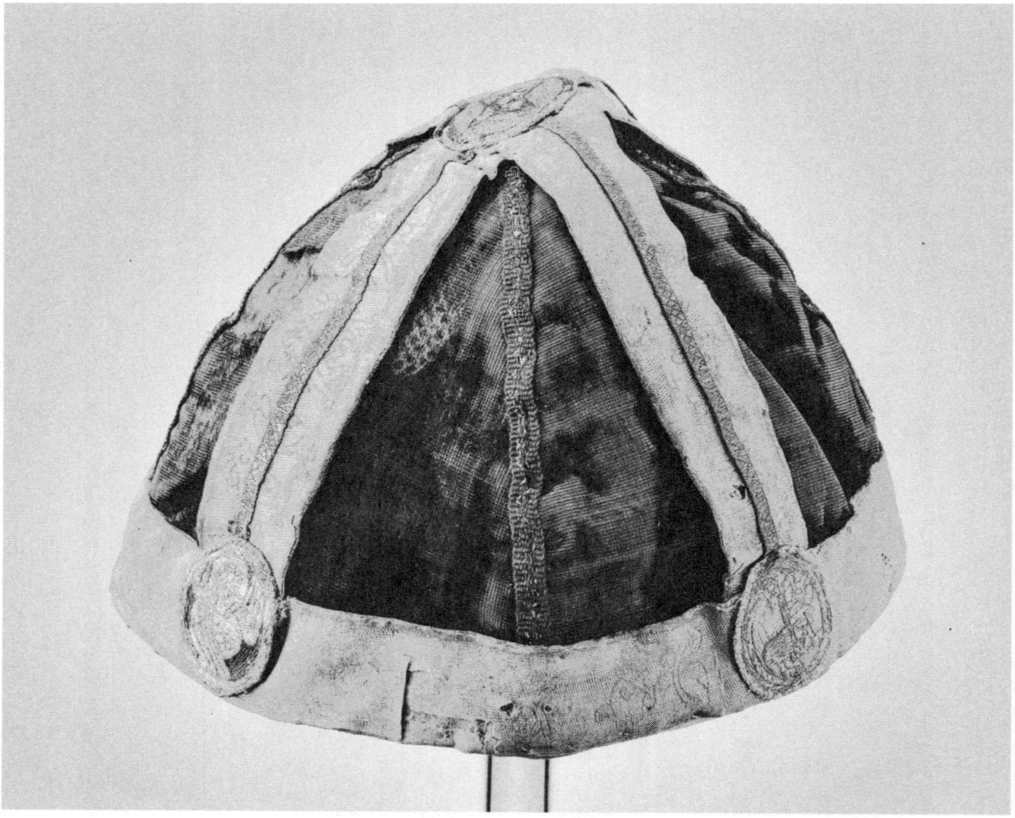

Figure 2.9. This is the only nun's crown known to survive from the Middle Ages; it is now in the collection of the Abegg-Stiftung in Riggisberg, Switzerland, Inv. Nr. 5257. Two bands of twelfth-century silk cross over the head and are held in place with a silk circlet that goes around; five appliqués in gold thread are attached at the joinings. The blue cap that provides support underneath is, however, sixteenth or seventeenth century.

unknown provenance.[54] (See figure 2.9.) Two bands of lovely twelfth-century silk cross over the head and are held in place with a silk circlet. (The blue cap that provides support underneath is sixteenth or seventeenth century.) Attached are five appliqués in gold thread: the lamb of God, an angel, a cherub or seraph, a king with raised hands (probably Solomon), and (on the crossing) a star (possibly a reference to Stella Maris). In a sensitive analysis, Evelin Wetter goes beyond the suggestion that the crown constructs the nun as Christ's bride and argues that it fashions her into similitude to the Virgin herself, crowned as queen of heaven by her son at her Ascension.[55]

The texts and objects that survive from late medieval women's cloisters help us to understand the multiple ways in which "crowning"—whether of the young nun herself or of the statues of Mary and the saints, whether with a physical crown of silk or gold wire or with a "fictive" wreath or *corona* of prayers—actually shaped the one crowned and bound her into a reciprocal relationship. Giving to the queen of heaven yet another crown was a participation in her eternal crowning and inclined her to give gifts to the giver in return. A bestowal of the consecrated nun's crown, whether embroidered with the saving wounds of Christ or with the angels who celebrate Mary's place at the right hand of her son, lifted the young nun toward the glory to which she aspired by her virginity. Yet we should be careful not to go too far in understanding the crowns offered to Mary, Christ, and the saints as literally the accoutrements of heaven or in assimilating the crowned nun here on earth to her heavenly reward. Both the texts and the objects show us that the nuns themselves saw a gap between earth and heaven.

On Earth and in Heaven

Gertrude the Great (d. 1301 or 1302) of the Saxon convent of Helfta, whose *Spiritual Exercises* provide a lengthy commentary on the nun's crowning, speaks of the nun's consecration as a process toward heaven. Christ promises: "I will make you a robe of the noble purple of my precious blood; I will crown you with the choice gold of my bitter death." And the young sister prays in response: "Make me to go on my way to you in my nuptial gown among the prudent virgins."[56] The crown is both the crown of thorns and the bridal wreath. The crowning is reciprocal: Christ and the nun are clothed with each other, and this is completed only in heaven.[57] The nun prays: "And after this life, may I deserve to receive the crown of chastity in a long white gown among a lily-like band, following you, lamb without spot, son of the Virgin Mary, wherever you go."[58] In the homier stories of Gertrude's *Legatus*, much of which was written about her by her sisters, Gertrude questions why a certain person who has died receives the garment of glory immediately while an equally worthy person, still alive, is not yet clothed with the "marvelously embroidered" robe of Christ.[59] The implication is clear: on earth the garment can still be soiled and wrinkled. The crown the nun receives at her earthly investiture both is — and is not yet — her crowning in heaven.

Crowning rituals from the Lüneburg cloisters show the same awareness of both the collapsing together and the distinction of earth and heaven. In a notice about the nuns' crowning of 1464 at Ebsdorf, a sister describes why Easter and the five Sundays after are all suitable for the "twofold espousal" of the nun to her bridegroom. The text closely assimilates the crowns Christ wins for souls by his precious blood and the crown the nun receives both now and "in the future" as reward for her virginity.[60] But a passage from a Middle Low German prayer book from the neighboring convent of Medingen makes clear in the nuns' own words that the coronation is completed only after death. The Easter liturgy is here understood as a dialogue between Christ and the soul, in which the nun's crown becomes an attribute of the resurrected body.[61]

> When our dear Lord hears the praise offered by Holy Christendom, he says to the devout soul: *Resurrexi et adhuc tecum sum* — I am risen from the dead and have taken back to me all the glory [*clarcheit*] and honor which I have had from the beginning of the world. *Et adhuc tecum sum* — and I am still with you, o devout soul, by my grace, and I shall sustain in you the blessedness which you will receive from me when I take you from this world to me, because you take me now to you in true commitment. Then I shall lay upon you the hand of my honor and shall crown you because you bear . . . some grief when remembering my suffering, and therefore you will be with me in eternal joy. Then you will be shown to the angels, since I will create anew your mortal body in the image of the *clarcheit* of my body. This you will receive after this life as I have received it twofold in my resurrection, in my Godhead and my humanity.[62]

The crowning is reciprocal, both present and future. Christ and the nun each enfold the other in love, but the final crowning is in heaven, when the mortal body is created anew in the gifts of the resurrection.[63] We are reminded of those medieval depictions of the Last Judgment in which naked figures rising from the dead are still distinguished in status by their headgear.[64]

This proleptic and processual quality is also seen in what the crowns actually looked like. Even the elegant surviving crown now at Riggisberg, although it may in form be a kind of *Bügelkrone* with gold embroidery, does not physically point upward as do royal crowns of the type we see on the processional and apocalyptic Madonnas at Wienhausen (figures 2.4 and 2.5) or on the multitude of saints and martyrs depicted on the Wienhausen ceiling. Indeed, if we compare the nun's crown (a simple cap) worn by the abbess in the image of the convent's founders on the Wienhausen vaults with adjacent images of the twenty-four golden-crowned elders of the Apocalypse or the diadem used by Christ to crown his mother in heaven, they do not appear to be the same sort of crown at all. (See figures 2.10a–b.) The contrast is even more striking if we consider an image of 1519 from Marienstern, which shows a novice being shorn. Beside her, a nun holds the simple cap she will later receive as her crown. Above, breaking out of the picture space, hovers the very different sort of golden crown she will receive only in heaven.[65] (See figure 2.11.)

The image most frequently used by scholars to illustrate the medieval nun's crown shows the same contrast. (See figures 2.12a–b.) A panel (about 1330) from the Altenberg Altar pairs a Premonstratensian nun as donor wearing her modest crown and venerating St. Elizabeth of Thuringia with a panel above on which Christ crowns Mary in heaven with a golden diadem whose pinnacles gleam, thrusting upward. Over Elizabeth, an angel hovers with the crown of glory she supposedly wears in heaven, but even it has not quite come to rest on the saint's head. Depicted as eternally giving clothes to beggars as she did while on earth, even the departed and sanctified Elizabeth seems almost still in process toward the coronation Mary has achieved in heaven. The little donor nun in the left-hand corner wears a crown, but not yet a crown of glory.

Indeed, the Mary depicted on the vaults of Wienhausen, like the processional Madonna whose wooden crown was safe from confiscation by reformers (figure 2.4), were themselves foreshadowings of heaven. Many scholars have recently emphasized the living quality of late medieval objects and the tactility and visuality of medieval

Figures 2.10a–b. Paintings for the Nuns' Choir at Wienhausen. Initial painting soon after 1380; restored 1488 by the nuns; restored again, 1867–68, within original outlines.

a. Here we see the martyrs receiving their crowns in heaven. Nonnenchor, Deckenmalerei, "Die 24 Ältesten."

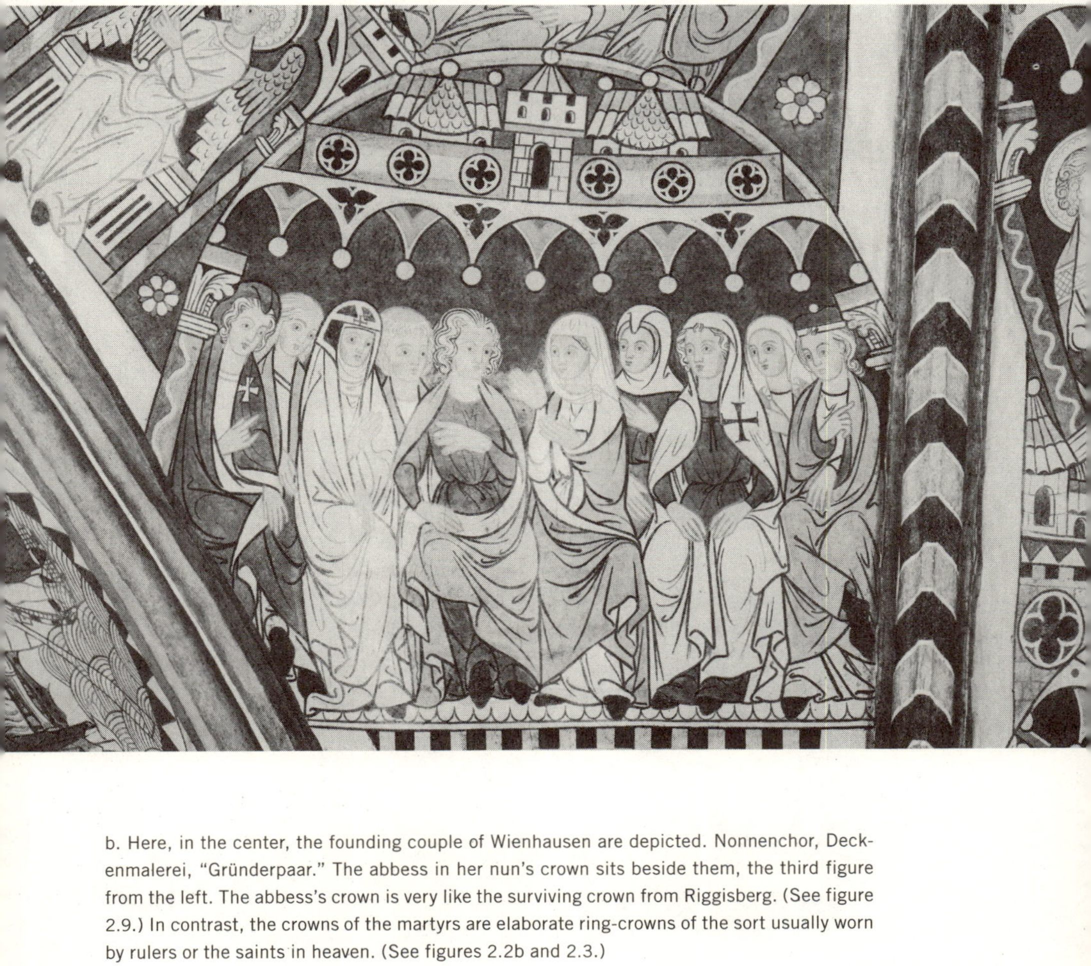

b. Here, in the center, the founding couple of Wienhausen are depicted. Nonnenchor, Deckenmalerei, "Gründerpaar." The abbess in her nun's crown sits beside them, the third figure from the left. The abbess's crown is very like the surviving crown from Riggisberg. (See figure 2.9.) In contrast, the crowns of the martyrs are elaborate ring-crowns of the sort usually worn by rulers or the saints in heaven. (See figures 2.2b and 2.3.)

Figure 2.11. Marienstern Ms. Oct. 1, fol. 59v. The image shows a novice being shorn almost as if she is being tonsured. Beside her, a sister holds the simple cap she will later receive as her nun's crown. Its shape is very like that of the Riggisberg crown. Above, breaking out of the picture space, hovers a very different sort of crown—the golden one she will receive only when she reaches her eternal reward in heaven.

devotion. This emphasis is not wrong. It mattered to nuns to think that what they gave to the Virgin was a wreath of prayer-flowers just as it mattered to wear on earth a crown of white silk that signaled a special place already reserved in heaven. The power of objects was at the center of late medieval piety. At its very heart lay the assumption that part contains whole and vice versa, that past, present, and future each not merely mirrors but contains the others. Without this, there cannot be hope of the salvation of the soul and the resurrection of the body. Such assumptions made the crowns of statues and the crowns of nuns both transient and permanent, both earthly and heavenly. Just as Mary was understood to be delighted and obligated by the goldsmith's crown, so the young nun was bound and molded for heaven by her white silk crown. In a sense, her crown, won by her perpetual virginity, *is* the crown of the Madonna. Confiscation of it or of Mary's crown is a threat to the nun's monastic identity.

Nonetheless, we should be careful about taking such assumptions too literally, lest we fall back into the description of late medieval piety as static and quantitative that is often attributed to Johan Huizinga.[66] Medieval nuns may not all have thought in the sophisticated terms voiced by Gertrude of Helfta when she quoted a text attributed to Hugh of St. Victor, but they were all aware of the temptations of daily life and the depredations of time that consume objects. Gertrude, or the nun recording her visions, argues that invisible things cannot be understood without visible images. Thus, we need "images of milk and honey," just as the Apocalypse of John tells us that the heavenly Jerusalem is "adorned with gold and silver and pearls and other kinds of gems." But "we know that there is nothing of this sort there, where however there is nothing lacking. For if no such things are there in outward appearance [*per speciem*], they are all there in likeness [*per similitudinem*]."[67] Hence, neither the nun's earthly crown nor the crown stolen from the enthroned Madonna *is* Mary's crown in heaven.

Whether or not they quoted such abstract theories of presence and representation, the nuns of the Lüneburg Heath thought in terms of two espousals, earthly and heavenly, and saw a deep as well as a literal significance in their crowns. Crowns mattered as literal objects but not only as literal objects. In the liturgy and in inner devotion, nuns and their statues were "crowned with many crowns." Proleptically

Figures 2.12a–b.

a. Right wing of the Altenberg Altarpiece from about 1334 showing St. Michael, the Coronation of the Virgin, St. Elizabeth, and the Death of the Virgin. In the coronation of the Virgin on the upper right panel, Christ crowns Mary in heaven with a golden diadem whose pinnacles thrust upward.

b. Detail of the lower left panel. Here we see a Premonstratensian nun as donor wearing her modest crown and venerating St. Elizabeth of Thuringia. Over Elizabeth, an angel hovers with the crown of glory she supposedly wears in heaven, but even it has not quite come to rest on the saint's head. The artist was a Rhenish master, active c. 1330. Now in the Städel Museum, Frankfurt am Main, Germany.

and processually, the crowns of earth were and were not the crowns of the eternal Jerusalem. But it mattered that they were crowns.[68] Understanding the many crowns of fifteenth-century piety and practice helps us understand a little better why the Wienhausen nuns, who tried to model themselves on the Mary crowned in heaven, felt spiritual as well as economic deprivation when her crowns were confiscated in the 1469 reform.

CHAPTER THREE

The Sacrality of Things: An Inquiry into Divine Materiality in the Christian Middle Ages[1]

For much of the twentieth century and increasingly in the last two decades, anthropologists, students of comparative religion, historians, and art historians have been interested in exploring materiality.[2] From such discussion, it seems clear that religions are characterized in a special way by materiality — that is, by the presence of specific things (not necessarily the same from one religion to another) that are charged with a significance we can call sacral or sacred. Such things are set apart from the ordinary; they provide access to and act for the divine. As anthropologist Webb Keane observes: "Religions may not always demand beliefs, but they will always involve material forms."[3] Indeed it is usually through its materiality — temples, relics, altars, sacred books, sand patterns, inscriptions — that we first gain access to a religion different from our own.

In recent studies of sacred objects, two examples have been especially popular as providing a paradigm: the eye-opening ritual in Hinduism and the *mīs pî* ceremony of mouthwashing in the ancient Near East. I take the Indian example first. Many Indian texts describe the coming to life of images of gods and goddesses as a series of rites or processes, from the initial selection of appropriate material for carving (wood from a male tree for a male god, for example) to its awakening by the chiseling and painting in of its eyes.[4] The image is then bathed, dressed, and adorned with unguents, and the devotee both recognizes and is recognized, locking eyes with the god (*darshan*).[5] Although the image is "made" by those who carve and anoint it, the god is also, as a devotional poem to Vishnu puts it, in the image "as butter lies hidden in fresh milk."[6] In ancient Mesopotamia, a new cult object similarly underwent a series of rituals, culminating in this case in the *mīs pî* (mouthwashing) ceremony, after which the artisans flung away their tools and chanted: "I did not make it; I swear I did not make it."[7] Scholars have struggled with a variety of concepts, such as "distributive agency" and "representation," to express what is happening in these ceremonies, but whatever refinement of terminology one prefers to use, it is clear that the power of an Other is emerging in the material object we call an image.[8]

To take as a paradigm for divine materiality these two examples of three-dimensional objects enlivened at the moment when eyes or mouth (two crucial portals of human communication) are provided raises a host of issues. How far is a devotional object anthropomorphic or iconic? If anthropomorphic, is it thus in some way "like" the god it bodies forth? If it is not "like" the divine, how is it recognized as especially related to the divine? Does it act for the god and if so, how? Is this agency manifested in events extraordinary to its materiality such as crying or bleeding — actions and events sometimes conceptualized as miracles or wonders?[9] What authorizes it to act for the divine? Is a ritual process or consecration necessary for the emergence of the divine in the material, and if so, is a role for and control by a priestly class necessary to the process? I shall return below to such questions, but first I must provide some background concerning the recent study of Christian images.

Recent Approaches to Christian Images

The standard textbook account of the development of Western Christian art over two millennia runs as follows.[10] Early Christians inherited the Second Commandment: "Thou shalt not make to thyself a graven thing, nor the likeness of any thing that is in heaven above, or in the earth beneath, nor of those things that are in the waters under the earth. Thou shalt not adore them nor serve them" (Exodus 20:4–5). But despite their detestation of statues of the pagan gods, Christians also inherited Roman iconographic traditions such as doves, lambs, fish, and shepherds that seemed appropriate to signify the peace of the afterlife, God's concern for humankind, and so forth.[11] After a flare-up of attacks on images in the Eastern Church between the sixth and eighth centuries, images were accorded acceptance by the Christian Church because of two basic arguments: first, that Christ, because God and human, can be depicted in his human form, and second (as theorized by John of Damascus and Thomas Aquinas, among others) that images point to the divine but do not instantiate it. They are not God but merely trigger a devotional turn toward or rise to God.

Much about this account is misleading or incorrect, not least because it takes the words of a few theorists to describe the practice of a wide range of European Christians, who often behaved as if statues, mosaics, and wall paintings were in fact divine. It certainly does not account for the distrust of images that erupted in northern Europe in the fifteenth and sixteenth centuries.[12] After all, the Second Commandment had been around a long time; why should it suddenly have been taken seriously? Nor does the traditional account adequately describe the intense presence — the "is"-ness — of the images that were attacked in the iconoclasm of the European reformations or reined in by the final decrees of the Council of Trent.[13] Indeed if we consider such an account in the context of a broader theorizing that takes rituals such as the *mīs pî* as the paradigm, Christian images would be anomalous — less mysterious, threatening, and powerful than other religious images. Yet what we know of the behavior of images in the Christian West and the behavior of many devotees toward them sounds more like the behavior of gods and adherents in present-day Bengal or ancient Mesopotamia than like the quiet meditating of a monk or nun who was, in theory at least, to mount upward away from the carved statue or prayer card to an Other circumscribed by and attainable in no word or figure.[14]

Moreover, if images are only triggers of reactions but in themselves do not incorporate the divine, the question of the source of their power becomes more pressing. As David Freedberg observed in his justly admired *The Power of Images*, Western images are not consecrated.[15] Some are blessed and sprinkled with holy water, but full consecration is limited to altar vessels, the top of the altar table, the ground of cemeteries and space of churches, the oil, water, bread, and wine used in the sacraments, and the personnel (the clergy) who perform them.[16] Where, then, does the sacrality of such objects as wall paintings and statues come from? Having asked the question this way, art historians have had to resort to explanations that attribute the power of images to something injected into them from outside.

Frequent explanations include the claim that the earliest freestanding statues in the West (such as the figures of Virgin and child known as the Throne of Wisdom and early monumental crucifixes) contained relics inside, as if pieces of the saints conveyed to the statues their holiness.[17] Another explanation, suggested by Hans Belting in his influential *Bild und Kult*, relates the authorization of images to stories that certain icons were *acheiropoieta* (not made by human hands) or in other ways miraculous in origin—that is, handed down by angels from heaven, or painted in miraculous circumstances by artists who actually saw Christ or his mother, or imprinted on cloth by Christ's own body or face.[18]

Explanations that stress social function or psychological need have also become popular, and such interpretation need not imply that claims to miraculous images were fraudulent, although we can document that they sometimes were. Images, like visions and other miraculous manifestations, often speak to the disadvantaged or socially marginal (children, women, the sick and disabled, or even criminals).[19] They can thus be analyzed as bypassing the clergy to bring Jesus or his mother Mary directly into contact with the religiously dispossessed. They can also be understood as useful to the powerful. Images were politically and economically important to communities competing for pilgrimage revenues, and they served as inspiration to armies mounting wars for Christ, such as the Reconquista, military missionizing in the northeast of Europe, and crusades to the holy land. As historians have pointed out recently, animated images were often older ones, in obscure or neglected sites, whose revival could empower or re-empower the individuals and communities that suddenly began to venerate them.[20]

None of this analysis is wrong. And it is pertinent to efforts to go beyond explanations that see images as simply triggers of devotion, inducements to something beyond or other than the images.[21] Nonetheless, much of the recent study of Western images seems to be adducing the wrong parallels. All this focus on image and idol as the place where materiality should be explored for the first 1500 years of Western Christianity is the wrong focus. When we use paradigms such as the eye-opening ceremonies of Hinduism to ask questions about Christianity, as I am proposing to do, we see that the parallel to image is not necessarily image. It is wrong to take the elaborate *mīs pî* ceremony as a parallel, in any simple sense, to the sixteenth-century frenzy to venerate the Schöne Madonna of Regensburg, for example, or other late medieval/early modern cults of the Christian image.[22] (See figure 3.1.) Nonetheless it is useful to try to understand the divine materiality of the European Middle Ages through some of the sophisticated questions scholars have raised about the *mīs pî*, as long as we recognize that image in one culture may not be the best analogy to image in another culture. The most intense devotion to and anxiety about representations of the holy did not, in the Western Christian tradition, accrue around images at all but around relics (pieces of holy people that became central to cult) and around sacraments and sacramentals (materials, such as water, oil, rings, staves, and bread, that conveyed a power they did not "depict," in the sense of having similitude to, but rather "represented," in the sense of making present).[23]

Even in periods when what we call art flourished more or less unquestioned, there was debate about how the holy was present in relics; and from circa 1050 to 1600 there was persistent conflict over the Eucharist. Controversy about whether, and how, bread and wine really become God led to more and more literalist and materialist explanations and to the miraculous behavior of the materials themselves. The iconoclasm of the fifteenth- and sixteenth-century European north, which was not practiced by all Protestant groups, was accompanied by far more widespread rejection of medieval practices vis-à-vis relics and the Eucharist. Indeed even in Catholic areas, much of earlier practice about holy matter was discarded or redefined. "Idols" were not only, perhaps not even primarily, statues and stained glass. For example, when a group of Protestant Visitors came to the nunnery of Zehdenick in the north of Germany to insist that the nuns surrender the "idol" they worshipped, they referred not to an image at all but to a glass container that supposedly held a miraculous host.[24] The anxiety in what we refer to as early modern "iconoclasm" was not so much over the first phrase of Exodus 20:4: "Thou shalt not make to thyself a graven thing" as over the second: "nor the likeness of any thing that is in heaven above, or in the earth beneath, nor of those things that are in the waters under the earth."[25] In other words, the anxiety was over materiality itself: How can the divine be reflected in the cosmos, in matter in all its manifestations? And specific aspects of matter—its changeableness and friability—were crucial in the medieval discussion.[26] What did it mean for the Other to be present in bread, in stone, in bones and dust?

Figure 3.1. Michael Ostendorfer, woodcut, 1610. British Museum, 1895,0122.77. This woodcut, of which a number of copies survive, shows the frenzied devotion of what many consider to be the last great medieval pilgrimage (1519–21): the cult of the Schöne Madonna of Regensburg in southern Germany. The object of devotion was at first a supposedly miracle-working painting, but the city soon erected a stone statue of the Virgin on an outdoor column that drew even more frenzied crowds.

All this came to a head most acutely in debates about and devotion to the Eucharist. It is the Eucharist that is, in the Western Middle Ages, the most appropriate parallel to images in other parts of the world. It is the Eucharist that is claimed in theology to become God, that is experienced by the faithful as a place of special access to God by seeing as well as ingesting, and that, particularly in the centuries of the later Middle Ages but still in some places today, allegedly manifests itself as the body of God by miracles of transformation such as bleeding. (See figure 3.2.) Thus it is apropos the Eucharist that the questions I outlined earlier as raised by the ceremony of *mīs pî*—questions about agency, similitude, consecration, and so forth—are most tellingly raised.

The Eucharist as Divine Materiality: The Relics of Johannes Bremer

That the Eucharist is understood and apprehended as divine materiality will seem obvious to modern Roman Catholics. But if we consider some of the questions raised by comparative study, we see how bizarre this concept is. In a religion whose theology stresses incarnation (that is, the coming of God into a human being) in ways other religions do not, it is odd that the focal point of revelation and agency is foodstuff, understood to be invisibly—but only invisibly—flesh and blood.

In the mid-fifteenth century, the Franciscan theologian Johannes Bremer underlined the issue. Writing in the midst of a controversy about divine materiality—a controversy in which Franciscans played a key role in defending the presence of various kinds of material traces of Christ's body—Bremer discussed three types of holy objects found in his region of northern Germany. He called all three "relics." I cite the discussion both to demonstrate the range of devotional objects Bremer saw as divine presences and to show how sophisticated, philosophically as well as theologically, discussions of the Christian material divine could become. Bremer writes:

> There are, in the church militant, great and precious relics [*reliquiae*]: the clothing of Christ, the cross, and other of his arms [*arma*—the instruments of the passion]. And there are, so the pious believe, major and more noble relics, that is, the flesh and blood of Christ reserved under their proper species [that is, the foreskin and blood relics of Christ]. And there are the greatest and

Figure 3.2. The miraculous bleeding host of Dijon in its monstrance. Folio 17v, Ogier Bénigne's Book of Hours, Baltimore, Walters Art Gallery, MS W.291. Given by Pope Eugene IV to Duke Philip the Good of Burgundy in 1433, the host was housed in a magnificent gold monstrance made for it in 1454. It came to be associated in some obscure way with anti-Jewish propaganda. This depiction of it was added to a Book of Hours in about 1500 by the family of Ogier Bénigne. Miracles in which bread turned into flesh and blood illustrate the complex manner in which late medieval devotion located encounter with and manifestation of the divine in aniconic or nonrepresentational stuff, even if such stuff was sometimes, as in this case, stamped with the human figure.

> most noble relics, in which it is necessary to believe for salvation — that is, the flesh and blood of Christ under the sacrament of the Eucharist [*sub Eucharistiae sacramento*]. The first are great, because they are Christ's *arma* and the instruments of our redemption, although separated. The second are greater, because they are something of the humanity of Christ and were joined to the divinity.[27] The third are greatest and most precious because they are united in the *supposito divino* by the act of divinity [that is, they are Christ's humanity assumed by the divine Logos].[28]

Six aspects of Bremer's claims are telling.[29] First, none of the objects is what we would call an image. It is true that the *arma Christi* (the instruments of Christ's passion: nails, whips, thorns, and so forth) were a popular iconographic motif, often found on altarpieces and church walls, in books of hours and other devotional texts.[30] As such, they did serve as aids to prayer and meditation. But in Bremer's discussion, such images are not relevant to the defense of divine presence in matter. The *arma Christi* that he refers to are actual relics of the Crucifixion: objects that had been in contact with Christ's body. To Bremer, it is not images but rather other sorts of objects that most closely reflect God.

Second, the word that Bremer uses is "relics" (*reliquiae*) — what remains of something. The devotional objects that Bremer finds central to worship are what modern theorists (following Peirce) would call indexes, not icons — objects that do not so much refer to as actually exist in contact with the holy.[31]

Third, the highest instantiation of the divine to Bremer is one that is not visibly animate. The host and chalice — that is, the bread and wine — he points to are not miraculous transformations. Bremer came from an order whose members tended to take a theological position in support of such transformations, and he was involved in university debates about and defenses of both blood relics and miraculously bleeding hosts. But here his emphasis is on invisible presence in material stuff.

Fourth, the highest instantiation of the divine is not anthropomorphic or even representational in the sense of iconic. Bread does not look like flesh. Wine (if red) may bear some similarity to blood, but it does not image or represent blood in any one-to-one sense. Similitude (in the sense of "looking like") does not matter to Bremer. What matters is presence.

Fifth, the highest "relic" is not genetically or genealogically linked to past holy bodies or holy objects. Unlike the first sort of relics Bremer mentions (the *arma Christi*: contact relics of Christ) and the second sort of relics (bodily relics of Christ: his foreskin or blood), the Eucharist is not physically derived from Christ's human body or contact with it. The first two sorts of holy objects that Bremer mentions are to him lower, less close to the divine, although they are more closely linked to body and more representational as well. In a sense we might say that, to Bremer, the stuff that is least close to the incarnate god (neither a part of him nor an object that has touched him) is the place where the divine arrives and is found.

Sixth, the bread and wine Bremer speaks of as the highest of relics are not signs or symbols in the sense of something more or less arbitrarily chosen to refer to something else. Neither index nor icon, they are also not sign. They *are* the divine. That which is least "like" or connected to the incarnate holy is thus its most immediate presence. Indeed, to this theologian (as to many of his contemporaries), the nonvisibility may be key. The divine is present "under the sacrament [*sub . . . sacramento*]" of the bread and wine. Despite the proliferating Eucharistic miracles in Bremer's own region of Germany, he prefers presence hidden, not manifest, in material stuff.

If we bear in mind both Bremer's discussion of the Eucharist and the questions about religious materiality that comparative study of rituals such as the Hindu eye-opening ceremony raises, our understanding of late medieval Eucharistic practice and belief immediately becomes deeper and the theoretical template we use to analyze materiality becomes more complex. In what follows, I want to suggest four ways in which late medieval Eucharistic theology and devotion raise large questions about the nature of the intersection of the material and the divine.

Dissimilitude and Divine Materiality

My first point is simply to underline the dissimilitude between the incarnate God and the material stuff in which that God is understood to be most completely present or instantiated. This dissimilitude requires more attention than we usually give it. So much recent discussion of late medieval piety has been devoted to the new and insistent stress on Christ's physical and emotional humanity that we sometimes neglect to notice that the same period saw an equally insistent emphasis on the literal presence of the incarnate God in the basic foodstuff of the Mediterranean diet — bread and wine — and a radical increase of miracles in which this holy food animated itself by bleeding, levitating, or glowing and was preserved, still visibly as foodstuff (although altered foodstuff), to provide a locus of pilgrimage. Yet bread and wine, even miraculously altered to a red-spotted wafer or a vessel of viscous liquid, are not in any simple sense "like" the figure of Christ seen on crucifixes, pietàs, or wall paintings of the *arma Christi*. (See figure 3.3 for an example of the devotional attention to the human Christ that was characteristic of the late Middle Ages and has been much emphasized recently by scholars.)

Much recent theoretical work on divine materiality raises the question of the anthropomorphism or iconicity of religious objects and argues that those that are closest to the human form are most apt to be the locus of the holy and to come alive for the faithful either in ritual or by miraculous self-assertion. This has led to a good deal of use, in the study of religion, of research from the new area of cognitive science. Scholars relate such ceremonies as the Hindu eye-opening ritual and the concomitant importance in Indian piety of *darshan* (the intense gaze between devotee and god) to the fact that babies tend to smile at ovals with only the eyes and mouth drawn in.[32] Research on robots has established what is known as the "uncanny valley effect" — that is, the fact that people can be demonstrated to respond differently to humanoid or humanlike figures, on the one hand, and machines or clearly inanimate objects, on the other.[33] Some cognitive scientists have even argued that anthropomorphism is a necessary stage in the evolution of religion.[34] Art historians and literary scholars have used this sort of research to assume a Pygmalion effect in religious art — that is, a tendency to privilege the human figure, or what approaches to the human figure, as a locus of the divine.

There are problems with this approach. I leave aside the well-known fact that neither in India nor in the ancient Near East is the anthropomorphic always the place where the divine arrives. We have only to think of the Shiva linga — the stone cylinder at the heart of Shaivite Hinduism.[35] I merely point out here that the centrality of the Eucharist in Christianity provides a powerful counter case to such simple conclusions.

It is worth noting here that even when we study Christian images (statues and wall paintings) that are claimed in the later Middle Ages to come alive, there is no correlation between three-dimensionality

Figure 3.3. Meister Francke, *Schmerzensmann* (Man of Sorrow or Man of Suffering) (c. 1430), 92 × 67 cm. Now in the Hamburger Kunsthalle. In this image of an androgynous Christ, gentle, sorrowing, yet in intense pain, the red cloak held by angels almost appears to be flayed skin. The painting is an example of the devotional attention to the human Christ that was characteristic of the late Middle Ages and has been much emphasized recently by scholars.

and tendency to animate, or between realism of depiction and animation. Nor is there a correlation between naturalism and success at stimulating devotion. The Madonna of the Prison in Prato, for example, that allegedly walked and wept in 1484, is a flat, rather ordinary wall painting like many others of its date and in no way more lively, beautiful, or womanly.[36] But the non-anthropomorphism, so to speak, of Eucharistic bread and wine—its nonsimilitude (in any visual or morphological sense) to the human figure of Christ—is even more telling.

To emphasize the non-anthropomorphism of consecrated bread and wine is not to argue that there are no anthropomorphic elements in devotion to the Eucharistic species. Not only did the faithful increasingly claim that the elements did on occasion manifest their reality as human flesh by miracle, liturgists spent much time elaborating the symbolism of the material stuff in ways that underlined its human physicality. The grains of wheat gathered in the wafer were regularly interpreted as the gathering of Christians into the church, and the grapes gathered (and crushed) to make wine were sometimes also so interpreted. The spilling out of blood in birthing, or wounding, or feeding (since breast milk was understood as processed blood) was related to the redness of wine/blood in the chalice. Medieval theologians in (to our tastes offensive) supersessionist arguments held that Christians were superior to Jews because they ate real human flesh, whereas Jews sacrificed only animals, but Christians were also superior because their sacrifice was invisible (hence bloodless), whereas Jewish sacrifice was literal and bloody.[37] All this symbolic interpretation draws on an understanding of the Eucharistic elements as human flesh and blood, however hidden as such.

Moreover, the well-known fact that the later Middle Ages saw increasing claims to visions in which the host, and sometimes the wine of the chalice, appeared as a human figure—the infant or the adult Christ—might be seen as a sort of "return of the [anthropomorphic] repressed." (See figure 3.2.) Nonetheless, there was ambivalence from both clerical authorities and the faithful about such experiences partly because of the suggestion of cannibalism. Women who saw visions of the infant Christ in the host usually cradled him in their arms as a substitute for receiving communion. When Colette of Corbie saw the Christ Child carved like a piece of meat, she brooded over the vision in horror and interpreted it as Christ's reparation for our sins, beating her own body in response.[38] Indeed, Eucharistic visions were sometimes seen as evidence of God's wrath, and priests who themselves experienced them or met with such claims from the faithful were often enjoined to pray that the elements return to the form of bread and wine. For example, the reforming Premonstratensian Eberhard Waltmann argued in the mid-fifteenth century that the appearance of a bloody finger in the chalice in the tale of the Mass of St. Gregory was as horrible (*horribilis*) as the blood-plague in ancient Egypt and an indication that all transformation miracles should be questioned.[39] When miraculous matter endured as bloodlike or fleshlike or even as reflecting a human face or body (as, for example, in the corporal at Walldürn), it induced at least as much anxiety over how to revere or preserve it as pride in its possession. All this suggests that, even when overlaid with visions of the human Christ or eruptions of flesh and blood, the Christian Eucharist was not in any simple sense anthropomorphic. Thus the Eucharist, if brought into the center of cross-cultural discussions of divine materiality, becomes a major case study in the questioning of recent generalizations about the importance of anthropomorphism in the genesis of sacral objects.

Second, as I suggested earlier in my discussion of images, the Eucharist should raise for us questions about the role of consecration in the coming of the holy into material stuff. According to Christian theologians, of course, consecration was necessary to the transformation of foodstuff into the body of Christ. Moreover, there was complex preparation for this moment of entry not only through the ritual of the mass (including its appeals to all the senses through chant, light, incense, and so forth) but also through previous extraliturgical preparation of the materials as the bread was baked and the wine pressed.[40] In all this, the centrality and control of the clergy is clear. Indeed as the theological emphasis on the Eucharist as sacrifice became more literal in the later Middle Ages, the priest came to be understood as in some sense Christ himself; hence the divine was present in sacrificer as well as sacrificed. So highly charged, so literally divine, were the elements on the altar that only the divine itself could bring about their transformation or handle and distribute them.[41] At least in theory. Nonetheless, there was anxiety over exactly the role of the priest and the nature of the instantiation of the divine in food. From the eleventh century on, controversy raged in Western Europe over how exactly to interpret the Eucharist. Transubstantiation, defined at the Fourth Lateran Council in 1215, was interpreted quite variously in the course of the later Middle Ages, and radically different theories of the Eucharist were a driving force in the fragmentation of Western Christendom in the sixteenth century. Many scholars have seen the proliferation of Eucharistic miracles from the twelfth century on as a response to increasing doubts about the increasingly literalist understanding of real presence.[42] I shall return to this. What I want to underline here is the fact that, even in the later Middle Ages, there was no simple relationship between consecration and the arrival of the divine. In many of the Eucharistic visions we know of through *exempla* collections and the important new genre we call nuns' books, Christ bypasses the clergy to bring himself to the person (more often than not a woman) who desires his presence after being denied the Eucharist.[43] In a number of the transformation miracles reported between the fourteenth and sixteenth centuries, there was heated controversy over whether the miraculous object (usually a bleeding host) had been consecrated or not.

The question of consecration was, for example, an element in the Wilsnack controversy—the century-long conflict over one of the most popular and contested pilgrimage sites of the later Middle Ages. From the beginning, there was confusion over whether or not the three wafers found intact and red-spotted after the church burned to the ground in 1383 had been consecrated. To the theologians, there was clearly a problem if Christ had manifested himself in nonconsecrated bread. But a pilgrimage had already developed. Thus the nearby bishop was sent to reconsecrate the hosts, just in case. According to early chronicle accounts, however, the hosts bled to demonstrate their power before the bishop arrived—a fact that could be interpreted either as proof that they had indeed been consecrated or as an assertion that they did not need to be. As this story makes clear, even in a religion where consecration ritual and the attendant clerical control are central in theory, the arrival of the divine can be understood as slipping out of such control.[44]

My third point is that the coming of the divine into matter in the Christian Eucharist contributes to a general, comparative-religion question about the respective roles of theology and practice in the encounter of God with matter. This is especially true for the later Middle Ages. As I said earlier, the proliferation of Eucharistic miracles in Western Europe, and even their increasing prominence as inducement to and justification of persecution of Jews, has usually been interpreted as a response to the definition of transubstantiation at the Fourth Lateran Council of 1215. According to this argument, the literalism of the definition — that is, that substance changes but accidents remain the same — led both to increasing expectation of the revelation of God in the elements and to increasing Christian doubt about the literalism of the doctrine, even to guilt about experiencing such doubt.[45] In such interpretation (as in the interpretation of Christian images as mere signs or triggers of devotion), theology is seen as driving practice.

It is true that one of the common scenarios for Eucharistic miracles is skepticism about the presence of Christ in wafer or chalice, followed by transformation of the stuff into blood or less frequently flesh. There are many other scenarios that do not relate to revelation as proof of doctrine, but that is not my point here. My point is that, according to many of the most sophisticated theologians of the period, there should not be such miracles at all. Transubstantiation meant by definition that the substance of the Eucharistic elements (what they are in their nature — that is, breadness and wineness) changes, but the accidents (the visible characteristics of that sort of stuff) remain the same. According to theological analysis, there could not be change of appearance. Eucharistic transformation could not simply be a revelation of the substance that was, in Bremer's words, "under" the bread and wine. It was its *in*visibility that guaranteed divine presence. Christ came as substance, not accidents. Hence, complex theorizing was necessary to explain miracles of the change of accidents; such change had to be attributed to a second divine act, either a miracle added to the consecrated material to put a sign of what was "under" on top, so to speak, or a miracle worked in the minds of those who perceived the transformation to make them see the blood.[46]

The tendency in much cross-cultural analysis of divine materiality has been to search for the theological underpinnings of rituals in which the divine is in some way instantiated. Cultures that have left no written theology have been assumed to be more opaque to analysis. Historians have felt that they need texts in order to understand objects. The gap between late medieval theological analysis of transformation miracles and the fact of such miracles complicates such assumptions. Whether or not exposure to the doctrine of transubstantiation led some people to assume or to doubt that God would appear in the matter of the Eucharist (and much of our evidence even for popular understanding of such miracles comes from writing for a highly specialized audience of clergy or cloistered religious), doctrine and theological explication of it are clearly not the explanation for the events or the piety surrounding them. First, we should note that there is a chronological problem. Accounts of Eucharistic miracles appear before the definition of 1215 (which is far less precise and Aristotelian than it is often represented as being).[47] Indeed it may well be that proliferating claims to miracles of Eucharistic transformation were an inducement to theological pronouncement rather than the other way around. Second, for reasons I have just explained, formal theology should have reined in such miracles even if they were owing to expectations raised by doctrine or to doubts about it. Theology cannot have been the driver of practice or the instigator of miracles. Thus the particular form that divine materiality took in the twelfth to sixteenth centuries in Western Christendom should lead us to question the assumption that we understand or explain religious practice when we find theological texts that pronounce upon it. This leaves far more open than before the pressing question of why particular holy objects come at certain periods and places to manifest, or spill out in visible ways, the divinity they possess or convey.

Christian Materiality in Comparative Perspective

With this observation I come to the final argument that I wish to make about the relation of the Christian Eucharist to comparative study. I am never satisfied with monocausal explanations. Therefore, I am unwilling to say that the political and economic utility of powerful things, theological teaching about the holy, or mind/brain research on human responses to various kinds of form or material explains the special significance of certain objects understood to be the instantiation of the divine in matter. I think specific rituals and specific objects can be understood only in specific settings. That bread and wine became the central manifestation of the divine in late medieval Europe is the consequence of many factors — not least the origins of Christianity in the Mediterranean basin where bread and wine were the basic diet, the model of the Jewish Passover, the theology of sacrifice in Exodus and Leviticus, and the clericalization of the late medieval church. What I want to pursue here is not so much a full explanation of the prominence of a particular kind of holy matter and the concomitant increase in transformation miracles as the observation that divine materiality must be understood as part of a culture's general sense of materiality, nature, and the cosmos. We cannot understand religious attitudes to matter—that is, special material revelations of the divine—unless we look at attitudes toward matter more generally.

To say this is not to argue that all objects should be understood as equally significant, nor is it to reduce religion to culture. But it is to remind us that holy matter is always a window not just into the divine but also into the material universe. Interpretations of late medieval Christianity have often forgotten this. Christianity has been criticized for privileging the body and the human in the humanity of Christ and thus putting "man" at the center of the universe. But late medieval religiosity made the material—relics and a wide range of devotional objects as well as the Eucharist—a special avenue to communication with God.[48] The power of this piety is attested by the strength of the reaction against it: both the new turn to interior devotion that rejected external aids and the vigorous objection to relics, images, and the Eucharist as divine presence that was voiced by dissidents from the twelfth to the sixteenth centuries (Albigensians, Lollards, and Hussites, for example) and by reformers (including some Catholic reformers, such as Erasmus) of the sixteenth century. Moreover, the special efficacy of the material was part of a late medieval sense of the universe as labile and revelatory—a sense manifested in werewolf stories, a new enthusiasm for alchemy and astrology, and the return of Neoplatonic conceptions of all physical reality as ensouled. Probably at no time in Western history has the sense of the material as alive and in constant metamorphosis been as strong as in the folk story and folk practice, the learned scientific literature, the magical and mineralogical theory, and the courtly poetry of the late Middle Ages.[49]

In this sense of matter as alive, we find something specific to the culture of Western Europe at a particular moment. Yet it is also relevant to wider comparative study. I propose two stories for comparison.

In the late thirteenth century, the nun Mechtild of Hackeborn saw a vision in which the vestments of a priest who was celebrating mass were covered with every blade and twig, every hair and scale, of the flora and fauna of the universe. She expressed surprise. But when she looked she realized that "the smallest details of the creation are reflected in the holy Trinity by means of the humanity of Christ, because it is from the same earth that produced them that Christ drew his humanity." In other words, the celebrant is, in a ritual context, clothed with the stuff of the universe, and this is glossed by Mechtild's sister nun, who records the vision, as the enclosure of all the flora and fauna of the world in the Christ who is present on the altar.[50]

There is an Indian text that is both parallel and not. In the *Bhāgavata Purāna*, an extant version of which is dated to south India in the ninth or tenth century, Krishna (an avatar of Vishnu) is a child living among goatherds when some of his friends tell his mother Yaśodā that he has been eating dirt. Krishna denies this. "If their words are true," he says, "look in my mouth for yourself." When his mother looks in, she sees the entire cosmos: the earth with all its mountains and seas; the sun, moon, and stars; the five material elements; the sense organs and the objects of sensation. Yaśodā is so frightened that Krishna must spread over her his "illusion" (*māyā*) so she once again sees only the everyday.[51]

The two stories are not the same and cannot be analyzed in the same way. They have different subtexts about the nature of revelation and the nature of reality. But each makes it clear that revelation through and within matter is related to a larger sense not only of the divine but also of the significance of the material in the religion in question. Both tales situate a piety in which things are holy in the context of a divine that chooses to manifest itself as containing the entire material universe (whether as redeemed through humanity or as reality beyond the illusion of the everyday). Revelation in these stories is not only *in* the material; it is also *of* the material. We cannot understand the place of divine materiality in such cultures without a larger sense of their attitudes toward materiality itself.

To summarize: I have tried to destabilize common scholarly assumptions and arguments about the Christian Eucharist by juxtaposing it to some recent questions that scholars have asked about divine materiality in other cultures. In doing so, I have wanted to illuminate both the Eucharist and the broader scholarly conversation about holy things. I have tried to redirect our attention to the fact that the Eucharist is the revelation of God in food. That such a revelation is the central example of divine materiality in late medieval Europe is not, I have argued, owing to what scholars have often assumed to be the explanations not only for Christian devotional objects but also for devotional objects in other cultures: anthropomorphism or some other form of morphological similitude to the divine; consecration by a priestly elite; or theological doctrine prescribing a certain sort of revelation. All of these factors are part of the context, but they do not explain the particular form of the material divine. Nor indeed does the doctrine of creation or the pervasive sense in late medieval Europe (extending far beyond the religious context) that the material world is in itself labile and revelatory. I have ended with Krishna's revelation to his mother and Christ's revelation to Mechtild in order to end with the questions raised by cross-cultural study left open. The prominence of objects, and especially of non-anthropomorphic objects, in religious practice and understanding is far stranger than we like to admit.

In closing then, I underline the strangeness of the visions of Yaśodā and Mechtild, the questionable nature of the miracle hosts of Wilsnack and the idol at Zehdenick, and the impressive yet confusing analytical precision of the Franciscan Johannes Bremer. My goal has been twofold: to make Western scholars think again about a central Christian rite by undermining conventional assumptions about it and to suggest that anthropologists, art historians, students of comparative religion, and even cognitive psychologists, who are just beginning to explore the aniconic and noniconic material divine, may have conveniently to hand in the Christian Eucharist a case study worth pursuing. Hence, I hope I have opened up new questions about the role of objects in Western Christianity and cast doubt on whether scholars of religion have, as yet, understood the full range of the issue of divine materiality.

CHAPTER FOUR

The Presence of Objects: Medieval Anti-Judaism in Modern Germany[1]

On the southwest corner of a large brick Gothic church in the little town of Sternberg in northern Germany is a curious stone. Mortared into the wall of a chapel that juts out beside what was once the main portal of the church, the stone bears, deeply embedded in it, large prints of two bare feet, on the edges of which chisel marks are visible. A photocopied church guide, available on a table inside the porch, mentions it only briefly, explaining that the stone, which was incorporated into the wall in 1496, is one on which the wife of the Jew Eleazar is said to have stood when she tried to sink a desecrated host in the nearby creek. Unable to cast away the host, she supposedly sank into the stone. (See figure 4.1.)

Located in the green and beautiful Mecklenburg landscape, Sternberg, like most areas of the former German Democratic Republic, is now suffering from massive unemployment and the flight of its youth to the west and to urban areas.[2] Its train station is closed; even local buses run there only on weekdays. Yet in the early sixteenth century, it was a prominent enough pilgrimage site to be singled out for attack in Martin Luther's famous *Open Letter to the Christian Nobility of the German Nation*. The cause of its pilgrimage was the objects that Eleazar's wife allegedly attempted to destroy by drowning: consecrated hosts (communion wafers) provided to the Jews by a priest in order to redeem a pawned cooking pot. (According to one account, the pot actually belonged to his concubine.) Those hosts were supposedly stuck with knives or nails until blood flowed from

Figure 4.1. Footprints supposedly left by Rabbi Eleazar's wife when she attempted to desecrate a Eucharistic host by throwing it into a creek. The stone is mortared into the outer wall of the Mary Church at Sternberg in Mecklenburg, Germany.

them and then, when they could not be sunk in water, were buried on the grounds of the former court of the duke. Revealed finally to the local clergy, they were found, blood-spotted, and worked miracles. Sixty-five Jews were tortured and confessed to the host desecration. Twenty-seven were executed by burning in a place still known as the Judenberg, on the edge of which was, in modern times, the cemetery of the Jewish community. (The priest was burned a year later in Rostock.) The remaining Jews were expelled from Mecklenburg, where they were not found again until the eighteenth century.[3]

The point of this chapter is not the story of the Jews of Sternberg nor of the pilgrimage. That story is certainly worth telling for English-speaking audiences, and many Germans today are unfamiliar with Sternberg and the many similar stories from the states of Mecklenburg and Brandenburg. Even when such incidents are known, they are often thought (quite incorrectly) to be characteristically south German. But in the past two decades scholars have written much about such events and their accounts are readily available. Recent scholarship agrees that in the thirteenth and fourteenth centuries pogroms often came first, giving rise subsequently to stories that Jews had desecrated Eucharistic hosts, whereas by the fifteenth century such stories, which were on the increase, tended to be elicited by torture in carefully regulated judicial procedures. The rise of legal process transformed legends and lynchings into evidence and judicial murder.[4] Scholars also agree in attributing complex political and economic motives to the protagonists in such events, disagreeing only about who benefited in particular cases from the expulsions and pilgrim revenues (secular princes, ecclesiastical ones, townspeople and merchants, or local clergy?). In other words, recent research has concentrated on historical fact (what happened?), recent interpretation on political, economic, or functional explanation (who or what group profited?).[5] My point here is not, however, events such as those of 1492 but the objects that still stand in German churches bearing witness to these events. For the odd stone with its large footprints is not the only physical object in the Mary Church at Sternberg that carries in its very stuff slander and outrage. Nor is Sternberg the only site where such objects persist. These objects raise insistent questions not only about what happened long ago but also about why the contemporary response has been what it is.

I want to pose some questions about the response of German and Anglophone tourists to such sites in order to consider how such objects are (and/or should be) memorialized, preserved, and displayed. Involved in these questions are others about the differences and similarities between images and objects and about the differences and similarities between medieval attitudes and modern ones. I begin with examples of the variety of present-day German treatments of such objects as the Sternberg footprints and end this part of the discussion with a consideration of the recent installations in the Jewish Museum in Berlin. Because the legends and sites of which I shall speak are obscure to English-speaking readers and the objects in question are very strange, there is much that needs explanation. I therefore proceed slowly, mixing accounts of present-day efforts to remember and forget with some discussion of scholarship on long-ago events. Only after I have described several sites and the rather different issues they raise do I turn to an elaboration of the medieval background necessary to understand them and then finally to a consideration of the inevitable complexity of contemporary response.

The Commemoration of Objects: Sternberg, Iphofen, Deggendorf, and Poznań

First, then, the other objects at Sternberg. Inside the church, close to the entrance, in what is now the baptismal chapel but was for centuries known as the holy blood chapel, stand what the little church guide refers to as "witnesses to the supposed Sternberg host desecration and . . . gruesome judicial murder of 1492." These objects are a large tabletop, heavily scored with knives, on which is inscribed "Dit is de tafele dar de Joden dat hillige sacrament up gesteken und gemartelt hebt tom sterneberge im Jar 1492," and a badly eroded wooden relief of the burning of the Jews.[6] (See figure 4.2 for the tabletop.) In the early sixteenth century, the awls or nails with which the host was pierced and the iron pot the priest Peter Däne tried to redeem by providing hosts to the Jews were displayed alongside the tabletop.[7] The pot and awls were, according to one account, carried off by marauding Swedish soldiers in 1638; the relief of the execution was severely damaged in a fire in 1741.

The objects in which the crime was supposedly inscribed, the hosts, were, in the sixteenth century, kept in a tall, painted, and gilded tabernacle in the holy blood chapel that was rapidly constructed

Figure 4.2. Tabletop on which Jews supposedly martyred a consecrated host in 1492. Displayed in the baptismal chapel, Mary Church, Sternberg.

for them in the parish church; the duke then built a second chapel and established a cloister on the place where the buried hosts had been found. (This multiplication of sites makes clear the competition for pilgrimage revenues.) An account by the humanist Nikolaus Marschalk in the early sixteenth century, written in order to credit the local princes (perhaps incorrectly) with the major initiative in getting rid of the Jews, charges the bishops and local clergy with negligence and disbelief, and suggests that they even considered consuming rather than preserving the miraculous blood-flecked hosts (a procedure for which there was actually considerable support in canon law). But the hosts became the center of a widespread cult, and records from the early sixteenth century tell of gorgeous *ex-votos* hung round them, including a little silver model of the city of Colberg.

Within forty years, the cloister was closed. Gifts for maintaining the eternal light before the shrine had dried up. A Protestant visitation in 1535 "forgot to ask" about the miraculous hosts.[8] Although an unreliable account says that the hosts were consumed as communion in 1539, it appears that the holy matter that was at the center of the frenetic pilgrimages of the 1490s was not so much destroyed as neglected, then forgotten. Only a few decades earlier, however, the charge that clergy wanted to destroy (that is, consume) the hosts could be used by Marschalk as evidence of lukewarm religiosity. Passionate debates between Protestant and Catholic scholars over the miraculous or superstitious nature of the original events survived into the eighteenth century. And the tabletop and nails, which had allegedly been in contact with the body of Christ as it suffered a reenactment of the Crucifixion and were marked with his blood, continued to be displayed, as did, of course, the footprints. If the hosts themselves (attacked by Luther and problematic in Protestant Eucharistic theology) at some point disappeared (perhaps conveniently), the contact relics (table, stone, and so on) survived. An elderly gentleman I met at a cocktail party in Berlin told me that his wife went to school near Sternberg in the 1930s and saw the tabletop with its ostensibly factual description of host abuse every Sunday when she went to church with her classmates, although she "never thought much about what it was."

Objects such as the tabletop and the footprints are of course now deeply troubling to the church at Sternberg. A recent, popular account of the history of German anti-Semitism describes the pastor in the 1980s as embarrassed, "burdened" by the objects, which he shows "but not willingly."[9] Although little is said in the photocopied guide about the footprints, the baptismal chapel serves now as a memorial to the Jews murdered in 1492 and by the Third Reich. A large menorah stands opposite the tabletop, and a plaque beneath the wooden relief, titled "The Sternberg Pogrom Against the Jews," states that murder took place in 1492 on the occasion of "a supposed host desecration" and declares the chapel a "reminder" of 1492 and of the Holocaust. The response is, we might say, scholarly; the impulse is to set the record straight. The host desecration did not happen. The judicial murder did. These are facts that viewers should not — should never — forget.

Perhaps the response is enough. It is more complex than the response to such objects in many places. In a number of European museums and churches, altar pieces depicting Jewish host desecrations have simply been removed from view without comment. A painting of the Regensburg host-finding in the Germanisches Nationalmuseum in Nuremberg, which I saw in the late 1990s, is currently not on display; wings which show the Pulkau host desecration are also not on view, although the altar by Nicholas Breu (c. 1520) is.[10] Moreover, in some places, the erasure of false history has itself been, either deliberately or accidentally, erased. For example, in a little village near Deggendorf (in Lower Bavaria), site of a famous host pilgrimage, a tin plaque fixed in the eighteenth century over a Crucifixion relief at the crossroads stated (quite fictitiously) that "here" the burghers took an oath on July 30, 1337, to revenge themselves on "the godless Jews" for "what they did to the host in Deggendorf." When American troops arrived in 1945, two armed soldiers forced a local painter to go to the crossroads and cover over the word "Jews" with black paint. The so-called "swearing column" with its black erasure stood until 1968 when a new crossing was built. Now the relief, broken in the process of removal, and the plaque with its crude but vivid reinterpretation are simply gone.[11]

If objects have sometimes been suppressed without comment, in other places they remain, also without comment. At Iphofen (near Würzburg), for example, where the legend of host desecration seems clearly to have been a projection back onto the fact of a pogrom, certain fairly late accounts tell of Jews throwing the abused Eucharist into a latrine, where it was saved from filth by a spiderweb. Despite the fact that no latrine or well appears in the earliest account (itself of dubious historical value) by Rudolf of Schlettstadt, a deep depression or hole cut into the floor of the Holy Blood Church was still revered in 1996, and a new altar designed and put into place in 1984 has a bronze grate in the form of the legendary spiderweb.[12] However silent now the legend, it lives on in that bronze web. (And who knows what accounts emerge when guides explain such decorative motifs to tourists, priests to parishioners, or parents to children?)

When, in December 2002, I visited the Corpus Christi Church, just north of the Old Market in the city of Poznań in Poland, I was not able to get into the crypt to see the well into which the Jews supposedly threw a desecrated host in 1399. But, I was told, the well is there; on this spot stood the house of Swidwa the Jew (although the location is outside the known bounds of the old Jewish quarter). Until a hundred years ago, it was said to work miracles. "What would a guide tell a tourist today?" I queried. "He'd just say," 'I was told, there is a legend. . .'" "So no exculpatory or expiatory reference is provided?" I asked. "Of course not. It's just the past, a part of history. Everyone understands that." And yet objects and sites have carried the Poznań story for hundreds of years. In 1620, in the same supposed house of Swidwa, a tabletop was found walled up in a pillar and was thought to be that on which the Jews pierced the host. It was carried in festive procession to the Carmelite Church. (A little entry survives in the city records noting shot and powder provided for the procession.) In 1750 the queen saw the miraculous hosts of Poznań, now understood to be three in number, in a little monstrance. In the early nineteenth century a Jewish scholar named Wolf Meyer Dessauer, whose account of events appears to be partly fabricated, reported that Jews were, in the early eighteenth century, required to march in the Corpus Christi procession carrying knives and a tablet which recounted the story of the host. That Jews were required to carry such objects is not certain; what *is* certain is that requiring such objects seemed credible Christian behavior. Whether or not it happened, Dessauer could believably argue that the past was made present—humiliatingly present—by objects. Thus we might well ask whether, for those standing at the end of such a tradition, it makes sense just to keep the crypt closed, especially if everyone knows the well is there.[13]

The silence—the absence of memorialization—at Iphofen and Poznań can be understood as cleansing; it can also be an effort to forget. So can reinterpretation, even expiatory reinterpretation. Take, for example, the case of Deggendorf. The story of the "Deggendorfer Gnad"—precious goal of pilgrimage until the early 1990s—seems to have originated in the pogrom of 1337 and the construction of the Corpus Christi or Holy Sepulcher Church, which began just afterward. Early accounts of the murder of Jews mention no violation of the Christian sacrament and no miracle. One early chronicle comments for the year in question, without suggesting a causal connection, that there was a plague of grasshoppers and the Jews were burnt. The first reference to miraculous hosts comes more than thirty years later and says simply that God's body was found, which the people saw; they therefore decided to build a church on the spot. An elaborate legend of Jewish host desecration, and of the miraculous host preserved without decay that testified to it, bloomed in the sixteenth century and created extensive pilgrimage and cult in the eighteenth and nineteenth centuries. The Deggendorf pilgrimage was permitted, even encouraged, by the Nazis, who attempted as a matter of policy to suppress Catholic pilgrimage sites but encouraged Deggendorf exactly because of its anti-Semitic connections. By the 1970s the cult had almost completely died. It was then deliberately revived as an expiatory Eucharistic pilgrimage, cleansed (the authorities said) of "all indications of host desecration."[14] There was much discussion of what sort of memorial tablet to install and whether to transfer the pilgrimage to a different week in order to break historical continuity. Finally, however, in 1992, the bishop of Regensburg, against popular resistance, discontinued the pilgrimage.[15]

The problem at Deggendorf was not merely the anti-Semitic propaganda that had accompanied the pilgrimage. It was the host itself. And the problem was historical as well as moral. Something stimulated the building of the Corpus Christi (or Holy Sepulcher) Church at Deggendorf, but evidence of claims to the finding of "Christ's body" appear only later (sometime before 1388). Regardless of who did or did not attack it, it is not clear that an object was, at the beginning, there.

The question of the authenticity and the religious meaning of Eucharistic miracles is not a new one. Hosts that resist corruption and drip blood have been vigorously debated by learned theologians and historians since the Middle Ages. According to the Catholic theological position established in the fifteenth century, the real presence of Christ in the Eucharist lasts only as long as the species—the externals—are unchanged. Hence authorities came to require, in a series of councils, that wonder hosts be displayed alongside freshly consecrated ones to avoid any possibility of idolatry; if miracle hosts decayed, they were to be replaced by newly consecrated wafers. In the vigorous debates between the 1390s and 1550s over the wonder hosts at Wilsnack, most popular of all German pilgrimage sites (and, like many wonder hosts, never associated with Jewish desecration), even the Franciscan defenders of the sacred objects argued not that these, or any, hosts *were* authentically Christ's blood but that they *could be*, and that pilgrimage to them was spiritually useful.[16] The Deggendorf host, supposedly undecayed after 650 years, was displayed, alongside a newly consecrated one, until 1990. But the monstrance had been opened several times, the holy objects scrutinized and cleaned of mold; clearly (as is entirely in accord with canon law, if not with popular belief) they had been replaced. Those who supported the postwar pilgrimage could argue only, as did the Franciscans at Wilsnack, that the hosts, whatever their provenance, were religiously useful—useful as penance, useful as acknowledgement of guilt, useful as expiation.[17]

Indeed, in the light of its own traditions, one might see the cult at Deggendorf as Eucharistic, not anti-Semitic, in origin and interpret the projection of host legends back onto a riot against the Jews less as an excuse for killing (which in many places at the time seemed hardly to need an excuse) than as a claim to miraculous presence—the stuff not only of pilgrimage (with all its economic and political benefits) but also of deeply felt devotion. To contemporaries, it may have been more a matter of seizing on the slaughter of Jews as an opportunity for miracle than crafting the miracle as an excuse (before or after the fact) for slaughter. Horrible though it seems to say it now, the Jews may have been "useful" in the Middle Ages not only as moneylenders and merchants, not only (in theological and exegetical terms) as the chosen remnant who must be preserved for a conversion that would herald the end of time, but also as creators (or—in theological terms—revealers) of holy matter.[18] The emergence of such matter—miraculously resisting decay and destruction as if nonmaterial, yet bleeding as if alive—was often in the earlier Middle Ages a response to superstition, naivete, or credulity, to accidents or mistakes in ritual. But increasingly in the later Middle Ages it was seen as the result of specifically Jewish doubt, malice, or abuse. It is quite possible to argue that the heart of the matter was matter—holy matter—not an excuse for attacks against the Jews.

Perhaps then it made some sort of historical as well as theological sense to transform the pilgrimage with its anti-Semitic overtones into Eucharistic reverence, as ecclesiastical authorities attempted to do in the 1970s and 1980s. Christ's death on the cross was understood, in late medieval and also in some modern Christian theology, as a sacrifice, a blood payment, an expiation for the sins of humankind. The mass reenacts that sacrifice.[19] To those who supported revival of the pilgrimage, viewing the host could thus be seen as repentance for all sin, an acknowledgement of human responsibility for error and malice, an offering up of Christ's complete sacrifice in place of humankind's always inadequate efforts at reparation. It could even have been understood (although it was not, to my knowledge, so interpreted) as expiation for anti-Semitism, the pogrom of 1337, and the Holocaust.

And yet, no matter how much authorities spoke of Deggendorf as Eucharistic devotion—as the veneration of Christ's body and blood present in every consecrated host—the heart of the cult was, historically, something different. The story that precipitated the pilgrimage was of a specific host that protested some sort of violation (even if it was only the violation of being lost or buried) and insisted, by its defiance of normal processes of change and decay, on its sacrality. Unless its specialness—its holy-object-ness—had endured, there was no reason for pilgrimage to Deggendorf in particular rather than to any altar on which was reserved a consecrated host.[20] And something particular did, at least in the eyes of many, survive. Frescoes of the host finding had been renewed as recently as 1976–77.[21] The same pastor who in 1961 recounted that forty years earlier the pitiful, decayed remains of the Deggendorf wonder had been replaced with a fresh consecrated wafer reported a new relic in 1959. In the parish church of Bad Hall (in Upper Austria), he was shown a piece of linen with a dark fleck, blood from the martyring of the hosts. Although no tradition, oral or written, survived, the parish paper of Deggendorf referred to this object in October 1959 as the blood of Christ; anonymous "desecrators" now replaced "Jews" in the account. The priest wrote that he was deeply moved to stand before the reliquary containing the holy cloth and hoped it would bring new life to the Deggendorf miracle, "as was the Holy Father's wish."[22] It seemed that, no matter how often the host in the monstrance was replaced, claims for miracles and associated holy matter would tend to emerge.

In the end, as the author of a massive and learned study devoted to the cult argued,[23] authorities could not cleanse the legend from ahistoricity by emphasizing expiation or wipe out its anti-Semitic overtones simply by referring to other perpetrators. As long as the object itself was the goal and center of cult, the connotations of violation and accusation it had carried for hundreds of years continued to circle round the pilgrimage. Anti-Semitism seemed to lurk in the miracle host itself. And yet at the core there was no retrievable story, no original desecration, perhaps no decay-resisting miracle at all (certainly not one that had perdured). Suppression not just of problematic provenance and anti-Judaism but of the object itself seemed necessary. Today at Deggendorf, there is no miracle host; there is instead a museum devoted to educating the public about the destructiveness and horrifying devotion it once engendered.

The Judensau

In contrast to silent removal or embarrassed reinterpretation, the efforts at memorialization in Sternberg and Deggendorf seem more considered. Instead of erasure, there is scholarly correction. Instead of decontextualized, antihistorical interpretation, there is historicizing. But more needs to be said. To consider the issue further, one might begin by wondering why there has been so little public discussion of objects such as the tabletop and footprints at Sternberg. After all, the past decade has seen in Germany not only discussion but also demonstrations against another anti-Semitic object: the "Judensau" or "Jew pig."

The Judensau is a particularly disgusting image found almost exclusively in German churches and broadsides of the fourteenth century and later; it depicts Jews sucking from the teats of a sow and a Jewish leader examining, placing his seal on, or even eating and drinking from the anus and genitals of a female pig. At first one animal image among many in the cycle of virtues and vices and carrying as its primary meaning the accusation that all sinners are Jews in their greed and lasciviousness, it became dissociated from such cycles and by the fifteenth and sixteenth centuries served as what German historians call a "Schandbild," an image intended to satirize, humiliate, and accuse. The association of Jews with an animal they considered unclean and with the filth (dung) of economic profit was drawn out explicitly.

Recently, in several German cities (among them Cologne, Frankfurt am Main, Bayreuth, and Nuremberg), there have been tumultuous demonstrations against such images, accompanied by vitriolic charges of murderous anti-Semitism on the one hand and of anti-intellectual, antihistorical image burning on the other.[24] In Lutherstadt Wittenberg, where an inscription attributing to "the rabbis" a garbled Kabbalistic name of God was added to the relief sometime after Luther discussed it enthusiastically and made a horrid joke on the Hebrew letters, a plaque has been installed of the sort we find at Sternberg: "God's true name, the here slandered Schem HaMphoras [Shem HaMephorasch] which the Jews saw as too holy to speak before Christians, died under the sign of the cross in six million Jews."[25] Although a *Kunstaktion* (artists' protest demonstration) against the Church of St. Sebaldus in Nuremberg accused the church of leaving information about the offensive image unobtrusive because it is available only in a pamphlet one picks up inside the church, the pamphlet itself (from March 2002) minces no words about either the historical tradition or the modern response.

> The Judensau is a shaming and abusive image. With other humiliating images, it is part of our history that we neither can nor wish to deny or thrust aside. Today they are for us a warning that earlier errors must not live on and that we must stand against all anti-Semitic language. . . . The anti-Semitic representations in the St. Sebaldus church are part of the world of pogroms of 1298, 1349 and 1499. Until today these images from a different time defame and harm even when many people no longer understand their symbolic meaning. . . . The Evangelical Church of Nuremberg sets for itself the challenge which this inheritance poses. It does not play down or weaken in any way the evidence of this blindness even when the images are aesthetically beautiful stone or glass. [Here the pamphlet refers to images in the windows of Jews depicted in their Jewish hats.] They remain warning signs which cry to heaven, call to penitence, and sharpen awareness. . . . Whoever represses evil and wants to forget promotes — however unconsciously and without willing it — new inhumanity.[26]

Why such impassioned discussion of the Judensau, which is after all one might say only an image, however disgusting? The tabletop at

Sternberg has elicited little concern and certainly no *Kunstaktion*, although it was evidence of an alleged crime for which we know twenty-seven people were unjustly executed in excruciating pain, and its surface displayed to Christians for hundreds of years an implausible and hideous accusation.

There are many answers to this rhetorical question, and they have to do, among other things, with the difference between a poor little town in Mecklenburg and the rich, thriving cities of Cologne, Frankfurt, and Nuremburg. Furthermore, the obscene and scatological nature of the Judensau perhaps, in some awful, titillating way, draws attention. It is, moreover, inaccurate to suggest that the Judensau is "only an image." It cannot be "only a picture" because, as powerful recent discussion by David Freedberg and others has taught us, art is never "only pictures."[27] Images have power. That is why they are burned, mutilated, dynamited. The Judensau was not merely anti-Semitic propaganda, the conveyer and inducer of attitudes. It effected as well as suggested action. In the early modern period it was placed on the doorways and porches of churches, the gates of cities, and the gables of inns to announce that Jews were unwelcome; it was even thought to ward off their presence in a talismanic way and insure that they would not return from exile.[28] Hence, this image lurks somewhere on the border between image and object. Not only a stimulus and record of hate, it is also evidence of the historical fact of expulsion and an amulet, powerful in itself, against the crossing of boundaries, the violation of Christian space.

Nonetheless it seems that the current outrage against the Judensau is outrage at what we might call the content of the image, not its talismanic quality or its specific historical role, which is mostly unknown. And that content seems particularly sinister because of a quality that has adhered to images since the later Middle Ages: their duplicability.[29] The Judensau was spread in early modern Germany through the new medium of print, just as word of it and of the *Kunstaktionen* against it is today spread via the new medium of the internet (often, in the latter case, without the image being reproduced at all). To current sensibilities, a scatological image (even when unseen) seems more offensive and dangerous than a tabletop, however slanderous the charges inscribed upon it. And in the sixteenth century, the Judensau was reproduced and distributed; the tabletop was not.

The Heiligengrabe Panel Paintings and the Jewish Museum in Berlin

This discussion of image and object brings me to the installations at the Jewish Museum in Berlin. I explain my point both autobiographically and somewhat circuitously by discussing my visit in November 2002 to Heiligengrabe.[30]

On the northern rim of the Mark Brandenburg, not far from the competing cult sites of Wilsnack, Beelitz, Zehdenick, Marienfliess, and Nauen,[31] Heiligengrabe was one of a series of Cistercian women's houses founded by the Margraves to lay claim to borderlands. It is already referred to in documents as "Zum Heiligengrab" in 1317, but the legend of its founding took on a clearly anti-Semitic character only in the early sixteenth century when the abbess—in competition with other cult sites and in a frenzied effort to preserve old belief in the face of the encroaching Reformation—had a new blood chapel built (1512) and a series of fifteen panels depicting the host desecration painted and hung in the church. (The panels, made in 1532, were based on earlier pamphlet material in Latin [1516] and German [1521]; several examples of the German version are still extant.) According to this late version, a Jew who stole or acquired a host found his hands covered with blood and buried the holy object, ground into fragments, at a place of execution beneath a gallows. He later confessed and was himself broken on the wheel. Miracles and visions in which blood figures prominently induced the bishop, the Margrave, the pastor at nearby Pritzwalk, and nuns from a neighboring house to establish a cloister on the site where the miraculous host fragments had been found, bleeding and reassembled.

Many sites in Protestant Mecklenburg and Brandenburg survive only as the vaguest of memories. (Tourists now visit the church at Güstrow to see a replica of Barlach's swinging angel, destroyed by the Nazis as degenerate art, not the once-acclaimed holy blood.) But Heiligengrabe—located, like Sternberg, in a depressed area of the former GDR, or East Germany—still draws visitors not only because of its lovely brick Gothic gables but also because of traces of the wonderful matter to which medieval pilgrims flocked. Excavations in 1984–86 in order to install heating under the floor of the Pilgrim Chapel that stands opposite the church revealed, in the middle of the rectangular nave of the first building on the site (from the end of the thirteenth century), a holy grave: a brick vault, too small to contain a human body, over which lay a stone inscribed with the date 1287. The little grave was found under a red (that is, blood-colored) plaster floor in which were stuck as if by accident several thirteenth-, fourteenth-, and fifteenth-century coins — evidence it was the site of pilgrim offerings. (See figure 4.3.) Further excavation revealed the vault to be positioned over several severely mutilated bodies, suggesting that the chapel was indeed built on a place of death — whether of legal execution or of lynchings, either of Jews or non-Jews, is unclear.

Recent scholarship (mostly local, archaeological, and antiquarian) disagrees about whether the little grave enclosed the wonder host of legend, revered on the spot where it was found and its alleged violator allegedly executed, or whether it was a replica of the Holy Sepulcher at Jerusalem of a sort known in German churches from the fourteenth and fifteenth centuries and used in the Easter week liturgy for the burial of the host during the *triduum* (the three days from Good Friday through Easter Sunday).[32] In a brilliant and unjustly neglected study from 1931, Romuald Bauerreiss called attention to the association of cemeteries, execution sites and pits or depressions in the earth with Holy Sepulcher churches and legends of host abuse (both Jewish and non-Jewish) and hence to the complicated connection many medieval people felt between blood-spilling as expiation and blood-spilling as retribution. Such ideas could make contact with the blood of criminals salvific and execution sites (particularly sites of the lynchings of Jews and host abusers) places of reparation for the sins of all humankind. Bauerreiss's perception would suggest that the legend of a miracle host or of host desecration at Heiligengrabe could have been triggered by the presence of a place of gallows and wheel.[33] And several scholars have suggested that the vault itself — which need not have been for a Maundy Thursday host but could have contained a relic from the Holy Land, such as earth — might have given rise to the chapel name or to the legend of a miraculous host. But references to the name "holy grave" and to a wonder host predate any Holy Sepulcher imitations known (and all of these are of a rather different type from the little vault at Heiligengrabe), whereas claims to wonder hosts were emerging in Brandenburg and Mecklenburg around 1300.

In any case, whatever the origins of the Pilgrim Chapel of Heiligengrabe, the site raises insistently questions about matter and memorialization. Although we may never be certain what was in the

Figure 4.3. Holy grave found under the floor of the Pilgrim Chapel at Heiligengrabe, in Brandenburg, Germany. In the Middle Ages, Heiligengrabe was a convent for Cistercian nuns; today it is a Protestant foundation dedicated to social and educational good works. The first mention of a holy grave comes from about forty years after the founding. The abbey was from very early on associated with a story of Jewish host abuse.

Figure 4.4. One of the surviving original panel paintings (made in 1532) of a supposed Jewish host desecration. Hanging in situ in the church at Heiligengrabe.

little grave, the accounts that survive, and were clearly intended in this case to induce pilgrimage not persecution, all stress the centrality of holy matter: the host fragments (either asserted to be miraculously reassembled or, by the doctrine of concomitance, to be every one of them fully Christ) and the bleeding earth with which the host was mixed. We are even told that, in the early sixteenth century, there was preserved in the chapel as a sort of contact relic a piece of the gallows under which the Jew supposedly buried the host. Similar holy objects (earth and wood) are found in competing cloisters in the same period.[34] In the neighboring Cistercian house of Zehdenick, what was revered was bloody earth from the site where a woman had allegedly buried a host under a beer keg. And the most important Cistercian monastery in the Mark, Lehnin, displayed a piece of the tree under which Graf Otto I had a dream about the founding of the cloister. When, however, the issue of memorialization is raised today about Heiligengrabe, it is raised not about these now absent holy objects but about the pictures. (See figure 4.4 for an example.)

In November 2002 I went to Heiligengrabe to see both the little grave and the panel paintings. The representative of the Protestant foundation who showed me the chapel was circumspect (as is the church literature) about the vault in the floor and its contents. She claimed only that scholars don't know what it was. In contrast, the paintings, which hang in the porch of the church (six survive), are accompanied by an explicit and painful gloss. A plaque, erected in 1996 by the Curatorship Committee of the Convent (which is charged with the reconstruction of cloister buildings), states that the Christian prejudice against Jews revealed in the legend of Heiligengrabe has influenced history, preparing the way for the genocide of the twentieth century. "In recognition of Christian guilt and with grief at its results, we wish to put the record straight and with this to give a sign of a renewed bond between Christians and Jews." The approach of the Curatorium at Heiligengrabe, like that of the Mary Church at Sternberg, the Sebaldus Church in Nuremberg, and even to some extent the Deggendorf pilgrim site, is historicizing and expiatory. There was no host abuse by Jews. Christians today castigate themselves for the consequences, over centuries, of stories that have damaged, shamed, and incited to murder.

I was surprised, however, to discover on my visit to Heiligengrabe that only two of the surviving original pictures were there. The other panels on display were replicas. Where were the other originals? In the Jewish Museum in Berlin, I was told. I did not remember such an exhibit from the Jewish Museum, but when I returned to the city I went to look. I could not find the panels from Heiligengrabe.

There has been much criticism of the present installations in the Jewish Museum. The controversial Libeskind building is itself a sculpture; and many believe that for all its beauty, it is ill suited to house anything. In any case, to almost any eye, the current exhibits are squeezed in awkwardly; the installations fight visually with the building, whose slanted windows, absolutely integral to the design, are nonetheless sometimes covered over to make wall space. Perhaps partly because of space constraints, the exhibits seem sketchy and, to many viewers, overly didactic. The Middle Ages receive little attention. The massacre of Jews at the time of the First Crusade is noted; charges of host desecration, of ritual murder, and of well-poisoning tend to be conflated but some space is, quite appropriately, given to the host-desecration charge in Berlin in 1510 (a case very similar to the Sternberg trials).[35] I was, however, puzzled not to find the Heiligengrabe panels, supposedly on loan to the museum. I expected these images to be the center of a display, their vivid color and cartoonlike drawing riveting passersby in their rush from one case to another. This was the actual paint and wood that recorded a lie passed down to posterity for hundreds and hundreds of years. The only reason for their absence I could think of was that they had already been returned to the cloister. So I asked.

No, I was told, the paintings are still here. But they're in the basement. We borrowed them only in order to scan them into the computer. If you want to see reproductions, go down to the educational center and call up the computer entry on host desecration. This I did, and saw a perfectly adequate and well-intentioned computerized presentation, taken mostly from a perfectly adequate and well-intentioned book about anti-Judaism in German history.[36]

But what about the objects? Does it matter that they are stored away in the basement, with only a digitalized version available? The reproductions in the computer presentation are small and muddy—no clearer to my eye than the reproductions in the book from which the text was taken. But one could make bigger and sharper computerized images. The paintings are hardly great art. They were copied from woodcuts in pamphlet literature, which were duplicable through the new medium of printing. One could argue that their digitalization only carries further what the author of the pamphlet and its patron the abbess had in mind. Moreover, if the best reaction to such material from the past is to historicize it, to set the record straight, what good is the exhibiting of a panel or two? Is it not better to make a video or an online program that can be sent widely to schools so children will see that legends and rumors they may still hear are not true? Is it not, in any case, more important to take action against evil language that associates Jews with pigs or with hunger for blood (whether or not one sees images) than against a painting or tabletop from an obscure Mecklenburg village? Perhaps display of the panels would only pander to a sentimental and elitist attachment to originals that is increasingly out of step with our throwaway culture. Attendance figures tell, after all, and the Jewish Museum with its didactic and digitalized exhibits is crowded — more crowded even than that tourist mecca, the Pergamonmuseum. (Berlin museums such as the Gemäldegalerie and the Kunstgewerbemuseum offer, on an ordinary day, only echoing silences.)

While I do not want to second-guess the curators at the Jewish Museum, who know far better than I the needs and reactions of their patrons, both Jewish and non-Jewish, I want to argue that, at least to scholars, the original objects do matter. This is for two reasons. First, we cannot hope to understand the medieval and early modern periods if we look only at *narratives* from the past. Recent work on medieval host-desecration sites has been, as I suggested above, mostly historicist, positivistic, and reductive. What happened? Who managed events? Who profited? How was group identity formed? Even work that concentrates on how memory constructed and preserved the legends (as it surely did) focuses quite naturally on how the historical accounts are fashioned, hence on texts.[37] But to a medieval pilgrim, theologian, innkeeper, or Markgraf, it was the matter, the stuff, the object, that was the center of it all — a powerful and dangerous center.[38] Hence, to historians who wish to understand why persecution and belief occurred so long ago, the *things* at stake are crucial. The vault at Heiligengrabe where something is absent, the Deggendorfer monstrance where something was present — a stone, a tabletop, a cooking pot, a carved gable or capital, a panel painting — these are not all parallel objects, and I shall say more about that below. But it was the need for holy matter, for some tangible way of encountering a God who was also far away, that drove Christian piety on the eve of the Reformation and incited preachers to efforts to manipulate, control, or discredit it. Stories of Jews, serving women, or criminals violating a wafer are stories that *create* the holy matter they assert to be violated. To say this is not to discount other motives for action or to ignore or excuse horror and pain. To focus on the objects is rather to see the pain and the danger *in them*, the blood still there.

This leads me to my second argument. For it seems to me that the very nature of these objects as objects, and not merely their medieval context, suggests that their display can have important educational and moral impact. All objects — the things human hands make and invest with function and significance, even the things human beings find and imbue with meaning — carry their history with them. Objects are specific, although mass-produced objects may seem virtually interchangeable and images of particular objects may be very widely disseminated. Nonetheless, as they are used and abused, objects take on marks that carry and convey their particular history. This capacity of carrying specificity is characteristic to some degree of all objects, I shall argue, but it is especially so for the objects I discuss in this essay — objects that have been used to inflict or justify evil. Hence even today it matters whether they, in all their specificity, are chiseled away, suppressed without comment, or replaced with digitalized images. It may be better to leave them where they have always stood, although washing away the blood they carry in such complicated ways is not as easy as setting up a menorah opposite them or canceling a pilgrimage. Perhaps indeed the importance of the objects lies exactly in the fact that they cannot be cleansed.

The Medieval Background

The medieval objects treated above — bits of trees, stones, tables, cooking pots, blood-spotted bread, paint on wood — are all in some sense relics, and relics are a particular kind of object. First collected and revered in the late third century, they were pieces of the bodies of the martyrs (and later of other saints), material fragments (earth, cloth, and the like) that had been in contact with those bodies, and bits taken from holy sites, especially those associated with the life of Christ (stones from Golgotha, for example, or earth from the Potter's Field, known as "the field of blood"). Venerated spontaneously by the Christian faithful, they were considered especially powerful witnesses to and contact with God's presence.[39] Although it is not quite correct to say, as scholars sometimes do, that bodily relics *were* the saint (or at least one must qualify this statement by adding that the saint was also in heaven before the throne of God), the holy matter of bodies and sites was at the very center of early medieval religion, absorbing older pagan traditions of holy trees, earth, wells, and so forth. Indeed objects were crucial not only in establishing but also in conveying sacrality. Pilgrims, for example, brought the empty tomb of Christ back from the Holy Land by bringing a linen strip measured to its length or a bit of its earth.[40] Moreover, we have evidence from as early as the seventh century of claims to the relics of Christ's body: his blood soaked into the column of the flagellation or collected on Golgotha, even his baby teeth or the flesh of his foreskin.[41] None of these holy objects authenticated itself entirely or simply by its material presence. Something testified to its history, to its contact with the sacred; but the testimony was not necessarily in our modern terms "historical." It could be a parchment or inscription that accompanied the object, an oral tradition, a dream directing the discoverer to discover it, or a miracle it suddenly worked.

As G. J. C. Snoek has argued, the Eucharist was in many ways a sort of super-relic throughout the Middle Ages.[42] Not only was it treated, liturgically and devotionally, as a relic (buried in altars with relics, used as an amulet against disaster, and so forth); it was divine power present in matter, and surrounding objects absorbed its power, as did the wood and earth of holy graves. Because it was, like the bodies of the saints, taboo, it could in the technical sense of the term be polluted; touching it was mortally dangerous if one was impure.[43] Yet the consecrated bread and wine were also more than, other than, relics; and many theologians worried about the parallel. As the "real presence" of Christ in the Eucharist was increasingly emphasized and then, in highly technical discussions (from the eleventh to the fifteenth centuries), elaborated and disputed as "transubstantiation," the consecrated elements came to be understood as holy matter exactly in their unseeability. Christ was present in the sacrifice of the mass on the altar—and fully present in every fragment and in both kinds—but the species covered and hid as well as manifested. Although, as Peter Dinzelbacher has argued, relic and Eucharist were both "real presences," Eucharist *was* Christ in substance and essence, relics were not.[44] Moreover, relics were visually what they were—the bones were St. Francis's bones, the tunic of Mary was Mary's cloak—whereas what the Eucharist was (flesh and blood) was hidden under bread and wine in order to avoid terrifying the faithful.

When the bleeding body of Christ veiled in the Eucharist erupted into visuality in miracles or visions of the bleeding host, ordinary Christians felt themselves in touch with the horror and splendor of God, but theologians were deeply worried, some so much so that they developed elaborate theories to assert that what was seen in such visions and miracles could *not* be the real presence. (What changed in transubstantiation was substance, not accidents. Thus according to the ingenious Thomistic formulation, if the accidents changed, what appeared would not "really" be Christ but a special visualization overlapping the real accidents of bread and wine.) Fifteenth-century synods and councils not only insisted that a freshly consecrated host be displayed alongside a supposed miracle host and suggested replacement of any wonder host touched by decay, as I explained earlier; they also supported the suppression of such objects by consuming them or walling them up in depositories where soiled altar linen was placed.[45] (The miraculous finds of Christ's blood or contact relics in pillars or altars—for example, the hosts at Andechs, the tabletop at Poznań—are perhaps the consequence of such earlier deposits.) Charges such as Marschalk's that ecclesiastical authorities wanted to destroy God's miraculous body by consuming it clearly reflect conflict among Christians about proper veneration of such supposed manifestations of God's presence.

In relics, too, we see a complicated dynamic of seen and unseen. Yes, the bone of the Magdalen was the Magdalen's bone, but from the early thirteenth century, "naked display" of relics was forbidden, and the containers (reliquaries) in which the bones or bits of cloth were preserved are characterized by a complex disjunction. Increasingly reliquaries became what German historians call "speaking reliquaries," ostensibly manifesting the shape of what was within (arm, foot, skull, and so forth). But, as Cynthia Hahn has shown, what is inside is often not the shape that is spoken. (Arm reliquaries can contain bits of skull or feet, for example.) Moreover, the very stuff of reliquaries contradicts and sublimates what is inside. Encased in gold and crystal, studded with gems whose color glistens forever, frozen and incorruptible, the blood of Christ and the bones of the martyrs are denied the corruptibility of earthly existence. The covering contradicts as well as expresses the nature of the human remnants within. Many saintly bodies supposedly declared their sanctity at autopsy or upon exhumation by manifesting incorruptibility, but even where no such claim was made, the reliquary spoke not fragmentation and putrefaction but triumph over it.[46] Miraculous hosts—holy matter—also spoke their immateriality. Bread, they nonetheless defied their accidents by bleeding as does living flesh, and by resisting the decay to which all matter is condemned.[47]

As Hans Belting has shown, paintings and sculptures in the Middle Ages partook of something of the quality—the holy stuff-ness—of relics.[48] Our earliest freestanding sculptures in the Middle Ages, the Throne of Wisdom statues of Mary and the Christ Child, are probably reliquaries.[49] Early crucifixes and panel paintings had relics in the head of the Christ figure or in the panel itself. Some icons were understood to be literally images of Christ or Mary, either painted from a vision that appeared to the painter or handed down directly from heaven (and hence, in an absolutely literal sense, objects from above). Whether or not bits of holy matter were imbedded in them, images were holy matter in the later Middle Ages. They warded off evil as amulets; they bled when attacked by heretics. Many were accorded indulgences, so that the very act of viewing them could provide exactly calculated numbers of days or even years of freedom from the expiatory suffering of purgatory. Indeed, images not only represented objects; they also, as Bauerreiss suggests, generated objects. The powerful Schmerzensmann (a dying or dead Christ, upright and bleeding in his tomb) surrounded by the *arma Christi* (the instruments of his torture) may have been the source not only of legends of Jewish violation of the host but also of those churches where depressions or pits (tombs) are revered as finding-spots of wonder hosts. If icons of a bleeding Christ rising from a pit in the earth could provide days or years of expiation, then it was only a little step to finding a physical pit from which a bleeding Christ (a wafer or waferlike object) arose.[50]

All this makes it clear that the objects once revered and still displayed in German churches—although not all relics in the same sense—participate nonetheless in a powerful sense of holy matter we moderns understand only imperfectly and at a distance. Panel paintings, tabletops, and wonder hosts were not conceptually so far apart as they seem today.

It was such holy matter that Jews (and others) supposedly violated in host desecration. It is, in fact, highly improbable that Jews acted as Christians charged. Christians accused them of scheming to acquire consecrated wafers in which they deliberately perpetrated a second Crucifixion of the body of Christ. And indeed we do have evidence both that they mocked the "superstitious" Christian idea that bread could become God's body and that they viewed the Eucharist as a dangerous or taboo object.[51] But we have no reason to think they tested Christian claims or "crucified" a stuff that they did not believe to be God. Understanding the context makes clear, however, why in the later Middle Ages host desecration was to Christians a more frequent and more serious charge than ritual murder. Murder — even ritual murder — was homicide; host desecration was attempted deicide, murder of God. (In the Brandenburg-Berlin judicial process of 1510, Jews were burned for host desecration but a man who had confessed to ritual murder was allowed to enter a monastery.)[52]

This background helps to explain why descriptions of charges against the Jews focus less on their execution and expulsion than on the holy matter they were thought to provide.[53] It is striking, for example, that the panel paintings from Heiligengrabe do not include the execution of the Jew (although the woodcuts do) but concentrate on the miraculous matter the event produced. In the account itself, as in many other desecration legends, the death of the Jew stands apart as a separate incident at the beginning of the story; far greater attention is given to the wonder host and its subsequent history of miracles.

Theologically speaking, host desecrations could not "create" holy matter. Desecrations could occur only to consecrated hosts.[54] The appearance of blood was thus a revelation of the real presence of Christ effected by the words of consecration. In this sense, violation only made visible the transubstantiated substance by a special imposition of miraculous accidents. Yet it is also correct to say that, in the stories from Deggendorf, Sternberg, Heiligengrabe, and many other sites, desecration made the host enduring, incorruptible holy matter rather than a wafer that should be consumed (and would cease, once it decayed or was digested, to be Christ's body). Without violation, God remained hidden; desecration led to revelation — a revelation that lasted. As the provost Eberhard Waltmann of Magdeburg wrote to John of Capistrano in 1452 in a debate over the miracle host at

Wilsnack, matter changes to blood to reveal God's anger, to express disgust at sin and unbelief.[55]

In the course of the fifteenth century, host violation grew ever more dangerous to the violators. Early legends of wonder hosts often attribute them to the superstition of lower-class women, to ritual impurity, or to ordinary criminals, and in a number of such stories no perpetrator is punished or even sought out. As the bleeding hosts came to seem more and more powerful and accusatory, those who provided the occasion for such eruptions of blood appeared ever more sinister. Jews, who could be more easily condemned and executed, seemed the obvious perpetrators. But the horror they supposedly produced was also a miraculous manifestation of God—an object in which he could be seen and touched. Processes against the Jews (such as those at Sternberg and Brandenburg-Berlin) or legends telling of their guilt (such as the apocryphal stories at Deggendorf and Heiligengrabe) were not only opportunities for economic gain through the expulsion of hatred outsiders; they were also moments of special encounter with the flesh of Christ. And if the bleeding was truly Christ's blood, then objects such as tabletops, knives, or nails that touched it, even a stone that touched the feet of someone (such as Eleazar's wife) who had touched it or a panel which made vivid its presence under a gallows, were not just evidence of a crime. They were also an ambiguous sort of relic, saturated not so much with the evil of the violators as with the power of a God who revealed himself in its midst.[56] In a distorted and hideous version of the *felix culpa*, desecration produced the holy matter that led to special access to the divine.[57]

Objects and Images Today

I do not expect the little church guide at Sternberg or the exhibits in the Jewish Museum in Berlin to explain the medieval context of their objects at length as I have done here.[58] Nor do I deny the importance of simple outrage or of repentance simply expressed. Plaques and computer presentations that repeat the mantra "never forget" are obviously a better response than silently removing embarrassing material or rewriting legends to recast offensive language. It can, moreover, require considerable moral courage to call off a popular pilgrimage as was done at Deggendorf. But I would argue that the objects of which I have spoken have even today a power not fully recognized by digitalizing them, canceling accompanying devotions, or glossing them with historicizing statements. We need more than the knowledge that the associated charges are untrue. We need to confront the objects themselves.

An objection might be raised here, one adumbrated by the discussion above of the Judensau and of the panels from Heiligengrabe. For, as I have already suggested, images and objects are not quite the same. Even at Heiligengrabe, the panel paintings, the wonder host, and the holy earth represent and embody the sacral in somewhat different ways. Why then lump together paintings, carved capitals, bleeding hosts, and miraculous footprints in my discussion of response?

In modern museum practice, no theory would conflate image and object. We occasionally find catalogues that treat, for example, Degas's pictures of milliners as evidence of worker alienation; exhibits in historical museums frequently underline a particular shoe or arrowhead with boutique lighting, aestheticizing it and isolating it from the everyday.[59] But no contemporary theory would treat a modern painting as simply a piece of historical evidence or an object. The very word of choice used by contemporary art historians—"images"—suggests some vestige of "representation," of presenting something in a medium it isn't. Paint, wood, steel, and so forth, present to us as if they were, for example, apples or the color red (but they are not, and thus they call attention to the "notness"). Even minimalist, literalist, or pop art calls attention to the gap between itself and objects by in some sense questioning—or even insulting (by mimicking)—their objecthood.[60] As Hans Belting has argued, there is a gulf between the later Middle Ages, "the era before the era of art," in which pictures and statues, like relics, manifested a divinity they participated in, and the very self-conscious Renaissance playing with illusion, which calls attention to the non-objectness of art.[61] The gorgeous textile behind a medieval Madonna is a frame for, a declaration of, her sacrality; the painted Renaissance curtain, exactly because it is so precisely like a curtain, makes it clear that it is not a curtain. A medieval image is an object in a way a Renaissance or modern painting is not.[62] But modern viewers inevitably react with modern, not medieval, viewing habits and assumptions. Hence, however much image and object were conflated as holy matter or embodiment of sacrality in the Middle Ages, it could be argued that it is strained and simplistic to conflate them in a discussion of modern response.

It is significant, moreover, that in a number of places where holy objects were venerated in the later Middle Ages (hosts and the instruments that supposedly tortured them, figures that bled, sacred earth, and so forth), these objects have been replaced by images (statues and paintings, called by German historians *Gnadenbilder*) as the goal of pilgrimage.[63] Although such figures, often allegedly wonderworking, cross any line contemporary theory may attempt to draw between image and object or art and photographic reproduction, devotional focus has shifted from the nonrepresentational bone or bit of linen or wood to objects which "image" the salvation figures — Mary and Jesus — they evoke. And Catholic theology scrupulously draws a distinction between the "veneration" they may receive as reflections and reminders of the divine, and the "worship" due only to God. Even in a devotional context, then, modern response tends to distinguish image and object, privileging image. (This separation may help to explain why contemporary reaction to the Judensau is more virulent than to the Sternberg table and footprints.)

The duplicability of images has, furthermore, been capitalized upon, especially since the advent of printing. Not only have engravings and prayer cards of wonderworking statutes (for example, the Virgin of Altötting) circulated for hundreds of years; depictions of Jewish host desecrations have served widely as anti-Semitic propaganda. It was pictures of the pictures of the events at Sternberg and Heiligengrabe that circulated, not pieces of — or even images of — the footprints or the little vault. (The Sternberg events turned up depicted on the local inflation currency [*Notgeld*] in Mecklenburg in 1922.)[64] To be sure, pieces of the true cross, little containers of holy earth, bits of cloth impregnated with power from contact with the tombs of saints, and so forth, circulated too; but they aroused suspicion if mass produced, exactly because it seemed necessary that, as objects, they carry with them some specific materiality, some indication of derivation from a particular, historically locatable source. Both because of their intrinsic duplicability and because of their nature as representation of something other than their material, images seem different from objects; even medieval images might seem then to demand from modern curators and custodians a different treatment, and from modern viewers a different response.

Nonetheless, I would argue that there is both a historical and a conceptual connection between object and image. Cult objects and wonderworking statues blur the distinction still; the miraculous corporal at Walldürn, for example, was until fairly recently replicated on little silks that were touched by the relic, absorbing its power.[65] Even today, both the devout and the curious take away from shrines prayer cards with images of *Gnadenbilder* and little bags of holy earth. From such objects and replicas, it is not far to the small pieces of metallic cloth given out to onlookers when Christo and Jeanne-Claude wrapped the Reichstag in June–July 1995. The scraps of fabric were not mere mementoes to remind viewers of what they had seen; viewers participated in the art itself when they held and preserved these little pieces, so to speak, of the action.

In the modern museum as well, images partake of objecthood, if not in quite the way they did in medieval churches. They not only "represent"; they are. As I suggest above, our response to any painting involves in complex ways our sense of how its materiality, its "stuffness," its paint and canvas, create the image that both represents and deceives. Indeed, both medieval devotional objects and modern paintings have a more complex relationship to representation than we sometimes admit. If we compare, for example, reliquary (object) and portrait (art), we see that both, in ways we have not thought sufficiently about, are veiling and revealing. Just as the painted Renaissance curtain, or the Warhol tomato soup can, or even a Rothko white on white, both *are* and *are not* what we see, so the reliquary and the wonder host inside it are and are not what they appear. The consecrated bread is invisibly the body of God, whether or not one sees red drops or believes them to be blood; the crystal and gold frame the contents as glorified and imperishable, contradicting while revealing the "breadness" of the bread. For all the differences before and after "the era of art," even modern images are never only images, just as medieval objects are not only objects.

Hence, whether we look from a medievalist's perspective or a modern one, against the background of a notion of holy matter or in the context of the polysemy of the concept "object" itself, the footprints, wells, sculptures, hosts, relics, and monstrances I have discussed here are odd, frightening, and complex things. They are all, in some sense, objects but objects with overtones of image as well. Revealing and querying what they convey, they are what they are; yet each represents (if only partially) a horror that lies beyond. Despite the differences among them, the questions they raise about memorialization is essentially the same. It is the simple question I asked earlier: Does it matter whether the objects themselves are preserved and displayed?

My answer is finally based less in my scholarly study of medieval devotion, or in a consideration of theories of objects and art, than in an empirical observation about how we see and remember. For all the modern shift to image and duplicability, I do not think we have in fact forgotten the power of objects. Christian believers and nonbelievers who tour European churches not only wonder at the splendor and cost of the furnishings but often feel the ghostly presence of the past in the traces left by hands and lips on devotional objects—both relics and *Gnadenbilder*—kissed over the centuries by the pious. Jews whose parents may have fled Germany or failed to survive the genocide sometimes feel physically ill when confronting the now whitewashed walls of concentration camps or find themselves unable to visit German sites at all. Ordinary visitors to museums often prefer that concrete, specific, tactile things from the past (shoes, fans, pipes, commonplace books, and the like) not be replaced by videos and computerized presentations. Supplemented, yes, replaced, no. People watch *Antiques Roadshow* on television exactly because they may be present at the moment when an ordinary object is revealed to be a carrier of history; it is not only the economic value that titillates.

The power of objects becomes clearer if we contrast them with photographs. The little piece of cloth I treasure from the Wrapped Reichstag brings the Berlin of the mid-1990s back to me in a way no postcard picture can. Touching my grandmother's butter mold creates an immediate connection to my childhood that bears no relationship to the melancholy and rather diffuse sense of absence stimulated by photos of a plump woman in an Alabama farmyard three-quarters of a century ago. A photograph, an "image"—exactly because it captures, represents, a moment that was "then"—underlines for us the distance since it was made; what it images is not here. An object that *was* there and *is* here connects us with that *was* because it still itself *is*.[66]

There is a moment in W. G. Sebald's novel *Austerlitz* in which the hero, walking the streets of Terezín, where his mother died in a camp, comes to a closed emporium whose window sets out dozens of objects that in all probability belonged to the camp's victims:

paperweights, buttons, a miniature barrel organ, a lampshade, a stuffed squirrel, and so forth. Sebald writes:

> What secret lay behind the three brass mortars . . . the endless landscape painted round a lampshade . . . showing a river running quietly through perhaps Bohemia or Brazil? And then there was the stuffed squirrel, already motheaten here and there, perched on the stump of a branch . . . which had its beady button eye implacably fixed on me, and whose Czech name — *vererka* — I now recalled like the name of a long-lost friend. What, I asked myself, said Austerlitz, might be the significance of the river never rising from any source, never flowing out into any sea . . . what was the meaning of *vererka*, the squirrel forever perched in the same position . . . ? They were all as timeless as that moment of rescue, perpetuated but forever just occurring, these ornaments, utensils, and mementoes stranded in the Terezín bazaar, objects that for reasons one could never know had outlived their former owners and survived the process of destruction, so that I could now see my own faint shadow barely perceptible among them.[67]

I would argue that, even without the mirroring glass of a shop window, we find ourselves reflected in the objects that survive from the destructive European past. This is exactly because what we find is the objects themselves.

Yet, the little vault at Heiligengrabe that, some thought, contained a tortured god; the table at Sternberg; the Judensau on the bridge at Frankfurt with its talismanic message of expulsion; the well in Poznań — these objects carry not the pathos of Sebald's squirrel or painted lampshade but a deeper horror. They are not in shop windows or even museums but in churches — institutions in which live the traditions and beliefs that led to the persecutions and pogroms of long and not so long ago. They are vestiges of the perpetrators, not the victims. What is inscribed in them is accusation, not loss. The self they connect us with is a self from the recent European past — a self that persecuted and killed.[68] The Sternberg table and the panels from Heiligengrabe are not just objects; they are horrible objects — evidence for and record of scapegoating, fear of the other, inflicted pain, opportunism, warped devotion, and deep belief. In the words inscribed upon them and the ghostly traces of blood supposedly shed long ago, they bear the marks of moments in history that lived into the twentieth century. The same wood that testified to and stimulated atrocities at Sternberg in 1492 and Heiligengrabe in 1532 is still there today.

Local residents, tourists, curators, pastors, scholars, and Holocaust survivors will confront such objects very differently and may disagree about whether they should be removed or displayed. But stories about them will continue to be told, memories will lurk, we — whether we are descended from perpetrators or victims or are merely curious passersby — may hear rumors of magic footprints or atrocious executions. What seems clear, therefore, is that at Sternberg, Iphofen, Frankfurt, Poznań, and other sites of persecution and horror, there must be some memorialization, and it should include something more than the distancing of historical correction. Glosses should say more than that the events were other than legend tells; repentance should acknowledge more than that the legacy of false history does damage. Whatever the ultimate goal of tourist pamphlets, artists' protest actions, historical or art historical conferences, or exorcizing liturgies, those involved must recognize that neither erasure nor contextualizing will remove the infamy of such things from memory. Thus, it is hard for me as a historian not to feel that it is best for us to encounter the objects themselves.[69]

CHAPTER FIVE

Avoiding the Tyranny of Morphology: Or, Why Compare?[1]

I am a student of Christianity in the twelfth to fifteenth centuries whose recent scholarly work has focused on northern Germany.[2] But I spent five weeks in India in the fall of 2009, hoping to immerse myself as far as possible in Hindu religious culture. As a medievalist, I expected some comparisons to the European Middle Ages to emerge. Two years later, while I was discussing this with a distinguished historian of modern Europe, she suddenly turned to me and asked: "What do you get out of this? I don't understand what you're learning about the Western Middle Ages that you didn't already know." That turns out to be a profound question. It challenged me to think harder than I had done before about making comparisons. This essay is an effort to provide a provisional and partly autobiographical answer to the question: What do scholars of religion do when they compare things, and why do they do it?

Scholarly Treatments of Comparison

In 1928, at the Sixth International Congress of Historical Sciences, the medievalist Marc Bloch made a plea for comparative history. But as John Elliott has pointed out in his elegant little book *History in the Making*, the plea was pretty much ignored for more than fifty years.[3] Historians had other things on their minds for much of the twentieth century. It seems to me, however, that comparisons crop up more frequently now in European studies, in large part owing to the pressure we all feel to globalize either spatially or temporally — that is, to study world cultures or write "deep" (also called "big") history.[4] References to other cultures, even when they are only what scholars have called "soft" or "asymmetrical" comparisons or illuminating asides,[5] can help us claim that we are attuned to the challenges of adjusting our teaching and our scholarship to what we used rather blindly to refer to as "the rest of the world."[6]

In contrast to the academic study of history, comparison has long been at the heart of a number of social science fields, in which sociologists and economists—especially those of a somewhat earlier generation such as Shmuel Eisenstadt, Barrington Moore, Douglass North, Robert Bellah, and Charles Tilly—have sought to ferret out largescale developmental trends. Such generalizing studies have been useful to humanists in posing research agendas to be pursued or hypotheses to be tested.[7] Nonetheless, efforts to establish universal developmental patterns (as in, for example, recent discussions of the "axial age" in the history of religions) have not appealed to most humanists.[8]

Ever since the 1960s, however, humanists have been fascinated by the sort of comparisons cultural anthropologists have undertaken, although they have been wary—as anthropologists themselves have been wary—of any tendency either to essentialize cultures in defining their differences or to universalize cultural responses, institutions, or phenomena as a basis for finding similarity. Moreover, there are humanistic fields such as comparative literature or comparative religion whose very titles incorporate comparison. Recent theoretical discussion in these fields and in other areas of the humanities such as literary criticism and art history has been skeptical of any universalizing conclusions, tending rather to assume that the point of comparison should be to elucidate difference. Perceived similarities—whether formal, structural, phenomenological, or functional—are often suspected of being either an imposition (even if a subconscious one) by Western cultures on non-Western ones or a result of superficial perceptions.

Sometimes the very suspicion of similarity has become theoretically useful. Art historians, for example, are currently fascinated by the category of "pseudomorphism"—that is, things that have "formal similarities where there is no similarity of artistic intent."[9] The point of such an analytical category is to jar the viewer into a new response by the stimulus of unexpected—or false—analogy. Indeed, the stimulus is based in a realization that, as Donald Judd put it: "A lot of things look alike, but they are not necessarily very much alike."[10] In literary circles, recent consideration of figures of speech, especially of metaphor, has focused on the effect achieved by the difference of the things compared. In such discussion, metaphor is understood to emphasize what is absent as much as what is present in the comparandum, and the two terms of the analogy are understood to pull against each other, illuminating through tension and difference.[11] Perhaps aware of such trends and in any case conditioned by their inevitably specialized and narrowly focused initial training, cultural historians have tended to distrust perceived similarities, despite their newfound desire to expand their activity as professionals in "deep" or global directions. The American historian George Fredrickson, writing in the introduction to his essay collection *The Comparative Imagination*, has even queried whether comparison is possible in the humanities given what he sees as postmodernism's stress on "the particular and unique."[12]

Anglophone religionists have been particularly concerned to stress difference, even incommensurability, between religious practices and traditions. Finding it difficult to escape from the worry that their subject matter is inevitably and insidiously inflected by Western Protestant assumptions, they try to avoid universalizing categories such as "secularization" or "religion" itself, fearing that whatever they discover, it is somehow their modern Protestant or post-Protestant selves. For example, in a fine volume on religion and materiality published in 2010, much of which deals with non-Western topics, David Morgan considers it necessary to open his introduction with a lengthy and anxious survey of discussions, mostly from the 1970s, of why the Christian concept of "belief" is inappropriate.[13] Recent treatment of devotional movements within Hinduism has asked repeatedly whether the category of "devotion" (*bhakti*) is a Western and universalizing importation — a colonial creation that mirrors only modern British researchers and not Indian history.[14] With his characteristic poetic intensity, Indologist David Shulman puts what seems to be the current scholarly goal thus: "What is at stake is singularity. One pares away likeness and is, with a little luck, left with the unique."[15]

The theoretical discussions I have just mentioned are quite diverse; I do not imply that they focus on the same issue. Nonetheless, there seems to lurk behind them an assumption that the comparanda with which one starts are in some way given or obvious. Thus, the important move is ferreting out and delineating difference. Similarity is either an obvious parallelism or a sort of trick or illusion; the goal is to move beyond it. One starts with two red squares, two female "idols," two mystics, or two terms in a poetic phrase ("love" and "red, red rose," to take a banal example). The challenge is to say why the squares or the idols are not the same, how the mystics' experiences are in some way different (because of a factor such as theology or gender), or how the poet achieves appropriate tension by juxtaposing incommensurate or dissimilar things. Find the "look-alikes," whether they are pseudomorphic or not; exploring the similarities will jar one into the difference one is looking for.

Even more than their fellow humanists, scholars in religious studies have tended to assume that finding the "likes" is the easy part. The question "How do you know where to start?" is seldom raised. If you're interested in women and religion, compare goddess figures. If you're interested in idolatry or iconoclasm, compare statues. Depending on your question, the choice of comparanda would appear to follow quite easily.[16] But choosing comparanda may be more complicated than it initially appears. It may be circular, on the one hand, or unproductive on the other. If we choose statues to compare we will find differences in them *qua* statues; if we choose male and female mystics, we will find them different *qua* mystics. Conversely, if we compare a hand painted by Rembrandt with one calling the reader to attention in the margin of a medieval manuscript, we will find them different but not different *qua* hands or *qua* "art" or perhaps *qua* any other interesting category; the comparison may thus be a waste of time. In such moves, we may have assumed an answer not because of the variety of the material before us but by the way we have posed the question. We have assumed that it is statues that raise crucial questions about religious representation, that mysticism is a central factor in gendered devotional experience, or that four fingers and a thumb are the important aspect of a certain shape drawn on a surface. But is this the best way to explore female versus male devotional response, religious presence, or hands?

I do not mean by this to argue that we can escape from building some assumptions about answers into our questions. That is how research proceeds. But I want to argue that, as my historian colleague suggested about my forays into Indian history, the issue of comparison is more difficult than we usually admit. Even before we come to delineating differences, we need to think far more carefully than we often have about the likenesses we start with. Morphology or visual similitude — that is, "looking like" — may not be the best basis for a comparative study that must, in the final analysis, consider both similarity and difference to be problematic if it is to illuminate either side of a comparison.[17] The tyranny of morphology — whether pseudo- or not — has operated too long in comparative study.[18]

Of course, morphology is not the only category that has operated tyrannically to obscure more subtle questions. Gender, function, and even some vague sense of "psychological need" have also been taken as obvious, and hence unexamined, points of departure. For example, comparing possessed women or apotropaic objects can seem a natural move, needing no methodological justification, yet in differing cultural contexts, it may be far from obvious whether a given phenomenon should be denominated "spirit possession" or a given object an "amulet." My discussion here focuses on the problem that a concentration on morphology, shape, or optical similitude can entail, but I am not arguing that we should reject comparison, even formal comparison. Rather, I argue both for making explicit the grounds — formal, functional, structural, psychological, cognitive, or devotional — of any comparison drawn and for admitting that the choice of a starting point in any study that juxtaposes two objects, phenomena, events, or developments is complicated and needs more explicit consideration than it is usually given.

In the remainder of this essay, I wish to explore three examples that demonstrate various approaches to choosing comparanda.[19] The first example makes an obvious choice of things to compare — one that has often been made by students of comparative religion. It takes statues of female sacred figures that not only "look alike" but also seem to behave similarly and moves in the conventional way to argue for difference. My point here is that the difference we discover may be so radical as to suggest that we did not choose the proper similarity to start with. The second considers a Western medieval devotional object that is frequently interpreted by modern viewers as a sexual body part but that raises acutely the question of whether this modern interpretation is a case of "pseudomorphism." I compare this image, understood against its medieval background, to a Hindu devotional statue not because the Western and non-Western images are like each other but because, taken in their religious contexts, they raise similar issues. The two cases push us to ask what it means to think one sees morphological "likeness" and to ruminate on how misleading it can be to assume, without sophisticated knowledge of context, that shapes or forms are either like or unlike. The third example returns to consider, at least in part, the material of the first. I now juxtapose Hindu and Christian devotional objects in order to show that things morphologically similar are not necessarily similar in phenomenological or religious impact; there may, however, be comparanda that are not morphologically similar, the exploration of which can push our understanding of objects to a deeper level than do either of the first two cases. In other words, what literary scholars find in metaphor—that is, morphological unlikes juxtaposed to illuminate while pulling against each other—may be a more useful way of probing the meaning of things than simply either exploring or rejecting morphological or pseudomorphological similarity. But we must be able to say why those particular comparanda are chosen in the first place.

A Comparison of Goddess Processions

I begin with processions of images, a phenomenon often explored by students of religion and one on which I shall bring my own Indian trip to bear. In his now classic study, *The Madonna of 115th Street* (1985), Robert Orsi describes the festival of Our Lady of Mount Carmel as practiced in the middle of the last century in New York City's East Harlem.[20] As he explains, a colorful replica, which looks nothing like the church's primary statue of the Madonna, was used in most years for the outdoor procession. On the 100th anniversary of the church's founding, which Orsi himself attended, the Madonna herself—that is, the statue that usually resides in a niche over the main altar—came out into the streets. On all festivals dedicated to her, however, Mary of Mount Carmel is understood to be present, whether she or a replica processes. She is carried up and down every block in Italian Harlem, and considerable effort is exerted to make sure each street is covered. Penitents walk at the rear of the procession. The devout, among whom women are especially numerous, laugh, cry, sing, and reach out to touch the statue's robes. Once the tour of Harlem is completed, the Madonna is greeted with fireworks, and when she returns to the church, gifts of money, gold, candles, and *ex-votos* are laid at her feet in thanksgiving for miracles worked, evils and adversities overcome. The female divine, pure and yet a mother, enacts, says Orsi, a paradoxical "psychodrama" of disintegration and reintegration, of the suffering of exile and the victory of return.[21]

In her study of reliquaries, *Strange Beauty* (2012), art historian Cynthia Hahn describes a similar festival at Saintes-Maries-de-la-Mer in the Camargue in the south of France, which she attended in October 2003. After a sermon and a series of prayers and hymns, two large carved and painted female figures in a small boat are carried from the church where they usually reside above and behind the main altar to a nearby beach and held above the waves, after which, escorted by the crowd of worshippers, they are returned to the church. The festival commemorates the miraculous arrival from the Holy Land, in a boat without sail or oars, of the saints Mary Jacobus and Mary Salome, relatives of the Virgin Mary, who were supposedly present with her at the Crucifixion of Christ. (See figure 5.1.)[22]

When I attended the festival of Durga Puja (the word "*puja*" means "the ritual of worship") in Varanasi in October 2009, much of what I experienced seemed similar to Catholic saints-day processions such as those I had myself witnessed or read of in the accounts of other scholars. (See figure 5.2 for a North American example and figure 5.3 for Durga Puja.) At the height of the festival, statues of the many-armed goddess Durga, warrior against the buffalo-demon, were carried through the streets on litters borne on the backs of men or on flatbed trucks; music, often from boomboxes, blared; faces focused so intently on the goddess herself that, although squeezed in among thousands of men (and they were mostly men), I felt not so much out of place as invisible.[23] Gorgeously clothed with jewels, flowers, and gauzy draperies, like Madonnas paraded today in Harlem or in Boston's North End, and bearing the same sort of bright, fixed, plastic smile, Durga made her way through the streets of Varanasi down to the river Ganga. And Durga Puja was ushered in over several days, as was the festival of the Madonna of 115th Street, by the preparation of special foods and the setting up of booths for festival-related goods. Images of Durga, constructed from river clay by artisans in special rites, were painted and adorned with clothes and jewels, and worshipped with dance, flowers, and song in the temporary temples or "pandals" made for them and found on hundreds of street corners for days before the final ritual procession.[24]

Figure 5.1. In the festival of Saintes-Maries-de-la-Mer in the Camargue in the south of France, the figures of St. Mary Jacobus and St. Mary Salome (relatives of the Virgin) are carried in a small boat from the church where they usually reside to a nearby beach and held above the waves, after which, escorted by worshippers, they return to the church.

Figure 5.2. A statue of the Madonna delle Grazie bearing the Christ Child, both figures decorated by adherents with flowers, crowns, jewelry, and money, is carried in procession through the North End of Boston.

Many scholarly considerations of such rites, whether in Europe, North America, or Southeast Asia, use anthropological models, especially those of Victor and Edith Turner, to stress the ways in which processions move adherents from ordinary time through moments of special encounter with the power of an "other," thereby creating communities and reinforcing boundaries.[25] Warrior yet mother, Durga can be seen to encapsulate the paradox of the fierce and the gentle, of that which both divides and defends community, in ways that parallel the Madonna of 115th Street as understood by Robert Orsi. Religious processions in Varanasi as in Harlem or Provence can be understood to move adherents through the liminal space theorized by the Turners. Moreover, both the hundreds of Durgas in Varanasi and the Marys in Boston, New York, or Provence are each fully a holy presence, although usually not in a generalized way.[26] The Marys are specific Marys (the Mary of Mount Carmel or the Madonna delle Grazie of Boston's North End)—instantiations of specific appearances of Our Lady more than of Mary herself—just as Indian temple statues are often not so much Ganesha or Hanuman, for example, as a specific aspect of Ganesha or Hanuman, tied to a particular geographical place. Thus both Durga in Varanasi and Our Lady of Mount Carmel in Harlem are examples of the complex way in which part is whole in many religions, whether one expresses this in the technical phrase "the distinctive devotional logic of presence" or as what I have elsewhere called the "concomitant habit of mind."[27]

Recently, scholars have also tended to employ theories, such as those of Alfred Gell, that see religious images as agents, not symbols or signs pointing to an Other but themselves actors and presences. In such interpretations, processions are not so much ritual reenactments of particular moments in a sacred story (although elements of reenactment cling to the procession in song and movement) as participations in an immediate and palpable power.[28] Each god or goddess statue is thus an example of what some adherents of "object-oriented ontology" or "thing theory" characterize as the living power of images or the agency of objects.[29] The words of J. P. Waghorne, describing Hindu images and temples, could equally well be used by current students of Western images. Waghorne says that images, "freed from their status as inanimate things," thus gain "power to transform and to recreate their creators."[30]

And yet there are not only hundreds of small differences between

Durga Puja and summer festivals of the Virgin Mary, there is a large and glaring one. The Marys leave their churches and return to them; even Mary Jacobus and Mary Salome in the Camargue, whose miraculous arrival by water is celebrated hundreds of years later, merely visit the ocean before returning to their niche over the altar. But Durga, made from the clay of the river Ganga, returns to the sacred waters.[31] The hundreds of Durgas I saw traveling to the river in Varanasi were, at the end of the festival, thrown in. When I journeyed the next day on the river, I saw plasticized body parts, bits of gauzy clothing, bright faces and fingernails floating and disintegrating in the water. (See figures 5.4 and 5.5.) One cannot imagine throwing the Madonna of Mt. Carmel into the Hudson River or the two Marys of Saintes-Maries-de-la-Mer into the Atlantic Ocean. However much the Marys of Catholic worship may represent the paradox of fertility and purity, they do not come from or return to mud.

Although a number of Hindu festivals take statues from temples in ritual performance and return them thereto in what seems parallel to Western Christian processions, in certain crucial Hindu festivals, such as the Durga Puja I attended, the goddess figure returns to the organic world from which she arose. As David Shulman puts it, describing another goddess festival that takes place in Andhra Pradesh over many months:

> Twice a year, the goddess Paidi Talli, "Golden Mother," has her festival.... Like other goddesses, Paidi Talli undergoes a natural, annual cycle. In May she emerges—as a spark in the hands of one of her devotees—from the turbid water of the Big Lake. She is then carried, latent, in mud drawn from the lake, to her main temple.... There she will incubate and ferment, infusing a series of clay and metal pots with her essence, for some three months. Afterward these pots, a full form of the goddess, will make the rounds... preparing the city for her arrival in yet another form. In early October, she comes in a dream to her chief priest and informs him that she is "growing" as a tree in such-and-such a grove.... This tree will be worshiped, recognized as Paidi Talli, and gently uprooted.[32]

Or, as Linda Hess explains, describing the annual dramatic performance of the ancient Ramayana story:

> The belief that God is everywhere... that God is in you and me or a stone, that God has physical and mental attributes, that he takes on those attributes to

Figure 5.3. The goddess Durga is carried in procession by male bearers in the festival of Durga Puja, in Kolkata, West Bengal, India.

Figure 5.4. The figure of the goddess Durga thrown into the river Hooghly in Kolkata, West Bengal, at the culmination of Durga Puja.

Figure 5.5. The figure of Durga disintegrating in the river after her immersion at the end of her festival. Kolkata, West Bengal, India.

> make himself accessible to his devotees—is . . . broadly inculcated and deeply imbibed. . . . "Symbolic" is too flat a word for this type of consciousness. . . . In this universe . . . God enters the shape of Ramchandra, Ramchandra enters the body of the boy . . . the earth enters the form of a cow.[33]

Western Christian imagery is, of course, often organic; the doctrine of creation underlines God's making of and love for the world. Theologians such as Bonaventure and charismatic reformers such as Francis of Assisi saw God's footprints in the entire creation. Francis, as is well known, preached to birds and wolves and, as is less well known, argued that it would be appropriate to smear the walls of the church with meat on Christmas so that the very building would feast.[34] In the late thirteenth century, the nun Mechtild of Hackeborn saw a vision in which the vestments of a priest who was celebrating mass were covered with every blade and twig, every hair and scale, of the flora and fauna of the universe; the nun who recorded the vision glossed it as showing that "the smallest details of the creation are reflected in the holy Trinity . . . because it is from the same earth that produced them that Christ drew his humanity."[35]

But the divine is not *in* the physical in Western piety in the same way in which it is in the world to the authors of Hindu devotional poetry.[36] Exploring transcendence as well as immanence, the Vishnaivite saint and poet Nammāḻvār (dates uncertain but probably fifth to ninth century) writes:

> Great one, who became all things,
> starting with the primal elements:
> wind, fire, water, sky and earth.
> Great one, wondrous one,
> you are in all things
> as butter lies hidden in fresh milk.[37]

Such metamorphosis of the divine into the natural does not play the same role in Western medieval images. The Marys of Catholic worship do not manifest themselves as, or transform into, trees as Paidi Talli does. However complex the Christian iconography of the Tree of Jesse may be, with various male relatives of Jesus and the Virgin Mary depicted on its branches, one cannot imagine the Madonna herself as a tree. The Tree of Jesse is a genealogical diagram presented in pictures, not an image of the divine.[38]

Thus, the parallel between the Hindu goddess and the Catholic saint, although their processions can each be elaborated with anthropological or "thing" theory, turns out to be relatively superficial. However much we may be confronted in both cases with an intense presence of something we can call power, general theories of "living pictures" or even of "liminality" do not take us very far when wood, mud, paint, and the female form occur in such different specific contexts and carry with them such different penumbra. Once one begins to allow the singularity to emerge, as Shulman puts it, one finds vastly divergent assumptions about the world.

I am not arguing, at this point, that comparing image processions is useless. Indeed, as I hope I have made clear, the comparison of Durga and Mary has taken me some distance toward understanding two more structural and phenomenological questions. First, where does supernatural power reside? And second, what conceptions of the material world condition what we might call religious presence? I return to these questions in the final example that follows, which argues for different, more subtly chosen comparanda. But in the meantime I take a detour to consider morphology or visual similitude a little further. For perhaps one should reject formal similarity far more radically than I have done so far. Perhaps Durga and Mary are only cases of pseudomorphism: female forms venerated in religious ritual but not really "very much alike." If so, our task would be to probe whether the religious shapes we think we see are in fact either similar or, in any meaningful way, different. Why do the apparent look-alikes look alike? And does it matter that they do? But this poses the deeper question raised by the concept of "pseudomorphism" itself. We can posit formal similarity in order to query it, but how do we know that something, even falsely or misleadingly, "looks like" something else? Do the shapes in fact look alike?

We can, of course, use categories from cognitive psychology: "red" is a certain wave length; an oval or mandorla is a shape that makes a certain portion of the brain light up on a scan; an outline of a circle with dots for eyes is recognized as a human face by a test group of babies.[39] But the latter example immediately makes it apparent that such categories are ambiguous. For any meaningful kind of humanistic inquiry, such a drawn circle is irrelevant — neither "like" nor "unlike" a human face. I do not want here to plunge into current discussion about the general validity of the cognitive turn in humanistic scholarship but merely to suggest that it hardly suffices, at this point in the development of research, to tell us how we identify similarity.[40] Even if the juxtaposition of things that are only spuriously alike can stimulate new interpretive moves for us and make us see in strange and radical ways, there must still be some reason why we start with the pairs we start with.[41] The category of "look-alikes" — even false look-alikes — is more complicated and more contextually conditioned than we tend to assume.

The Problem of Pseudomorphism: When Are Shapes Really Alike?

To illustrate this complexity, I wish to consider a Western medieval devotional image that has drawn much attention in recent years. I see it as raising in acute form the question of whether we can ever be sure we know that something "looks like" — even falsely looks like — something else. Once I've explored this image in its Western context, I shall turn to a Hindu one that raises, in its Indian context, similar issues. Thus, my comparison here is not a direct East-West comparison but rather, one might say, "relational" or "proportional." I consider two images, understanding each as a formal structure and considering it in comparison to other possibly "similar" forms that occur in its own context; I question how far we can go in either case in assuming what the original image "looks like." I then suggest that there may be a productive comparison not between the two images per se but between the ways in which each is embedded in, and raises questions about, its own cultural context. As a mathematician might say, A:B::A':B'. The comparison here is not between A and A' but between the two relationships.[42] All this will be a good deal clearer in the examples that follow than it is in this abstract description.

The Western image I wish to consider is the side wound of Christ, venerated in the high Middle Ages as part of devotion to the five wounds inflicted on Christ in the Crucifixion (two in the hands, two in the feet, one in the right side) but increasingly in the fifteenth century revered alone — in both iconography and devotional text — as a special entry into Christ's body as refuge, love, and salvation.[43] In some manuscript illuminations, woodcuts, and prayers, the side wound appears in isolation as a large oval shape. Sometimes it is treated as an exact measure (called a length) that gives the actual size of the wound or that, multiplied (usually by forty), gives the length of Christ's body. (See figure 6.9.) Sometimes it is placed horizontally and appears to be a mouth, speaking accusation. (See figure 5.6.)

But sometimes the oval is placed vertically and has reminded modern viewers of a vagina with labia, giving rise to elaborate feminist and/or queer interpretations of the image as erotic and/or gendered.[44] (See figure 5.7.) My question is: What do we make of this supposed look-alike, which is not in any simple way glossed on the images as erotic or sexual or female?

Before we reject or embrace the similarity, we have to ask: *Are* these things similar? As Silke Tammen has pointed out, the vertically placed side wound is a mandorla and can be seen as an opening in Christ's tunic, thus evoking medieval theories of sight as penetration and echoing the associations in many religious traditions of the mandorla with revelation and meditation.[45] In both Eastern and Western Christianity, the mandorla is often a frame for holy figures, and in present-day theosophy, based loosely on Hindu and Buddhist practice, the mandorla is a meditational device. Thus, someone in a Roman Catholic or Greek Orthodox tradition might well respond: "That's that funny-shaped frame for Jesus I've seen in churches"; or someone in a theosophist tradition, or even an American new age one, might react just as immediately: "That's an image for meditation."[46] Does the wound really look like a vagina or is this only a case of pseudomorphism?

There are a number of medieval texts that do associate Jesus's body with the female body as lactating, conceiving, and giving birth. Salvation is understood in poetry and biblical exegesis as nestling within the bowels or side of the savior, and in some especially theologically acute writers, it is glossed as being born from him. The most explicit textual identification of the side wound with vagina or womb is with it as container and source of life, and direct visual identification is most obvious in objects such as birthing girdles that use the wound as an amulet against difficult childbirth. Such girdles — thin strips of vellum bearing an image of the wound with drops of blood — were bound around the stomach of a woman in labor to ease her pain and were believed to have the power of inducing a similar slit, the vagina, to open.[47]

But what about the erotic overtones? Beyond modern, decontextualized, psychoanalytic responses, is there any contextualized reason for seeing the image as erotic or sexual rather than, or in addition to, maternal or physiological? The answer is yes, and in two very different senses.

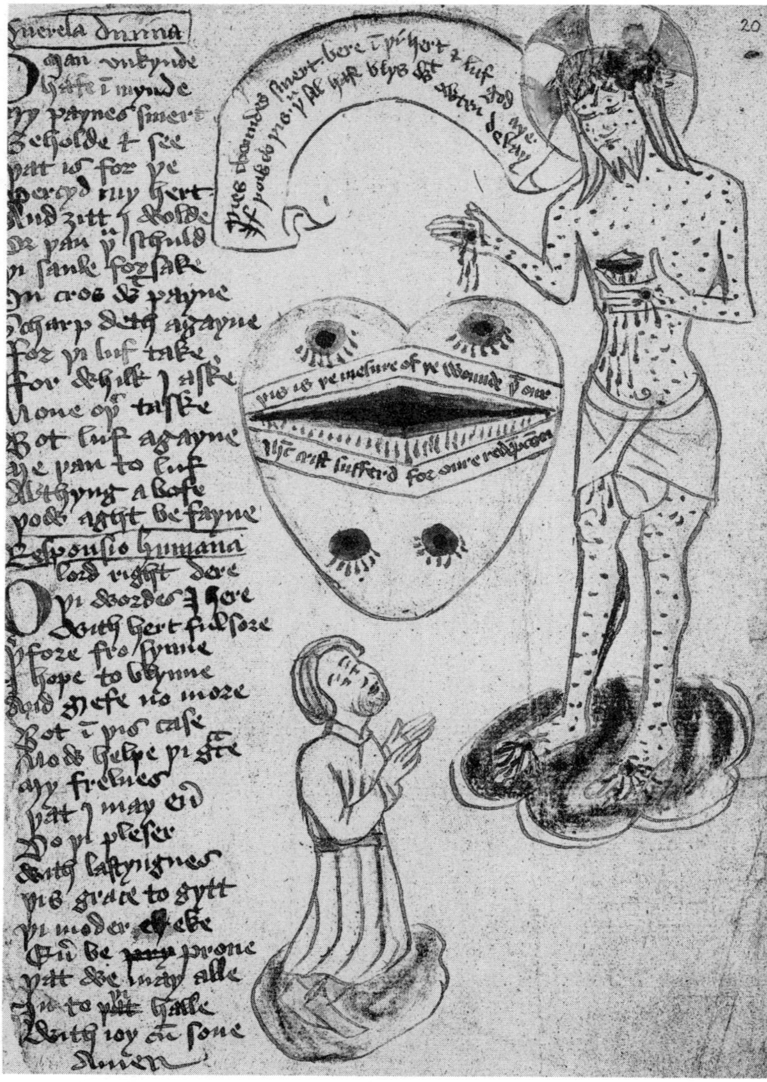

Figure 5.6. Folio 20r, MS Brit. Lib. Add. 37049, fifteenth century. The miniature depicts the bleeding Man of Sorrows, who offers his heart to a little lay figure and complains: "O man unkynde, hafe in mynde, my paynes smert. Beholde and see, that is for the, percyd my hert." Bearing all five wounds, the heart becomes Christ's whole body. The side wound, placed horizontally, becomes a mouth, speaking accusation, but it also announces itself to be the wound that Jesus suffered in a literal sense, because it is the wound's exact "mesure."

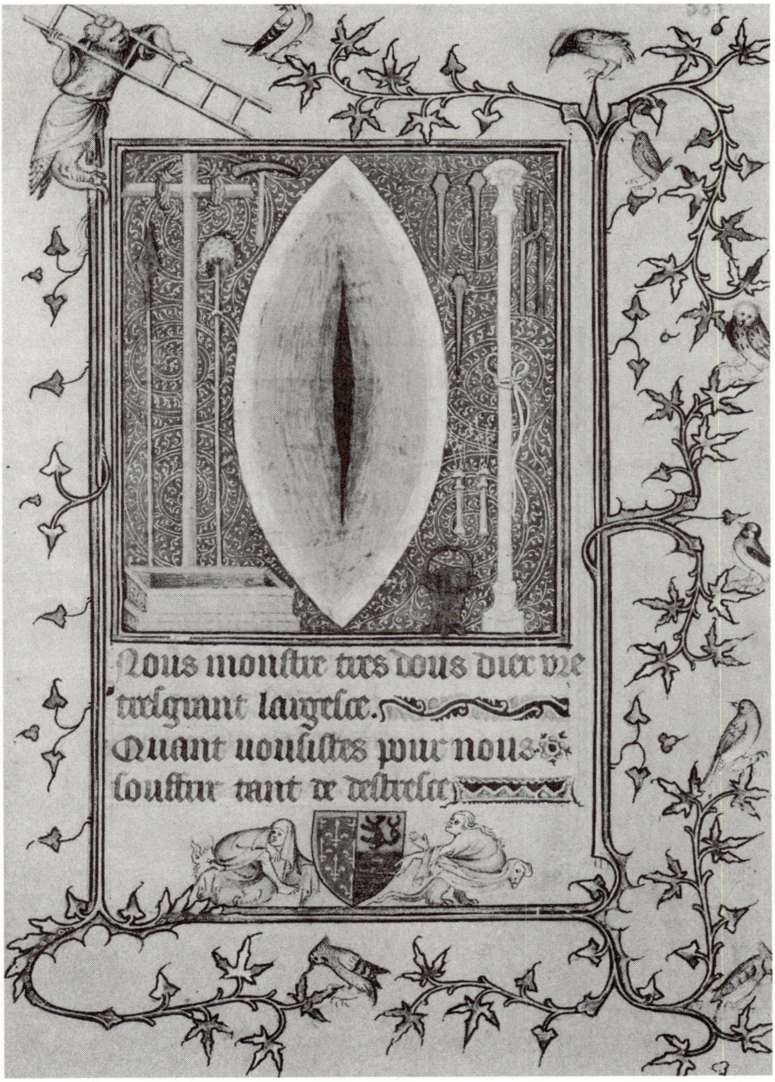

Figure 5.7. Psalter and Hours of Bonne of Luxembourg, fol. 331r. The Metropolitan Museum, the Cloisters Collection, acquisition number 69.86. From before 1349. Surrounded by the *arma Christi*, the vertically presented and flamboyantly red side wound has been interpreted by some modern scholars as drawing a parallel between Christ's gift of salvation and a vagina, understood as the opening from which the salvation of the world was born and into which saved souls return to rest in the center of Christ.

First, we must note that by the high Middle Ages, responses to the wounds and blood of Christ were elaborately and explicitly erotic both in a sense we might call polymorphous — that is distributed over the entire body — and as genitally focused. It is impossible not to see sexual overtones in the homey and erotic images of the popular fourteenth-century Middle English treatise *A Talkyng of the Loue of God*:

> I leap at Him swiftly as a greyhound at a hart. . . . I suck the blood from his feet. . . . I embrace and I kiss, as if I was mad. I roll and suck I do not know how long. And when I am sated, I want yet more. Then I feel that blood in my imagination as it were bodily warm on my lips and the flesh on his feet . . . so soft and so sweet to kiss.[48]

A much commented on passage in the probably somewhat earlier *Prickynge of Love* complicates the physiological image of conceiving and birthing in a way that is not so much feminizing as eroticizing and genderbending. The images of wounds as doorways in the *Prickynge* are almost all of entry, sometimes implicitly sexual. Christ opens doors and windows so that the soul (which in a clearly erotic passage becomes the lance that pierced Christ's side) may enter and remain within in the "tabernacle" of the body; to be born is to be cast forth from paradise, a poor substitute for remaining ecstatically within the body of God.[49]

This is textual imagery. But there is visual evidence as well. Surviving examples of apparently quite popular objects that appear to mock both Holy Wound piety and relic devotion suggest that the sexual and fetishizing overtones were apparent to contemporaries.[50] A little lead badge, cast about 1400 and now in the Cluny Museum in Paris (one other example, from Rotterdam, is known), shows three penises carrying a vagina in procession, just as reliquaries of holy arms, feet, and heads were carried (and are still carried) in the sort of saints-day processions I discussed above.[51] (See figures 5.8 and 5.9.) When placed in the context where it certainly belongs — that of other insignia mocking the delights and temptations of pilgrimage and the sexual transgressions of the clergy — the little badge seems to parody contemporary piety. Visual parallels between it and vertical, mandorla-shaped images of the side wound are striking. For example, the isolated and apparently swollen wound in one of the Bohun Books of Hours (Pommersfelden, Graf von Schönborn Schlossbibliothek

MS 348 [2934], fol. 9v), lifted upward in resurrection by angels as if it were the body of Christ, bears a striking resemblance to the little vagina borne by penises in the badge now at Cluny.[52] The bawdy and misogynist implications of such insignia (even suggesting rape fantasy) complicate our response to the very different and yet similar visual images of Christ's wound understood as the whole Christ, violated—even captured—by the lance at the Crucifixion for the salvation of sinners. More than pseudomorphism, there is a complex dialogue of likeness and unlikeness here between slit, wound, mandorla, and vagina that leads us to query what sort of relationship between body part and whole body is implied by such veneration.[53]

If one moves from this to a consideration of the cylindrical-shaped Shiva linga revered in Shaivite Hinduism, similar issues arise. The question of what the linga is—like the question of what we see when we see the wound of Christ—is a complicated one. There has been much heated dispute between Western and Hindu scholars over many decades about what one sees when one sees the linga, whether clothed in worship with cloths and flowers or unclothed. The basic meaning of the word "linga" is sign, distinguishing mark, symbol (with no sexual referent), and Sanskrit texts describe the object as an endless pillar representing the entire universe, as cosmic energy, or as Shiva's phallus, lost and recovered. In certain representations (and some of these are among the most ancient), it is depicted as an erect penis, with the physiological details carefully carved. (See figure 5.10.) In some early images, it is paired with the yoni (which can be understood as the vulva). But there are also aniconic lingas: found stone objects that bear little resemblance to a body part, cylindrical-shaped hills, and ice lingas formed like stalagmites by dripping and freezing water.[54] (See figure 5.11.) Moreover, when decorated and clothed in ritual, the linga has a different, less physiological appearance, and there are examples in which it is combined with the face or the full figure of the god in ways that either enhance or obscure its apparent phallic detail.[55] (See figures 5.12 and 5.13.) The linga does not go out in procession, suggesting in its immobility that it is a root, a core, a font of worship.

Clearly the question of pseudomorphism arises once again. Although some lingas appear, especially to Western eyes, to be erect penises, the perception has produced such outrage in certain quarters so that authors and publishers of general descriptions, such as

Figure 5.8. Participants in the seven-yearly historic *Heiligdomsvaart* (relics pilgrimage) in Maastricht, the Netherlands, in June 2018. On both Sundays during the ten-day festival, a procession is held in which the main relics and other devotional objects are exhibited and paraded. Here members of the bell-ringers guild carry the reliquary bust of one of the sixth-century bishops of Maastricht.

Figure 5.9. Three penises carrying a vagina in procession. Lead badge. 5.4 × 4 cm. End of the fourteenth or beginning of the fifteenth century. Such bawdy badges parallel the insignia collected by pilgrims to memorialize their journeys and sometimes mock pilgrim hypocrisy. It is rare to find one that parodies actual holy objects, but this badge is clearly a visual takeoff on holy-wound devotion and treats the often revered body part as if it has been captured and carried in a procession of the sort seen in figures 5.1, 5.2, and 5.8.

Figure 5.10. Linga with one face of Shiva, seventh to early eighth century, Thailand (Phetchabun Province, Si Thep). Stone, 140 cm high. The Metropolitan Museum of Art, Gift of Evelyn Kossak, The Kronos Collections, 1994, accession number 1994.510. Monumental lingas of the seventh and eighth centuries are found throughout Thailand. Kings would establish lingas as a religious act and as a means of legitimizing their claims to power over newly conquered territories. The circular pillar is implicitly the cosmic axis; its phallic character expresses fertility and power. The face of Shiva, recognizable by the crescent in his hair and by his vertical third eye, provides a focus for veneration. Above his face is the glans of the penis.

Figure 5.11. Ice linga, revered in Amarnath cave, located in Jammu and Kashmir, India, about 88 miles (141 km) from Srinagar. According to legend, Bhrigu Muni, one of the seven great sages, was the first to have discovered the Amarnath linga. It is believed that in the eleventh century Queen Suryamati gave sacred emblems to this temple. Pilgrimage continues today and reaches its peak when the iced stalagmite attains the apex of its waxing phase in the summer months.

Figure 5.12. Gudimallam linga, found in a famous temple, popularly known as "the Parasurameswara Temple," in a small village in the Chittoor District of Andhra Pradesh, India. Carved out of a hard dark brown indigenous stone, the linga is about five feet in height and one foot in thickness and is located in the innermost sanctuary of the temple. It has been claimed that this linga is the earliest discovered so far, and it can possibly be dated to the third century BCE. In this version, the phallic quality of the linga seems clear, and is both complicated and emphasized by the figure of Shiva standing in front with a penis that is nonerect but a central focus. The god stands on a dwarf and bears in his right hand a ram and a small vessel in his left.

Figure 5.13. This Shiva linga, called Kubera linga, is found at the Jambukeswara temple in Thiruvanaikaval, near Srirangam, in India. The temple is a famous Shiva shrine built by Kocengannan (Kochenga Chola), one of the early Chola rulers, around 1,800 years ago. Here the linga is clothed and decorated in a way that obscures the phallic associations.

those in encyclopedias, have been reluctant to elaborate the parallel.[56] Moreover, texts associate the object with the ascetic as well as the erotic Shiva—the Lord of the Dance (Nataraja) who dances both the dance of passion and the dance that destroys the universe. In a well-known myth about the origins of linga worship quoted here from the *Brahmānda Purāna*, Vishnu speaks:

> Once upon a time . . . I lay . . . alone, with all the creatures in my belly. Then, all of a sudden, I saw the four-headed Brahma, who said to me, "Who are you? . . . I am the maker of the worlds." I said to him: "*I* am the maker of the worlds, and also the one who destroys them, again and again." As the two of us were talking together in this way, each wishing to get the better of the other, we were amazed to see a flame arising in the north. Its brilliance and power made us cup our hands in reverence and bow to it. The flame grew, and Brahma and I ran up to it. It broke through heaven and earth, and in the middle of the flame we saw a linga, blazing with light.
>
> Then Brahma said to me: "Quickly, go down and find the bottom of this linga. I will go until I see its top." I agreed. I kept going down for a thousand years, but I did not reach the bottom of the linga, nor did Brahma find its top. We turned back and met again, amazed and frightened; we paid homage to Shiva, saying, "You create the worlds and destroy them."[57]

As in the case of the wound in Christ's side, so in the case of the Shiva linga; context is all-important to understanding. We may think the sexual connotations of the linga more apparent than those of Christ's wound, but even if we see an erect penis in the linga, we do not really see what is there unless we encounter it in both its textual and its ritual setting. Like the wound of Christ, the linga is generative as well as erotic in its sexual connotations. To really see this stone cylinder, we must see it decorated with flowers, cloths, and ghee (clarified butter) and revered in hymn and prayer as font of both life and destruction. Yet to say that the phallus and the linga are merely pseudomorphic also makes it impossible to see. If we encounter only stone or ice, cloth or flowers, we fail to see the fertility and the power.

Like the wound of Christ, the Shiva linga raises complex questions about the complete presence of god in what appears to be a fragment (a fragment that sometimes even visually becomes the whole) and about physiological images (both like and not like a body part) as anthropomorphizing the sacred. These are issues to which I shall return. My point here has not been to compare Christ's wound with

Shiva's linga but rather to raise apropos both devotional objects the question of pseudomorphism and context. The comparison I draw is relational. I suggest that the problem raised by the linga in its context is analogous to the problem raised by the side wound in its. The parallel is between the relations of objects to their context not between the objects themselves. Thus, both cases complicate notions of sameness. Querying how we might ascertain that certain forms are isomorphic or pseudomorphic is a way of underlining my argument that the fundamental problem of comparison for humanists is not finding the differences that learning and research will inevitably discover; it is understanding what it means to start with two "similars." Is morphology (shape, appearance) the place to start?

A Better Question: Where Is Presence?

With this question, I return to the comparison of Durga and Mary with which I began. I want now not merely to suggest that comparing images is not necessarily the right comparison; I want to explore what sort of comparison we might put in its place. I suggest that what we should ask is not "How is image in one culture like or not like image in another culture?" but rather "Where (in what place, object, or person) do religious presence and power reside?" In other words, the ground of comparison becomes phenomenological or structural or "representational" (in the sense of representing or making present).[58] Rather than assume that we should begin our exploration of presence with what scholars have tended to denominate "images," I propose that we start with the question: Where is the power? In what does it appear or adhere? But before I propose and explore what I take to be the better comparison, I should consider a bit further recent work on images.

As I pointed out earlier, a number of Western historians have recently drawn parallels between the "lives" of Indian and Western images and have used non-Western understandings to provide arguments for taking Christian images as animate presences, possessing an agency, both frightening and empowering, that shapes their adherents.[59] As David Freedberg puts it:

> By means of the proper rites, the deity is induced to inhabit a piece of inanimate [*sic*] matter. Then it becomes an object suitable for worship and capable of bestowing help . . . a receptacle for [the] god. This is what happens in

> Hinduism, on the West Coast of Africa, and among the Maori in New Zealand. It is also what happens in the case of the main monotheistic religions.

Calling the ceremony a "consecration rite," Freedberg remarks: "It is significant that many [such] rites involve the last stages of completing an image and bringing it to life."[60] Scholars have recently struggled with a variety of concepts, such as "distributive agency" and "representation,"[61] to express what is happening in these ceremonies, but whatever refinement of terminology they use, they stress that the power of an Other is here emerging in the material object we call an image.

For Freedberg and for many other scholars, the eye-opening ritual in Buddhism, Hinduism, and ancient China has provided a paradigm.[62] In fact, the Indian example makes it clear that the process is lengthier and more labile than a focus on providing eyes suggests. Indian images come to life in a series of rites or processes, from the initial selection of appropriate material for carving (wood from a male tree for a male god, for example) to awakening by the chiseling or painting in of eyes. Although the image is "made" by those who carve and anoint it, the god is latently present, lying, as Nammāḻvār put it, like "butter . . . in fresh milk." The image is then bathed, dressed, and adorned with unguents, and the devotee both recognizes and is recognized, locking eyes with the god (*darshan*).[63] Presence depends on the lengthy process of handling the god and on the expectation, which itself must be prepared, of the devotee.

Recent discussions of the parallels between Western and non-Western images have helpfully complicated earlier descriptions of the art of the European Middle Ages. As I have discussed elsewhere, standard textbook accounts of the iconoclastic controversy in the early Middle Ages have been misleading in their tendency to focus on theology more than practice.[64] Nor do traditional accounts adequately describe the awe-ful potency of the images that were increasingly feared and rejected in the fifteenth and sixteenth centuries.[65] Thus, it has been crucial for historians to jettison formulations that see Western images as simply triggers of devotion, inducements to something beyond or other than the images.[66] Non-Western cases have helped European medievalists rediscover the power of images themselves.

Nonetheless, much of the recent study of Christianity seems to me to adduce the wrong Western/non-Western comparisons. Not only is it misleading to compare Durga and Mary as if their processions were parallel, it seems misleading to assume that we will probe the nature of sacred presence most deeply if we compare statues. As I explained earlier, much recent work is predicated on the assumption that comparanda are, and should be, morphological — that is, visually similar. Indeed, in all this work, scholars have tended to treat the really interesting parallel as that of anthropomorphic image to anthropomorphic image; the starting point is thus "look-alikes," especially human "look-alikes." Implicated in this is the use, especially by art historians, of the term "image" (*imago*) to designate what has come in the West to be considered "art," although historically the term refers to figures of speech and ontological relationships as well.[67] Yet surely what we should be comparing is "presences" — that is, objects or places in which the holy is understood to be encounterable, palpable, "there." We should ask not "What looks like a god?" but "Where is the power, phenomenologically, structurally, religiously?"

Asking the question this way leads to a very different set of comparanda between Hindu and Christian piety. The most intense devotion to representations of the holy did not, in the Western Christian tradition, accrue around images at all but around relics (pieces of holy matter that became central to cult) and around sacraments and sacramentals (materials, such as water, oil, rings, staves, and bread, that conveyed a power they did not "depict," in the sense of having similitude to, but rather "represented," in the sense of making present).[68] Relics and Eucharist — neither of them anthropomorphic or perhaps even iconic in any simple sense — were more central to the Western Christian sense of sacred presence than were images and can be analyzed as more precise parallels to Hindu rituals of inducing the god or goddess in matter. The foot of St. Margaret *was* St. Margaret in a way a statue of her was not; the bread and wine of the Eucharist *were* Christ, a more telling parallel than any crucifix (even a moving or speaking one) to the presence of Vishnu or Shiva in statue, milk, or wood.

Suppose then that we take as comparanda Hindu images of gods and goddesses (both iconic and aniconic), on the one hand, and the Christian Eucharist on the other.[69] The Hindu material immediately suggests two issues. First, in what sort of material does god emerge? Second, how is this emergence effected or realized? Is it found or induced? Thus the parallel I now draw between Hinduism and Christianity — the deep parallel of religious presence — leads, I argue, to better questions, and the questions lead in turn to more apposite and illuminating understandings of difference. In considering these issues, however, my point is not so much to provide specific answers even for Western material as to suggest why these are better questions than those raised by simply accepting or rejecting morphological similarity.

If we consider the material locus of the divine in the Christian Middle Ages in the light of these questions, we see anew the strangeness of the Christian ideas of "real presence" (that Christ is literally present in the elements on the altar after consecration) and "transubstantiation" (that the "substance" — that is, the nature — of the bread and wine are transformed into Christ's flesh and blood, although the outward appearance or "accidents" remain unchanged). In so incarnational a religion (that is, one whose theology stresses the coming of God into a human being), it is odd that the focal point of revelation and agency is food. So much recent discussion of late medieval piety has been devoted to the new and insistent emphasis on Christ's physical humanity that we sometimes neglect to notice that the same period saw an equally insistent emphasis on the literal presence of the incarnate God in the basic foodstuff of the Mediterranean diet — bread and wine — and a radical increase of miracles in which this holy food animated itself by bleeding, levitating, or glowing and was preserved, still visibly as foodstuff (although altered foodstuff), to provide a locus of pilgrimage. Yet bread and wine, even miraculously altered to a red-spotted wafer or a vessel of viscous liquid, are not in any simple sense "like" the figure of Christ seen on crucifixes, pietàs, or wall paintings.[70]

To emphasize the non-anthropomorphism of consecrated bread and wine is not to argue that there are no anthropomorphic elements in devotion to the Eucharistic species, just as a move to complicate our understanding of the Shiva linga is not to deny anthropomorphic references in texts and images relating to it. Christian theologians spent much time elaborating the symbolism of the Eucharistic elements in ways that underlined it as flesh and blood, however hidden as such. Moreover, the period from 1100 on in the medieval West saw increasing claims to visions or physical transformations in which the host, and sometimes the wine of the chalice, appeared as the infant or the adult Christ.[71] Such visionary experiences and miraculous eruptions were fraught with more anxiety, however, than scholars often recognize. When miraculously transformed matter was thought to endure as bloodlike or fleshlike or even as reflecting a human face or body (as, for example, on the wine-spotted corporal at Walldürn), it induced at least as much anxiety over how to revere or preserve it as pride in its possession.[72] Even when overlaid with visions of the human Christ or eruptions of flesh and blood, the Christian Eucharist was not in any simple sense anthropomorphic.

In chapter 3 I discussed some recent scholarship that sees the anthropomorphism of religious objects as the locus of, or generator of, their power to mediate the divine Other to humankind.[73] As I explain there, even for Hindus, whether or not an image (such as the linga) is anthropomorphic depends on viewer response and ritual setting as much as on what the object might be thought to look like per se.[74] Some scholars even suggest that Durga is present at her ceremony not so much in the clay figures as in the nine plants that are ritually bathed at the beginning of her festival.[75] Thus, even the goddess may be most present when she looks least like a human. Taken in the context of this discussion, the centrality of foodstuff in Christianity—even foodstuff theorized as human flesh—contributes to the questioning of generalizations about the importance of anthropomorphism in the genesis of sacral objects.

If we turn to the second issue I suggested earlier—that is, how the sacred is found, or induced to appear, in the material—we find again that the parallel is between Hindu rituals surrounding images and Christian ceremonies relating to the Eucharist.

The ritual by which Durga is induced to enter her statue is lengthy: performances of prayer, song, and dance are offered; food, flowers, jewels, and textiles clothe and anoint her. In similar fashion, as Richard Davis explains, the god begins to emerge in a male statue carved for a temple at the moment when the artisans search for the appropriate male tree in the forest.[76] Paidi Talli is carried from the river to ferment in pots before she emerges as a tree. The aniconic linga found in nature as a stone or mountain or dried riverbed manifests itself as divine. It is not so much consecrated as accorded worship. It manifests its power in activities such as bleeding, glowing with light, providing food, drinking milk—activities that almost imperceptibly cross the line into transformation or miracle.[77] Whatever importance chiseling in the eyes of a statue may have, the appearance of the sacred in the material is a process not a moment; the god is both found and induced to appear.

As Freedberg observed, Western images are not consecrated.[78] Some are blessed and sprinkled with holy water, but full consecration is limited to altar vessels, the altar table, the ground of cemeteries and churches, the oil, water, bread and wine used in the sacraments, and the personnel (the clergy) who perform them.[79] Assuming that consecration must be a defining act has led art historians to worry about its absence vis-à-vis images and hence to propose various theories to explain the undoubted power some images acquired, arguing that they were made holy by implanting relics in them or by attributing to them miraculous origins. I would suggest rather that holiness was sometimes *found* in statues or wall paintings or saints' bodies in the West, as it was in stones or riverbeds in India. But the real parallel to the consecration process in Hinduism lies in the central locus of holiness in late medieval Christianity: the consecration of the Eucharist. That process is far more like the preparation of Durga or even the finding of Paidi Talli than we have recognized. For all the emphasis of theologians and canon lawyers on consecration by the clergy as a moment of transformation from bread into flesh, the encounter with god in foodstuff was prepared for materially and experientially.

By the later Middle Ages, the communion wafer was no longer home-baked bread offered by housewives but a flat, thin, almost transparent disk, often stamped with an image of the crucified Christ. (See figure 3.2, where such a figure becomes the basis for a host miracle.) It was ritually prepared by clergy or monks, and according to some monastic customs, the wheat was selected kernel by kernel, the mill hung with curtains, and the millers specially garbed; the bakers either sang hymns while preparing it or kept silent lest their breath touch the bread.[80]

Not only was the consecration of the bread prepared for, as the wood was prepared before the carving of a Hindu god, encounter with the Eucharist was for the faithful a process in some ways similar to the encounter with Durga in festival and song. A number of developments between the eleventh and the fourteenth centuries in Europe tended to move the Eucharist away from a communal meal and toward a mystery whose impact came when a hidden something was revealed. The words of consecration became less audible; the priest now stood in front of the altar with his back to the congregation. By the thirteenth century, pierced screens that functioned to direct as well as to limit the gaze were erected between the ordinary laity and the apse where the altar was located.[81] The focal point of the mass came to be not the consecration but the moment when the priest elevated — that is, lifted up — the host.[82] Nor was the revelation of the host only visual. Through incense, music, genuflections, and candles, all the senses were over the course of the mass awakened. Increasingly then, the central Christian ritual involved a kind of synesthesia.

Moreover, the consecrated host, paraded in Corpus Christi processions or exposed on the altar outside the mass in gorgeous crystal and gold monstrances, became a holy object in and of itself, inspiring terror as well as devotion. Whether or not miracles of sensible transformation were reported, the holy was encountered as intense, reverberating presence.[83] So powerful was this holy stuff that wafers, sometimes even unconsecrated wafers, were used by the populace as apotropaic objects to increase fertility in beehives, fishponds, and fields. In such a religious climate, what was at stake even in many cases of miraculous appearances of Christ was less a stark moment of metamorphosis into the anthropomorphic than a sense of the palpable and encompassing emergence of the divine.

Having found a better comparandum for the Hindu statue in the Christian Eucharist, I have actually come to see the Eucharist in a new way — as less anthropomorphic and more processual than I understood before. But the fact that I have found more appropriate and telling "likes" by asking "Where is the sacred?" does not obscure the radical singularity of things. Although the Eucharist — whether reserved as a wafer in a tabernacle or monstrance or displayed as a blood-picture at Walldürn — is a better parallel to Durga than are the statues of the two Marys revered in the Camargue, a probing of better "likes" leads nonetheless to differences — indeed to even deeper differences. Materiality itself raises different questions for Christianity and Hinduism.

As we saw in considering Durga's procession to and immersion in the Ganga, a different sense of the organic is at play in Catholic and Hindu worlds; fragmentation and decay raise different questions. In contrast to Durga's or Paidi Talli's emergence from and return to mud, one thinks of Christian miracles in which cracks in crucifixes are healed by the application of the Eucharistic host or visions in which the broken hand of a statue of the Christ Child is left behind as a relic, proof to the worshipping visionary that even pieces are permanent presences.[84] Indeed, it was exactly because fragmentation was so threatening that statues and stained glass were not only rejected but also smashed at periods of iconoclasm.[85] And although Christians in Western Europe increasingly broke relics of the saints into pieces in order to distribute their holiness, they felt a need to assert — through theories of concomitance — that part is really whole.[86] Moreover, the tiny pieces found in reliquaries were assembled into vast collections rather than isolated as bits, thus reflecting the community of the holy in heaven more than fragmentation or individuation on earth.[87]

If we turn from statues and relics to the materiality in which the divine itself was instantiated, the contrast is even starker. According to the theory of transubstantiation, bread and wine are the flesh and blood of the God-man; yet foodstuff, which supports life, also decays. Whereas Durga and Paidi Talli are born from and joyfully return to the organic, the process of generation and corruption is a problem for Christian theology. This problem led occasionally to what seem to modern ears ridiculous debates over whether the God in the Eucharist could be digested and excreted or piled into mountains of stuff that grew larger with each consecration. The quandary posed was even greater when miraculously transformed wafers or wine, preserved as revelations of God's body, showed signs of rot. Clergy sometimes denied evidence of change or surreptitiously replaced deteriorating wafers with new and undecayed ones.[88] But my point is not that certain formulations of anxiety sound silly or certain actions questionable — charges medieval contemporaries themselves made — but rather that anxiety about materiality was central. Such anxiety is reflected even today in the requirement that Catholic churches possess a *sacrarium* or *piscina* (a sink connected directly to the ground, not to the public sewage system) in which holy things, such as the water used to cleanse the Eucharistic vessels, are to be disposed of without danger of contact with garbage or human waste.[89] The controversy that erupted around the Madonna by Chris Ofili in the *Sensation* exhibition at the Brooklyn Museum in 1999–2000 because of its use of a resin-covered lump of elephant dung and of phallic symbols has a long history behind it. Although some

Hindu, like some Christian, sages and contemplatives seek to transcend the material world in ways too complicated to explore here, a comparison of divine materiality in the two traditions suggests that the presence, even the representation, of god in organic stuff has been threatening to Western Christians in a way it is not to Indian devotees of Shiva and Vishnu.[90]

Thus, my answer to the historian colleague who asked whether I had learned anything about the West by going to India is that I did. But it was only by finding the right similitudes to start with that I was able to use increased understanding of the Hindu divine to ask new questions about, and hence probe more deeply into, the strangeness of Western practices I had studied for so long.

To conclude: comparison must start with similarities or it cannot begin. But deciding what is similar to what is far from obvious. Students of religion have been too cavalier in assuming that choosing comparanda is the easy part of any research. Obvious choices of parallels may result all too quickly in discoveries of difference that are not only obvious but finally unproductive. How, then, do I think students of religion should proceed in choosing things to compare? First, they should avoid assuming that "look-alikes"—either to explore or to dismiss—are the best parallels for understanding cultures. Second, they should seek structural, functional, phenomenological, or devotional—rather than purely morphological—parallels, prepared for the possibility that startling similarities may emerge between things that look radically different. Third, they should place each of the carefully chosen comparanda in its own context before drawing out the comparison of these things-in-context with each other.

In the end, however, scholars will find difference as much as sameness, and the more careful the decision about comparanda the more telling will be the differences disclosed. Even when the comparison is as sensitive to the complexity of two traditions as we can make it, the terms will inevitably pull against each other, each asserting its strangeness and its integrity. And it is in the pulling against, as well as the sameness, that each will shed light on, and indeed change our understanding of, the other. As literary critic James Wood says about metaphor, "As soon as you liken x to y, x has changed, and is now x + y, which has its own parallel life."[91] Once understood as similar to as well as different from a Hindu statue, the Christian Eucharist never looks the same again.

Metaphor, or what one of the greatest of Christian theologians called "dissimilar similitudes," is thus the best image I can find for true comparison.[92] We must seek such dissimilar likenesses—that is, things like each other at some level deeper than appearance. We must then allow these things to pull away from each other because of the unlikeness and yet each to become part of our understanding of the other because of the deeper similitude. If we do this, we will conclude not by dismissing mistaken parallels or identifying superficial incongruities but by penetrating, with learning and thoughtfulness, to true cultural singularity, which is never, given the human condition, only singular.

CHAPTER SIX

Footprints: The Xenophilia of a Medievalist[1]

As a child, I fantasized about the apparently deserted island of Robinson Crusoe, as did the children of Arthur Ransome's *Swallows and Amazons*, my favorite book.[2] I wandered around my backyard in a circle that I drew in the mud under the swing set to represent my island and pretended that, like those children, I found mysterious footprints. My pretending was emphatically not because I wanted to barricade myself against a threatening and foreign other; rather, it was because the discovered footprints pointed to something strange and a little out of reach but also recognizable and therefore inviting investigation. Once drawn, the footprints in the mud became my puzzle—as mysterious to me as were the footprints of Man Friday found by Crusoe or the traces of interlopers found by the children of the Swallows camp on their desert island. Of course, I articulated to my eight-year-old self no theory of the footprint. I remember only drawing it and spending hours "exploring my island." But the footprint has remained with me as an image of the foreign, distant, strange, or other (*xenos*) that I circle around when I research and write about the past. It seems an appropriate object to consider for a symposium on xenophilia.

A footprint like Man Friday's is not only a trace of something human that has been present; it is, as itself, still present physically. Yet it points beyond, toward something not present any longer—something of which it is, as a modern theorist might say, a trace,[3] or as a medieval theologian would put it, a vestige.[4] Eagerly following such footprints is not the opposite of fear; rather, such exploration subsumes fear, impelled by desire for a knowledge that will perhaps be dreadful and shocking, or enticing and provocative, once even partly obtained. In itself, the footprint stimulates desire (*philia*) and dread (*phobia*). It is, in itself, a paradox — both an absence and a presence. And the part (foot) it makes both present and absent signals the existence of a whole (a body) that has gone away. As itself, the footprint is familiar, yet tantalizingly partial, hence strange. But it points beyond itself to something that is foreign, dissimilar, and hence even stranger.[5]

It is my suggestion that medieval European veneration of the footprints of Christ, supposedly left on the Mount of Olives at his Ascension into heaven, can provide a specific and incisive model for thinking both about xenophilia and about the sort of comparative study Europeanists find themselves drawn to recently. For the holy footprint, as medieval devotees understood it, was active; it bodies forth the agency, the challenge, the provocation of the other in a way modern theories of the "trace" do not. Hence, there are aspects of medieval veneration that make the medieval footprint a better starting point for thinking about both "the other" and "the trace" than that provided by many of the general discussions of otherness, likeness, or simulacra available today.

Comparative Footprints

It is, of course, impossible to raise questions about the other, whether desired or avoided and even abhorred, without addressing the issue of comparison. For all scholars stand in their own time and place on the globe as they look toward something outside themselves. We are all always comparativists. The footprint as object is, however, a particularly appropriate inducement to considering the nature of cross-cultural comparison — specifically the issue I have addressed elsewhere: What should one choose when beginning to compare? Should one start with morphology — that is, with objects or images that "look alike"?[6] Footprints raise this question because morphology seems the obvious place to start when considering them. Indeed, if one looks around the world and across time, it is the morphology (that is, the shape or appearance) of the footprint that seems to induce, even determine, the cult that arises around it. The popular book *Footprints in Stone* by Janet Bord, published in 2004, details hundreds of supposed imprints of the feet of giants, heroes, saints, devils, monsters, and gods and goddesses in places all over the globe.[7] The fact that the indentations look like feet has clearly in many cases been enough to give rise to the stories about them.

At the most obvious level of consideration, such stone impressions show how the same object can be differently interpreted in different cultures. For example, the almost six-foot-long footprint on Adam's Peak in southwest Sri Lanka is interpreted by Muslims as the place where Adam landed when he was expelled from Paradise. To Buddhists, it is the footprint left by the Buddha at the moment of his final contact with the world from which he was departing. To some Hindus, it is the print of Shiva. To Chinese Taoists, it is that of the first ancestor. Christians claim that the mark has been left by St. Thomas, apostle to south India.[8] In a parallel case, Jacob Kinnard has studied sculptural images of footprints in Bihar that are revered by both Buddhist and Hindu pilgrims, who attach very different identities and significance to the same objects. Kinnard argues that the issue of to whom the footprints belong does not arise among worshippers because the footprint's identity depends on the ritual context within which it is located and the religious affiliation of the participant.[9]

Even a quick glance at footprints in various religious traditions of the world makes clear that they are often visually rather different in presentation. Footprints of Christian figures such as Christ, Mary, or the saints are usually plain, although many of the transportable copies of them that survive are inscribed with identifying information about source or attributed power.[10] (See figure 6.1 for the footprint of Christ on the Mount of Olives in Jerusalem and figure 6.8 for a transportable copy.) Even the prints at the Tomb of Jesus in Srinagar, Kashmir, have chiseled into them only the marks of the Crucifixion nails. (Jesus supposedly returned to Kashmir, where he was known as Yuz Asaf, after his Crucifixion and taught there.)[11] In contrast, the footprints of the Buddha are usually highly decorated, often with the so-called Seven Appearances representing his Enlightenment. (See figure 6.2.) Many representations of the footprints of the Hindu god Vishnu are incised with multiple symbols as well.[12] Hence, it is clear that, in comparison to Christianity, footprints often serve a more elaborate instructional and even ritual function in some other religions, manifesting complex information about doctrine and practice.

Nonetheless, footprints — however specifically and differently identified by their adherents and the traditions within which they are found — are all prints of feet, and as Anthony Cutler has suggested,

Figure 6.1. Stone supposedly marked with one of Christ's footprints, Church of the Ascension, on the Mount of Olives, Jerusalem. An octagonal aedicule surrounds the Ascension rock, which is said to contain the right footprint of Christ, the section bearing the left footprint having been taken to the Al-Aqsa Mosque in the Middle Ages. The imprint is venerated by Christian pilgrims as the last spot on earth touched by the incarnate Christ.

Figure 6.2. Footprints of the Buddha (Buddhapada). From Pakistan, Gandhara region; Kushan Empire, 30–375 CE. 86.36 × 125.1 × 6.35 cm. Yale University Art Gallery, gift of the Rubin-Ladd Foundation under the bequest of Ester R. Portnow 2015.141.1. In contrast to Christ's footprints, the footprints of the Buddha are usually highly decorated, often with the so-called Seven Appearances representing his Enlightenment. In this relief, auspicious motifs such as wheels, swastikas, and shrivastas (wheels with hornlike tops) fill the soles and toes of the Buddha's footprints. The snakelike heads of the two devotees in the niches on either side indicate that they are demi-divinities.

they have some morphological similarity and functional parallels across cultures.[13] They are proofs of presence — that is, proofs that Vishnu, Shiva, Buddha, Jesus, St. Patrick, or the Virgin Mary were really there where the prints endure. Such assertions of presence are particularly important in cases where the marks have allegedly been left by apparitions or visions, such as the footprints at the Church of Domine Quo Vadis in Italy, supposedly left by the Christ who appeared to St. Peter fleeing persecution, or those of the archangel Michael in the Church of Monte Sant'Angelo sul Gargano,[14] although it is interesting to note that claims about the form in which the divine figure was present are often unimportant to the teller of the story of an apparition.[15] Moreover, copies of the prints attest to successful pilgrimage made to them or to proper veneration performed at their shrine. Visitors take home copies that have been touched to the original footprints or copied from them. Pilgrims sometimes leave behind their own bodily traces — footprints or handprints — at various sites to affirm that they were there.

Feet are significant in many religions. Just as the head is usually seen as the highest part of the person, so feet are often seen as the lowest because they touch an earth understood as polluting — the opposite of the sacred or the celestial.[16] In many religions, the gods and their avatars or servants are not permitted to touch the earth, and in Hinduism and Buddhism images of footprints are sometimes in fact images of sandals worn by the god or goddess to prevent contact with the ground.[17] Moreover, footwashing is a purification ritual in many parts of the world.[18] Jesus's washing of the feet of the disciples on the Thursday of the Last Supper was understood not only as a model of his humility but also as a sign of his human physicality. It was a sort of reverse or paradoxical purification rite — a sign of his willing choice of contact with the impurity of soil and corruption. Although Christian stories usually consider footprints to be proofs of the presence of holy beings, they sometimes treat feet and the earth they touch as negative, even as a sign of evil or contamination. In chapter 4, I discuss the alleged footprints of a rabbi's wife preserved at Sternberg in northern Germany as proof that she sank deep into a stone under the weight of an abused host and was not able to rise. (See figure 4.1.) In contrast to accounts of angelic or saintly footprints, these marks reflect a sense that entrapment in earth is accusatory, a proof of evil intent.[19]

This brief comparison of footprints across religions illustrates at once that much more is at stake than mere similarity of form. Deeper questions, such as conceptions of earth and physicality and of access to the Other of spiritual power, at once emerge.[20] Moreover, if we turn to the footprints on the Mount of Olives, revered since the days of the early church, we quickly see that morphology is not the most important aspect of this object's power.

Christ's Footprints on the Mount of Olives: A Brief History

Modern theorists of the trace, vestige, or imprint assume that the entity to which it owes its existence in the first place is always already gone. A trace is by definition a simulacrum that refers beyond itself.[21] A footprint gestures toward something that cannot be present; if the foot were there, we would not see the footprint. In mechanical reproduction, this is also the case. When a seal is imprinted in wax, an object formed in a mold, or a print made from an engraved metal plate or woodblock, the mold or matrix or plate must be removed in order for the copy to exist. The object that informs the material shapes it so that model and impression are "like" each other, although sometimes as mirror images. Hence, absence is the condition of presence; the reproduction or trace exists only when the modeling object is gone but leaves a hint, a simulacrum, of what it is like.

It is clear that absence — not vanishing or ephemerality but absence — is at the heart of early Christianity. Indeed, Christianity can be said to have been established, authenticated, even proven, by an absence: the empty tomb. The nonpresence of a dead body at a specific site demonstrated the Resurrection: "He [Jesus] is not here but is risen" (Luke 24:6). As Eusebius argued in the fourth century — and Christians have repeated many times since — the empty tomb was "the revered and all-hallowed testimony of the Saviour's resurrection . . . testifying by facts louder than any voice to the resurrection of the Saviour."[22] Similarly, the footprints on the Mount of Olives proved the Ascension: he was here but he has gone up into heaven.

When we look at encounters with Christ's footprints in the Holy Land, however, we find that medieval traces are not primarily absences but also, and emphatically, presences. The copies or bits of footprints carried away by the devout are significant not because they conjure up something (a mold or pattern or a charismatic person) that has gone away but because something (a substance, holiness, or power) is present. They are not primarily remembrances or mnemonic devices or even proofs of attendance by pilgrims at shrines; they are agents. The very word *vestigia* (steps, tracks, prints, vestiges, even moments or instances) was employed by medieval theologians such as Bonaventure to argue for God's action in the world. Used down into the early modern period by reformers such as John Calvin, the idea that we encounter traces of the divine plan in nature became a paean of praise to God's glory that almost amounted to an argument from design.[23] Those who viewed or touched such traces experienced something insistently and permanently there. Moreover, the traces not only endured, they also replicated themselves. They acted and traveled. Their presence was understood to be carried across time and space not only by bits of the footprints themselves but also by measures (such as pieces of leather or linen) that did not resemble feet in anything except length.

Gospel accounts of Christ's Ascension are very short (Luke 24:50–53; Mark 16:19), and the account in Mark is generally thought to be a later interpolation. The lengthiest biblical account is in Acts 1:9–12:

> And when he had said these things, while they looked on, he was raised up; and a cloud received him out of their sight.
>
> And while they were beholding him going up to heaven, behold, two men stood by them in white garments.
>
> Who also said: Ye men of Galilee, why stand you looking up to heaven? This Jesus who is taken up from you into heaven shall so come as you have seen him going into heaven.
>
> Then they returned to Jerusalem from the mount that is called Olivet, which is nigh Jerusalem, within a sabbath's day journey.

A church was built on the site of the Ascension very early and dedicated in 378.

According to art historian Andrea Worm, the earliest visual representations of Christ rising up from what is clearly a stone on the Mount of Olives is in a manuscript now in the British Library, perhaps from Trier or Hirsau, made a little after 1100.[24] (See figure 6.3.) There are a number of twelfth- and thirteenth-century examples of depictions of such stones, which sometimes appear to resemble altars, although many images show Christ departing from a hillock or

Figure 6.3. Gospel Lectionary, British Library Egerton MS 809, fol. 33v. Germany. Possibly from the abbey of St. Maximin at Trier, or the abbey of Hirsau in Swabia, first quarter of the twelfth century. This is probably the earliest visual representation of Christ rising up from what is clearly a stone on the Mount of Olives.

mountain, not a stone. By the mid-twelfth century we find illustrations in which Christ leaves behind one or two footprints, on either a hillock or a stone, and such representations proliferate in northern Europe in the later Middle Ages.[25] (See figures 6.4a–b.) In a number of cases, the depiction of Christ as vanishing upward so that only his feet remain visible comes to be combined with the presence of the prints. This pairing of traces with disappearance clearly underlines visually the juxtaposition and complementarity of absence and presence, departure and perdurance.[26] Moreover, we should not fail to note that the passage from Acts specifically illustrated in such images is a pledge of return, of even greater presence. Those who behold Christ going up into heaven are promised: "He shall *so* come as you have seen him going." The returning Christ will be like the Christ of the departure, a palpable human presence.

Textual evidence complicates and enriches the understanding of the footprints we derive from images. Veneration of Christ's footprints in the church on the Mount of Olives is first mentioned in the early fifth century in a letter that bishop Paulinus of Nola (d. 431) wrote to his friend Sulpicius Severus, based not on eyewitness experience but on reports from someone living in Jerusalem. According to this account, the footprints could not be covered in marble but sprang into view again when workmen attempted to cover them.[27] On this report, Sulpicius based the account in the second book of his chronicle of 402, asserting that the footprints of Christ remained undisturbed so that the faithful might adore where his feet had been impressed in the dust, despite the fact that pilgrims continuously took particles of earth with them from the holy place.[28] In the thirteenth century, James of Voragine's *Golden Legend*, one of the two or three most widely read books in the later Middle Ages, repeated Sulpicius's account, stressing that the footprints refused to be covered over with marble flooring and underlining their permanence as proof of Christ's presence on earth after the Resurrection: "Footmarks in the dust there prove that the Lord had stood on that spot: the footprints are discernible and the ground still retains the depressions his feet had left."[29]

Our first report of the church after the ravages of the early seventh century comes from an account by Adamnan, abbot of Iona in Scotland, whose *De locis sanctis libri tres* was based on the oral account of the Gallic bishop Arculf, who had visited Jerusalem about 680 and whose evidence concerning the city and its monuments is considered by modern historians to be reliable.[30] Arculf describes a protective cover reaching as high as a person's neck with a large opening in the middle through which one could see the footprints of the Lord clearly impressed in the dust (*vestigia pedum Domini . . . impressa in pulvere*). And those entering can, he says, come easily to the place of the holy dust (*adire locum sacrati pulveris*) and take particles (*particulas*) in their outstretched hands.[31]

After the siege of Jerusalem in 1099, references to stone footprints replace those to traces in sand. Although we have accounts of pilgrims visiting and kissing a stone in the first decade of the twelfth century,[32] our first explicit reference to the stone as imprinted with feet seems to be written by a pilgrim from Iceland in about 1150 that asserts that "in Michael's church stands a high rock in which lies the stone that the Lord stepped on when he ascended to the heavens, and one can see the imprint of his left foot, fourteen inches long, as if he has stepped barefoot into clay."[33] The curious reference to the precise length suggests that the pilgrim has been told the exact dimensions or has perhaps even measured the imprint himself. After the fall of the Crusader kingdom in 1198, Salah al-Din gave the Church of the Ascension to two of his followers; it remained in use as a mosque for more than three hundred years. Christian pilgrim accounts down into the early modern period show confusion over how much of the building survived, how many footprints remained, and, if only one, which footprint.[34] A late thirteenth-century account by Burchard of Mount Sion says that the prints were blocked by a stone in such a way that they could be touched but not seen; in a fifteenth-century report, Nicolas of Poggibonsi asserts that there are two prints of bare feet but that Christ ascended from another stone outside the church. Seventeenth-century accounts refer to a single footprint, and one reports that the second print had been removed to Haram ash-Sharif.[35] At present, a slab that supposedly contains the right footprint is revered inside the Chapel (or aedicule) of the Ascension, on the floor, in an asymmetrically placed frame.[36]

It is clear from these accounts that the traces were significant not only as proof of presence but also (as both the Acts of the Apostles and James of Voragine's account stress) as proof of the *physicality* of presence. As I indicated earlier, feet are associated in many cultures with earth and hence with physicality (although the implications of

Figures 6.4a–b. German woodcuts from the late fifteenth century that show the vanishing Christ leaving behind one or two footprints. The varying iconographical traditions may reflect pilgrim experiences of seeing either one or two footprints since accounts from the period differ about how many footprints are present and, if only one, whether it is the left or the right.

a. The Ascension of Christ, from Jean de Mandeville, *Reysen und Wanderschaften durch das Gelobte Land*, Basel, c. 1481. From *The Illustrated Bartsch*, vol. 83: *German Book Illustration before 1500: Anonymous Artists, 1481–82*, 8381.1481/1034 [21.428], p. 206.

b. The Ascension of Christ, from Bertholdus, *Horologium devotionis*, fol. 92v, Nuremberg, 1489. From *The Illustrated Bartsch*, vol. 87: *German Book Illustration before 1500: Anonymous Artists, 1489–91*, 8789.1489/393 [4.2780], p. 116.

Figure 6.5. *Belles Heures du Duc de Berry*, fol. 149v. 1405–1408/1409; Paris, France. The Limbourg Brothers (Franco-Netherlandish, active France, by 1399–1416). The Metropolitan Museum of Art, the Cloisters Collection, 1954; Accession Number: 54.1.1a, b. Mary Magdalen swoons over the feet of Christ at the Deposition from the cross. The feet of Christ had complex symbolic significance as images of his humanity and humility; they were therefore places of special access and devotion to him.

physicality vary according to tradition, ritual, and theology). The many medieval depictions of the most prominent saints of Christendom (above all Mary Magdalen and Francis of Assisi) curled around the feet of Christ in devotion suggest that in the Middle Ages feet were a special place of encounter with the physicality of the holy.[37] (See figure 6.5 for Mary Magdalen swooning over the feet of the dead Christ.) So much was this so that we even have depictions of the *Noli me tangere*, Christ's injunction to Mary Magdalen after the Resurrection not to touch him, that show Mary reaching for or touching Christ's feet. (See figures 6.6 and 6.7.)[38] The mark of Christ's bare feet in direct contact with earth (whether dust or stone), protected by neither sandal nor carpet, was proof that a god had been historical, bodily, human.

Not just proof of a holiness once present or of the physicality of that holiness, the footprints themselves were active, self-replicating, transportable power.[39] Moreover it is not clear that their shape or appearance (what I have called "morphology") is crucial to this carrying power. Their holiness—not only what they signified but what they *were*—could be transported through space and time either by bits of themselves (those self-duplicating and perpetuating *particulas* referred to in the *De locis sanctis*) or by measurements (such as the mathematically precise measure noted by the Icelandic pilgrim) that replicated their length.

Iconic and Aniconic Representations of Christ's Footprints

We do not have any early accounts of measures of the footprints from the Mount of Olives (although the precision of the Icelandic pilgrim's later reference to length suggests that they were made) but an account by an anonymous pilgrim from Piacenza in c. 570 describes the practice of measuring and transporting other footprints. According to this account, the prints of Jesus's feet survive on an oblong stone in the Church of St. Sophia in Jerusalem where he was forced to stand while Pilate heard his case. The author wrote that "he has a well-shaped foot, small and delicate... and pilgrims take the measure of the prints [*vestigia*] of his feet, which they hang about themselves and are cured of various diseases."[40] The author similarly describes the marks of Christ's breast and hands on the column of the flagellation in the Church of Holy Sion, whose measures (*mensurae*) are also taken away and hung around the neck to cure illness.[41] Right down

Figure 6.6. So important devotionally did the feet of Christ become that Christ's injunction to Mary Magdalen not to touch him (John 20:17) is often in fact illustrated by images of her reaching toward or almost touching his feet. On fol. 75v of the *Bernward Gospels*, a richly decorated evangeliary now housed in the Hildesheim Cathedral Museum and made for the monks of Hildesheim in the early eleventh century, the Magdalen's hand seems to slide behind or on Jesus's feet, avoiding touch (if it does) only by an odd trick of perspective.

Figure 6.7. Prayer book of Ursula Begerin, fol 134r. Strasbourg, later fifteenth century. Despite the injunction not to touch, the Magdalen reaches for Christ's feet, here still marked by the blood of open wounds.

into the early modern period measures of Christ's footprints—often in the form of outlines with prayers or indulgences inscribed inside—circulated widely in Catholic Europe.[42] The Bayerisches Nationalmuseum in Munich possesses a linen token from c. 1600, cut exactly to the shape and length of the footprint on the Mount of Olives and touched to the original. (See figure 6.8.) Folklorist Lenz Kriss-Rettenbeck has discussed such reproductions of the footprints of both Jesus and Mary and speaks of their wide diffusion in early modern Europe.[43]

According to medieval understandings, such objects were relics; they literally and materially absorbed power. Gregory of Tours's description of the practice by which pilgrims to Rome acquired cloth objects known as *brandea* from St. Peter's tomb is well known:

> Whoever wishes to pray comes to the top of the tomb after unlocking the railings that surround the spot . . . inserts his head in the opening and requests whatever is necessary. . . . If someone wishes to take away a blessed relic, he weighs a little piece of cloth . . . and lowers it into [the tomb]; then he keeps vigils, fasts, and earnestly prays. . . . If the man's faith is strong, when the piece of cloth is raised from the tomb it will be so soaked with divine power that it will weigh much more than it weighed previously.[44]

But measures brought back from the Holy Land were more than contact relics, soaking up the power of an original through being pressed upon it. Some of the prayers that ask Christ to shield believers through his measurement speak as if Christ's length *is* his person:

> Oh Lord Jesus, I beg you, because you have sheltered me with your length . . . protect and shield us poor sinning people. . . . Hide me in your length . . . as your godhead hides itself in your humanity. . . . Hide me in your holy wounds and be my protection against all my enemies.[45]

Linen or paper strips cut to the exact height of Christ or his mother Mary were said to hide devotees in Christ's side, protect them from "wounds and injuries, fire and water, robbers and poisoners, hail, thunder, and magicians," and to give to "all pregnant women" an "easy birth."[46]

Moreover, contact between token and original was not essential. Although several of the surviving linen or paper measures were supposedly touched to the original, it is not clear that physical contact with alleged presence was necessary to empower a token.

Figure 6.8. Pilgrim's token of the footprint of Jesus Christ from the Mount of Olives in Jerusalem, cut to the exact shape and size of the footprint and touched to the original. Length: 260 mm. Linen, c. 1600. From Lenz Kriss-Rettenbeck, *Bilder und Zeichen religiösen Volksglaubens* (Munich: Georg D. W. Callwey Verlag, 1963), plate 215. Although pilgrims' tokens, like modern souvenirs, tend not to survive, historians think these measures of Christ's footprint traveled to Europe from the Holy Land in large numbers in the later Middle Ages and the early modern period.

Measurement itself came to be — and convey — person. In a woodcut from circa 1490, brilliantly analyzed by David Areford, we find that a measure of Christ's side wound stands in visually for his entire body, connecting face, hands, and feet.[47] (See figure 6.9.) The wound is treated explicitly as a measuring rod. The scroll to Christ's right reads, "This is the length and width of Christ's wound which was pierced in his side on the Cross. Whoever kisses this wound with remorse and sorrow, also with devotion, will have as often as he does this, seven years indulgence from Pope Innocent." The scroll on Christ's left, which refers to the cross shown inside the wound, reads, "This little cross standing in Christ's wound measured forty times makes the length of Christ in his humanity. Whoever kisses it with devotion shall be protected from sudden death or misfortune."

Here, the length of Christ becomes Christ himself.[48] This example is more complex than it at first appears both because the length itself acts (it grants indulgences — that is, remission from punishment for sin — and physical protection) and because it is basically aniconic or noniconic (although it is imaged in this example as if it is Christ's body). In a different but related European devotional practice, a length of cord or leather was often treated as if it were the devotee. A standard donation to churches in the later Middle Ages was a measure of wick or candle wax calibrated to the height, girth, or weight of the person giving it, as if quantity of measure were self.[49] Hence it is clear that, to medieval Christians, measures of Christ's foot or body, shoulder or knee, did not have to look like the body part in question in order to transport it through time and space.[50] A more abstract similitude of measurement was enough.

If we return to accounts from the Mount of Olives, we find that the earliest form in which evidence of Christ's presence was taken away was not any sort of image or token but simply bits of the stuff itself. The footprint was mostly not understood to be either established as present elsewhere or transported to another place by a "look-alike." Although sometimes conveyed by a form that imaged it, it was, in its earlier period, more often conveyed by a particle of sand or dust that looked nothing like the shape of Christ's foot from which it was taken. Pilgrims such as Arculf carried off bits — *particulas* — of the footprints, which nonetheless forever remained. As the modern historian Ora Limor puts it, the earth had a will of its own. Insisting on enduring, it preferred to stay shaped just as Christ's foot had made it. Or, as

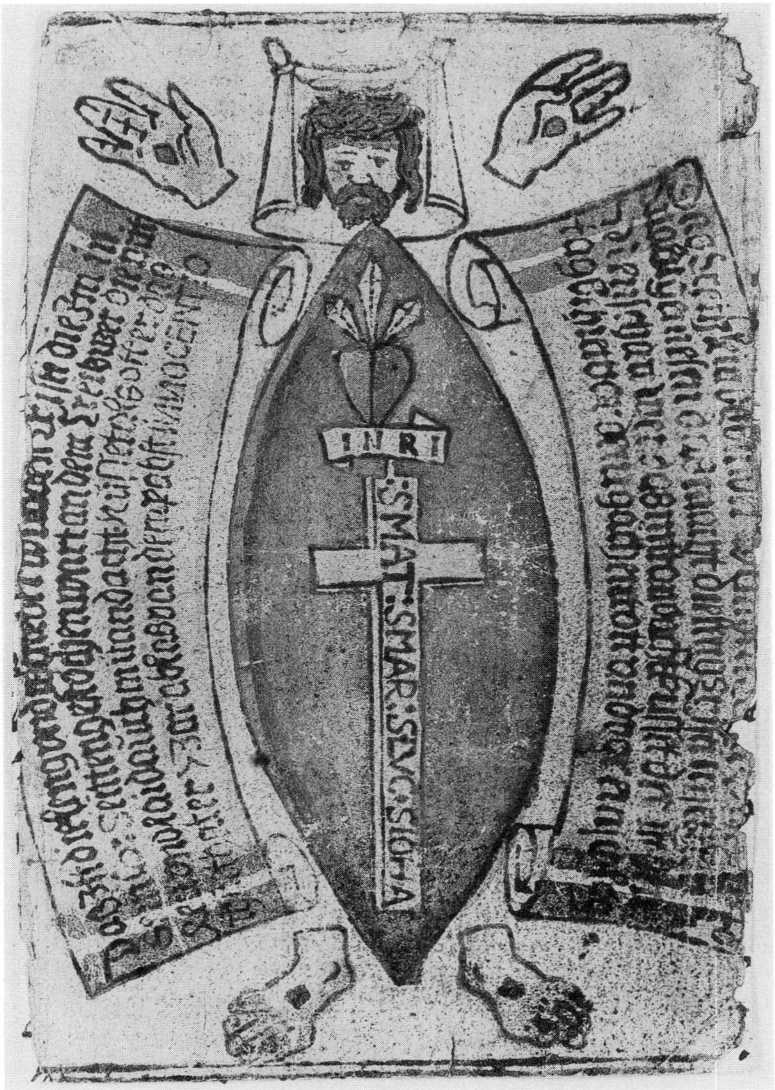

Figure 6.9. Wounds of Christ with symbols of the Passion, woodcut, about 1490; Rosenwald Collection 1943.3.831, National Gallery of Art, Washington, DC. Tipped vertically, the side wound visually becomes the body of Christ, binding the wounds in the feet and hands into a whole. It is also materialized into a measuring stick and an amulet. The scroll to the right states that the little cross in the wound, multiplied by forty, gives the true length of Christ and, when kissed, protects against disaster; the left-hand scroll promises seven years indulgence for kissing the wound.

Sulpicius Severus put it in his pilgrim's guide: "The sand of the place suffers no injury . . . as if it had been sealed by the footprints impressed upon it."[51] Although it permitted no sign of alteration or diminution, the footprint could be carried abroad by a minute particle of itself.

Earth was, of course, portable and easily acquired. Moreover, it not only absorbed holiness through contact with holy figures or bodies; it also conveyed presence to other earth. Augustine wrote in the *City of God* of a certain Hesperius, who received a bit of sacred earth from Jerusalem and hung it in his bedroom to ward off an invasion of demons. The earth was later buried and that site became a place of miraculous cures, the earth itself having transported power from Jerusalem to a bedroom near Hippo and beyond that to a burial site.[52] The sixth-century pilgrim from Piacenza reports that, at the Holy Sepulcher, earth was brought in from elsewhere and became holy through contact with the tomb. The same Gregory of Tours who recounted the story of the cloth at St. Peter's in Rome told how the ground at the tomb of the Lord in Jerusalem "is [often] covered with a natural radiant brightness; then it is sprinkled with water and dug up, and from it tiny [clay] tokens are shaped and sent to different parts of the world."[53] The tokens cured illness and warded off snakes. Earth from Akeldama, the Potter's Field, purchased with Judas's thirty pieces of silver and saturated with the blood of his bowels, was allegedly carried to Rome as early as the fourth century, conveying with it the power to decompose bodies quickly and without smell. According to a guide written between 1480 and 1526, it not only decomposed the bodies of foreigners but also regurgitated any locals buried there. There were later, less successful efforts to transport Akeldama (and Akeldama as it resided in Rome) to Ireland and Germany. Such efforts to transport holiness through transporting noniconic physical stuff derived from holy places raise complex questions about under what circumstances physical holiness attenuates and whether or how it is diluted.[54]

The transfer of holiness through transferring actual pieces did not cease when the Ascension footprints changed from sand to stone. Bits of the site on the Mount of Olives continued to show up in relic collections in Europe. To cite only two examples, both from the exemplary study by Andrea Worm: The inventory of a twelfth-century reliquary of the head of Pope Alexander now in Brussels lists "a relic of the stone on which the Lord stood when he ascended into the sky." A relic capsule from the capital of a column in the cathedral at Braunschweig supposedly includes a bit of the stone "from which the Lord ascended to heaven."[55] Thus, the change of medium mattered less than modern theories suggest it should have. From the earliest accounts, sand is treated as perduring stuff, and stone is fragmented. In both cases, part(icle) transfers whole. Although differently malleable, sand and stone equally retain presence, transfer holiness, and endure rather than dissipate. The footprints of Christ from Jerusalem are not so much reminiscences or gestures toward something else; they are themselves material presences, agents; they are media that transport power from one place, one object, one body, to another; they heal and redeem recipients. If they are proofs, they are not so much proofs of past occurrences as proofs of the intersection of human and divine (incarnation and creation) and of events to come: personal remission of punishment for sin or the Second Coming.[56]

This consideration of the footprints on the Mount of Olives suggests that attention to shape or form or morphology can be a barrier as well as an aid to understanding. What was revered at, or carried from, a specific place in the Holy Land to Europe by a traveler in the years after Christ's alleged Ascension was sometimes shaped like a foot and sometimes not. The place of the Ascension appears to have been revered before there were claims that footprints had been left there, either in sand or stone. And the footprint that was carried away from that place by pilgrims or visitors could be a pattern or copy that images a footprint, but it could also be a bit of sand or stone or a measure of length that bears no resemblance to a foot.

I have here considered only Christ's traces on a single spot, not comparing them to his other supposed footprints, such as those at Domine Quo Vadis, much less to footprints of the Virgin Mary or St. Michael or dozens of other non-Christian figures understood to exist where certain sorts of depressions or marks in the earth are found. But it seems clear that a study of comparative footprints is a less useful context for understanding the objects I have discussed here than a consideration of how other relics of the Holy Land, such as bits of the earth from Akeldama or the Holy Sepulcher, were transported to Europe. If we compare only those physical traces understood to be footprints, we miss all the nuance that has emerged from looking instead at the history of how a mark or set of marks has impact, acts, has power, or travels, regardless of what the relic that carries the marks looks like.

Moreover, if we simply compare footprints as look-alikes across different religious cultures, we may miss even more crucial divergences. As I have mentioned, prints of feet can be of feet bare or feet shod — with different implications for ideas of the earth and of the divine.[57] They can be plain or highly decorated. As supposed traces left by gods or powerful figures in earth or stone, footprints may be primarily loci to which the devout travel, or loci from which stuff (object or particle) is taken, or both. The primary attraction of a footprint can be as a sign that the holy made contact with humans, that sacred events (including departures) occurred. The print thus marks a place to which pilgrimage should be made. Or the print and its representations or physical particles (outlines, measures or drawings, bits of sand or stone, or even records of a journey made) can be valued primarily as a relic — that is, as an object that transports a god's power or plan or presence on earth. In this case, the devout will feel inspired and entitled to take bits of it away. As records of divine or even demonic presence, traces of footprints can convey information about favor gained, about instruction or warnings received, or about devotion performed. If one really wants to compare footprints across the religious traditions of the world, one must compare iconic footprints with other kinds of noniconic or aniconic traces; one must also study the relative importance of place and object (that is, in a certain sense, of pilgrimage and relic) in the traditions in question.[58]

As a medievalist exploring xenophilia, my task is not, however, to provide a general theory of cross-cultural comparison, to explore the relative importance of holy object and sacred place across religions, or to describe in broad terms the similarities and differences of the iconic and the aniconic as purveyors of sacrality. Exploration of the footprints of Christ on the Mount of Olives suggests all these general questions and I have tried to adumbrate some considerations and even tentative answers here. But my topic in this chapter is what "love of" and encounter with the Other might mean as a model for research in the history of the European Middle Ages, and I now return to it. Christ's footprint as I have explored it here seems to me a moving and graphic depiction of what the Other (*xenos*) is.

The Iconography of the Footprint and the Gap

The medieval footprint is more complex than the footprint of Man Friday found by Robinson Crusoe or the trace found by the Walker family in the book *Swallows and Amazons* I loved as a child. It is more complex — more literally an agent — than the trace theorized by modern interpreters. Not merely gesturing toward an Other that cannot be present because the object or person forming it has departed, the medieval footprint has power *as itself.* It not only evokes, hints at, gestures toward an Other — the foot — that has departed; that foot itself gestures toward — adumbrates — the fully human Christ, who himself rises toward the Other of heaven.[59] So in this medieval understanding, trace adumbrates the form that makes it, which form itself (foot), as part, adumbrates the whole (body) to which it belongs. But it not only adumbrates in these two senses what lies beyond; it itself has power. It brings the Mount on which it is located and the Christ who left it there to the one who encounters or carries away the trace. It conveys — it *is* — presence as well as absence. Surely then it provides an image of and an analogy to the *xenos* we study and yearn toward in xenophilia.

If we return to the medieval iconography of the footprints of Christ, we find something even more telling, however. We find an emphasis on the gap between the trace and that which has left it behind. The depiction that becomes increasingly common in the north of Europe positions us the viewers of the image *with* the apostles who stand "looking up to heaven" (Acts 1.11). With them, we look not so much at the cloud that hides the disappearing Christ as at the gap opening up between us and the savior being hidden in heaven.[60]

As I explained earlier, there are many medieval depictions of Christ's Ascension. In some he rises from a stone, in some from a hillock, in some even from an altar. (See figure 6.3.) By the thirteenth century, we begin to find representations of his ascent in which his body has disappeared; only his feet remain in view.[61] (See figure 6.10.) It is as if the apostles, gazing upward, have as their last glimpse of the savior the feet that have indicated to them his full humanity — the feet that walked the dusty road to Emmaus, the feet that Mary Magdalen (as medieval people understood the story) anointed with oil, the feet that later saints would stroke and revere.[62] From the early thirteenth century, a number of the northern European representations that show Christ rising out of the picture space come to be paired with a footprint or footprints left behind on the stone or the hill of the Ascension.[63] (See figures 6.4a–b, 6.11, 6.12, and I.17.) Although it used to be said that the so-called disappearing Christ

Figure 6.10. Rüdiger Schopf, *The Ascension of Christ*. MS Basel, Universitätsbibliothek, A II 12, fol. 5r. 1405–1407. This is an example of the type of Ascension image known as "the vanishing Christ." Standing as if with the apostles, we the viewers see only the disappearing feet.

and the depiction of footprints appeared simultaneously as iconographic motifs, the study of many examples shows that the argument for their coincidence does not completely hold.[64] Nonetheless, when the motifs are combined, as they often are, the image underlines the Ascension as a moment of both loss and gift, as not only absence and departure but also a presence left below of what has gone. It also clearly aligns the viewer of the woodcut or miniature with the apostles who stand below and look up. What we, the viewers of the image, are positioned to see is what they saw: not a son received by his father into heaven or a king reigning there, but a figure disappearing into the clouds. As the description in Acts 1:10 underlines: "They were beholding him going up to heaven."

In two well-known, sixteenth-century woodcuts by Altdorfer and Dürer, the Christ who departs, seen only in his vanishing feet, feels heavy with holiness, as if he is still pressing down into the rock as he rises. (See figures 6.11 and 6.12.) The departing feet almost appear to be a seal matrix that has stamped an impression into the ground below. The disappearing Jesus leaves behind not emptiness but presence. The trace is *itself* both the Christ it represents and that Christ's gone-awayness. Moreover, what is particularly striking is the way in which these images and their precursors focus the gaze of the viewer on neither the departing columnar feet nor on the marks left below but on the space in between. It is true (as Meyer Schapiro and Robert Deshman have both emphasized) that we, the viewers of such woodcuts, are able to see only the vanishing Christ the apostles saw. In this particular iconography, his triumphant entry into heaven is not depicted. But in these images, the apostles mostly do not look all the way up to the vanishing Christ; rather they gaze into the space between the footprint and the feet.[65] What they encounter is the widening gap between what remains and what departs. And we who view the woodcut also see a gap between heaven and earth.[66] Indeed, that gap is often the focal point, the central space, of the image. What stands in the middle is an emptiness that underlines the distance between what departs and what remains.

These two woodcuts by German masters come at the culmination of a long tradition of iconographic development. In an extremely popular book, *The Mirror of Human Salvation*, that circulated widely in late medieval Europe in both manuscript copies and blockbooks, we find a great deal of evidence of the widespread use of the combined

Figure 6.11. Albrecht Altdorfer, *Christ's Ascension*, in *The Fall and Redemption of Man* series. Woodcut, c. 1513. The National Gallery of Art, Washington, DC., Rosenwald Collection: 1943.3.362. Although the image depicts ascent, Christ's feet seem to press heavily downward and almost appear as if they are protruding from a column.

Figure 6.12. Albrecht Dürer, *The Ascension of Christ.* Woodcut, 1509–11. In this well-known woodcut, of which a number of copies survive, the Christ who departs, seen only in his vanishing feet, feels heavy with holiness. The departing feet almost appear to have stamped an impression into the ground below. Thus, the disappearing Jesus leaves behind not emptiness but presence. The trace is itself both the Christ it represents and that Christ's gone-awayness.

motifs of Jesus's feet vanishing above, his footprints left below, and the centrality of the space in between.[67] Of the approximately sixty examples of the *Mirror*'s illustration of Christ's Ascension found in the Warburg Institute Iconographic Database, fifty-two have the disappearing Christ rather than the full figure.[68] Almost all have some sort of mountain, sometimes enormously tall and rearing up into the picture like a column, and almost all have footprints, although almost none of the footprints or the disappearing feet show wounds or blood.[69] Although some of the illustrations are too crude for us to be sure where the gaze of the assembled apostles and Mary is directed (and there is one odd example where the viewers stand behind the flattened mountaintop almost as if it were a table in front of them with the footprints spread out there), in a large number of the images there is a gap between the heavens into which Christ ascends and the mound or rock below where his prints are visible (and sometimes quite large). The viewing apostles seem to gaze into the space between heaven and earth or at the traces left behind. (See figures 6.13 and 6.14.) The three images that usually in this text accompany the Ascension — Jacob's vision of a ladder to heaven, the Good Shepherd who leaves ninety-nine sheep to search for one who is lost, and Elias carried up into the sky — all emphasize comfort and salvation. But the depiction of the Ascension itself highlights instead the tangible promise Christ leaves behind and a space that seems to image humanity's distance from and yearning toward a savior who disappears.

Even more complicated is the way in which Christ's Ascension is depicted in the part of the *Mirror* (chapter 44) devoted to the Seven Sorrows of Mary. Conventionally understood as grieving because left behind when Christ ascends to his father, Mary is depicted in the original composition (which was later often copied) as surrounded by objects from the life of Christ arranged in a frame or in a set of little frames. (See figure 6.15.) In a variant, she is shown with things that signify Christ's passion and look very much like the *arma Christi*. (See figure 6.16.) Both variations usually include a small hill adorned with footprints.[70] Clearly a little hump (usually green) with two footprints on it has become a kind of attribute or icon or symbol standing in for the Ascension.[71] In the context of earthly sorrowing, it is an object, the left-behind footprints and not the clouds above or the disappearing Christ, that has *become* the biblical event. In another variant, we find Mary situated in the traditional Ascension iconography; nine of the ten examples of this version have the footprints. Only one later variant shows Mary mourning without any objects; two show Mary or Mary and John grieving with only a single object of sorrow: the little hill with its footprints standing under the disappearing Christ. (See figures 6.17 and 6.18.)[72] The waiting mother and Christ's friend gaze into the space left between presence and absence.

Some of these representations also are too crudely drawn for us to be sure about where the gaze of the group focuses, but in a number of the images the assembled followers, including Mary and even the angels flanking the scene, gaze into the gap.[73] A few anomalous depictions have departing feet and mountaintop touching, but most emphasize a space — often a wide space — in between. Taken together, the images stress a distance between the Christ who rises to heaven and the relic left behind, which is sometimes faintly sketched but often demands attention by its sharp outline or dark color. Moreover, despite a certain variety in the placement of the viewers inside the image, we the viewers of the manuscript or blockbook are clearly drawn to the gap in between. What we focus on at the center of the image, before we look to see what is above and what below, is the picture space in the middle: the space between what remains and what has gone. If we try to look, read, and pray as medieval users of such images would have done, we need to concentrate with the grieving mother on the *distance between* the absent Christ and the present trace. Mary's seventh sorrow is, after all, as the text explicitly tells us, the fact that she is left behind.

Conclusion: The Footprint as a Model of What and How We Study

Employing the footprint as medieval theorists and worshippers understood it, I suggested earlier that the print or trace or vestige is useful as a model of what we study when we study another culture. We study absences, in that the objects, texts, and images we consider always point elsewhere to an other we cannot fully grasp. They are always partial, gesturing toward a whole that is foreign and outside. But we study these traces also as presences. They are not merely placeholders for what is not there. They are there as themselves. What they *are* is present, has power, acts. They are like those medieval footprints that point to what has departed but also in themselves — in their outlines, in their lengths, in their physical particles — have

Figure 6.13. MS from Avignon, first half of the fourteenth century. Rome, Biblioteca Corsiniana 55.K.2 (Rossi 17), fol. 42v. Gift of Evelyn Silber. Illustration of the Ascension of Christ from the very popular medieval book, the *Speculum humanae salvationis* (Mirror of Human Salvation). This depiction highlights the tangible promise Christ leaves behind in his footprints. The large space in the middle of the image seems to represent humanity's distance from yet yearning toward a savior who disappears.

Figure 6.14. The Ascension of Christ from the *Speculum humanae salvationis*. MS from Cologne or Westphalian, c. 1360. Darmstadt, Universitäts- und Landesbibliothek—Hs 2505, fol. 62v, provided to the Warburg Database by the Universitäts- und Landesbibliothek Darmstadt (CC-BY-NC-SA 3.0). Although the space between the departing Christ and the little green hill is smaller than in some images, the apostles and Mary are not so much looking into heaven as focused on the footprints and the space in between them and Christ's feet.

Figure 6.15. Mary is surrounded here by objects alluding to Christ's life, presented in small frames. A little hill marked with footprints, rather than the vanishing Christ or his feet or an unadorned rock, stands here for Mary's sorrow at the Ascension. From chapter 44, "The Seven Sorrows of Mary," in the *Speculum humanae salvationis*. Manuscript from the Rhineland, Steinhaus monastery near Wuppertal, c. 1390. Brussels, Bibliothèque royale de Belgique—281–283 (cat. no. 2140), fol. 50r. Gift of Evelyn Silber.

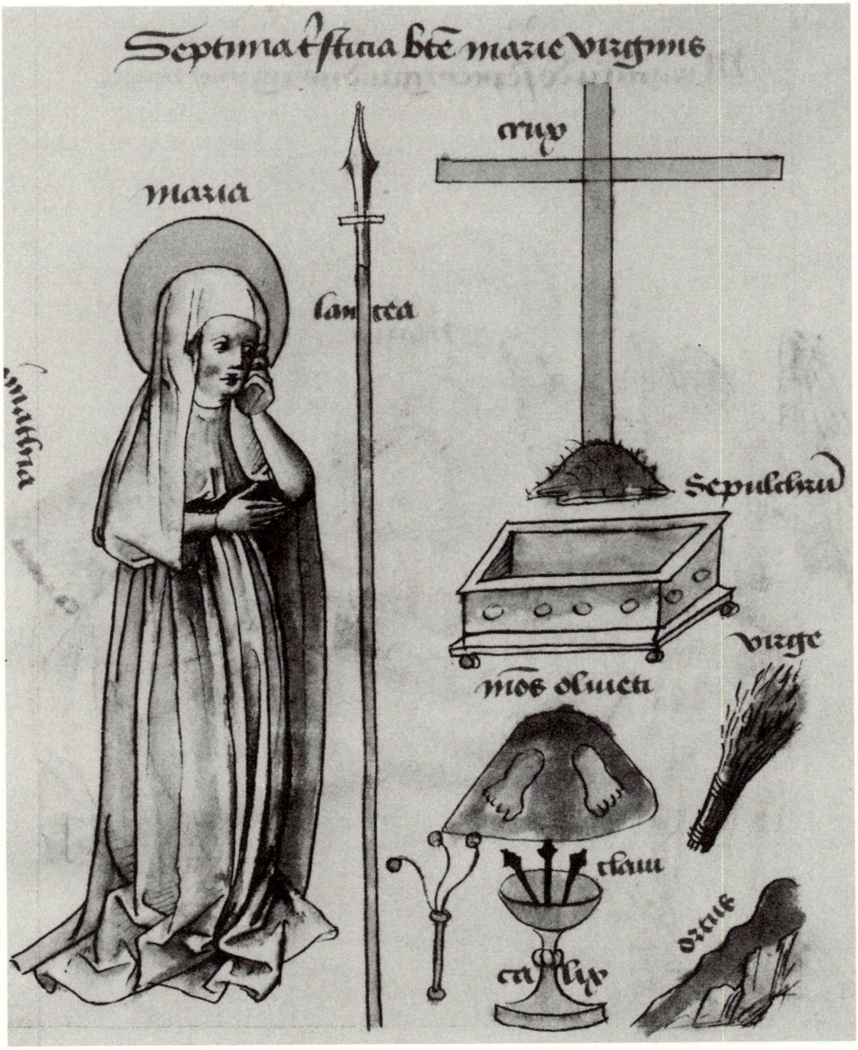

Figure 6.16. Paris, Bibliothèque nationale de France, lat. 512, fol. 49r. Manuscript from Basel, early fifteenth century. Mary is surrounded by a version of the *arma Christi*, to which the footprints on the Mount of Olives have been added as her "seventh sorrow"—that is, her suffering at being left behind when Christ departs. Hence an object—that is, a little green hill with footprints—has become a standard image of the loss yet presence of Christ to those left behind.

Figure 6.17. Mary left behind after the Ascension grieves for her son. Her gaze is clearly fixed not on the departure but on the footprints Christ left and on the space between them and the vanishing Christ. Manuscript Bavarian or Austrian, c. 1440–66. Munich, Bayerische Staatsbibliothek—Cgm 3974, fol. 49.

Figure 6.18. Paris, Bibliothèque nationale de France, lat. 511, fol. 47r. Manuscript Alsatian, c. 1370–80. In the image on the right, Mary and the beloved apostle John are seen sorrowing at Christ's departure. The focus of the depiction is clearly on the space between the departure and the trace left behind. Mary's grief at her son's vanishing into heaven is, in illustrations of chapter 44 of the *Speculum humanae salvationis*, often paired with a Pietà, as it is here. Thus, Mary grieves at two losses: the loss of her son in death and then, after the Resurrection, the loss of his departure into heaven. But the marks of Christ's feet remain behind to comfort all Christians.

frightening and exalting power.[74] Further reflection suggests to me that what we scholars gaze at is often neither the thing beyond in a different culture, time, or place, nor the trace (that is, the evidence) it has left behind, but the gap in between. At least when we theorize, we are often talking about the gap, and recent interest in theoretical discussion tends to draw our attention to it. The challenge for us is therefore to accomplish something like what the illustrations in the *Mirror of Human Salvation* or Altdorfer and Dürer accomplish: that is, to keep our attention focused both on what is absent and on what remains while being ever mindful of the gap in between.

I return, in closing, to a childhood self, fascinated by stories of children or shipwrecked sailors who find, on apparently deserted islands, footprints that frighten, challenge, and intrigue, ever beckoning toward the unknown. Such footprints provide an image of what we seek in xenophilia — that is, in loving and desiring the other. But the footprint I have explored here is more complicated because more active and transformative than the marks found by Robinson Crusoe or the children of *Swallows and Amazons*. As depicted by medieval artists and used by medieval devotees, it not only possesses the sort of agency some modern theorists wish to attribute to objects, but it also evokes an awareness of the perspectival location of viewers and theorists characteristic of modern literary and historical analysis at its best.

Hence the medieval footprint in its many guises and permutations can perhaps serve as a metaphor for what all scholars pursue — with *phobia* as well as *philia*.[75] The other we seek to know, whether text or object, is paradoxical — on the one hand, a conjuring up of an absent something that has left only a trace, yet on the other hand, a thing powerful in and of itself. After all, there would be no other to pursue if something strange — whether wonderful or fearsome — did not hover beyond, forever just out of our reach, whole although we encounter only a part. But we would have no access to that other if something, by its very absence, had not left behind a specific, powerful in itself, and very much present part — a vestige, or trace, or footprint.

Notes

INTRODUCTION

1. On the image, see Thomas Lentes, "Die Gewänder der Heiligen — Ein Diskussionsbeitrag zum Verhältnis von Gebet, Bild und Imagination," in *Hagiographie und Kunst: Der Heiligenkult in Schrift, Bild und Architektur*, ed. Gottfried Kerscher (Berlin: Reimer, 1993), pp. 120–51, at pp. 124–25; and Jeffrey F. Hamburger, *Nuns as Artists: The Visual Culture of a Medieval Convent* (Berkeley: University of California Press, 1997), p. 76.

2. Gift of J. Pierpont Morgan, 1917 (17.190.504). See in this chapter fig. I.2 and pp. 42–43. See Maria D. Murray, "Reverse-painted and Gilded Glass Through the Ages," *The Connoisseur* 180 (July 1972), pp. 201–12; Jane Hayward, compiler, *Glass in the Collections of the Metropolitan Museum of Art* (New York: Metropolitan Museum of Art, 1982), pp. 14–15, fig. 9; Timothy B. Husband, entry on the Magdalen reliquary in Stefano Carboni et al., "Ars Vitraria: Glass in the Metropolitan Museum of Art, Medieval Art and the Cloisters," *The Metropolitan Museum of Art Bulletin*, n.s., 59.1 (Summer 2001), p. 36; and Martina Bagnoli, Holger A. Klein, C. Griffith Mann, and James Robinson, eds., *Treasures of Heaven: Saints, Relics, and Devotion in Medieval Europe* (Baltimore, MD: Walters Art Museum and Cleveland: Cleveland Museum of Art, 2010), pp. 196–97. Most of the scholarly attention has been to the glass medallion.

3. On Wilsnack, see Caroline Walker Bynum, *Wonderful Blood: Theology and Practice in Late Medieval Northern Germany and Beyond* (Philadelphia: University of Pennsylvania Press, 2007), ch. 2, pp. 25–45. On the general question of the role of consecration in constituting things as holy, see chapters 3 and 4 in this book.

4. On relics and reliquaries, see (among much that could be cited) Nicole Herrmann-Mascard, *Les reliques des saints: Formation coutumière d'un droit* (Paris: Klincksieck, 1975); Peter Dinzelbacher, "Die 'Realpräsenz' der Heiligen in ihren Reliquiaren und Gräbern nach mittelalterlichen Quellen," in *Heiligenverehrung in Geschichte und Gegenwart*, eds. Peter Dinzelbacher and Dieter Bauer (Ostfildern: Schwabenverlag, 1990), pp. 115–74; Arnold Angenendt, *Heilige und Reliquien: Die Geschichte ihres Kultes vom frühen Christentum*

bis zum Gegenwart (Munich: C. H. Beck, 1994); Anton Legner, *Reliquien in Kunst und Kult: Zwischen Antike und Aufklärung* (Darmstadt: Wissenschaftliche Buchgesellschaft, 1995); Henk W. van Os, *The Way to Heaven: Relic Veneration in the Middle Ages* (Baarn, The Netherlands: De Prom, 2000); Thomas Head, "Relics," in *Dictionary of the Middle Ages*, ed. Joseph R. Strayer (New York: Charles Scribner's Sons, 1982–2004), vol. 10, pp. 296–99; Alexandra Walsham, ed., *Relics and Remains*, Supplement 5 to *Past & Present* 206 (2010); Bagnoli, Klein, Mann, and Robinson, eds., *Treasures of Heaven*; Julia M. H. Smith, "Portable Christianity: Relics in the Medieval West (c. 700–1200)," *Proceedings of the British Academy* 181 (2012), pp. 143–68; Cynthia Hahn, *Strange Beauty: Issues in the Making and Meaning of Reliquaries, 400–circa 1204* (University Park: Pennsylvania State University Press, 2012); Cynthia Hahn, *The Reliquary Effect: Enshrining the Sacred Object* (London: Reaktion Books, 2017); and Renana Bartal, Neta Bodner, and Bianca Kühnel, eds., *Natural Materials of the Holy Land and the Visual Translation of Place, 500–1500* (London: Routledge, 2017). See n. 22 in this chapter on relics of the Crucifixion. For stones and plants brought back from the Holy Land as relics, see Nina Gockerell, "Pilgerandenken aus Jerusalem," in *Dona Ethnologica Monacensia: Leopold Kretzenbacher zum 70. Geburtstag*, eds. Helge Gerndt, Klaus Roth, and Georg R. Schroubek (Munich: Bayerisches Nationalmuseum, Institut für deutsche und vergleichende Volkskunde, 1983), pp. 163–79, esp. p. 171; and Elina Gertsman and Asa Simon Mittman, "Rocks of Jerusalem: Bringing the Holy Land Home," in Bartal, Bodner, and Kühnel, eds., *Natural Materials*, pp. 157–71. For more on relics, see chapter 6.

5. For an example of a relic of similarity, see the column of the flagellation in Bologna: Figure I.15. For a case of a relic touched to the original, see the linen footprint in figure 6.8. For an embedded relic, see the Karlštejn Chapel, which has relics inserted into the image of the Crucifixion itself and also a relic box inserted below the figure of the Suffering Christ, discussed in Barbara Drake Boehm and Jiří Fajt, eds., *Prague: The Crown of Bohemia, 1347–1437* (New York and New Haven, CT: Metropolitan Museum of Art and Yale University Press, 2005), pp. 10–15. In terms of efficacy, it does not seem to have mattered whether the relics were unseen (for example, inserted into the pedestal of a statue or behind the surface of a panel painting) or displayed openly (for example, through crystal). Display behind crystal, as in figure I.2, increased in the later Middle Ages. On embedded relics, see Caroline Walker Bynum, *Christian Materiality: An Essay on Religion in Late Medieval Europe* (New York: Zone Books, 2011), pp. 117–20. In modern canon law, a first-class relic is something directly associated with Christ's life or the physical remains of a saint; a second-class relic is an item a saint wore or frequently used; a third-class relic is an object touched to a first- or second-class relic, often a piece of cloth called *ex brandea*.

6. I have discussed the question of what gives certain things the spark or charge of holiness in Caroline Walker Bynum, epilogue to *Religious Materiality in the Early Modern World*, eds. Suzanna Ivanič, Mary Laven, and Andrew Morrall (Amsterdam: Amsterdam

University Press, 2019), pp. 247–55, which considers non-Christian as well as Christian objects. I suggest there that the qualities of paradox and tactility I discuss later in this introduction tend in other religious cultures also to imbue objects with holiness and religious power.

7. On the danger felt by church authorities that unconsecrated objects might slip out of clerical control, see Bynum, *Christian Materiality*, p. 162, and n. 3 in this chapter. As Brigitte Bedos-Rezak has recently shown, another important artifact, seals and their presence on charters, also proliferated from the twelfth century on. Although not religious objects of the sort I am studying here, seals carried the presence and authority of the person doing the sealing to distant venues in a manner somewhat parallel to the believed ability of relics or body parts to convey power across distance. See Brigitte Miriam Bedos-Rezak, *When Ego Was Imago: Signs of Identity in the Middle Ages* (Leiden: Brill, 2011), esp. p. 55. See Bynum, *Christian Materiality*, p. 193, on ways in which the widely dispersed burial of body parts (for example, hearts, heads, even viscera) of members of aristocratic or even clerical elites was also understood to convey and distribute their presence, although such bodily fragments were not usually considered holy.

8. On objects such as the blessed oats, which are known as sacramentals, the classic study is Adolph Franz, *Die kirchlichen Benediktionen im Mittelalter*, 2 vols. (Freiburg: Herder, 1909). On the wide variety of objects that could carry the holy, see Lenz Kriss-Rettenbeck, *Bilder und Zeichen religiösen Volksglaubens* (Munich: Georg D. W. Callwey, 1963) based on the collection of folk material in the Bayerisches Nationalmuseum in Munich. For examples of stones and plants brought from the Holy Land, such as those in figure I.4, see Kriss-Rettenbeck, *Bilder*, p. 68 and plates 212 and 213. On birthing girdles, see Mary Morse, "Seeing and Hearing: Margery Kempe and the mise-en-page," *Studia Mystica* 20 (1999), pp. 15–42. In Bynum, *Christian Materiality*, fig. 46, I have reproduced a copy of the images in Wellcome MS 632, computer-generated by Stephen Morse and recreated by permission.

9. On the principle of *similia similibus*, see Stephen Wilson, *The Magical Universe: Everyday Ritual and Magic in Pre-Modern Europe* (London: Hambledon and London, 2000), p. xxiv, and Marcel Mauss, *A General Theory of Magic*, trans. Robert Brain (London: Routledge, 1972 [1902]), pp. 91–92. Wilson relies on Frazer's *Golden Bough* as well as Mauss. For a critique of Frazer, see Ludwig Wittgenstein, "Remarks on Frazer's *Golden Bough*," in Wittgenstein, *Philosophical Occasions, 1912–1951* (Indianapolis: Hackett, 1993), pp. 118–55, esp. pp. 133, 139, and 143. On homeopathic medicine, which uses the same principle, see S. Paranthaman, "What Is Similia Similibus Curantur?" *Times of India*, March 9, 2009, https://timesofindia.indiatimes.com/What-is-similia-similibus-curantur/articleshow/4240036.cms (accessed January 8, 2020). I have dealt with this further in "Interrogating 'Likeness': Fake Friends, *Similia Similibus*, and Heavenly Crowns," *Historische Anthropologie* 28.1 (2020), pp. 31–56.

10. Images that depict Christ as an object, such as Christ in the Winepress or the Host-mill, are discussed in Bynum, *Christian Materiality*, pp. 83–85. For a brilliant discussion of

the increasing importance of religious images for educating and shaping knowledge, practice, and perception after the Fourth Lateran Council of 1215, see Aden Kumler, *Translating Truth: Ambitious Images and Religious Knowledge in Late Medieval France and England* (New Haven, CT: Yale University Press, 2011).

11. On Mechtild's images, see Caroline Walker Bynum, *The Resurrection of the Body in Western Christianity, 200–1336*, expanded edition (New York: Columbia University Press, 2017), pp. 337–41. On theologians and spiritual directors who privileged the unseen over the seen, see n. 37 in this chapter.

12. Rachel Fulton Brown, *Mary and the Art of Prayer: The Hours of the Virgin in Medieval Christian Life and Thought* (New York: Columbia University Press, 2017), p. 76.

13. Cited in Fulton Brown, *Mary*, p. 76, from *In antiphonam Salve regina*, sermo 3.2, *Patrologia latina* 184, col. 1069. See also Fulton Brown, *Mary*, p. 510 n. 124. Fulton Brown translates *rerum vocabulis* as "words of things." Perhaps "words from things" makes the meaning clearer. Although the origin of these names is biblical, they are used not so much because they have been used traditionally as because they are, as the commentator says, appropriate to what Mary *is*.

14. James Wood, *The Broken Estate: Essays on Literature and Belief*, with a new introduction (New York: Picador, 2010), p. 51. For more on metaphor, see chapter 5 at nn. 11 and 91.

15. See chapter 2, pp. 107. For the dressing of statues generally, see chapter 1, nn. 75–77, and on the dresses at Wienhausen, see Caroline Walker Bynum, "Are Things 'Indifferent'? How Objects Change Our Understanding of Religious History," *German History* 34 (2016), pp. 88–112, esp. pp. 97–110.

16. The phrase *ex-voto* comes from *ex voto suscepto* and refers to a suppliant's vow to make an offering when the requested assistance comes from the god. Votive objects can be petition for, or gratitude for, assistance or gifts in a wider sense made to express hope or intention. See Ittai Weinryb, ed., *Agents of Faith: Votive Objects in Time and Place* (New York: Bard Graduate Center, 2018), published in conjunction with the exhibition "Agents of Faith in Time and Place," held at the Bard Graduate Center Gallery from September 14, 2018, to January 6, 2019. On the religious gift exchange often called *do ut des* — that is, the idea that a suppliant gives in order that God may give in return — see chapter 2, n. 28, and Christopher S. Wood, "The Votive Scenario," *Res* 59–60 (Spring–Autumn 2011), pp. 206–27.

17. See Kriss-Rettenbeck, *Bilder und Zeichen*, plate 81 for a measure of the arm of St. Francis Xavier, plate 84 for a measure of the Christ Child of Loreto, plates 83 and 85 for measures of the length of Mary and Christ, and plates 82 and 215 for measures of the footprints of Christ and Mary.

18. On measures as transporting the presence of a holy person, see Adolf Jacoby, "Heilige Längenmasse: Eine Untersuchung zur Geschichte der Amulette," *Schweizerisches Archiv für Volkskunde* 29.1 (1929), pp. 1–17, and *Schweizerisches Archiv für Volkskunde* 29.4 (1929), pp. 181–216; Kriss-Rettenbeck, *Bilder und Zeichen*, pp. 40–41, 68, 115, 137–38, and plates 81–85,

215, and 240; David Areford, "The Passion Measured: A Late-Medieval Diagram of the Body of Christ," in *The Broken Body: Passion Devotion in Late-Medieval Culture*, eds. A. A. MacDonald, H. N. B. Ridderbos, and R. M. Schlusemann (Groningen: Egbert Forsten, 1998), pp. 220–21 and 238; and Louis Gougaud, "La prière dite de Charlemagne et les pièces apocryphes apparentées," *Revue d'histoire ecclésiastique* 20 (1924), pp. 211–38. For measures of the Holy Sepulcher, see Gockerell, "Pilgerandenken aus Jerusalem," pp. 165–66. For people giving themselves by giving lengths or weights of themselves, see Franz, *Die kirchlichen Benediktionen,* vol. 2, pp. 456–57, and Bynum, *Christian Materiality*, pp. 98–99. The length of the body or the length or circumference of a body part (sometimes the girth of a pregnant woman's belly) was measured with a cord, which then became the wick of a candle made to the measure. See Bartal, Bodner, and Kühnel, eds., *Natural Materials*, on the transfer of presence by physical objects, mimetic and nonmimetic. See also nn. 30–32.

19. See Giles Constable, "The Cross in Medieval Monastic Life," in *Christianity and Culture in the Middle Ages: Essays to Honor John Van Engen*, eds. David C. Mengel and Lisa Wolverton (Notre Dame, IN: University of Notre Dame Press, 2015), pp. 236–50.

20. On the crucifix as inducing stigmata, see Bynum, *Christian Materiality*, pp. 112–21.

21. On Bremer, see chapter 3.

22. The phrase *arma Christi* meant "arms" in all the senses of the word: weapons of our defense against sin, instruments of torture used to execute Christ, and "coats of arms" or symbols of group membership or identification. By the later Middle Ages, the term also referred to the assemblage of physical relics of the Crucifixion, such as pieces of the sponge, thorns, lance, etc. For an example of the *arma Christi* sculptured as relics, see Nadine Mai, "Place and Surface: Golgotha in Late Medieval Bruges," in Bartal, Bodner, and Kühnel, eds., *Natural Materials*, pp. 190–206, esp. fig. 11.4, p. 104. For the *arma Christi* as relics, especially as discussed by the late medieval theologian Johannes Bremer, see chapter 3, pp. 135–38.

23. Robert Suckale, "*Arma Christi*: Überlegungen zur Zeichenhaftigkeit mittelalterlicher Andachtsbilder," *Städel-Jahrbuch* N. F. 6 (1977), pp. 177–208. See also Rudolf Berliner, "Arma Christi," *Münchner Jahrbuch der Bildenden Kunst* ser.3, 6 (1955), pp. 35–152.

24. See Gertrud Schiller, *Iconography of Christian Art*, trans. J. Seligman, 2 vols. (Greenwich, CT: New York Graphic Society, 1972); Berliner, "Arma Christi," p. 68; and Caroline Walker Bynum, "Seeing and Seeing Beyond: The Mass of St. Gregory in the Fifteenth Century," in *The Mind's Eye: Art and Theological Argument in the Middle Ages*, eds. Anne-Marie Bouché and Jeffrey F. Hamburger (Princeton, NJ: Department of Art and Archaeology, Princeton University, 2005), pp. 208–40, at pp. 220–22.

25. See discussion of *The Mirror of Human Salvation* in chapter 6. For the Virgin Mary sorrowing beside the little green hill, see figs. 6.16–6.18.

26. The narrativity of medieval devotion has been overemphasized, in my opinion. On the difference between image (*imago*) and narrative (*historia*), see Jean Wirth, *L'image à l'époque romane* (Paris: Éditions du Cerf, 1999), p. 29, although he does not make the point I make here.

27. The amassing of relics and wonders by the nobility and prelates of the church was also a form of conspicuous consumption, intended to display wealth and power. On relic collections, see J. Smith, "Portable Christianity." On cabinets of wonders, see Oliver Impey and Arthur MacGregor, eds., *The Origins of Museums: The Cabinet of Curiosities in Sixteenth- and Seventeenth-Century Europe* (Oxford: Clarendon Press, 1985), and Paula Findlen, *Possessing Nature: Museums, Collecting and Scientific Culture in Early Modern Italy* (Berkeley: University of California Press, 1994).

28. See nn. 6 and 7. In addition to biblical, theological, and devotional understandings of God and creation, basic assumptions about nature and materiality also underlie this. To a medieval person, nothing is completely inanimate. Stones and gems were thought to "grow" in the body of the earth. Dirt, dung, and rot could "give birth" to life as spontaneous generation. For more on this, see Bynum, *Christian Materiality*, pp. 213–16, 231–41, 250–60, 282–86, and 378 n. 50.

29. The way of thinking according to which part can transfer whole or mimetic object can transfer that which it "represents" is sometimes called by students of religion "the devotional logic of presence" or "the contagion of holiness." See Robert A. Orsi, *The Madonna of 115th Street: Faith and Community in Italian Harlem, 1880–1950*, 3rd ed. (New Haven, CT: Yale University Press, 2010), p. xvi, and Janet Bord, *Footprints in Stone: The Significance of Foot- and Hand-prints and Other Imprints Left by Early Men, Giants, Heroes, Devils, Saints, Animals, Ghosts, Witches, Fairies and Monsters* (Loughborough, UK: Heart of Albion Press, 2004), pp. 6–7. It is related to what I have called the "habit of concomitance"; see Bynum, *Christian Materiality*, pp. 208–15.

30. On the column, see Mai, "Place and Surface," pp. 190–206, at p. 199. And see Anthony Cutler, "The Relics of Scholarship: On the Production, Reproduction, and Interpretation of Hallowed Remains in Late Antiquity, Byzantium, Early Islam, and the Medieval West," in *Saints and Sacred Matter: The Cult of Relics in Byzantium and Beyond*, eds. Cynthia Hahn and Holger A. Klein, Dumbarton Oaks Byzantine Symposium and Colloquia (Washington DC: Dumbarton Oaks Research Library and Collection, 2015), pp. 309–45, at p. 320.

31. See Mai, "Place and Surface," pp. 190–206. For other examples of objects that partake of the power of an original because of "likeness" to it, see Mai, "Place and Surface," p. 205 n. 47. I am grateful to Nadine Mai for sharing "Material, Materialität, Authentizität: Materialrezeption in der Nachbildung der Heiligen Stätten Jerusalems," ch. 4 in "Jerusalem — Transformationen," Ph.D. diss., University of Hamburg, 2016. Although many of the lengths that survive refer to being touched to an original relic or measure (such as the length of Christ at the Holy Sepulcher), not all measures that carry presence seem to have been "activated," so to speak, by touch. See Kriss-Rettenbeck, *Bilder und Zeichen*, pp. 40–42, 68.

32. On the church of St. Stephano in Bologna as an imitation of Jerusalem, see also Robert Ousterhout, "Flexible Geography and Transportable Topography," in *The Real and Ideal Jerusalem in Jewish, Christian and Islamic Art: Studies in Honor of Bezalel Narkiss on the Occasion*

of His Seventieth Birthday, ed. Bianca Kühnel, special issue of *Jewish Art* 23–24 (1997–98), pp. 393–404; and Bianca Kühnel, "Virtual Pilgrimages to Real Places: The Holy Landscape," in *Imagining Jerusalem in the Medieval West*, eds. Lucy Donkin and Hanna Vorholt, *Proceedings of the British Academy* 175 (Oxford: Oxford University Press, 2012), pp. 243–64. It is clear that the column, like the other exact echoes of the Holy Sepulcher and its surrounds in Jerusalem, was not thought to "be" (in a modern sense) the original it echoed but it is also clear that such things gained power through similitude. To note this is not, however, to argue that all similitude is visually "looking like." For more on this, see nn. 80–81. On measurement as similitude, see chapter 6, p. 240. As Kühnel points out, attention to what Mai rightly calls "similarity relics" has focused on architectural echoes of Jerusalem in Europe because of Richard Krautheimer's focus on the issue earlier in the twentieth century.

33. See n. 17.

34. See n. 8. On the iconography of the wound in Christ's side, see chapter 5, n. 44.

35. Scholars now tend to emphasize that there is no sharp break between the "Middle Ages" and the "Reformation," even in Calvinist, iconoclastic England. See Eamon Duffy, *The Stripping of the Altars: Traditional Religion in England, c. 1400–c. 1580* (New Haven, CT: Yale University Press, 1992); Eamon Duffy, *Marking the Hours: English People and Their Prayers, 1240–1570* (New Haven, CT: Yale University Press, 2006); John Bossy, *Christianity in the West, 1400–1700* (Oxford: Oxford University Press, 1985); David Aers, "A Whisper in the Ear of Early Modernists; or, Reflections on Literary Critics Writing the 'History of the Subject,'" in *Culture and History 1350–1600: Essays on English Communities, Identities, and Writing*, ed. David Aers (Detroit: Wayne State University Press, 1992), pp. 177–202; James Simpson, "The Rule of Medieval Imagination," in *Images, Idolatry, and Iconoclasm in Late Medieval England: Textuality and the Visual Image*, eds. Jeremy Dimmick, James Simpson, and Nicolette Zeeman (Oxford: Oxford University Press, 2002), pp. 4–24; and Sarah Stanbury, *The Visual Object of Desire in Late Medieval England* (Philadelphia: University of Pennsylvania Press, 2008). Thomas Lentes, "'Andacht' und 'Gebärde': Das religiöse Ausdrucksverhalten," in *Kulturelle Reformation: Sinnformationen im Umbruch, 1400–1600*, eds. Bernhard Jussen and Craig Koslofsky (Göttingen: Vandenhoeck & Ruprecht, 1999), pp. 26–67, brilliantly carries fourteenth- and fifteenth-century concerns forward into Reformation developments.

36. This argument uses an interesting understanding of "representation," one to which I return at p. 45. For even if Christ's body is literally present in the Eucharistic wafer (according to the theory of transubstantiation), God does not "look like" a circle. On the emblem "IHS" as popularized by Bernardino of Siena, see Daniel Arasse, "Entre dévotion et hérésie: La tablette de saint Bernardin ou le secret d'un prédicateur," *Res* 28 (1995), pp. 118–39, and John van Engen, "Multiple Options: The World of the Fifteenth-Century Church," *Church History* 77.2 (2008), p. 280.

37. See Jeffrey F. Hamburger, "The Visual and the Visionary: The Image in Late

Medieval Monastic Devotions," in Hamburger, *The Visual and the Visionary: Art and Female Spirituality in Late Medieval Germany* (New York: Zone Books, 1998), pp. 111–48 and 427–67; Jeffrey F. Hamburger, "Seeing and Believing: The Suspicion of Sight and the Authentication of Vision in Late Medieval Art and Devotion," in *Imagination und Wirklichkeit: Zum Verhältnis von mentalen und realen Bildern in der Kunst der frühen Neuzeit*, eds. Alessandro Nova and Klaus Krüger (Mainz: Philipp von Zabern, 2000), pp. 47–70; and Herbert Kessler, *Neither God nor Man: Words, Images, and the Medieval Anxiety about Art* (Freiburg im Breisgau: Rombach Verlag, 2007). As Aden Kumler puts it in *Translating Truth*, p. 103, the imperceptible as "soteriologically superior" was "something of a truism" in the later Middle Ages.

38. Proponents of new approaches, such as object-oriented ontology, thing theory, and various sorts of "new materialism," do not agree on what the current material turn is or should be. For some examples, see the references in chapter 3, n. 2, and Paul M. Graves-Brown, ed., *Matter, Materiality, and Modern Culture* (London: Routledge, 2000); Bill Brown, "Thing Theory," *Critical Inquiry* 28.1 (2001), pp. 1–22; Elisabeth Arweck and William Keenan, eds., *Materializing Religion: Expression, Performance and Ritual* (Oxford: Ashgate, 2006); Bynum et al., "Notes from the Field: Materiality," *The Art Bulletin* 95 (2013), pp. 11–37; and Aden Kumler, "Materials, Materia, 'Materiality,'" in *A Companion to Medieval Art: Romanesque and Gothic in Northern Europe*, 2nd ed., ed. Conrad Rudolph (Hoboken, NJ: John Wiley & Sons, 2019), pp. 95–117. See also https://en.wikipedia.org/wiki/Object-oriented_ontology (accessed January 7, 2020), and https://www.researchgate.net/post/What_is_the_material_turn_in_the_social_sciences (accessed January 7, 2020). Recent work by historians includes Paula Findlen, ed., *Early Modern Things: Objects and Their Histories, 1500–1800* (London: Routledge, 2013), and Henning Laugerud, Salvador Ryan, and Laura Katrine Skinnebach, eds., *The Materiality of Devotion in Late Medieval Northern Europe: Images, Objects, Practices* (Dublin: Four Courts Press, 2016). There is also scholarship, both older and recent, that focuses on various types of specific material used by medieval artists and artisans. See, for example, Günter Bandmann, "Bemerkungen zu einer Ikonologie des Materials," *Städel-Jahrbuch* 2 (1969), pp. 75–100, and Ittai Weinryb, *The Bronze Object in the Middle Ages* (Cambridge: Cambridge University Press, 2016). From my extended treatment in Bynum, *Christian Materiality*, it will be clear that I come to the topic of materiality from the fields of art history and the history of religion. For the vast amount of literature on the topic from social anthropology, much of it fascinating but not directly related to my interests, see Dan Hicks and Mary C. Beaudry, eds., *The Oxford Handbook of Material Culture Studies* (Oxford: Oxford University Press, 2010), and Daniel Miller, *Stuff* (Cambridge: Polity Press, 2010). There are helpful observations in Carl Knappett, *Thinking through Material Culture: An Interdisciplinary Perspective* (Philadelphia: University of Pennsylvania Press, 2005), esp. pp. 163–70, but to engage with this whole conversation would take me too far afield.

39. Peter Browe, *Die eucharistischen Wunder des Mittelalters* (Breslau: Müller & Seiffert, 1938), Gavin Langmuir, "The Tortures of the Body of Christ," in *Christendom and Its*

Discontents: Exclusion, Persecution, and Rebellion, 1000–1500, eds. Scott Waugh and Peter Diehl (Cambridge: Cambridge University Press, 1996), pp. 287–309, and Langmuir, "At the Frontiers of Faith," in *Religious Violence between Christians and Jews: Medieval Roots, Modern Perspectives*, ed. Anna Sapir Abulafia (Basingstoke, UK: Palgrave, 2002), pp. 138–56. See also chapter 3, nn. 42, 44, and 47.

40. This is a position that Robert Orsi, among others, has taken; Robert A. Orsi, *History and Presence* (Cambridge, MA: Harvard University Press, 2016). See my review in *Common Knowledge* 23.3 (2017). For the argument that attitudes toward the material and toward transformation generally, not Eucharistic theology, are the proper context for understanding late medieval ideas of change, see chapter 3, pp. 138–45. For a sophisticated treatment of late medieval pictorial representation and vernacular theology that privileges Eucharistic theology, see Kumler, *Translating Truth*, ch. 4.

41. For discussion of the centrality of material objects and their transformation in our understanding of the profound differences between medieval Christianity, on the one hand, and Judaism and Islam on the other, see chapter 6, p. 326, n. 58 below, and Bynum, *Christian Materiality*, pp. 273–79. It is worth noting that Catholicism after the Council of Trent also turned away from some of these late medieval devotional emphases.

42. On the increasing confidence in the possibility of transformation, including species transformation, in the later Middle Ages, see Caroline Walker Bynum, *Metamorphosis and Identity* (New York: Zone Books, 2001). For more on somatic expressions of spiritual experience such as stigmata, miraculous anorexia, and mystical pregnancy, see Caroline Walker Bynum, *Holy Feast and Holy Fast: The Religious Significance of Food to Medieval Women* (Berkeley: University of California Press, 1987).

43. Martin Gaier, Jeanette Kohl, and Alberto Saviello, eds., *Similitudo: Konzepte der Ähnlichkeit in Mittelalter und früher Neuzeit* (Munich: Fink, 2012), argues that "similitude" has been theorized little. Focused on art historical image theory, this volume is more philosophical and theoretical than my treatment here, although it is similarly based in case studies. I am grateful to Paul North for sharing with me portions of his book *Bizarre-Privileged Items in the Universe: The Logic of Likeness*, forthcoming from Zone Books. I have dealt with some of these issues further in Bynum, "Interrogating 'Likeness.'"

44. All citations to the Bible in this book are to the Latin Vulgate and/or the Douay translation of 1609.

45. Robert Javelet, *Image et ressemblance au 12e siècle, de saint Anselme à Alain de Lille*, 2 vols. (Paris: Letouzey et Ané, 1967). Javelet's now classic work studies the ways in which twelfth-century theologians and spiritual writers, building on patristic neo-Platonic ideas, understood the human being's return to the image and likeness of God in which he/she has been created, however much the original likeness has been obscured by sin. Although it has many meanings in twelfth-century discussions, "likeness" always carries some idea of ontological (not visual) resemblance and some connotations of dynamism.

See esp. *ibid.*, vol. 1, pp. xix–xxiii. On the idea of image and likeness in Augustine, on which later medieval thinkers build, see John Edward Sullivan, O. P., *The Image of God: The Doctrine of St. Augustine and Its Influence* (Dubuque, Iowa: The Priory Press, 1963), pp. 3–37. Ideas of likeness are also involved in discussions of predication, see nn. 69–73 in this chapter.

46. Crucial on the complex varieties of meanings of *imago* in the twelfth and thirteenth centuries is Bedos-Rezak, *When Ego Was Imago*. In theology, *imago* referred to both the human being's relationship to God, his maker, and to the Son, God in human form. In linguistics, *imago* included textual metaphors. In psychology, it referred to perceptions (including cognitions and dreams).

47. On traces in nature, see Friedrich Ohly, *Zur Signaturenlehre der Frühen Neuzeit: Bemerkungen zur mittelalterlichen Vorgeschichte und zur Eigenart einer epochalen Denkform in Wissenschaft, Literatur, und Kunst*, eds. Uwe Ruberg und Dietmar Peil (Stuttgart: Hirzel, 1999). See also John Calvin, *Institutes of the Christian Religion*, ed. John T. McNeill, trans. F. L. Battles, 2 vols. (Louisville, KY: Westminster Press, 1977), vol. 1, pp. 51–69, on how knowledge of God shines forth in the creation. But see also *ibid.*, ch. 11, pp. 99–120, against images.

48. Johan Huizinga, *The Waning of the Middle Ages*, trans. Fritz Hopman (Garden City, NY: Doubleday, 1954 [1923]). A full and more accurate translation appeared in 1996: Johan Huizinga, *The Autumn of the Middle Ages*, trans. Rodney J. Payton and Ulrich Mammitzsch (Chicago: University of Chicago Press, 1996). Much of the reception has, however, been influenced by the earlier version. For the reception history, see *ibid.*, pp. ix–xiii. As often happens with classics, Huizinga's work has been routinely criticized recently by art historians, who charge him with "crystallizing" or "reifying" medieval devotion. Such criticisms seem to me insensitive both to his thoughtful awareness of what needs might have led many people to petition and even manipulate heaven and to his vast learning in devotional literature (Latin and vernacular) as well as in art—a learning that was partly obscured by the truncated English translation of 1923.

49. Huizinga, *Autumn of the Middle Ages*, p. 174.

50. *Ibid.*, pp. 174–92. Jeffrey F. Hamburger has discussed Huizinga in *The Visual and the Visionary*, pp. 113–14 and 392.

51. See, among much that might be cited, Erwin Panofsky, *Studies in Iconology: Humanistic Themes in the Art of the Renaissance* (New York: Harper & Row, 1972). As is the case with Huizinga, it has become fashionable recently to criticize Panofsky, without due recognition of the power and perceptiveness of such works as *Gothic Architecture and Scholasticism* (New York: New American Library, 1957) and *Renaissance and Renascences in Western Art* (New York: Harper & Row, 1972) not only as analyses of art objects but also as basic interpretations in cultural history. Crucial recent works on late medieval art include Herbert Kessler, *Spiritual Seeing: Picturing God's Invisibility in Medieval Art* (Philadelphia: University of Pennsylvania Press, 2000); Herbert Kessler, *Seeing Medieval Art* (Orchard Park, NY: Broadview Press, 2004); and Kumler, *Translating Truth*.

52. On Peirce, see https://en.wikipedia.org/wiki/Semiotic_theory_of_Charles_Sanders_Peirce#II._Icon,_index,_symbol (accessed January 7, 2020). See also Cynthia Hahn, "Objects of Devotion and Desire: Relics, Reliquaries, Relation, and Response," in the catalogue *Objects of Devotion and Desire: Medieval Relic to Contemporary Art*, ed. Cynthia Hahn (New York: Hunter College, 27 January–30 April 2011), pp. 8–19, here p. 13, who uses Peirce's categories. Peirce did not, of course, create his categories in order to describe medieval material.

53. On the altarpiece, see Marjorie O'Rourke Boyle, *Divine Domesticity: Augustine of Thagaste to Teresa of Avila* (New York: E. J. Brill, 1997), pp. 178–91, esp. p. 188. For a stimulating discussion of the triptych, I am indebted to Elizabeth Parker, "The Merode Annunciation Triptych: So Much for the Mousetrap," from "Paradigms and Personae in the Medieval World: A Symposium in Honor of Elizabeth A. R. Brown," New York, March 16, 2018. Marilyn Aronberg Lavin identifies the wood in Joseph's hand as another domestic object (although there are clearly two traps represented in the painting); see "The Mystic Winepress in the Merode Altarpiece," in *Studies in Late Medieval and Renaissance Painting in Honor of Millard Meiss*, eds. Irving Lavin and John Plummer (New York: New York University Press, 1977), pp. 297–301.

54. For a parallel case of the supposed tooth of the Buddha, see Hildegard Diemberger, "Powerful Objects in Powerful Places: Pilgrimage, Relics and Sacred Texts in Tibetan Buddhism," in Ivanič, Laven, and Morrall, eds., *Religious Materiality*, pp. 67–84.

55. For more on how reliquaries construct friable, broken, and decayed bits of bodies and matter as heavenly and eternal, see chapter 4, pp. 172–73. I discuss "dissimilar similitude" at nn. 68–69 in this introduction.

56. The garment the nun weaves in prayer is not a depiction that looks like chastity nor, of course, a piece of a chaste body, but it is a real garment, not just an arbitrarily assigned symbol of completeness. On index, icon, and sign, see n. 52.

57. See, for example, Stewart Guthrie, "A Cognitive Theory of Religion," *Current Anthropology* 21.2 (1980), pp. 181–94; and Stewart Guthrie, *Faces in the Clouds: A New Theory of Religion* (Oxford: Oxford University Press, 1993), esp. pp. 103–12. See also Eric R. Kandel, *The Age of Insight: The Quest to Understand the Unconscious in Art, Mind, and Brain, from Vienna 1900 to the Present* (New York: Random House, 2012), and Robert Turner, "Ritual Action Shapes Our Brain: An Essay in Neuroanthropology," in *Ritual, Performance and the Senses*, eds. Michael Bull and Jon P. Mitchell (London: Bloomsbury Academic, 2015), pp. 31–44. For my reservations about such cross-cultural generalizing, see chapter 3, p. 139, and Bynum, "Are Things 'Indifferent'?" esp. pp. 93–95. I expressed reservations about the psychological reduction of medieval literalizings or somatizings as long ago as my discussion of parallels and nonparallels between medieval religious inedia and modern anorexia nervosa in Bynum, *Holy Feast and Holy Fast*. There are obviously some parallels between what psychiatry calls "conversion phenomena" and medieval bodily events and it can be helpful

to consider them, but differences in conceptualizations of such phenomena (including different understandings of their causation and trajectory) must be noted as well.

58. See Alfred Gell, *Art and Agency: An Anthropological Theory* (Oxford: Oxford University Press, 1998), published posthumously and enormously influential recently for its stress on culture as social interaction. Gell criticized Panofsky's focus on meaning and symbolic communication and saw all art as "a system of action intended to change the world" (*ibid.*, p. 6). On Gell, see Christopher Pinney and Nicholas Thomas, eds., *Beyond Aesthetics: Art and the Technologies of Enchantment* (Oxford, New York: Berg, 2001); Robert Layton, "Art and Agency: A Reassessment," *Journal of the Royal Anthropological Institute* 9.3 (2003), pp. 447–64; and Robin Osborne and Jeremy Tanner, eds., *Art's Agency and Art History* (Oxford: Blackwell, 2007). On attention to images as performative, see Alain Dierkens, Gil Bartholeyns, and Thomas Golsenne, eds., *La performance des images* (Brussels: University of Brussels, 2010). The most influential statement of the theory of art's agency has been David Freedberg, *The Power of Images: Studies in the History and Theory of Response* (Chicago: University of Chicago Press, 1989). On the agency of objects, see also Bruno Latour, "The Berlin Key or How to Do Words with Things," in Graves-Brown, ed., *Matter, Materiality and Modern Culture*, pp. 10–21; and Bynum, *Christian Materiality*, pp. 280–84. On recent "thing theory," which has some affinity with these ideas, see n. 38.

59. Lambros Malafouris and Colin Renfrew, eds., *The Cognitive Life of Things: Recasting the Boundaries of the Mind* (Exeter: McDonald Institute for Archaeological Research/Oxbow Books, 2010), pp. 1–12. Another approach through networks is the so-called Actor-Network Theory (ANT), discussed and used by Carl Knappett, *An Archaeology of Interaction: Network Perspectives on Material Culture and Society* (Oxford: Oxford University Press, 2011), esp. pp. 7–10. I have not been able to take account of this theory in this volume.

60. Glenn Peers, "Object Relations: Theorizing the Late Antique Viewer," in *The Oxford Handbook of Late Antiquity*, ed. Scott Fitzgerald Johnson (Oxford: Oxford University Press, 2012), p. 988. Peers's way of looking at religious objects is currently very widespread and tends to be applied across cultures. For bibliography on this, see chapter 3, nn. 2–3.

61. On the footprints of Christ, see chapter 6, pp. 227–44; on the clothing rituals of Wienhausen, see chapter 2, pp. 111–12; on the Judensau, see chapter 4, pp. 160–62.

62. Aden Kumler, "*Imitatio Rerum*: Sacred Objects in the St. Giles's Hospital Processional," *Journal of Medieval and Early Modern Studies* 44.3 (Fall 2014), pp. 469–502.

63. Here I find helpful what the painter Frank Auerbach asserts in discussing the portrait. Although a painting transforms its subject in paint, it never loses touch with the subject's specificity and remains contingent on it; hence a portrait must be "like nothing else on earth, but like [its subject]." Quoted by Mark Prince in "Magnetism in Perpetual Motion" (review of a book and an exhibit by Frank Auerbach), *Times Literary Supplement* (January 1, 2016), pp. 17–18. See also Johannes Endres, "Unähnliche Ähnlichkeit: Zu Analogie, Metapher und Verwandtschaft," in Gaier, Kohl, and Saviello, eds., *Similitudo*, pp. 29–58.

64. For more on iconoclasm, see chapter 3, pp. 130–31, and Bynum "Interrogating 'Likeness.'" For more on the complexity of the relationship of object to image, see chapter 4, pp. 175–81.

65. Two decades ago, the idea of "representation," considered in a political context, was complicated by identity politics. Was it necessary for someone or something to look like or be like something else in order to "represent" that someone or something else? See Bynum, *Metamorphosis and Identity*, pp. 19–21, 163–66, and Caroline Walker Bynum, preface to Bartal, Bodner, and Kühnel, eds., *Natural Materials*, pp. xix–xxi. In these days, given our new emphasis on intersectionality, the political issue is both easier and harder to resolve. Any individual has multiple identities and can therefore (and should) "represent" multiple positions.

66. The conference "Beyond Representation: An Interdisciplinary Approach to the Nature of Things," September 27–29, 2012, Bard Graduate Center and Institute of Fine Arts, New York University, New York, organized by Jaś Elsner, Finbarr B. Flood, and Ittai Weinryb, did not so much reject "representation" as expand the concept.

67. I do not mean to give the impression that most stigmatics claimed to have the nails of the Crucifixion in their flesh. In most cases, what appeared were simply Christ's wounds.

68. See chapter 2, pp. 119–28, for further discussion. The passage is from Gertrude, *Legatus divinae pietatis* 1.1, in *Revelationes Gertrudianae ac Mechtildianae,* eds. Monks of Solesmes, 2 vols. (Paris: Oudin, 1875-77), vol. 1, pp. 10–11. It is also in Gertrude, *The Herald of Divine Love,* trans. Margaret Winkworth (New York: Paulist Press, 1993), 1.1, p. 89, and Gertrude, *Oeuvres spirituelles* 2: *Le Héraut, livres 1–2,* ed. Pierre Doyère, *Sources chrétiennes* 139 (Paris: Éditions du Cerf, 1968), 1.1, pp. 126–27. Book 1 of the *Legatus* was written by one of Gertrude's fellow nuns. No scholar who has worked on the passage has found a source in Hugh of St. Victor.

69. See chapter 5, pp. 219–20, for further discussion. The citation is from pseudo-Dionysius (or Denis) the Areopagite, *La hiérarchie céleste*, eds. René Roques, Günter Heil, and Maurice de Gandillac, *Sources chrétiennes* 58 (Paris: Éditions du Cerf, 1958), ch. 2, sections 3–4 (140C–141D), pp. 78–81.

70. On Augustine, see Sullivan, *The Image of God*, pp. 7–11 and 17–20, and Margaret W. Ferguson, "St. Augustine's Region of Unlikeness: The Crossing of Exile and Language," *Georgia Review* 29 (1975), pp. 842–64, esp. p. 856. On twelfth-century theories of *imago*, see Bedos-Rezak, *When Ego Was Imago*, esp. pp. 171–73.

71. Thomas Aquinas, *Summa contra Gentiles*, trans. with introduction and notes by Anton C. Pegis, F.R.S.C. (Notre Dame, IN: University of Notre Dame Press, 1955), bk 1, ch. 32, paragraphs 1–2, p. 143.

72. *Ibid.*, bk 1, ch. 29, paragraphs 1–5, pp. 138–39. See also James F. Anderson, *Introduction to the Metaphysics of St. Thomas Aquinas: Texts Selected and Translated* (Chicago: Henry Regnery, 1953), pp. 36–43; and E. Jennifer Ashworth, "Medieval Theories of Analogy," in

The Stanford Encyclopedia of Philosophy (Fall 2017 Edition), ed. Edward N. Zalta, https://plato.stanford.edu/archives/fall2017/entries/analogy-medieval (accessed December 9, 2019.)

73. Likeness was also central in debates about iconoclasm. See Bynum, "Interrogating 'Likeness,'" and n. 64 in this chapter.

74. I do not go into here the question of how far such a notion of resemblance draws on Neoplatonic ideas of "participation" — a topic on which scholars of Augustine, as well as of pseudo-Dionysius, have written much. See n. 70. I would argue indeed that there is more of an element of Neoplatonic participation in Thomas Aquinas's discussions of "likeness" than many scholars hold; see the passage quoted at n. 72. I have had to leave discussion of several issues concerning "likeness" to "Interrogating 'Likeness.'" I am grateful to the editors of the journal in which it appears, Simon Teuscher and Caroline Arni, for many perceptive comments.

75. Moreover, as I remark in considering the experiences of the Wienhausen nuns on the eve of the Lutheran Reformation, objects can sometimes guide us to discovering spiritual experiences and concerns that we do not find in documents because the surviving documents are not of the type to reflect or recount such concerns. See chapter 2.

76. Jacqueline Jung, "The Tactile and the Visionary: Notes on the Place of Sculpture in the Medieval Religious Imagination," in *Looking Beyond: Visions, Dreams, and Insights in Medieval Art and History*, ed. C. Hourihane, Index of Christian Art Occasional Papers 11 (Princeton, NJ: Index of Christian Art, 2010), pp. 203–40.

77. Lorraine Daston, ed., *Things That Talk: Object Lessons from Art and Science* (New York: Zone Books, 2004) and a number of other publications have referred to objects as "speaking" to express their agency. This has long been true in the lengthy discussions of "speaking" reliquaries. For a correction to this, see Cynthia Hahn, "The Voices of the Saints: Speaking Reliquaries," *Gesta* 36.1 (1997), pp. 20–31. I share the recent reservations about this metaphor because it tends to intellectualize such objects and make their significance too close to that of word or idea. Nonetheless, Daston's book has been helpfully influential in leading to a more labile sense of the agency of things.

78. For discussion of the linga and of Yaśodā's vision, see chapters 3 and 5.

79. On the duck-rabbit illusion, see Google's listings at https://www.google.com/search?client=firefox-b-1-d&q=duck-rabbit+illusion (accessed October 13, 2019).

80. See Cutler, "The Relics of Scholarship," p. 345, who cites Georges Didi-Huberman's idea of "dissemblance." See also Cynthia Hahn, *Strange Beauty*; Hahn, *The Reliquary Effect*; Jean-Claude Schmitt, "Les images et le sacré," in Dierkens, Bartholeyns, and Golsenne, eds., *La performance des images*, pp. 29–46; and Thomas Golsenne, "Parure et culte," in *ibid.*, pp. 71–85. This is a point I have been emphasizing since the mid-1990s. See Bynum, *The Resurrection of the Body*, esp. pp. 59–114 and 200–25, although I do not go so far as those who suggest that the reliquary makes the relic. See also the analysis of the Mary Magdalen reliquary at n. 54 in this chapter.

81. See nn. 17 and 18. I agree with a point made by Laura Kendrick, *Animating the Letter: The Figurative Embodiment of Writing from Late Antiquity to the Renaissance* (Columbia: Ohio State University Press, 1999), p. 188, where she stresses that the divine is often (especially early in the development of a tradition) revealed by unlike as well as by like objects, for example Christ imaged as a fish rather than a man in early Christianity.

82. On paradox, see Caroline Walker Bynum, "Why Paradox? The Contradictions of My Life as a Scholar," *The Catholic Historical Review* 98.3 (July 2012), pp. 432–55. Although this is a personal essay, it also argues that recognition of and encounter with paradox is central to what scholars do when they study religion.

83. See Bynum, *Wonderful Blood*, pp. 85–111. It is crucial to note that some medieval theologians held that there could not be miracles that revealed the holy substance produced in transubstantiation exactly because, according to theology, the accidents did not change. Modern scholarship has too often ignored this point. But see also the caveat in chapter 3, n. 46.

84. As I note in chapter 4, contemporary Germans have agitated and demonstrated against objects such as the Judensau. Treatment of host-desecration libels has been more complicated. The way in which actions and debates concerning such material provides parallels with contemporary debates in the United States over Civil War monuments is obvious, and people of good will have argued both sides of the conundrum: to retain such materials (while signaling, by providing context, the guilt in which they participate) or simply to remove them. For moving remarks on the issue of the Confederate statues, see Karen L. Cox, "What Changed in Charlottesville," *New York Times*, August 11, 2019. Michael Gorra, "A Heritage of Evil," *New York Review of Books* (November 7, 2019), pp. 10–13, makes the same argument about Confederate memorials in the United States that I make about German monuments in chapter 4.

85. This question echoes the issue of reducing religion or art to cognitive response that I refer to in n. 57.

86. For further discussion of the nature of comparison, see Yve-Alain Bois, "On the Uses and Abuses of Look-alikes," *October* 154 (Fall, 2015), pp. 127–49; Gaier, Kohl, and Saviello, eds., *Similitudo*; and Bynum, "Interrogating 'Likeness,'" pp. 31–56.

87. In "What's New about the Medieval?," the 2017 introduction to the expanded edition of my *Resurrection of the Body in Western Christianity*, pp. xxv–xxviii, I muse about the fact that European medievalists have not in general managed to make their insights relevant to specialists in other periods and geographical areas of history. In "Interrogating 'Likeness'" and the epilogue to *Religious Materiality*, I suggest that the characteristics of medieval Christian religious objects, especially their paradoxical aspects, should be considered by historians of religion, literature, and art as they theorize the "agency of objects," comparison, and "representation." Anthropologist Carl Knappett observes in *An Archaeology of Interaction*, p. 215: "A reader may find the case studies satisfactory at a certain level . . . but

that the relevance to his or her own . . . material appears slim at best." Historians often feel the same way. Nonetheless, I continue to believe that careful case studies of specific objects in their own contexts are a good place to start in formulating broader understandings of what religious objects do and how they are "like."

88. For more examples of such images, see chapter 6.

CHAPTER ONE: HOLY BEDS

1. A short version of this chapter was commissioned by the journal *Gesta* for its Encounters series and was published in *Gesta* 55.2 (Fall 2016), pp. 129–31, under the title "Encounter: Holy Beds." Essays for "Encounters" are supposed to focus on a scholar or a work of art that has significantly influenced the author. In the *Gesta* version, I began with my own visit in 1960, when I was an undergraduate at the University of Michigan, to the *Flanders in the Fifteenth Century* exhibit.

2. The cradle seems to have been acquired by Ruth and Leopold Blumka in 1947 and given to the Metropolitan Museum by Ruth Blumka in memory of her husband in 1974. It was originally in the possession of the Grand Béguinage in Louvain, which sold it to Jules Frésart in Liège in 1882. It was acquired before 1894 by Albert Figdor in Vienna and auctioned in 1930. The Blumkas acquired it from the Bondy Collection in Vienna in 1947. See Detroit Institute of Arts, *Flanders in the Fifteenth Century: Art and Civilization; Catalogue of the Exhibition, Masterpieces of Flemish Art, Van Eyck to Bosch* (Detroit: Detroit Institute of Arts/Brussels: Centre National de Recherches Primitifs Flamands, 1960), pp. 343–45. Peter Keller, *Die Wiege des Christuskindes: Ein Haushaltsgerät in Kunst und Kult* (Worms: Werner, 1998), p. 198, says that the Purchase Book of the Burrell Collection remarks in 1937 that a similar cradle, sold at the Figdor sale in 1930, brought an "enormous price."

3. Advertising for the exhibit focused on Rogier van der Weyden, Jan van Eyck, and Hieronymus Bosch.

4. Detroit Institute of Arts, *Flanders in the Fifteenth Century*, p. 343.

5. The category of "devotional object" was really put on the map of art history by the exhibit curated by Henk van Os in Amsterdam in 1994–95; see Henk W. van Os, *The Art of Devotion in the Late Middle Ages in Europe, 1300–1500*, trans. Michael Hoyle (Princeton, NJ: Princeton University Press, 1994).

6. In fairness to the Detroit curators, one must note that the much later discussion of the crib in the Metropolitan Museum's *Bulletin* itself, although it emphasizes that the function of such objects is "to lead to the belief that they [the beguines] were actually taking part in the sacred events," does not underline either the gendered or the experiential aspects of such objects. William D. Wixom, "Late Medieval Sculpture in the Metropolitan, 1400–1530," *Metropolitan Museum of Art Bulletin* 64.4 (2007), p. 3.

7. For bibliography on women and devotion, see Christiane Klapisch-Zuber, "Holy Dolls: Play and Devotion in Florence in the Quattrocento," in Klapisch-Zuber, *Women,*

Family, and Ritual in Renaissance Italy (Chicago: University of Chicago Press, 1985), pp. 310–31; Ulinka Rublack, "Female Spirituality and the Infant Jesus in Late Medieval Dominican Convents," *Gender and History* 6.1 (1994), pp. 37–57; Jeffrey F. Hamburger, "Am Anfang war das Bild: Kunst und Frauenspiritualität im Spätmittelalter," in *Studien und Texte zur literarischen und materiellen Kultur der Frauenklöster im späten Mittelalter: Ergebnisse eines Arbeitsgesprächs in der Herzog August Bibliothek Wolfenbüttel, 24.–26. Febr. 1999*, eds. Falk Eisermann, Eva Schlotheuber, and Volker Honemann (Leiden: Brill, 2004), pp. 1–43; Jeffrey F. Hamburger, *The Visual and the Visionary: Art and Female Spirituality in Late Medieval Germany* (New York: Zone Books, 1998); Jeffrey F. Hamburger, *Nuns as Artists: The Visual Culture of a Medieval Convent* (Berkeley: University of California Press, 1997); Eva Schlotheuber, *Klostereintritt und Bildung: Die Lebenswelt der Nonnen im späten Mittelalter. Mit einer Edition des 'Konventstagebuchs' einer Zisterzienserin von Heilig-Kreuz bei Braunschweig (1484–1507)* (Tübingen: Mohr Sieback, 2004); and Jeffrey F. Hamburger, Carola Jäggi, Susan Marti, and Hedwig Röckelein, eds., in cooperation with the Ruhrlandmuseum Essen, *Frauen-Kloster-Kunst: Neue Forschungen zur Kulturgeschichte des Mittelalters: Beiträge zum Internationalen Kolloquium vom 13. bis 16. Mai 2005 anlässlich der Ausstellung "Krone und Schleier"* (Turnhout: Brepols, 2007).

8. For the recent emphasis on materials and materiality, such as object-oriented ontology, thing theory, and various sorts of "new materialism," see the introduction, n. 38. On the recent attention to the agency of objects and to cognitive theories of response, see the introduction, nn. 57 and 58.

9. Rudolf Berliner, *Die Weihnachtskrippe* (Munich: Prestel Verlag, 1955); Rudolf Berliner, "The Origins of the Crèche," *Gazette des Beaux-Arts*, 6th series, 30 (1946), pp. 249–78; Keller, *Die Wiege*. See also Lenz Kriss-Rettenbeck, "Anmerkungen zur neueren Krippenliteratur," *Bayerisches Jahrbuch für Volkskunde* (1966/67): *Festschrift für Rudolf Berliner* (Volkach: Hart, 1967), pp. 7–36; Lenz Kriss-Rettenbeck, *Bilder und Zeichen religiösen Volksglaubens* (Munich: Georg D. W. Callwey, 1963), pp. 33 and 37–38; Markus Walz, *Weihnachtskrippen im Kölner Raum: Verbreitungsgeschichte—Funktionszuweisungen—Gestaltung*, Rheinisches Archiv 120 (Cologne: Böhlau, 1988); and Rüdiger Vossen, *Höhle. Stall. Palast. Weihnachtskrippen der Völker* (Hamburg: Christians Verlag, 1990).

10. Given by J. P. Morgan from the collection of his father, J. Pierpont Morgan, who had acquired it as part of the collection of Georges Hoentschel, a well-known French architect. Hoentschel had acquired it from a learned curator at the Louvre, Émile Molinier. The only detailed study of the object is William H. Forsyth, "Popular Imagery in a Fifteenth-Century Burgundian Crèche," *Metropolitan Museum Journal* 24 (1989), pp. 117–26. There is a brief mention in Wixom, "Late Medieval Sculpture in the Metropolitan, 1400–1530," pp. 1–48, at p. 22, and one in Stefan Roller, ed., *Heilige Nacht: Die Weihnachtsgeschichte und ihre Bilderwelt: Liebieghaus Skulpturensammlung, Frankfurt am Main, 12 Oktober 2016 bis 29 Januar 2017* (Munich: Hirmer; Frankfurt am Main: Liebieghaus, 2016), pp. 124, 126 fig. 63, 254 no. 42.

11. Forsyth comments in "Popular Imagery," pp. 120–21: "The manger's illogical height may be the result of the exigencies of the crowded composition. In any case, I know of no other crèche with this duplication of cribs." I have also not been able to find other examples in either sculpture or painting. Keller in *Die Wiege*, p. 211, item B.10 says there are other examples of the mother and child appearing in two different registers or planes of the depiction but gives no examples of double cribs or beds. An image of the Adoration of the Christ Child from the Walters Art Gallery, Baltimore (Kat. Nr. B 8) in Keller, plate 53, shows Mary adoring the child with an empty manger or eating trough above and an empty cradle below. The catalogue *Heilige Nacht* gives a number of northern European examples of mangers floating above the depiction of a Nativity below, but none of two beds. The exhaustive study by Giulia Puma of Italian paintings of the Nativity shows that it was fairly common to depict a manger with the baby in it above Mary in the picture space, Mary holding the baby beside an empty manger or laying him in it, or a manger with the baby above while one or two midwives below place the baby in a second container for a bath. There is no case of an empty cradle below a full manger. See Giulia Puma, "La *Nativité* italienne: Une histoire d'adoration (1250–1450)," Thèse de doctorat d'Italien, Université Paris 3 — Sorbonne Nouvelle (2012).

12. I am grateful to Griffith Mann, curator at the Metropolitan Museum in New York, and Cynthia Hahn, professor at Hunter College and the Graduate Center of the City University of New York, who arranged for me to be able to examine in detail the crib and its embroidered bedding.

13. See Keller, *Die Wiege*, p. 12 and passim.

14. In 1223, Pope Honorius III gave Francis permission to set up a manger with an ox and an ass in a cave in the woods at Grecio and preach about it. But Francis had no human figures in the ensemble, and Franciscans were not especially important later in spreading the practice of setting up crèches or in crib devotion. The prominence of animals in early scenes of the birth may be owing to the passage from Isaiah 1:3, "The ox knoweth his owner and the ass his master's crib." According to Gregory the Great, the ox represents the Jewish people, who carry a special weight of sin, and the ass represents the heathen. See Vossen, *Höhle. Stall. Palast*, p. 40.

15. Both Keller and Berliner think the crèche or Nativity scene emerges in the sixteenth century — that is, they date to that period the first cases of the full, freestanding depiction of the historical event of the birth in Bethlehem appearing in churches. Berliner argues that the earliest evidence of a Christmas crèche in a church is from 1562 in Prague. Both Keller and Berliner argue that Francis's manger should not be considered a crèche because no holy persons were represented, only the live animals and a straw-filled manger. Berliner, *Die Weihnachtskrippe*, pp. 15–16, argues that it is incorrect to assume that Nativity scenes were used only at Christmas but later scholars disagree.

16. Forsyth, "Popular Imagery," p. 125 n. 1, argues that Nativity scenes should be

distinguished from crèches. He holds that "crèche" originally referred only to a manger, whereas "Nativity" referred to one of a series of scenes common in retables of the period. According to such analysis, the Burgundian crèche is clearly a full Nativity scene (even though it has no wise men) and is earlier than the first Nativity scenes discussed by Keller and Berliner. To Berliner, Walz, and Kriss-Rettenbeck, the term *Krippe* refers to a group of three-dimensional, freestanding figures of Mary, Joseph, the child, and other attendants, which serves a devotional and educational purpose. According to this definition the Burgundian crèche is not a *Krippe*. See Walz, *Weihnachtskrippen im Kölner Raum*, p. 5. Keller, who makes a strict division between manger scene and cradle devotion, argues that the Nativity scene is late, becoming common in art only in the sixteenth century with Dürer, Altdorfer, and Grünewald. Keller, *Die Wiege*, pp. 157 and 193.

17. See Keller, *Die Wiege*, pp. 25–30, and Vossen, *Höhle. Stall. Palast*, p. 38.

18. Alois Döring, "'Lasst uns das Kindlein wiegen. . . ': Das Jesuskind-Wiegen, ein verschwundener Weihnachtsbrauch—und in aktueller Krippenkunst in Erinnerung gebracht," in *"Zur Krippe her kommet . . . ": Geschichten und Bräuche rund um die Weihnachtskrippe*, ed. Landesgemeinschaft der Krippenfreude in Rheinland und Westfalen e. V. anlässlich des 90-jährigen Jubiläums (1925–2015) (Münster/New York: Waxmann, 2015), pp. 85–99, at p. 91, says the German carol (based on Latin) comes from the second half of fourteenth century from a monk of Strasbourg. See also Vossen, *Höhle. Stall. Palast*, p. 38, and Keller, *Die Wiege*, p. 110.

19. We find depictions of the birth at Bethlehem as early as the fourth century on sarcophagi and in the catacombs. The earliest versions show the manger with an ox and ass, a shepherd and an angel. Mary and Joseph appear a little later. Then we have no depictions of the full scene for about eight hundred years. Vossen, *Höhle. Stall. Palast*, p. 38.

20. In the *De investigatione Antichristi* of 1160–63, Herrad of Landsberg was also critical of the practice. And Guerric of Igny refers to it. See Keller, *Die Wiege*, pp. 108–10.

21. Vossen, *Höhle. Stall. Palast*, p. 38.

22. *Ibid.*; Keller, *Die Wiege*, pp. 118–21. There is debate about whether Margaret saw an actual cradle or an illustration on parchment. See Döring, "'Lasst uns das Kindlein wiegen . . . ,'" p. 87. On Margaret, see Rublack, "Female Spirituality."

23. Van Os, *The Art of Devotion*, p. 102, and Keller, *Die Wiege*, pp. 134–39.

24. For examples from current practice, see *"Zur Krippe her kommet. . . ,"* pp. 7–84, 100–54. On the revival of the Christmas crib in Germany in the twentieth century, see Walz, *Weihnachtskrippen im Kölner Raum*.

25. For examples of cribs or mangers on altars in the place of the tabernacle, making clear the Eucharistic connection, see Berliner, *Die Weihnachtskrippe*, pp. 15–16 and plate 6. The fact that there are also examples of reliquaries shaped like cradles further underlines the significance of these little beds as places where earth and heaven meet. See Keller, *Die Wiege*, plate 31. Plate 8 is also possibly a cradle reliquary.

26. Keller, *Die Wiege*, pp. 148–49, and Döring, "'Lasst uns das Kindlein wiegen . . . ,'" pp. 85–92.

27. On this, see the introduction, pp. 40–41.

28. Berliner, "Origins," pp. 264–65, says that "rocking the child" often meant singing cradle songs. He argues that there is no evidence that the phrase meant physical rocking of an object until 1600.

29. Keller, *Die Wiege*, pp. 8–9 and 137–38; Berliner, "Origins," pp. 268–69. Cradles were also particularly popular with laywomen. According to Keller, of seventy-two known cradles from bourgeois houses in the Netherlands, forty-nine belonged to women and twenty-three to men.

30. Van Os, *The Art of Devotion*, pp. 100–103, 181. It is extremely rare to be able to trace provenance in this amount of detail.

31. See n. 42.

32. See n. 37.

33. See the discussion of Powell, Rublack, and Hamburger at nn. 75 and 77.

34. Christiane Klapisch-Zuber, "Holy Dolls," and Rublack, "Female Spirituality." For examples of the dolls, see van Os, *The Art of Devotion*, pp. 99–101. For an eighteenth-century painting of a Conceptionist nun holding her doll, see chapter 2, n. 51.

35. See chapter 2, pp. 110–12.

36. See Schlotheuber, *Klostereintritt und Bildung*; Eva Schlotheuber, "Klostereintritt und Übergangsriten: Die Bedeutung der Jungfräulichkeit für das Selbstverständnis der Nonnen der Alten Orden," in *Frauen-Kloster-Kunst*, pp. 43–55; and chapter 2.

37. David Herlihy, "Women in Medieval Society," The Smith History Lecture, University of St. Thomas, Houston, TX, 1971, reprinted in David Herlihy, *The Social History of Italy and Western Europe, 700–1500: Collected Studies* (London: Variorum Reprints, 1978), and Klapisch-Zuber, "Holy Dolls."

38. Jeffrey Hamburger, "Medieval Self-Fashioning: Authorship, Authority, and Autobiography in Suso's *Exemplar*," in *The Visual and the Visionary*, pp. 233–78.

39. See "Krippen," Bayerisches Nationalmuseum, http://www.bayerisches-nationalmuseum.de/index.php?%20id=287 (accessed December 12, 2019).

40. On bells used as pendants for children or on their cribs to ward off evils such as plague or accidents, see Kriss-Rettenbeck, *Bilder und Zeichen*, pp. 37–38.

41. Keller, *Die Wiege*, p. 107, expresses doubt about the function of a relic if one were placed here. Berliner, "Origins," p. 270, refers to two cradles or Nativity scenes that were reliquaries.

42. See Döring, "'Lasst uns das Kindlein wiegen . . . ,'" pp. 89–90, citing Berliner. Döring himself thinks the heads might be purely decorative.

43. See the introduction, n. 79.

44. See nn. 10 and 11.

45. On Joseph, see Charlene Villaseñor Black, *Creating the Cult of St. Joseph: Art and Gender in the Spanish Empire* (Princeton, NJ: Princeton University Press, 2006). See also Forsyth, "Popular Imagery," p. 118 and p. 125 n. 9.

46. See the introduction, p. 42, for more discussion of the Merode altarpiece.

47. See n. 24.

48. Keller, *Die Wiege*, pp. 29–30. For an image, see Joseph Malouel?, *Nativity*, oil on tempera (c. 1400), Museum Mayer van den Bergh, Antwerp, Belgium (courtesy Wikimedia Commons). Here, Joseph can be seen cutting one of his stockings with a knife as Mary watches and the infant Jesus waits in a manger. See also "Relic of the Holy Diaper: The Swaddling Clothes of Jesus," *Reliquarian*, December 18, 2014, https://reliquarian.com/2014/12/18/relic-of-the-holy-diaper-the-swaddling-clothes-of-jesus/ (accessed December 12, 2019).

49. Virginia Nixon, *Mary's Mother: Saint Anne in Late Medieval Europe* (University Park: Pennsylvania State University Press, 2004), gives many examples of the Holy Kinship and the Anna-Selbdritt. For two examples of the Anna-Selbdritt from the Metropolitan Museum that are not on display, see https://www.metmuseum.org/art/collection/search/471953 and https://www.metmuseum.org/art/collection/search/467724 (accessed May 6, 2018). For an example of the Holy Kinship in the National Gallery of Art in Washington, DC, see https://www.nga.gov/collection/art-object-page.123018.html (accessed December 12, 2019).

50. See Kathleen Ashley and Pamela Sheingorn, eds., *Interpreting Cultural Symbols: Saint Anne in Late Medieval Society* (Athens: University of Georgia Press, 1990); Nixon, *Mary's Mother*; and Jennifer Welsh, *The Cult of St. Anne in Medieval and Early Modern Europe* (New York: Routledge, 2017).

51. According to Ashley and Sheingorn, introduction to *Interpreting Cultural Symbols*, pp. 17–18, the change in the later Middle Ages from understanding Jesus's lineage as patrilineal to understanding it as matrilineal was owing to the emphasis on the maternal line in the extremely popular medieval work by James of Voragine, *The Golden Legend*.

52. On St. Anne and the Immaculate Conception, see Nixon, *Mary's Mother*, pp. 74–79.

53. The theme of Mary teaching the Christ Child to read or Anne teaching the Virgin reflects both the increasing literacy of women in the period and an emphasis on the female role in teaching young children. See Welsh, *Cult of St. Anne*, pp. 36–37, and Pamela Sheingorn, "'The Wise Mother': The Image of St. Anne Teaching the Virgin Mary," *Gesta* 32.1 (1993), pp. 69–80. For images, see the early fifteenth-century sculpture attributed to Claus de Werve of the Virgin teaching the Christ Child to read, in the Metropolitan Museum at https://www.metmuseum.org/toah/works-of-art/33.23/ and the sculpture of St. Anne teaching the Virgin, in the Philadelphia Museum at https://www.philamuseum.org/collections/permanent/43985.html (both accessed May 6, 2018).

54. On Mary, Anne, and Emerentia as providing images of normal female activity acceptable to God, see Merry Wiesner-Hanks, *Women and Gender in Early Modern Europe*

(New York: Cambridge University Press, 2000), p. 219, and Welsh, *Cult of St. Anne.*

55. As Forsyth suggests in "Popular Imagery," p. 121, there is a vertical division in the scene, with the mother on the side of the angels and the father paired with the shepherds. But this can hardly represent any simple division between beds, because both beds (the waiting and the full) are attended by angels. Moreover, the manger (filled with the revealed savior) is closer to the shepherds, while Mary attends the empty cradle.

56. To my knowledge, the sensual aspects of this sculpture have not been noticed before.

57. According to Forsyth, the Burgundian crèche is not the only image we have of the Christ Child sharing the warmth of the animals. Forsyth, "Popular Imagery," p. 124 and p. 126 n. 29. Keller, in *Die Wiege*, p. 211, item B.10, sees the ox as pulling on the swaddling clothes and says this motif is occasionally found. (He cites two examples.) The two animal figures are quite abraded so the exact gesture is hard to decipher, but the mouth of the animal on the left is clearly involved.

58. Jacqueline Jung, "The Tactile and the Visionary: Notes on the Place of Sculpture in the Medieval Religious Imagination," in *Looking Beyond: Visions, Dreams, and Insights in Medieval Art and History*, ed. Colum Hourihane, Index of Christian Art Occasional Papers 11 (Princeton, NJ: Princeton University, 2010), pp. 203–40.

59. Herbert Kessler, *Spiritual Seeing: Picturing God's Invisibility in Medieval Art* (Philadelphia: University of Pennsylvania Press, 2000); Herbert Kessler, *Seeing Medieval Art* (Orchard Park, NY: Broadview Press, 2004); Hourihane, *Looking Beyond*; Caroline Walker Bynum, "Seeing and Seeing Beyond: The Mass of St. Gregory in the Fifteenth Century," in *The Mind's Eye: Art and Theological Argument in the Middle Ages*, eds. Anne-Marie Bouché and Jeffrey Hamburger (Princeton, NJ: Department of Art and Archaeology, Princeton University, 2005), pp. 208–40; and Jacqueline Jung, "Beyond the Barrier: The Unifying Role of the Choir Screen in Gothic Churches," *The Art Bulletin* 82.4 (December 2000), pp. 622–57.

60. Glenn W. Most, *Doubting Thomas* (Cambridge, MA: Harvard University Press, 2007). Most's point is that the scriptural passage does not say that Thomas actually placed his fingers in Jesus's side, but in medieval and Renaissance accounts he is depicted as doing so, often graphically. On the pairing with the *Noli me tangere*, see Bynum, "Seeing and Seeing Beyond," pp. 219–20 and 232. The frontispiece to this book shows the Doubting Thomas (an image of Christ's graphic presence) paired with another depiction of absence, the Ascension of Christ into heaven.

61. Marguerite of Oingt, *Pagina meditationum*, chs. 30–39, *Les oeuvres de Marguerite d'Oingt*, eds. and trans. Antonin Duraffour, P. Gardette and P. Durdilly (Paris: Publications de l'Institute de Linguistique Romane de Lyon, 1965), pp. 77–79.

62. The Vulgate translates *floridus* as "flourishing," but the Latin word clearly conjures up flowers.

63. Jeffrey Hamburger, "'On the Little Bed of Jesus': Pictorial Piety and Monastic Reform," in *The Visual and the Visionary*, pp. 383–426; the poem is at p. 401. As Hamburger

points out (p. 392), the dominant erotic metaphor in such poems about the bed of the heart is not the bed but rather the chamber.

64. Hamburger, *Nuns as Artists*, p. 76.

65. See Keller, *Die Wiege*, pp. 7, 180–85; Roller, *Heilige Nacht*, pp. 46–51, 114–20, and 250–51; and Hamburger, "The Reformation of Vision: Art and the Dominican Observance in Late Medieval Germany," in *The Visual and the Visionary*, pp. 427–67; here at pp. 445–46. The motifs of Mary in childbed and of Mary (or the midwives) washing the baby go back to antiquity. For examples from the Nuremberg and Munich museums, and the Stiftsmuseum St. Florian, Austria, see https://commons.wikimedia.org/wiki/File:GNM_-_Maria_im_Wochenbett.jpg and https://www.zobodat.at/pdf/JOM_156_0049-0073.pdf (both accessed December 12, 2019).

66. Rublack, "Female Spirituality," p. 42.

67. See the introduction, n. 13. As Rachel Fulton Brown makes clear in her lengthy study *Mary and the Art of Prayer: The Hours of the Virgin in Medieval Christian Life and Thought* (New York: Columbia University Press, 2017), pp. 47–101, "temple," "house," "earth receiving the seed of Christ," and so on, are more common names for the Virgin than "stable" or "manger." But all the names stress containing and fertility.

68. Cited in van Os, *Art of Devotion*, p. 102, as *Van die gheestelijker kintheyt Jesu*, Antwerp 1488, BMH i14, Utrecht, Rijksmusuem Het Catharijneconvent. Available digitized as Universiteitsbibliotheek Gent 900000178752 (folios 104 and 105 missing): https://books.google.be/books?id=421PAAAAcAAJ&amp (accessed May 12, 2018). There are now about fifteen known copies of this book, of which five are in the Netherlands and four in Belgium. It was printed by Gerard Leeu. The Meditation on Jesus's Childhood (in eleven chapters) is the first of three meditations included. On the text, see Fons van Buuren, "'Van die gheestelike kintscheyt Jhesu ghemoraliseert': Een verkenning," in *Drukker zoekt publiek: Gheraert Leeu te Gouda, 1477–1484*, ed. Koen Goudriaan (Delft: Eburon, 1993), pp. 111–32, and Anna Dlabačová, "De houtsnede die niet bestond: Een gecorrigeerde afbeelding in het werk van Gerard Leeu," *Madoc. Tijdschrift over de Middeleeuwen* 30.3 (2016), pp. 28–40. I am grateful to Eleanor Goerss not only for directing my attention to this text and providing information about it but also for the analysis of the paradoxical quality of a meditation in which the praying woman is both lowly bed and the glorious throne of heaven. I am also grateful to Wijnie de Groot of the Department of Germanic Languages at Columbia University for help with the transcription and translation of this text.

69. See van Os, *Art of Devotion*, p. 102: "Men sal dit zuete kindeken ihesus nu opnemen ende heffen uut syn wiegelkyn. As hi selve seyt, men moet des menschen soen verheffen op dat alle die ghene die aen hem geloven niet en vergaen, mer hebben mogen dat eewige leven." In the digitized version, folios 23v–24r.

70. *Ibid.*, folios 37v–38r: "Men sal nu dit zuete cleyne kindeken wyeghen als het leyt in sijn crebbeken. Die deuote ziele voert hem alom ende leert hem wandelen ende bewaert

hem gelijc als dat licht van haren ooghen binnen in harer herten scrine staet gheset ihesus wyeghelken twelc sy bouenal wel wieghen ende wackelen can / . . . / so staet ihesus wieghelken / besloten in haer herteken Daer ihesus dit kindeken selue of spreket / ende seyt hyer wil ic ewelijc en altijt zijn." "Wackelen" is an archaic word for "rock."

71. *Ibid.*, folio 17r-v: "Niet met gulden laken behangen oft met duerbaer ghesteynte omset. maer in snooden doeckeren gewonden. In sulcker armoeden hebben syt gheuonden Ende dit kindeken hebben sij gheuonden in syn crebbeken. Glosa. Niet en sittet verheuen in conincckliker troonen. maer inder crebben Niet en regneert in des keysers pallays mer het is allendich in eenre couwer scueren."

72. *Ibid.*, folio 49r: "Och waer mijn lijf des hemels troon ende wel verciert met enghelen coren ende alle dinck daer in na sijn behoeren ende mijn herte waer daer af een palleys daer soude ghy int midden van dien pallayse eewlijc wonen. Ende soudet sijn mij heere ende ick u dienerse Ende oeck dat mijn beenen waren gulden pylarenen aen ene stoel ghewracht daer soudet ghy op sitten."

73. See n. 55.

74. See Keller, *Die Wiege*, p. 13; and n. 25 in this chapter.

75. Amy Knight Powell, *Depositions: Scenes from the Late Medieval Church and the Modern Museum* (New York: Zone Books, 2012), pp. 81–95, 167–209. On dressing statues, see Richard Trexler, "Der Heiligen neue Kleider: Eine analytische Skizze zur Be- und Entkleidung von Statuen," in Klaus Schreiner and Norbert Schnitzler, eds., *Gepeinigt, begehrt, vergessen: Symbolik und Sozialbezug des Körpers im späten Mittelalter und in der frühen Neuzeit* (Munich: Fink, 1992), pp. 362–402; Charlotte Klack-Eitzen, Wiebke Haase, and Tanja Weissgraf, *Heilige Röcke: Kleider für Skulpturen in Kloster Wienhausen* (Regensburg: Schnell & Steiner, 2013); and Caroline Walker Bynum, "Are Things 'Indifferent'? How Objects Change Our Understanding of Religious History," *German History* 34 (2016), pp. 88–112, esp. pp. 97–111. On moving and manipulatable figures, see Johannes Tripps, *Handelnde Bildwerk in der Gotik: Forschungen zu den Bedeutungsschichten und der Funktion des Kirchengebaudes und seiner Ausstattung in der Hoch- und Spätgotik* (Berlin: Gebr. Mann, 1998), and Berliner, *Die Weihnachtskrippe*, pp. 63–64.

76. Council of Trent, session XXV, in Theodore Alois Buckley, trans., *Canons and Decrees of the Council of Trent with a Supplement . . . Literally Translated into English* (London: George Routledge and Co., 1851), pp. 212–15. On Protestant reactions and how objects can carry earlier significances despite changes in theology, see Bynum, "Are Things 'Indifferent'?," esp. pp. 88–95.

77. Rublack, "Female Spirituality"; Jeffrey F. Hamburger, introduction to Klack-Eitzen, Haase, and Weissgraf, *Heilige Röcke*, pp. 7–8. See also Trexler, "Der Heiligen neue Kleider"; Klapisch-Zuber, "Holy Dolls"; and Jung, "The Tactile and the Visionary."

78. Thomas Lentes, "Die Gewänder der Heiligen — Ein Diskussionsbeitrag zum Verhältnis von Gebet, Bild und Imagination," in *Hagiographie und Kunst: Der Heiligenkult in*

Schrift, Bild und Architektur, ed. Gottfried Kerscher (Berlin: D. Reimer, 1993), pp. 120–51. For the painting, see pp. 124–25. For the example from Töss, see the introduction to this book, p. 120.

79. See the introduction, n. 37.

80. Hamburger, *Nuns as Artists*, p. 76

81. See n. 67.

82. See the introduction, pp. 49–53.

83. I have explored something of the same paradoxical quality in another late medieval devotional motif, the Gregory Mass; see Bynum, "Seeing and Seeing Beyond."

CHAPTER TWO: "CROWNED WITH MANY CROWNS"

1. This chapter was first published as "'Crowned with Many Crowns': Nuns and Their Statues in Late Medieval Wienhausen," *The Catholic Historical Review* 101.1 (2015), pp. 18–40. Volume 101 was the *CHR* Centennial issue edited by Maureen Miller, and I am grateful to her for the invitation to contribute and for her suggestions. I also thank Jeffrey Hamburger, Eva Schlotheuber, Evelin Wetter, and Henrike Lähnemann for generous assistance with images and Katharina Mauerhofer, who made the trip to the Abegg-Stiftung with me. The article is republished here with minor changes and additional images. The title of this essay is derived from the well-known hymn by Matthew Bridges (d. 1894), based on Revelation 19:12. In the hymn, the one crowned is Christ himself.

2. Seventeen cloisters and foundations are supervised by the Klosterkammer Hannover. See "Klosterkammer Hannover," https://www.klosterkammer.de (accessed April 15, 2014). In what follows I use material from the other five Lüneburg cloisters to supplement what we know about Wienhausen. On the Lüneburg cloisters, see Josef Dolle and Dennis Knochenhauer, eds., *Niedersächsisches Klosterbuch: Verzeichnis der Klöster, Stifte, Kommenden und Beginenhäuser in Niedersachsen und Bremen von den Anfängen bis 1810* (Bielefeld: Verlag für Regionalgeschichte, 2012), and Ida-Christine Riggert, *Die Lüneburger Frauenklöster* (Hannover: Hahnsche Buchhandlung, 1996).

3. On Wienhausen, see June L. Mecham, *Sacred Communities, Shared Devotions: Gender, Material Culture, and Monasticism in Late Medieval Germany*, eds. Alison I. Beach, Constance H. Berman, and Lisa M. Bitel (Turnhout: Brepols, 2014), with full bibliography. Mecham died, tragically young, before she was able to complete this volume. It remains indispensable for all scholars interested in German monasticism, women's history, and medieval devotional objects.

4. In the Lüneburg cloisters generally, the cult of the saints was forbidden and relics confiscated in 1555. Dieter Zimmerling, *Von Zeit und Ewigkeit: Die Lüneburger Klöster* (Braunschweig: Westermann, 1995), gives a good account of the Protestant Reformation. At Wienhausen, the relics of the main altar in the nuns' choir were removed in 1543. See Horst Appuhn, "Der Auferstandene und das Heilige Blut zu Wienhausen: Über

Kult und Kunst im späten Mittelalter," *Niederdeutsche Beiträge zur Kunstgeschichte* 1 (1961), pp. 73–138, at 78.

5. Horst Appuhn, and Christian von Heusinger, "Der Fund kleiner Andachtsbilder des 13. bis 17. Jahrhunderts in Kloster Wienhausen," *Niederdeutsche Beiträge zur Kunstgeschichte* 4 (1965), pp. 157–238, at 175 n. 24. For more on the statues' clothes, see Charlotte Klack-Eitzen, Wiebke Haase, and Tanja Weissgraf, *Heilige Röcke: Kleider für Skulpturen in Kloster Wienhausen* (Regensburg: Schnell & Steiner, 2013); and Caroline Walker Bynum, "Are Things 'Indifferent'? How Objects Change Our Understanding of Religious History," *German History* 34 (2016), pp. 88–112, esp. pp. 102–10.

6. See Horst Appuhn, *Kloster Wienhausen, 4: Der Fund vom Nonnenchor* (Wienhausen: Wienhausen Verlag, 1973); Appuhn and von Heusinger, "Der Fund"; and Wiebke Michler, *Kloster Wienhausen: Die Wandmalereien im Nonnenchor* (Wienhausen: Kloster Wienhausen, 1968), p. 59. The painting was probably initially done soon after the choir was built in 1308; the Chronicle tells us that it was renewed in 1488 by three nuns named Gertrude; it was again restored in 1867–68. Since the rather sharp black outlines of the figures long continued to show through, it is likely that the restorers followed the originals closely. Moreover, the paintings as we see them today follow the style of the late Romanesque of the region.

7. Johann Michael Fritz, "Die bewahrende Kraft des Luthertums—Mittelalterliche Kunstwerke in evangelischen Kirchen," and Günther Wartenberg, "Bilder in den Kirchen der Wittenberger Reformation," in *Die bewahrende Kraft des Luthertums: Mittelalterliche Kunstwerke in evangelischen Kirchen*, ed. Johann Michael Fritz (Regensburg: Schnell & Steiner, 1997), pp. 9–18 and 19–33, and Jeffrey F. Hamburger, "Am Anfang war das Bild: Kunst und Frauenspiritualität im Spätmittelalter," in *Studien und Texte zur literarischen und materiellen Kultur der Frauenklöster im späten Mittelalter: Ergebnisse eines Arbeitsgesprächs in der Herzog August Bibliothek Wolfenbüttel, 24.–26. Febr. 1999*, eds. Falk Eisermann, Eva Schlotheuber, and Volker Honemann (Leiden: Brill, 2004), pp. 1–43, at pp. 3–5. In her introduction to *Iconography of Liturgical Textiles in the Middle Ages*, ed. Evelin Wetter (Riggisberg: Abegg-Stiftung, 2010), pp. 7–15, Wetter comments on the large number of survivals in Protestant Hungary.

8. The goal of providing for daughters and widows was not the only reason for survival. Piety continued. See Wolfgang Brandis, "Quellen zur Reformationsgeschichte der Lüneburger Frauenklöster," in Eisermann, Schlotheuber, and Honemann, eds., *Studien und Texte*, pp. 357–91, at pp. 359–60, and Merry Wiesner-Hanks, introduction to *Convents Confront the Reformation: Catholic and Protestant Nuns in Germany*, eds. and trans. Merry Wiesner-Hanks and Joan Skocir (Milwaukee: Marquette University Press, 2004). But spiritual life slowly attenuated.

9. Horst Appuhn, *Kloster Wienhausen: Aufnahmen von Hans Grubenbecher, Dietrich Klatt und Jens Rheinländer* (Wienhausen: Wienhausen Verlag, 1986), pp. 22–23, 61.

10. Ulinka Rublack, "Female Spirituality and the Infant Jesus in Late Medieval Dominican Convents," *Gender and History* 6.1 (1994), pp. 37–57.

11. See Werner Williams-Krapp, "'Dise ding sint dennoch nit ware zeichen der heiligkeit': Zur Bewertung mystischer Erfahrungen im 15. Jahrhundert," *Zeitschrift für Literaturwissenschaft und Linguistik* 80 (1990), pp. 61–71, at pp. 66–67; and Claire Taylor Jones, "Rekindling the Light of Faith: Hymn Translation and Spiritual Renewal in the Fifteenth-Century Observant Reform," *Journal of Medieval and Early Modern Studies* 42.3 (2012), pp. 567–96, at pp. 570 and 592 n. 12.

12. *Chronik und Totenbuch des Klosters Wienhausen*, intro. Horst Appuhn, 3rd ed. (Wienhausen: Kloster Wienhausen, 1986). On sources generally, see Brandis, "Quellen."

13. See Klack-Eitzen, Haase, and Weissgraf, *Heilige Röcke*, p. 52. A dress for the naked Christ Child held by the so-called processional Madonna (discussed later in this chapter) also survives. *Ibid.*, p. 53. For an example of these dresses, see figure 1.17.

14. These garments have recently been published in a magnificent catalogue with detailed discussion; see Klack-Eitzen, Haase, and Weissgraf, *Heilige Röcke*.

15. *Chronik und Totenbuch*, pp. xlii, xliv, and lxi. (Page numbers refer to those of the original manuscript. Arabic numerals refer to the *Chronik*; Roman numerals refer to the *Totenbuch*. For the Chronicle, the editor has reordered the material to make it chronological.) Medieval memorial books record the date of death so the donor or his/her family could expect prayers on that day, but do not record year of death, that not being important for ritual remembrance. In some cases, historians can determine the year of death by cross reference to mentions of the person in other documents.

16. Klack-Eitzen, Haase, and Weissgraf, *Heilige Röcke*, pp. 21–23; Hamburger, "Am Anfang," pp. 33 and 35. The Christ Child from Heiligkreuz is still sometimes displayed with his crown.

17. *Krone und Schleier: Kunst aus mittelalterlichen Frauenklöstern*, catalogue for two exhibits: Ruhrlandmuseum, Essen: *Die frühen Klöster und Stifte, 500–1200*, and Kunst- und Ausstellungshalle der Bundesrepublik Deutschland, Bonn: *Die Zeit der Orden, 1200–1500* (Munich: Hirmer, 2005), pp. 394–95. On the parallel to bridal wreaths, see Désirée Koslin, "The Robe of Simplicity: Initiation, Robing, and Veiling of Nuns in the Middle Ages," in *Robes and Honor: The Medieval World of Investiture*, ed. Stewart Gordon (Basingstoke: Palgrave, 2001), pp. 255–74, which uses almost exclusively English material.

18. N. Gussone, "Krönung," and H. Laag, "Kranz," in *Lexikon der Christlichen Ikonographie*, 2 (Freiburg: Herder, 1970), cols. 661–71 and 558–60; and E. Vavra "Kleidung," and V. H. Elbern, "Krone," *Lexikon des Mittelalters*, vol. 5 (Munich: Deutscher Taschenbuch Verlag, 2002), cols. 1198–1200 and 1544–47.

19. *Krone und Schleier*, pp. 166–67. In 1474, Mary of York's wedding crown was presented to the cathedral at Aachen, where it is still today placed on a devotional statue at festivals; see Klack-Eitzen, Haase, and Weissgraf, *Heilige Röcke*, p. 21.

20. *Chronik*, pp. 22–23. According to Brandis, "Quellen," p. 391, the sixteenth-century reformers showed some bad conscience about later confiscations of the nuns' property.

21. On efforts by the reformers Johannes Meyer and Johannes Busch to curb private devotion, which also make clear that it continued, see Jeffrey F. Hamburger, *The Visual and the Visionary: Art and Female Spirituality in Late Medieval Germany* (New York: Zone Books, 1998), pp. 440–41.

22. Robert Suckale, *Die mittelalterlichen Damenstifte als Bastionen der Frauenmacht* (Cologne: Otto Schmidt, 2001).

23. *Chronik*, p. 32. The vision of St. Anne received by the ill abbess Katharina von Hoya shortly before 1433 is also instructive; *Chronik*, p. 14. Understanding herself to be chastised for spending lavishly on her private dwelling, the aristocratic abbess made that dwelling into a chapel. But the resplendent dress of the St. Anne who appeared to her was understood to be entirely appropriate. See June Mecham, "Katharina von Hoya's Saint Anne Chapel: Female Piety, Material Culture, and Monastic Space on the Eve of the Reformation," in *Frauen-Kloster-Kunst: Neue Forschungen zur Kulturgeschichte des Mittelalters: Beiträge zum Internationalen Kolloquium vom 13. bis 16. Mai 2005 anlässlich der Ausstellung "Krone und Schleier,"* eds. Jeffrey F. Hamburger, Carola Jäggi, Susan Marti, and Hedwig Röckelein in cooperation with the Ruhrlandmuseum Essen (Turnhout: Brepols, 2007), pp. 177–85.

24. Nowhere in late medieval piety is there the assumption that equality of religious value or of piety means sameness. However much the Observant reformers may have wished to enforce upon women's houses both claustration and poverty, no medieval Christian could fail to note (as both text and image clearly demonstrated) that even after the Last Judgment, resurrected bodies would bear their individuality and indicate their unequal statuses in their headgear. See n. 64. For an excellent discussion of the nuns' relationship to "property," both before and after the Observant reform, see Mecham, *Sacred Communities*, pp. 89–126.

25. Susanna Potstock (1470–1501), a reformer who was accepted by the convent, and Katharina Remstede (1501–1549), who was driven from the cloister for several years during efforts to impose the Lutheran Reformation.

26. See Appuhn, *Kloster Wienhausen: Aufnahmen*, plate 27.

27. Richard Trexler, "Der Heiligen neue Kleider: Eine analytische Skizze zur Be- und Entkleidung von Statuen, " in *Gepeinigt, begehrt, vergessen: Symbolik und Sozialbezug des Körpers im späten Mittelalter und in der frühen Neuzeit*, eds. Klaus Schreiner and Norbert Schnitzler (Munich: Fink, 1992), pp. 362–402; Christiane Klapisch-Zuber, "Holy Dolls: Play and Devotion in Florence in the Quattrocento," in *Women, Family, and Ritual in Renaissance Italy*, ed. Christiane Klapisch-Zuber (Chicago: University of Chicago Press, 1985), pp. 310–31; Rublack, "Female Spirituality and the Infant Jesus"; Hamburger, introduction to Klack-Eitzen, Haase, and Weissgraf, *Heilige Röcke*, pp. 7–8; Amy Knight Powell, *Depositions: Scenes from the Late Medieval Church and the Modern Museum* (New York: Zone Books, 2012), pp. 81–95, 167–209. See also chapter 1 and figure 1.17.

28. I borrow the phrase "devotional logic of presence" from Robert A. Orsi, *The*

Madonna of 115th Street: Faith and Community in Italian Harlem, 1880–1950, 3rd ed. (New Haven, CT: Yale University Press, 2010), p. xvi; I have called this way of seeing the "concomitant habit of mind" in Caroline Walker Bynum, *Christian Materiality: An Essay on Religion in Late Medieval Europe* (New York: Zone Books, 2011), pp. 208–15. *Do ut des* — I give that you may give — is frequently invoked as a fundamental characteristic of religious worship.

29. Thomas Lentes, "Die Gewänder der Heiligen — Ein Diskussionsbeitrag zum Verhältnis von Gebet, Bild und Imagination," in *Hagiographie und Kunst: Der Heiligenkult in Schrift, Bild und Architektur*, ed. Gottfried Kerscher (Berlin: Reimer, 1993), pp. 120–51. See also the introduction to this book, pp. 14–15.

30. Lentes, "Die Gewänder," pp. 124–25. On the development of rosary devotion in this period and its importance for nuns, see *Rosenkränze und Seelengärten: Bildung und Frömmigkeit in niedersächsischen Frauenklöstern*, ed. Britta-Juliane Kruse (Wiesbaden: Harrassowitz, 2013), especially Julie Hotchin, "Meditations for a Nun's Coronation from Wöltingerode," pp. 117–24. See also June Mecham, "Reading Between the Lines: Compilation, Variation, and the Recovery of an Authentic Female Voice in the *Dornenkron* Prayer Books from Wienhausen," *Journal of Medieval History* 29.2 (2003), pp. 109–28, at p. 121, with examples of nuns offering crowns of prayers to Mary. For the St. Ursula example, see Hamburger, *The Visual and the Visionary*, p. 78 n. 208.

31. *Chronik*, p. 142. We are told explicitly that this story concerns the crown that "was at the time of the first reformation taken out of the cloister along with many other things."

32. *Ibid.*, pp. 67–70.

33. Eva Schlotheuber, *Klostereintritt und Bildung: Die Lebenswelt der Nonnen im späten Mittelalter. Mit einer Edition des 'Konventstagebuchs' einer Zisterzienserin von Heilig-Kreuz bei Braunschweig (1484–1507)* (Tübingen: Mohr Siebeck, 2004); Eva Schlotheuber, "Ebstorf und seine Schülerinnen in der zweiten Hälfte des 15. Jahrhundert," in Eisermann, Schlotheuber, and Honemann, eds., *Studien und Texte*, pp. 169–221; Eva Schlotheuber, "Klostereintritt und Übergangsriten: Die Bedeutung der Jungfräulichkeit für das Selbstverständnis der Nonnen der Alten Orden," in *Frauen-Kloster-Kunst*, pp. 43–55; and Eva Schlotheuber, "Best Clothes and Everyday Attire of Late Medieval Nuns," in *Fashion and Clothing in Late Medieval Europe/Mode und Kleidung im Europa des späten Mittelalters*, eds. Rainer C. Schwinges and Regula Schorta with Klaus Oschema (Basel and Riggisberg: Schwabe Verlag and Abegg-Stiftung, 2010), pp. 139–54. See also Evelin Wetter, "Von Bräuten und Vikaren Christi. Zur Konstruktion von Ähnlichkeit im sakralen Initiationsakt," in Martin Gaier, Jeanette Kohl, and Alberto Saviello, eds., *Similitudo: Konzepte der Ähnlichkeit in Mittelalter und Früher Neuzeit* (Munich: Fink, 2012), pp. 129–46.

34. Quoted in Gil Bartholeyns, "Les objets contre les symboles: Une sociologie chrétienne et médiévale du signe," in *La performance des images*, eds. Alain Dierkens, Gil Bartholeyns, and Thomas Golsenne (Brussels: Éditions de l'Université de Bruxelles, 2010), pp. 137–56, at p. 142.

35. *Ibid.*, pp. 138–39 and 147. The case in 1199 concerned the practice of taking the

monastic habit at the end of life. Jean-Claude Schmitt, "Les images et le sacré," *ibid.*, pp. 29–46, and Thomas Golsenne, "Parure et culte," *ibid.*, pp. 71–85, are also helpful.

36. Schlotheuber, *Klostereintritt und Bildung*, pp. 139–40.

37. *Ibid.*, p. 160.

38. The idea that convents served primarily to educate the female children of the aristocracy before they left to marry is a mistaken interpretation by modern historians, who have extrapolated back from the post-Reformation period, although such uses of convents were undoubtedly sometimes made; see generally Schlotheuber, *Klostereintritt und Bildung*. She cites a late fifteenth-century chronicler who warns that secular girls with their "worldly clothing" in red and gold, with pearls and expensive headbands, would bring "corruption" for the future nuns (pp. 112–14).

39. At the Holy Cross cloister in Braunschweig, for example, the crucial term for transition to nun's status became the coinage *dies mansacionis* (from *mansare* or *manere*) — that is, the day on which the nun moved into her own cell. Schlotheuber, "Klostereintritt und Übergangsriten," p. 50. See also Julie Hotchin, "The Nun's Crown," *Early Modern Women: An Interdisciplinary Journal* 4 (2009), pp. 187–94.

40. J. Schneider, "Kleiderordnungen," in *Lexikon des Mittelalters*, vol. 5, cols. 1197–98, and Ulinka Rublack, *Dressing Up: Cultural Identity in Renaissance Europe* (Oxford: Oxford University Press, 2010), pp. 81–123.

41. Wetter, "Von Bräuten," p. 130, and Schlotheuber, "Best Clothes," p. 146. On head-covering as a sign of status, and its difference for men and women, see Gabriela Signori, "Veil, Hat or Hair? Reflections on an Asymmetrical Relationship," *The Medieval History Journal* 8.1 (2005), pp. 25–47.

42. Hotchin, "The Nun's Crown"; Wetter, "Von Bräuten"; Schlotheuber, "Best Clothes"; Koslin, "The Robe of Simplicity."

43. Schlotheuber, *Klostereintritt und Bildung*, p. 162 n. 204, and Schlotheuber, "Best Clothes," p. 153 n. 61.

44. Hotchin, "The Nun's Crown," p. 194 n. 19. The chronicler of the monastery of Heiningen near Hildesheim rejoiced, during a brief period of re-Catholicization: "We put on our crowns again."

45. The reference in Abelard is cited in Wetter, "Von Bräuten," p. 134 n. 24; Tengswich's letter is cited at p. 135 n. 27, and Schlotheuber, "Best Clothes," p. 153. For Hildegard's defense, which rests on the claim that her virgins are wedded to holiness, see Barbara Newman, *Sister of Wisdom: St. Hildegard's Theology of the Feminine* (Berkeley: University of California Press, 1987), pp. 221–22. The real veils and crowns described in Tengswich's letter are identical to those in Hildegard's vision in *Scivias* 2.5, see Hildegard of Bingen, *Scivias*, 2 vols., Corpus christianorum: continuatio mediaevalis, 43 and 43 A (Turnhout: Brepols, 1978), vol. 43, pp. 174–75 and plate 14.

46. Johannes Busch, "Liber de reformatione monasteriorum," in *Chronicon*

Windeshemense und Liber de reformatione monasteriorum, ed. Karl Grube (Halle: Hendel, 1886), p. 603.

47. I am grateful to Henrike Lähnemann for these references; she points also to Hildesheim Dombibliothek MS J 29 (H11) fol. 52r. See Ulrike Hascher-Burger and Henrike Lähnemann, *Liturgie und Reform im Kloster Medingen: Edition und Untersuchung des Propst-Handbuchs Oxford, Bodleian Library, MS Lat. liturg. e. 18* (Tübingen: Mohr Siebeck, 2013), pp. 99–103, at p. 101; Hans-Walter Stork, "Handschriften des ehemaligen Zisterzienserinnenklosters Medingen zur Zeit der Klosterreform im 15. Jahrhundert und in nachreformatorischer Zeit," in *Evangelisches Klosterleben: Studien zur Geschichte der evangelischen Klöster und Stifte in Niedersachsen*, ed. Hans Otte (Göttingen: V & R Unipress, 2013), pp. 337–60, at pp. 349–53 and fig. 6; and Henrike Lähnemann, "Schnipsel, Schleier, Textkombinatorik: Die Materialität der Medinger Orationalien," in *Materialität in der Editionswissenschaft*, ed. Martin Schubert, Beihefte zu editio 32 (Tübingen: De Gruyter, 2010), pp. 347–58, at p. 352. See also Henrike Lähnemann, Laura Godfrey, Joseph Leake, Gennifer Dorgan, and Micah James Goodrich, "The Medingen Manuscripts at Harvard: Houghton Library's MS Lat 395 and MS Lat 440," *Harvard Library Bulletin* 28.2 (Summer 2017), pp. 1-56.

48. For the little image of Bernward of Hildesheim venerated by a nun in her crown, see Appuhn, *Kloster Wienhausen*, 4: *Der Fund*, p. 33; for the vault painting, see Michler, *Kloster Wienhausen: Die Wandmalereien*, p. 59.

49. Elizabeth Perry, "Convents, Art and Creole Identity in Late Viceregal New Spain," in *Women and Art in Early Modern Latin America*, eds. Kellen Kee MacIntyre and Richard E. Phillips (Leiden: Brill, 2007), p. 338. The crowns worn by Latin American nuns look very much like some of the crowns that survive for medieval statues. See Hamburger, "Am Anfang," pp. 33 and 35, figs. 4, 7, and 8. At Marienstern in Saxony, the nuns who vow perpetual virginity are even today buried with their myrtle crowns; Marius Winzeler, "Die Bibliothek der Zisterzienserinnenabtei St. Marienstern. Zu Geschichte und Bestand einer frauenklösterlichen Büchersammlung des Mittelalters," in Eisermann, Schlotheuber, and Honemann, eds., *Studien und Texte*, pp. 331–56, here p. 342. For an image of the Bridgettines' crown, see https://en.wikipedia.org/wiki/Bridgettines (accessed November 30, 2013). For the Handmaids of the Precious Blood, who today wear circlets of real thorns at their profession and in death, see "Handmaids of the Precious Blood," https://nunsforpriests.org (accessed November 30, 2013).

50. For an eighteenth-century portrait by an unknown artist of a Conceptionist nun, who wears a silver crown adorned with what appear to be real roses, see Ilona Katzew et al., eds., *Painted in Mexico: 1700–1790: Pinxit Mexici*, Catalogue of Exhibit at Los Angeles County Museum and Fomento Cultural Banamex, A.C., Mexico City (Munich/London/New York: Delmonico Books/Prestel, 2018), p. 329, plate 85. The nun's own hair is modestly covered with a veil, which is itself covered with a heavy embroidered covering (a kind of second veil) that points downward; the crown rests on this covering. The nun herself clutches a doll of the sort discussed in chapter 1. The painting suggests to me that there is much to explore about

the clothing and material objects characteristic of early modern nuns in the New World.

51. Mecham, "Reading Between the Lines," and Mecham, *Sacred Communities*, pp. 205–60. On the "Find," see n. 5 in this chapter.

52. Schlotheuber, *Klostereintritt und Bildung*, p. 164 n. 217: "In corona sunt quattuor cruces rubee cum trans{ . . . }nant crucifixi sponsi nostri quinque vulnera, quod in signum Christi vulnerati gerebimus in capite, ut semper simus memores nostri sponsi, in canticis ubi dicit: 'Vulnerasti cor meum, soror mea sponsa,' scilicet per amorem."

53. *Ibid.*, p. 162. On the occasion of her nieces' investiture, an abbess of Medingen called the new nuns "co-citizens of the angels"; p. 166: "concives angelorum."

54. As this book was going to press, news broke of the claim, made by Evelyn Wetter, Curator at the Abegg-Stiftung, and Philippe Cortez, a Paris art historian, that the crown was one made for Hildegard of Bingen at the end of her life. See the article "Schweiz: Nonnenkrone der Hildegard von Bingen identifiziert," in *Vatican News* (February 20, 2020), at https://www.vaticannews.va/de/kirche/news/2020-02/schweiz-deutschland-hildegard-von-bingen-geschichte-kirche-orden.html. I have not been able yet to acquire the Wetter and Cortez monograph. For a color image, see Schlotheuber, "Best Clothes," p. 146 fig. 7. We owe the discovery that the textile is a nun's crown to Schlotheuber.

55. Wetter, "Von Bräuten."

56. Gertrude of Helfta, *Oeuvres spirituelles*, 1: *Les Exercices* 3, eds. Jacques Hourlier and Albert Schmitt (Paris: Éditions du Cerf, 1967), pp. 98 and 104; also Gertrude the Great of Helfta, *Spiritual Exercises* 3, trans. Gertrud Jaron Lewis and Jack Lewis (Kalamazoo: Cistercian Publications, 1989), pp. 43 and 47. And on Gertrude's use of clothing metaphors, see Michael Bangert, "The Metaphor of the Vestment in the Writings of Gertrud of Helfta (1256–1302)," in *Iconography of Liturgical Textiles*, ed. Wetter (see n. 6), pp. 129–39.

57. See Gertrude, *Legatus divinae pietatis* 3.18, eds. Monks of Solesmes, *Revelationes Gertrudianae ac Mechtildianae* (Paris: Oudin, 1875–77), vol. 1, p. 151: Christ speaks: "Ecce jam induor te ad hoc ut delicatam manum meam illaesam extendere possim inter hispidos peccatores, ad benefaciendum eis; et vestio te meipso ad hoc, ut omnes quos in tua memoria ad meam ducis praesentiam . . . ad illam trahas dignitatem, ut eis secundum meam regalem munificentiam benefacere possim."

58. Gertrude, *Les Exercices* 3, p. 118; *Exercises* 3, p. 54.

59. Gertrude, *Legatus* 3.65, pp. 241–42.

60. Schlotheuber, *Klostereintritt und Bildung*, pp. 164–65 nn. 220–23.

61. Staatsbibliothek zu Berlin — Preussischer Kulturbesitz MS germ. oct. 265, fols. 90v–92r, which is Medingen BE 3, a Middle Low German prayer book from the Cistercian Convent of Medingen, Lower Saxony; probably written by a lay sister. I thank Henrike Lähnemann for calling my attention to this.

62. "Wan de leve got horet dat loff der hilgen cristenheit so secht he to der innigen sele also: 'Resurrexi et adhuc tecum sum' — Ick bin upgestan van dem dode unde hebbe wedder

to mi genamen alle de clarcheit unde ere, de ik gehad hebbe van ambeginne der werlt. 'Et adhuc tecum sum' — unde bin noch mi di, o innige sele, virmiddelst miner gnade unde an mi is behude salicheit, de du van mi nemen scholt, wan ik van desser werlt di to me neme darumme dat du mi nu to di nimpst in waren loven. Denne wil ik up di lecghen de hant miner ere unde wil di kronen, darumme dat du underwilen mine hant drichst vei wesen in der ewigen froude. Denne scholtu wunderlick openbaren den enghelschen gheisten, wan ik dinen sterfflicken licham wedder schippen wille, lick gebildet der clarcheit mines lichammes. Dit scholtu tomalen emfangen na dessem levende, alse ik in miner upstandinge twevolt entfangen hebbe an miner gotheit unde an miner minscheit." Transcription by Henrike Lähnemann; translation by Lähnemann and Bynum.

63. *Clarcheit* or *claritas* is one of the four gifts with which the immortal soul endows the resurrected body, according to scholastic theology; see Caroline Walker Bynum, *The Resurrection of the Body in Western Christianity, 200–1336*, expanded edition (New York: Columbia University Press, 2017), pp. 131–32.

64. See, for example, Bynum, *Resurrection of the Body*, plate 33.

65. Winzeler, "Die Bibliothek," p. 343, fig. 3; see n. 48 in this chapter.

66. Johan Huizinga, *The Autumn of the Middle Ages*, trans. Rodney J. Payton and Ulrich Mammitzsch (Chicago: University of Chicago Press, 1996). See the introduction to this book, pp. 40–41.

67. Gertrude, *Legatus* 1.1, pp. 10–11. A translator of the work, whose translation of the passage in question differs from mine, reports that she has found no work by Hugh of St. Victor to which the author might refer here. Gertrude, *The Herald of Divine Love,* 1.1, trans. Margaret Winkworth (New York: Paulist Press, 1993), p. 89 n. 8. Gertrude, *Oeuvres spirituelles* 2: *Le Héraut,* 1.1, ed. Pierre Doyère (Paris: Éditions du Cerf, 1968), pp. 126–27, gives no reference.

68. It is worth underlining the importance given to glory, heavenly marriage, and resurrection in the piety of northern German convents, especially at Wienhausen with its numerous depictions — in glass, wall paintings, sculpture, and small devotional images — of the risen Christ. See Appuhn, "Der Auferstandene." The emphasis in much of the scholarly literature on suffering, violence, and pain in late medieval spirituality is, at least for these houses, considerably overdone.

CHAPTER THREE: THE SACRALITY OF THINGS

1. This essay was first published as "The Sacrality of Things: An Inquiry into Divine Materiality in the Christian Middle Ages," *Irish Theological Quarterly* 78.1 (2013), pp. 3–18. It is reprinted, with minor revision and additions, by permission of Sage Publishing. I thank Salvador Ryan of St. Patrick's College, Maynooth, for the invitation to deliver the lecture that became this essay and for his hospitality during my trip to Ireland. I thank Richard Davis for his generosity in sharing ideas during several conversations about Indian images.

2. Among many recent collections of essays on the topics of materiality and material culture, I find especially important Lorraine Daston, ed., *Things That Talk: Object Lessons from Art and Science* (New York: Zone Books, 2004); Daniel Miller, ed., *Materiality* (Durham, NC: Duke University Press, 2005); David Morgan, ed., *Religion and Material Culture: The Matter of Belief* (London: Routledge, 2010); and Suzanna Ivanič, Mary Laven, and Andrew Morrall, eds., *Religious Materiality in the Early Modern World* (Amsterdam: Amsterdam University Press, 2019). The caveats of Tim Ingold are apposite; see Tim Ingold, "Materials Against Materiality," *Archaeological Dialogues* 14 (2007), pp. 1–16. The much-cited article by Bill Brown, is, in my judgment, too general to be very helpful; see Bill Brown, "Thing Theory," *Critical Inquiry* 28 (2001), pp. 1–22. See the introduction to this volume, n. 38.

3. Webb Keane, "The Evidence of the Senses and the Materiality of Religion," *Journal of the Royal Anthropological Institute* 14 (2008), pp. 110–27, at p. 124. See also Elisabeth Arweck and William Keenan, "Introduction: Material Varieties of Religious Expression," in *Materializing Religion: Expression, Performance and Ritual*, eds. Elisabeth Arweck and William Keenan (Oxford: Ashgate, 2006), pp. 1–20.

4. On the eye-opening ceremony, see Richard H. Davis, *Lives of Indian Images* (Princeton, NJ: Princeton University Press, 1997), pp. 33–37; Stephen P. Huyler, "The Experience: Approaching God," in *The Life of Hinduism*, eds. John Stratton Hawley and Vasudha Narayanan (Berkeley: University of California Press, 2006), pp. 33–41; and Wendy Doniger, *The Hindus: An Alternative History* (New York: Penguin, 2009), p. 352.

5. Linda Hess, "An Open-Air Ramayana: Ramlila, the Audience Experience," in Hawley and Narayanan, eds., *The Life of Hinduism*, pp. 128–29, and Huyler, "Experience," p. 36.

6. Davis, *Lives*, p. 39.

7. Josh Ellenbogen and Aaron Tugendhaft, eds., introduction to *Idol Anxiety* (Stanford, CA: Stanford University Press, 2011), pp. 1–2; and Beate Pongratz-Leisten, "Divine Agency and Astralization of the Gods in Ancient Mesopotamia," in *Reconsidering the Concept of Revolutionary Monotheism*, ed. Beate Pongratz-Leisten (Winona Lake, IN: Eisenbrauns, 2011), pp. 137–85, esp. pp. 149–50.

8. On "distributive agency," see Beate Pongratz-Leisten, "A New Agenda for the Study of the Rise of Monotheism," in *Reconsidering the Concept*, pp. 21–22. On "representation," see Alfred Gell, *Art and Agency: An Anthropological Theory* (Oxford: Oxford University Press, 1998).

9. See Richard H. Davis, ed., *Images, Miracles, and Authority in Asian Religious Traditions* (Boulder, CO: Westview Press, 1998), especially Robert L. Brown, "Expected Miracles: The Unsurprisingly Miraculous Nature of Buddhist Images and Relics," pp. 23–36.

10. For one example of this, see Ellenbogen and Tugendhaft, eds., introduction to *Idol Anxiety*, pp. 8–9. In the Eastern Church, even after the iconoclastic controversy, images are understood to in some sense "participate in" and not merely represent the divine. On Eastern iconoclasm, see Leslie Brubaker, *Inventing Byzantine Iconoclasm* (London: Bristol

Classical Press, 2012), and Leslie Brubaker and John Haldon, *Byzantium in the Iconoclast Era, c. 680–850* (Cambridge: Cambridge University Press, 2011).

11. Laura Kendrick, *Animating the Letter: The Figurative Embodiment of Writing from Late Antiquity to the Renaissance* (Columbus: Ohio State University Press, 1999), p. 188, has pointed out that early in the development of a tradition, the divine is often revealed by unlike as well as by like objects.

12. On sixteenth-century iconoclasm, see Margaret Aston, *England's Iconoclasts*, vol. 1: *Laws against Images* (Oxford: Clarendon, 1988); Lee Palmer Wandel, *Voracious Idols and Violent Hands: Iconoclasm in Reformation Zurich, Strasbourg, and Basel* (Cambridge: Cambridge University Press, 1995); Peter Marshall, *The Reformation: A Very Short Introduction* (Oxford: Oxford University Press, 2009), pp. 72–76; Caroline Walker Bynum, "Are Things 'Indifferent'? How Objects Change Our Understanding of Religious History," *German History* 34 (2016), pp. 88–112; Bynum, *Christian Materiality: An Essay on Religion in Late Medieval Europe* (New York: Zone, 2011), pp. 269–73; and Bynum, "Interrogating 'Likeness': Fake Friends, *Similia Similibus*, and Heavenly Crowns," *Historische Anthropologie* 28.1 (2020), pp. 31–56. For the point that hostility to images is always an acknowledgment of the power lodged within them, see Jeremy Dimmick, James Simpson, and Nicolette Zeeman, introduction to *Images, Idolatry, and Iconoclasm in Late Medieval England*, eds. Jeremy Dimmick, James Simpson, and Nicolette Zeeman (Oxford: Oxford University, 2002), p. 1; and Horst Bredekamp, *Kunst als Medium sozialer Konflikte: Bilderkämpfe von der Spätantike bis zur Hussitenrevolution* (Frankfurt am Main: Suhrkamp, 1975), pp. 299–300.

13. *Sacrosancti et Oecumenici Concilii Tridentini Paolo III, Julio III et Pio IV, pontificibus maximis, celebrati canones et decreta: Pluribus annexis ad idem concilium spectantibus* (Mechelen: J. Hanicq, 1862), pp. 270–74. The Council also legislated against new miracles and new relics unless investigated by a bishop.

14. On the late medieval turn to inward devotion and the suspicion of sight, see Jeffrey F. Hamburger, "Seeing and Believing: The Suspicion of Sight and the Authentication of Vision in Late Medieval Art and Devotion," in *Imagination und Wirklichkeit: Zum Verhältnis von mentalen und realen Bildern in der Kunst der frühen Neuzeit*, eds. Alessandro Nova and Klaus Krüger (Mainz: Philipp von Zabern, 2000), pp. 47–70; Bynum, *Christian Materiality*, pp. 269–71 and p. 298 n. 1; and the introduction to this book at n. 37. The later Middle Ages also saw an important emphasis on taking in, even eating (*manducatio*), through sight that has parallels to the Hindu concept of *darshan*.

15. David Freedberg, *The Power of Images: Studies in the History and Theory of Response* (Chicago: University of Chicago Press, 1989), pp. 89–91. Blessed images are "sacramentals," as are holy water, blessed wheat or flowers, religious medals, and so forth.

16. See articles "Bénédiction" and "Consécration" in *Dictionnaire de droit canonique* (Paris: Letouzey et Ané, 1935–1965), vol. 2 (1937), cols. 349–74 and vol. 4 (1949), cols. 248–67, by Auguste Molien and Pierre Bayard, respectively.

17. On the question of how far such early statues do contain relics, see Ilene H. Forsyth, *The Throne of Wisdom: Wood Sculptures of the Madonna in Romanesque France* (Princeton, NJ: Princeton University Press, 1972).

18. Hans Belting, *Likeness and Presence: A History of the Image before the Era of Art*, trans. Edmund Jephcott (Chicago: University of Chicago Press, 1994). The title of the English translation does not quite capture the contrast of *Bild* and *Kult* in the German original, but the German *Bild* (picture, image, etc.) is hard to translate.

19. An excellent example of an account that stresses social control is Charles Zika, "Hosts, Processions and Pilgrimages: Controlling the Sacred in Fifteenth-Century Germany," *Past & Present* 118 (1988), pp. 25–64. Sociological or functionalist explanations, like those from cognitive science, are not on the same level of interpretation as those which refer to cultural intention, such as consecration or miraculous origin, and can, of course, coexist with them.

20. Erik Thunø and Gerhard Wolf, eds., *The Miraculous Image in the Late Middle Ages and Renaissance* (Rome: L'Erma di Bretschneider, 2004).

21. An especially effective contribution to the effort to turn our attention away from the visual and toward the tactile (or haptic) is Jacqueline Jung, "The Tactile and the Visionary: Notes on the Place of Sculpture in the Medieval Religious Imagination," in *Looking Beyond: Visions, Dreams, and Insights in Medieval Art and History*, ed. Colum Hourihane, Index of Christian Art Occasional Papers 11 (Princeton, NJ: Princeton University, 2010), pp. 202–40. See the introduction to this book, nn. 58–61.

22. Freedberg, *Power*, pp. 100–104. See also Christopher S. Wood, "Ritual and the Virgin on the Column: The Cult of the Schöne Maria in Regensburg," *Journal of Ritual Studies* 6.1 (1992), pp. 87–107.

23. On sacramentals, the classic work is Adolph Franz, *Die kirchlichen Benediktionen im Mittelalter*, 2 vols. (Freiburg: Herder, 1909).

24. Caroline Walker Bynum, *Wonderful Blood: Theology and Practice in Late Medieval Northern Germany and Beyond* (Philadelphia: University of Pennsylvania Press, 2007), p. 58.

25. Jan Assmann makes a slightly different point from mine here, arguing that it matters whether one sees the force of the injunction as "Thou shalt not make" or "Thou shalt not adore . . . nor serve." See Jan Assmann, "What's Wrong with Images?" in Ellenbogen and Tugendhaft, eds., *Idol Anxiety*, pp. 19–31.

26. The fundamental point of my book *Christian Materiality* is to underline the importance in the Western tradition of anxiety about matter as the locus of change.

27. Bremer says "*are* of the humanity" and "*were* joined." He would seem to be arguing here the traditional Franciscan position that the blood of Christ's body had been assumed by the Logos in the womb, but that shed blood was not united with the Logos during the *triduum* (the three days between Good Friday and Easter Sunday); hence, a bit of it could remain behind.

28. Ludger Meier, "Der Erfurter Franziskanertheologe Johannes Bremer und der Streit um das Wilsnacker Wunderblut," in *Aus der Geisteswelt des Mittelalters* (*Festschrift Grabmann*), eds. Albert Lang et al., Beiträge zur Geschichte der Philosophie und Theologie des Mittelalters: Texte und Untersuchungen, Supplementband 3 (Münster: Aschendorff, 1935), p. 1262 (from Braunschweig MS 48, fol. 209d).

29. Bremer shows ambivalence about the second sort of relic both in the phrase "so the pious believe" (which may suggest that it would be possible not to so believe) and in the phrase "something of the humanity of Christ" (which, from a theologian so given to precision, seems to be deliberately imprecise). On this point, see Bynum, *Christian Materiality*, pp. 165–67, which discusses Bremer from a different perspective.

30. On the *arma Christi*, see the introduction, pp. 31–32 and figure I.12.

31. I am using "icon," "index," and "symbol" as in Peircian sign theory, where the term "index" refers to something that gives evidence of one-time contact with that which it represents and thus retains some ability to act for it. On this, see Cynthia Hahn, "Objects of Devotion and Desire: Relics, Reliquaries, Relation, and Response," in the catalogue for *Objects of Devotion and Desire: Medieval Relic to Contemporary Art*, curated by Cynthia Hahn, New York, Hunter College, 27 January–30 April 2011, p. 13. In the introduction to this book, I suggest that there are some problems with using Peircian categories for medieval objects.

32. Robert L. Fantz, "Pattern Vision in Newborn Infants," *Science* 140 (1963), pp. 296–97; and Stewart Guthrie, *Faces in the Clouds: A New Theory of Religion* (Oxford: Oxford University Press, 1993), pp. 103–12. Guthrie, who sees anthropomorphism as the origin of religion, tends to argue in a circle. Defining religion as that which relates to gods or spirits, he excludes by definition experiences and phenomena that are not anthropomorphic. This is a problem especially for Buddhism. Justin L. Barrett and Rebekah A. Richert suggest that children can conceive of God in anthropomorphic and non-anthropomorphic ways. See Justin L. Barrett and Rebekah A. Richert, "Anthropomorphism or Preparedness? Exploring Children's God Concepts," *Review of Religious Research* 44 (2003), pp. 300–12.

33. Jerome Groopman, "Medical Dispatch: Robots That Care," *The New Yorker* (November 2, 2009), pp. 66–77.

34. Stewart Guthrie, "A Cognitive Theory of Religion," *Current Anthropology* 21 (1980), pp. 181–94; Guthrie, *Faces in the Clouds*; Justin L. Barrett and Frank C. Keil, "Conceptualizing a Nonnatural Entity: Anthropomorphism in God Concepts," *Cognitive Psychology* 31 (1996), pp. 219–47. On such explanations, see the perceptive critique by James Laidlaw, "A Well-Disposed Social Anthropologist's Problems with the 'Cognitive Science of Religion,'" in *Religion, Anthropology, and Cognitive Science*, eds. Harvey Whitehouse and James Laidlaw (Durham, NC: Carolina Academic, 2007), pp. 211–46.

35. There has been much debate on whether the linga is a penis and therefore anthropomorphic. As dressed and revered, its penile form is often hidden; but in some versions where the carving is unadorned, the similarity to a penis is clear. See chapter 5, pp. 203–11.

It is also important to note that non-anthropomorphic objects are important loci of the divine in Hinduism, and, significantly enough, these sacral "found" or "self-manifesting" objects do not have to be consecrated. See Davis, *Lives*, pp. 19–21 and 137–40, and Hess, "Open-Air Ramayana," p. 131.

36. Robert Maniura, "The Images and Miracles of Santa Maria della Carceri," in Thunø and Wolf, eds., *The Miraculous Image*, pp. 81–96.

37. Bynum, *Wonderful Blood*, pp. 234–47, esp. p. 243.

38. For Low Country examples of such visions, see Caroline Walker Bynum, *Holy Feast and Holy Fast: The Religious Significance of Food to Medieval Women* (Berkeley: University of California Press, 1987), pp. 115–29. On Colette, see Peter of Vaux, "Life of Colette of Corbie," in Joannes Bollandus and Godefridus Henschenius, *Acta Sanctorum . . . editio novissima*, eds. Joannes Carnandet et al. (Paris: Palmé, 1863), March, vol. 1, ch. 10, par. 84, p. 558, and ch. 11, pp. 560–62.

39. On Waltmann, see Bynum, *Wonderful Blood*, p. 39.

40. Joseph A. Jungmann, *The Mass of the Roman Rite: Its Origins and Development (Missarum Sollemnia)*, trans. Francis A. Brunner and Charles K. Riepe, revised and abridged edition in one volume (New York: Benziger Brothers, 1951), pp. 330–35.

41. Bynum, *Wonderful Blood*, p. 240.

42. Peter Browe, *Die eucharistischen Wunder des Mittelalters* (Breslau: Müller & Seiffert, 1938); Peter Browe, "Die eucharistischen Verwandlungswunder des Mittelalters," *Römische Quartalschrift* 37 (1929), pp. 137–69; Peter Browe, "Die Hostienschändungen der Juden im Mittelalter," *Römische Quartalschrift* 34 (1926), pp. 67–97; and Gavin Langmuir, "The Tortures of the Body of Christ," in *Christendom and Its Discontents: Exclusion, Persecution, and Rebellion, 1000–1500*, eds. Scott Waugh and Peter Diehl (Cambridge: Cambridge University Press, 1996), pp. 287–309.

43. Many examples are to be found in Bynum, *Holy Feast and Holy Fast*, pp. 113–86 and 219–44.

44. Claudia Lichte, *Die Inszenierung einer Wallfahrt: Der Lettner im Havelberger Dom und das Wilsnacker Wunderblut* (Worms: Werner, 1990); Bynum, *Wonderful Blood*, pp. 25–45; and Felix Escher and Hartmut Kühne, eds., *Die Wilsnackfahrt: Ein Wallfahrts- und Kommunikationszentrum Nord- und Mitteleuropas im Spätmittelalter* (Frankfurt am Main: Peter Lang, 2006).

45. Langmuir, "The Tortures of the Body of Christ."

46. Peter Browe, "Die scholastische Theorie der eucharistischen Verwandlungswunder," *Theologische Quartalschrift* 110 (1929), pp. 305–32, at p. 311 n. 2. The fact that theologians argued that the real presence under the accidents by definition could not be seen should not be used to obscure the fact that many visionaries "saw" the presence and artists depicted it. See Aden Kumler, *Translating Truth: Ambitious Images and Religious Knowledge in Late Medieval France and England* (New Haven, CT: Yale University Press, 2011), ch. 4, esp. pp. 103–105 and 158.

47. It is important to note that the concept and the term "transubstantiation" were not established as a basic ontology in 1215, as some interpreters seem to assume. "Transubstantiation" was debated as to both its meaning and its formulation well into the fifteenth century, and even the Council of Trent failed to find a full formulation of it. See Caroline Walker Bynum, "Seeing and Seeing Beyond: The Mass of St. Gregory in the Fifteenth Century," in *The Mind's Eye: Art and Theological Argument in the Middle Ages*, eds. Anne-Marie Bouché and Jeffrey F. Hamburger (Princeton, NJ: Department of Art and Archaeology, Princeton University, 2005), pp. 208–40, at pp. 208–15.

48. Relics — and the nature of their materiality — should be brought much more fully into the discussion, and I do so in chapter 5, nn. 68–69. Even more consideration of this issue would be useful. For recent work on relics, see *Past & Present* 206 (2010), Supplement 5: *Relics and Remains*, ed. Alexandra Walsham; *Objects of Devotion and Desire*, curated and ed. Hahn; Martina Bagnoli, Holger A. Klein, C. Griffith Mann, and James Robinson, eds., *Treasures of Heaven: Saints, Relics, and Devotion in Medieval Europe,* catalogue (Baltimore, MD: Walters Art Museum and Cleveland: Cleveland Museum of Art, 2010); and, somewhat unsatisfactory, Charles Freeman, *Holy Bones, Holy Dust: How Relics Shaped the History of Medieval Europe* (New Haven, CT: Yale University Press, 2011). For more bibliography on relics, see the introduction, nn. 4–5.

49. On this, see Bynum, *Christian Materiality*, ch. 4. As I argue in the introduction, to say that the Eucharist was one of the — if not *the* — central ritual objects in which God was instantiated in late medieval religion is not to argue that one should make transubstantiation the underlying ontology in late medieval–early modern sensibilities, as some scholars have done. See the introduction, p. 39.

50. Mechtild of Hackeborn, *Sanctae Mechtildis virginis ordinis sancti Benedicti Liber specialis gratiae*, bk. 4, ch. 3, in *Revelationes Gertrudianae ac Mechtildianae*, eds. Monks of Solesmes, 2 vols. (Paris: Oudin, 1875-77), vol. 2, p. 260.

51. Davis, *Lives*, p. 41.

CHAPTER FOUR: THE PRESENCE OF OBJECTS

1. This essay was written in 2002–2003 and published in the journal *Common Knowledge* in winter 2004. I have not attempted to rewrite it in light of recent bibliography or events but let it stand as a musing on problems concerning the display and interpretation of medieval objects that still have power to disturb and accuse. (See the introduction, nn. 83–84.) A major work that updates some of the history discussed here is Mitchell B. Merback, *Pilgrimage and Pogrom: Violence, Memory, and Visual Culture at the Host-Miracle Shrines of Germany and Austria* (Chicago: University of Chicago Press, 2013). For an excellent summary of the development of the Jewish host-desecration myth, which accounted for only a portion of the miracle host sites in the late Middle Ages, see Miri Rubin, "Desecration of the Host: The Birth of an Accusation," *Studies in Church History* 29 (1992), pp. 169–85. For help in acquiring

material for this chapter, I am deeply indebted to Yolande Korb, Gert Melville, and Mitchell Merback. As always, I am grateful to Joel Kaye, Karen Margolis, Dorothea von Mücke, and Stephen D. White for thoughtful readings. Some of this work was done while I was a fellow at the Hans Arnhold Center of the American Academy in Berlin in the fall of 2002. Special thanks to Guenther Roth, who made the trip to Sternberg with me, and to Gerhard Lutz, with whom I traveled to Heiligengrabe; each has taught me much about iconography.

2. Sternberg had 5,300 inhabitants around 1988. See Rosemary Schuder and Rudolf Hirsch, eds., *Der gelbe Fleck: Wurzeln und Wirkungen des Judenhasses in der deutschen Geschichte—Essays* (Cologne: Röderberg im Pahl-Rugenstein Verlag, 1988), p. 129. When I visited it in 2003, its population was 4,900. In 2018, it was 4,157. See https://de.wikipedia.org/wiki/Sternberg and https://en.wikipedia.org/wiki/Sternberg,_Mecklenburg-Vorpommern (accessed January 9, 2020).

3. On Sternberg, see Volker Honemann, "Die Sternberger Hostienschändung und ihre Quellen," in *Kirche und Gesellschaft im heiligen Römischen Reich des 15. und 16. Jahrhunderts*, ed. Hartmut Boockmann (Göttingen: Vandenhoeck und Ruprecht, 1994), pp. 75–102; Fritz Backhaus, "Die Hostienschändungsprozesse von Sternberg (1492) und Berlin (1510) und die Ausweisung der Juden aus Mecklenburg und der Mark Brandenburg," *Jahrbuch für Brandenburgische Landesgeschichte* 39 (1988), pp. 7–26; Schuder and Hirsch, eds., *Der gelbe Fleck*, pp. 129–44; Hermann Maschek, ed., *Deutsche Chroniken*, vol. 5 of *Deutsche Literatur: Sammlung literarischer Kunst- und Kulturdenkmäler in Entwicklungsreihen*, ed. Anton Pfatz (Leipzig: Philipp Reclam, 1936), pp. 134–38; K. Schmidt, *Das heilige Blut von Sternberg* (Halle: Max Niemeyer, 1892); G. C. F. Lisch, "Das heilige Blut zu Sternberg," *Jahrbücher des Vereins für meklenburgische Geschichte und Altertumskunde aus den Arbeiten des Vereins* 12 (Schwerin: Stillersche Hofbuchhandlung zu Rostock und Schwerin, 1847), pp. 187–307. I acquired the four-page photocopied guide "Kirchlicher Wegweiser" (Sternberg, n.d.) in October 2002. The accounts I cite here differ markedly about who profited from the pilgrim trade and about the role of the church authorities in Schwerin, but all agree in focusing on the question and in suggesting competition for revenues as a major motive in the events. Honemann, "Die Sternberger Hostienschändung," pp. 83–88 and 95, has an interesting discussion of the "material proofs" (that is, of the objects); his focus is on why they were convincing to sixteenth-century contemporaries.

4. For an English-language discussion of this, see Heiko A. Oberman, *The Roots of Anti-Semitism in the Age of Renaissance and Reformation*, trans. J. I. Porter (Philadelphia: Fortress Press, 1984), pp. 94–100, and 124. And see Wolfgang Treue, "Schlechte und gute Christen: Zur Rolle von Christen in antijüdischen Ritualmord- und Hostienschändungslegenden," *Aschkenas: Zeitschrift für Geschichte und Kultur der Juden* 2 (1992), pp. 95–116, esp. pp. 115–16. On blood cults and wonder hosts generally, see the splendid analysis by Mitchell B. Merback, "Channels of Grace: Pilgrimage Architecture, Eucharistic Imagery, and Visions of Purgatory at the Host-Miracle Churches of Late Medieval Bavaria," in *Art and Architecture of Late*

Medieval Pilgrimage in Northern Europe and the British Isles, eds. Sarah Blick and Rita Tekippe (Leiden: Brill, 2004), pp. 587–646; Caroline Walker Bynum, "The Blood of Christ in the Later Middle Ages," *Church History* 71.4 (2002), pp. 685–714; Nicholas Vincent, *The Holy Blood: King Henry III and the Westminster Blood Relic* (Cambridge: Cambridge University Press, 2001); Mark Daniel Holtz, "Cults of the Precious Blood in the Medieval Latin West," Ph.D. diss., University of Notre Dame, 1997; Karl Kolb, *Vom Heiligen Blut: eine Bilddokumentation der Wallfahrt und Verehrung* (Würzburg: Echter, 1980), which is unreliable in many of its details but gives an overview from a Catholic perspective; Johannes Heuser, "'Heilig-Blut' in Kult und Brauchtum des deutschen Kulturraumes: Ein Beitrag zur religiösen Volkskunde," Ph.D. diss., Bonn, 1948; Peter Browe, *Die eucharistischen Wunder des Mittelalters* (Breslau: Müller und Seiffert, 1938); Peter Browe, "Die eucharistischen Verwandlungswunder des Mittelalters," *Römische Quartalschrift* 37 (1929), pp. 156–57; and Romuald Bauerreiss, *Pie Jesu: Das Schmerzensmann-Bild und sein Einfluss auf die mittelalterliche Frömmigkeit* (Munich: Karl Widmann, 1931).

5. Miri Rubin, *Gentile Tales: The Narrative Assault on Late Medieval Jews* (New Haven, CT: Yale University Press, 1999), is an exception, dealing as it does with how the past is constructed in narrative and by memory, but the treatment is general, and objects are not its special focus. Particularly sophisticated versions of the political argument are Bruno Hennig, "Kurfürst Friedrich II. und das Wunderblut zu Wilsnack," *Forschungen zur brandenburgischen und preussischen Geschichte* 19 (1906), pp. 73–104, and Hartmut Kühne, "Der Harz und sein Umland: Eine spätmittelalterliche Wallfahrtslandschaft?" in *Spätmittelalterliche Wallfahrt im mitteldeutschen Raum: Beiträge einer interdisziplinären Arbeitstagung (Eisleben 7./8. Juni 2002)*, eds. H. Kühne, Wolfgang Radtke, and Gerlinde Strohmaier-Wiederanders (2002), https://edoc.hu-berlin.de/handle/18452/30 (accessed January 8, 2020). For economic and social interpretations, see Felix Escher, "Brandenburgische Wallfahrten und Wallfahrtsorte im Mittelalter," *Jahrbuch für die Geschichte Mittel- und Ostdeutschlands* 27 (1978), pp. 116–37, and Charles Zika, "Hosts, Processions and Pilgrimages: Controlling the Sacred in Fifteenth-Century Germany," *Past & Present* 118 (1988), pp. 25–64.

6. Schuder and Hirsch, eds., *Der gelbe Fleck*, p. 138, and Schmidt, *Das heilige Blut*, p. 27, give slightly different versions of the tabletop inscription, but it is clear to me from personal inspection and photographs that Schmidt's is the more accurate.

7. It is worth noting that the earliest accounts, including the confession of Eleazar's wife, say the martyring was done with knives, not nails; see Honemann, "Die Sternberger Hostienschändung," p. 83 n. 10. Presumably, knives metamorphosed into nails to accord more closely with accounts of Christ's Crucifixion.

8. Lisch, "Das heilige Blut," p. 224.

9. Schuder and Hirsch, eds., *Der gelbe Fleck*, p. 130. It would be interesting to know how recent such embarrassment is, not only at Sternberg and Deggendorf but generally. It is my impression that it developed only in the 1980s.

10. On Pulkau, see Rubin, *Gentile Tales*, p. 68 and pp. 222–23 n. 121. The legend of the Regensburg desecration is now obscure; the abuser was probably not thought to be a Jew.

11. Manfred Eder, *Die "Deggendorfer Gnad": Entstehung und Entwicklung einer Hostienwallfahrt im Kontext von Theologie und Geschichte* (Deggendorf/Passau: Passavia-Univ.-Verlag, 1992), p. 445.

12. See Merback, "Channels of Grace," pp. 609–12 ; Harald Schwillus, "Hostienfrevellegende und Judenverfolgung in Iphofen: Ein Beitrag zur Entstehungsgeschichte der Kirche zum hl. Blut im Gräbenviertel," *Würzburger Diözesan-Geschichtsblätter* 58 (Würzburg: Echter, 1996), pp. 87–109, esp. p. 95 n. 34; and Eder, *Die "Deggendorfer Gnad,"* p. 385 n. 703. A stone relief depicting the events was until 1979 located in the center of the church.

13. On Poznań, see Rodgero Prümers, "Der Hostiendiebstahl zu Posen im Jahre 1399," *Zeitschrift der historischen Gesellschaft für die Provinz Posen* 20.1 (1905), pp. 293–317; and J. Perles, "Geschichte der Juden in Posen," *Monatsschrift für Geschichte und Wissenschaft des Judenthums* 13 (1864), pp. 281–95, 321–34, 361–73, 409–20, 449–61.

14. Kolb, *Vom Heiligen Blut*, p. 144, commented in 1980 that there was "heute keine Rede mehr" of the original legend.

15. On Deggendorf, see Eder, *Die "Deggendorfer Gnad."*

16. The literature on Wilsnack is extensive. Especially useful are Hennig, "Kurfürst Friedrich II"; Ernst Breest, "Das Wunderblut von Wilsnack (1383–1552): Quellenmässige Darstellungen seiner Geschichte," *Märkische Forschungen* 16 (1881), pp. 131–301, and *Das Wilsnacker Wunderblut* (Barmen: Hugo Klein, 1888); Browe, *Die eucharistischen Wunder*, pp. 166–71; Ludger Meier, "Wilsnack als Spiegel deutscher Vorreformation, " *Zeitschrift für Religions- und Geistesgeschichte* 3.1 (1951), pp. 53–69; J. Fliege, "Nikolaus von Kues und der Kampf gegen das Wilsnacker Wunderblut," *Das Buch als Quelle historischer Forschung: Fritz Juntke anlässlich seines 90. Geburtstages gewidmet* (Leipzig: Bibliographisches Institut, 1977), pp. 62–70; Hartmut Boockmann, "Der Streit um das Wilsnacker Blut: Zur Situation des deutschen Klerus in der Mitte des 15. Jahrhunderts," *Zeitschrift für historische Forschung* 9 (1982), pp. 385–408; Zika, "Hosts, Processions and Pilgrimages"; Claudia Lichte, *Die Inszenierung einer Wallfahrt: Der Lettner im Havelberger Dom und das Wilsnacker Wunderblut* (Worms: Werner, 1990); Hartmut Kühne, "'Ich ging durch Feuer und Wasser. . .': Bemerkungen zur Wilsnacker Heilig-Blut-Legende," in *Theologie und Kultur: Geschichten einer Wechselbeziehung: Festschrift zum einhundertfünfzigjährigen Bestehen des Lehrstuhls für Christliche Archäologie und Kirchliche Kunst an der Humboldt-Universität zu Berlin*, ed. Gerlinde Strohmaier-Wiederanders (Halle: Andre Gursky, 1999), pp. 51–84; and Caroline Walker Bynum, *Wonderful Blood: Theology and Practice in Late Medieval Northern Germany and Beyond* (Philadelphia: University of Pennsylvania Press, 2007), pp. 25–45.

17. Kolb, *Vom Heiligen Blut*, pp. 192–94, prints a sermon given by Bishop Rudolf Graber at Walldürn on June 12, 1968, that makes exactly this argument apropos another famous Eucharistic relic: the corporal on which wine supposedly turned into Christ's blood. It

does not matter, he asserts, whether sanctified wood and cloth can be rationally explained or what the priest Otto actually did long ago. The objects and the site concentrate the prayers of believers and surround them not only with five hundred years of pilgrimage but also with all of salvation history.

18. In a strict theological sense, desecration reveals (not creates) sacrality. See the discussion at nn. 51–52. Some theologians argued (and argue still today) that at least a small number of the Jewish people must survive, since their conversion will be one of the signs of the Second Coming of Jesus.

19. Marius Lepin, *L'idée du sacrifice de la messe d'après les théologiens depuis l'origine jusqu'à nos jours* (Paris: Gabriel Beauchesne, 1926), pp. 3–331; Josef Geiselmann, *Die Eucharistielehre der Vorscholastik* (Paderborn: F. Schöningh, 1926), pp. 43, 88, 98–99, 411–12, and 427; P. J. Fitzpatrick, "On Eucharistic Sacrifice in the Middle Ages," in *Sacrifice and Redemption: Durham Essays in Theology*, ed. S. W. Sykes (Cambridge: Cambridge University Press, 1991), pp. 129–56; Donald L. Ehresmann, "Medieval Theology of the Mass and the Iconography of the Oberwesel Altarpiece," *Zeitschrift für Kunstgeschichte* 60 (1997), pp. 200–26; Caroline Walker Bynum, "The Power in the Blood: Sacrifice, Satisfaction and Substitution in Late Medieval Soteriology," in *The Redemption: An Interdisciplinary Symposium on Christ as Redeemer*, eds. Stephen T. Davis, Daniel Kendall S.J., and Gerald O'Collins S.J. (Oxford: Oxford University Press, 2004), pp. 177–204; and Bynum, *Wonderful Blood*, pp. 195–248.

20. Jan Hus in c. 1405 and Heinrich Tocke in 1412 and 1443 made exactly this charge against the Wilsnack host; see Breest, "Wunderblut" (published in 1881), pp. 169–72, 177, 188ff., and 212. The sermon referred to in n. 17 is a twentieth-century effort to meet exactly this sort of objection—that is, the objection that there is no reason for pilgrimage if the provenance and history of the relic are questioned or disproved.

21. Eder, *Die "Deggendorfer Gnad,"* p. 460.

22. *Ibid.*, pp. 432–34.

23. *Ibid.* I have not been able to visit the museum at Deggendorf.

24. A check under "Judensau" on the internet turns up dozens of entries. Among other sites, see https://en.wikipedia.org/wiki/Judensau (accessed January 9, 2020).

25. "Gottes eigentlicher Name der geschmähte Schem HaMphoras, den die Juden vor den Christen fast unsagbar heilig hielten, starb in 6 Millionen Juden unter einem Kreuzeszeichen." As the Wikipedia article cited in n. 24 points out, the inscription reads "Rabini Schem HaMphoras," which is gibberish that presumably garbles "shem ha-mephorasch."

26. Pamphlet "Judenfeindliche Darstellungen an der Sebalduskirche zu Nürnberg," March 2002. For recent action, see https://en.wikipedia.org/wiki/Judensau_at_the_choir_stalls_of_Cologne_Cathedral (accessed September 24, 2019).

27. David Freedberg, *The Power of Images: Studies in the History and Theory of Response* (Chicago: University of Chicago Press, 1989). See also the introduction to this book, pp. 43–45.

28. Isaiah Shachar, *The Judensau: A Medieval Anti-Jewish Motif and Its History* (London:

The Warburg Institute, 1974). A Judensau on the facade of a private house facing the main road in the little town of Kelheim near Regensburg was understood in local tradition to commemorate the expulsion of the Jews in 1442. It was removed sometime in the early nineteenth century by order of a local judge at the request of the Jews but was kept in the pharmacy and restored to the pharmacy facade in 1895 when the house was rebuilt. It was removed (probably chiseled off) in 1945 by order of the United States army. See Shachar, *The Judensau*, p. 38.

29. My interpretation differs somewhat from the well-known one of Walter Benjamin, "The Work of Art in the Age of Its Technological Reproducibility" (first published in 1936). For the second version of the essay, see Walter Benjamin, *The Work of Art in the Age of its Technological Reproducibility, and Other Writings on Media*, eds. Michael W. Jennings, Brigid Doherty, and Thomas Y. Levin, trans. Edmund Jephcott et al. (Cambridge, MA : Belknap Press of Harvard University Press, 2008). See also chapter 6 n. 3. Although dealing primarily with objects and not art images, I, like Benjamin, see a difference between the power or "aura" of the original and that of the reproduced. But I give greater attention to the sheer "presence"—especially the religious presence—of the original object and stress more the power—especially the propaganda power—of reproducible images. In my original article as in this slightly revised version, I develop my ideas without trying to intersect further with Benjamin's. I also do not consider here the distinction C. S. Peirce makes between "image," "index," and "symbol." On this, see the introduction, pp. 41–43.

30. On Heiligengrabe, see Lieselotte Kötzsche, "Das wiedergefundene Hostiengrab im Kloster Heiligengrabe/Prignitz," *Berliner Theologische Zeitschrift* 4.1 (1987), pp. 19–32; Christa and Friedrich Plate, "Die Ergebnisse der Ausgrabungen in der Wunderblutkapelle des Klosters Heiligengrabe, Krs. Wittstock," *Ausgrabungen und Funde: Archäologische Berichte und Informationen* 32 (1987), pp. 94–99; Gerlinde Strohmaier-Wiederanders, *Geschichte vom Kloster Stift zum Heiligengrabe* (Berlin: Nicolai, 1995); Treue, "Schlechte und gute Christen," pp. 113–14; and Hubert Faensen, "Zur Synthese von Bluthostien- und Heiliggrab-Kult: Überlegungen zu dem Vorgängerbau der Gnadenkapelle des märkischen Klosters Heiligengrabe," *Festschrift für Ernst Schubert*, Sachsen und Anhalt: Jahrbuch der Historischen Kommission für Sachsen-Anhalt 19 (Weimar: Böhlau, 1997), pp. 237–55. The Low German version of the legend with reproductions of the woodcuts (1521) is given in Johannes Simon, *Die Legende vom Ursprunge des Klosters Heiligengrabe in der Prignitz: Nach dem Drucke von 1521 neu herausgegeben und erläutert* (Heiligengrabe: Museumsverein Heiligengrabe, 1928), based on G. Schmidt, "Rostocker Drucke zu Halberstadt," *Jahrbücher des Vereins für meklenburgische Geschichte und Alterthumskunde* 53 (1888), pp. 339–50.

31. It is not even very far from the more northern blood cult sites of Sternberg, Güstrow, Krakow am See, Doberan, and Schwerin. On sites in Mecklenburg, see Karl Schäfer, "Märkische Fronleichnamsverehrung und ihre kulturelle Auswirkung vor Luther," *Wichmann Jahrbuch* 2/3 (Berlin, 1931–32), pp. 99–107; and Kirchner, "Das

Cisterzienser-Nonnenkloster zum heiligen Kreuz in Zehdenick," *Märkische Forschung* 5 (1857), pp. 109–83. Although it is without footnotes, Klaus-Martin Bresgott and Arnt Cobbers, *Reiseziele einer Region: Die Zisterzienserklöster im Land Brandenburg* (Berlin: Kai Homilius Verlag, 1999), is also useful. The indefatigable opponent of blood piety Heinrich Tocke made stick a charge of fraudulent host veneration at Wartenburg bei Wittenberg shortly after word of a miracle spread in 1429; see Heuser, "Heilig-Blut in Kult, " p. 31, and Ernst Breest, "Synodalrede des Domherrn Dr. Heinrich Tocke von Magdeburg," *Blätter für Handel, Gewerbe und soziales Leben (Beiblatt zur Magdeburgischen Zeitung)* 23 (Monday, June 5, 1882), pp. 175–76.

32. The best-known examples are Gernrode and Wienhausen. I have discussed the Holy Sepulcher at Wienhausen in Caroline Walker Bynum, "Are Things 'Indifferent'? How Objects Change Our Understanding of Religious History," *German History* 34 (2016), pp. 88–112, at p. 99.

33. Bauerreiss, *Pie Jesu*. See also Mitchell B. Merback, *The Thief, the Cross and the Wheel: Pain and the Spectacle of Punishment in Medieval and Renaissance Europe* (Chicago: University of Chicago Press, 1999).

34. For other examples of cloisters that revered holy earth, see Faensen, "Zur Synthese," p. 242. Faensen thinks the little vault at Heiligengrabe was built to shelter the finding-spot of the wonder host and was later part of a "cultic fusion" of Holy Sepulcher-cult and blood-cult — a fusion about which Merback, "Channels of Grace," also writes. For recent work on holy earth as transporting power, see Lucy Donkin, "Earth from Elsewhere: Burial in *Terra Sancta* beyond the Holy Land," in *Natural Materials of the Holy Land and the Visual Translation of Place, 500–1500*, eds. Renana Bartal, Neta Bodner, and Bianca Kühnel (London: Routledge, 2017), pp. 109–26.

35. On the Brandenburg-Berlin case, see Backhaus, "Die Hostienschändungsprozesse von Sternberg,“ and Oberman, *The Roots of Anti-Semitism*.

36. The presentation seems largely based on Schuder and Hirsch, eds., *Der gelbe Fleck*.

37. It is worth noting here that work on sites of host-desecration libels has been done by historians of many religious identities — Jews, Jesuits, Protestants, and those with no religious affiliation — and by those of several nationalities.

38. This is not the same as to say that medieval people — or some medieval people — really believed these stories, or that "belief" or "religiosity" was at the center of it all, as many historians do. The question remains: What kind of religiosity? What kind of belief? Otherwise one ends up saying only that religiosity is central to religion, which is not a very interesting conclusion.

39. Recent bibliography on relics is voluminous. See the introduction, n. 4, and Caroline Walker Bynum, *The Resurrection of the Body in Western Christianity, 200–1336*, expanded edition (New York: Columbia University Press, 2017), pp. 59–114.

40. Even ordinary adherents could convey self through object. In the later Middle

Ages, for example, penitents gave themselves to God by donating to his altar wax candles measured to the length of their own bodies. On the variety of objects that could convey self, see n. 34 and the introduction, n. 18.

41. See Bynum, "Blood of Christ," pp. 691–99.

42. G. J. C. Snoek, *Medieval Piety from Relics to the Eucharist: A Process of Mutual Interaction* (Leiden: Brill, 1995). On the competition between Eucharist and relics, see Yrjö Hirn, *The Sacred Shrine: A Study of the Poetry and Art of the Catholic Church* (London: Macmillan, 1912), pp. 135–36, and Jaroslav Pelikan, *The Growth of Medieval Theology (600–1300)*, vol. 3 of *The Christian Tradition: A History of the Development of Doctrine* (Chicago: University of Chicago Press, 1978), pp. 180ff. Snoek treats the parallels between them.

43. Hubertus Lutterbach, "The Mass and Holy Communion in the Medieval Penitentials (600–1200): Liturgical and Religio-Historical Perspectives," in *Bread of Heaven: Customs and Practices Surrounding Holy Communion: Essays in the History of Liturgy and Culture*, eds. Charles Caspers, Gerard Lukken, and Gerard Rouwhorst (Kampen, The Netherlands: Kok Pharos, 1995), pp. 61–81.

44. Peter Dinzelbacher, "Die 'Realpräsenz' der Heiligen in ihren Reliquiaren und Gräbern nach mittelalterlichen Quellen," in *Heiligenverehrung in Geschichte und Gegenwart*, eds. Peter Dinzelbacher and Dieter Bauer (Ostfildern: Schwabenverlag, 1990), pp. 115–74.

45. See Browe, "Die eucharistischen Verwandlungswunder"; Dinzelbacher, "Die 'Realpräsenz' der Heiligen"; Bynum, "Blood of Christ"; and Wolfgang Brückner, "Liturgie und Legende: Zur theologischen Theorienbildung und zum historischen Verständnis von Eucharistie-Mirakeln," *Jahrbuch für Volkskunde* 19 (1996), pp. 139–66. For the miraculous hosts at Andechs, see Bynum, *Christian Materiality: An Essay on Religion in Late Medieval Europe* (New York: Zone, 2011), pp. 15–17.

46. Bynum, *The Resurrection of the Body*, pp. 200–26 and 318–29; and Cynthia Hahn, "The Voices of the Saints: Speaking Reliquaries," *Gesta* 36.1 (1997), pp. 20–31.

47. Another aspect of the resistance of holy matter to change is the motif of survival through fire and water, on which see Kühne, "'Ich ging durch Feuer und Wasser...'"

48. Hans Belting, *Likeness and Presence: A History of the Image before the Era of Art*, trans. Edmund Jephcott (Chicago: University of Chicago Press, 1994). I should point out that from the time of the iconoclastic controversy on, medieval theologians, philosophers, and spiritual advisers discussed in sophisticated terms the distinction between image and the "reality" it represented. See, for example, Jeffrey F. Hamburger, "Seeing and Believing: The Suspicion of Sight and the Authentication of Vision in Late Medieval Art and Devotion," in *Imagination und Wirklichkeit: Zum Verhältnis von mentalen und realen Bildern in der Kunst der frühen Neuzeit*, eds. Alessandro Nova and Klaus Krüger (Mainz: Philipp von Zabern, 2000), pp. 47–70. Medieval theorists also discussed the difference between image and holy object (relic) and argued that relics had elements of representation; for Thomas Aquinas's sophisticated treatment of the topic, see P. Séjourné, "Reliques," *Dictionnaire*

de théologie catholique, vol. 13 (Paris: Letouzey et Ané, 1936), cols. 2312–67, esp. 2318–66; and the introduction, nn. 71–72.

49. Scholars have disagreed about this. See Ilene H. Forsyth, *The Throne of Wisdom: Wood Sculptures of the Madonna in Romanesque France* (Princeton, NJ: Princeton University Press, 1972).

50. For a powerful analysis connecting the finding-site of miracle hosts and images of the Schmerzensmann, see Merback, "Channels of Grace."

51. Michel Tarayre, "Le sang dans le *Specvlvm Maivs* de Vincent de Beauvais: De la science aux *miracvla*," in *Le sang au moyen âge: Actes du quatrième colloque international de Montpellier Université Paul-Valéry (27–29 novembre 1997)* (Montpellier: Université Paul-Valéry, 1999), p. 353, cites evidence that Jews may have required that Christian wet nurses abstain from nursing Jewish infants for three days after they had received communion. On the general matter of Jewish criticism of Christian belief and practice, see Gavin Langmuir, "The Tortures of the Body of Christ," in *Christendom and Its Discontents: Exclusion, Persecution, and Rebellion, 1000–1500*, eds. Scott Waugh and Peter Diehl (Cambridge: Cambridge University Press, 1996), pp. 287–309.

52. The two charges were sometimes conflated, as when Jews were accused of murdering Christians in order to extract consecrated hosts they had swallowed.

53. It is important to remember, however, that the broadsides that spread the stories were often intended to foment anti-Jewish action as well as to encourage pilgrimage. They informed those in other regions that Jews accused of host desecration might flee their way. See Honemann, "Die Sternberger Hostienschändung," pp. 90–93.

54. The issue comes up in the early retellings of the Wilsnack legend, where the miracle hosts have to defend themselves against the suspicion that they had not been consecrated and therefore could not be miraculous. When the bishop of Havelberg threatened to reconsecrate the hosts, they bled to ward off the *iniuria* of double consecration. See Kühne, "'Ich ging durch Feuer und Wasser . . .'"

55. Breest, "Wunderblut," pp. 260–62.

56. It is worth noting that, as at Sternberg, the tabletop in the Brandenburg case was revered along with the knife and a piece of the host in the cathedral. The tabletop on which a particle of the host sent to Spandau was supposedly tortured was venerated in the bishop's court chapel in Berlin.

57. The theological and devotional idea of the *felix culpa* held that Adam's sin was "fortunate" because it led to the salvation of humankind, won by the Crucifixion.

58. I do insist, however, that medievalists have not paid sufficient attention to ways in which attitudes toward sacrality and materiality created the conditions for the development of the particular anti-Semitism located in objects I stress here.

59. More could be said about museum practice. Although I do not agree with all of his distinctions, a start toward thinking about questions of the display of objects in museums

is found in Stephen Greenblatt, "Resonance and Wonder," in *Exhibiting Cultures: The Poetics and Politics of Museum Display*, eds. I. Karp and S. D. Lavine (Washington, DC: Smithsonian Institution Press, 1991), pp. 42–56.

60. See Michael Fried's classic essay "Art and Objecthood" (1967), republished in *Art and Objecthood: Essays and Reviews* (Chicago: University of Chicago Press, 1998), pp. 148–72. I am not concerned here with Fried's point about minimalist art as theater or with his valuing of various types of art, but rather with his statements about the way in which mid-twentieth-century art comments on "objecthood."

61. Belting, *Likeness and Presence*.

62. Recent discussion that emphasizes the "power" of all images gives even modern art a curiously medieval aura or presence. See, for example, Freedberg, *Power of Images*, many of whose most telling examples of images that act or elicit action are medieval. See also the discussion of the agency of objects in the introduction, pp. 43–45.

63. For example, Neukirchen beim Heilig Blut, Willisau, and Erding. On the change from relic to devotional image (*Gnadenbild*) as a goal of pilgrimage, see Kolb, *Vom Heiligen Blut*, pp. 160–83, and Alois Döring, "St. Salvator in Bettbrunn: Historische-volkskundliche Untersuchung zur eucharistischen Wallfahrt," *Beiträge zur Geschichte des Bistums Regensburg*, eds. Georg Schwaiger and Paul Mai (1979), vol. 13, pp. 35–234, esp. p. 120. On Erding, see Anton Bauer, "Eucharistische Wallfahrten zu 'Unserm Herrn,' zum 'Hl. Blut,' und zum 'St. Salvator,' im alten Bistum Freising," *Beiträge zur altbayerischen Kirchengeschichte* 21.3 (1960), pp. 37–71. One must be careful not to date this shift too early. In the fifteenth century, what one sees is competition between different kinds of blood relics (for example, between Schwerin, Zehdenick, Wilsnack, Marienfliess, Heiligengrabe, and so on). On the issue of duplicability, it is important to note that prayer cards and replicas undoubtedly did become both propagators and goals of pilgrimage in the later Middle Ages. On the general shift, in the early modern period, from relic to apparition as the trigger of pilgrimage: see William A. Christian, *Apparitions in Late Medieval and Renaissance Spain* (Princeton, NJ: Princeton University Press, 1981); Pierre-André Sigal, *L'homme et le miracle dans la France médiévale (XIe–XIIe siècle)* (Paris: Éditions du Cerf, 1985); and Philip M. Soergel, *Wondrous in His Saints: Counter-Reformation Propaganda in Bavaria* (Berkeley: University of California Press, 1993), pp. 20–30. Many historians relate this shift to the increased prominence of "visuality" in late medieval piety. The point is both correct and also, at the moment, overemphasized in scholarship. See Robert Scribner, "Vom Sakralbild zur sinnlichen Schau," in *Gepeinigt, begehrt, vergessen: Symbolik und Sozialbezug des Körpers im späten Mittelalter und der frühen Neuzeit*, eds. Klaus Schreiner and Norbert Schnitzler (Munich: Fink, 1992), pp. 309–36. Basic is still Anton Mayer, "Die heilbringende Schau in Sitte und Kult," in *Heilige Überlieferung: Ausschnitte aus der Geschichte des Mönchtums und des heiligen Kultes. Festschrift für Ildefons Herwegen* (Münster: Aschendorf, 1938), pp. 234–62. On bleeding hosts as on the borderline between objects and images, see Zika, "Hosts, Processions and Pilgrimages," p. 60.

64. Schuder and Hirsch, eds., *Der gelbe Fleck*, pp. 142–44.

65. On the pilgrimage at Walldürn, see Kolb, *Vom Heiligen Blut*, pp. 160–63. A striking example of the fusion of image and holy matter is a model of the Schmerzensmann at Erding from the eighteenth century that is actually molded from the holy earth of the host-finding-site. See Merback, "Channels of Grace," pp. 604–608.

66. A photograph can, of course, be treated as an object—that is, we can relate to it less because of what it images than because we remember the occasions on which we took it out and scrutinized it, etc. Noting this only, however, confirms my point both about how objects work for us and about the porous (but not nonexistent) line between image and object. For more on complex questions relating to display of objects (including racist images and objects), see the introduction, pp. 53–54.

67. W. G. Sebald, *Austerlitz*, trans. Anthea Bell (New York: Random House, 2001), pp. 195–97.

68. A character in a novel by Rachel Seiffert, *The Dark Room* (New York: Vintage Books, 2002), p. 207, cries out in horror and anguish that in today's Germany schoolchildren identify with the victims in the camps, not understanding that their grandparents were the killers, not the killed. (The novel is a complex depiction, of course, and does not necessarily espouse this particular perception.) Objects such as the tabletop at Sternberg, with its inscription, make it impossible to forget that Western Christian culture killed.

69. For a parallel discussion of what to do about Confederate memorials in the United States, see Michael Gorra, "A Heritage of Evil," *New York Review of Books* (November 7, 2019), pp. 10–13 and the introduction to this volume at n. 85.

CHAPTER FIVE: AVOIDING THE TYRANNY OF MORPHOLOGY

1. This essay was first published as "Avoiding the Tyranny of Morphology, or Why Compare?" *History of Religions* 53 (May 2014), pp. 341–68. It is republished here with minor revisions and with the addition of images. I thank Wendy Doniger, John Stratton Hawley, Brooke Holmes, Joel Kaye, and Guenther Roth for careful reading of earlier versions. I also thank the organizers of the workshop "Postcontextualism" held at the Max Planck Institute for the History of Science in Berlin, 21–22 June 2013, for opportunities to discuss the issue of comparison. I am grateful to Richard Davis for a very helpful conversation about Indian images in the spring of 2012, to Yve-Alain Bois for several discussions of pseudomorphism, to Lynn Hunt for discussion of comparison, and to Sashi Sekhar, Jyotirmaya Sharma, David Shulman, and Punam Zutshi for much guidance when I visited India. Elizabeth Blackmar, Neslihan Şenocak, Christopher Heuer, and Kevin Madigan, who have used the essay in discussions with American students, have provided helpful feedback, as have Simon Teuscher and Caroline Arni from a European perspective. As always, I am grateful to my doctor father, Giles Constable, who first taught me how to understand medieval religion in both its historical and its historiographical context. For further discussion of

these issues, see Caroline Walker Bynum, "Interrogating 'Likeness': Fake Friends, *Similia Similibus*, and Heavenly Crowns," *Historische Anthropologie* 28.1 (2020), pp. 31–56.

2. See chapter 2 in this volume and "Are Things 'Indifferent'? How Objects Change Our Understanding of Religious History," *German History* 34 (2016), pp. 88–112.

3. J. H. Elliott, *History in the Making* (New Haven, CT: Yale University Press, 2012), p. 168. George M. Fredrickson, "The Status of Comparative History," in *The Comparative Imagination: On the History of Racism, Nationalism, and Social Movements* (Berkeley: University of California Press, 1997), p. 35, emphasizes how little comparative history has been done by American historians.

4. Lynn Hunt, "Globalization and Time," in *Breaking Up Time: Negotiating the Borders between Present, Past and Future*, eds. Chris Lorenz and Berber Bevernage (Göttingen: Vandenhoeck & Ruprecht, 2013), pp. 199–215. See also the first three essays in Benjamin Z. Kedar, ed., *Explorations in Comparative History* (Jerusalem: The Hebrew University Magnes Press, 2009). For a perceptive critique of the recent turn to "deep" or neurohistory, see Ruth Leys, "The Turn to Affect: A Critique," *Critical Inquiry* 37.3 (2011), pp. 434–72.

5. Jürgen Kocka, "Comparative History: Methodology and Ethos," in Kedar, *Explorations*, p. 33. Kocka's "asymmetrical" is Kedar's "soft" comparison—that is, study that "focus[es] on one entity but widen[s] a historian's horizons by having recourse to secondary literature pertaining to another entity . . . so as to gain a wider perspective, think up new questions and elicit insights." Kedar, *Explorations*, p. vi.

6. Even such contrasts can be effective in warding off facile generalizations about human development or underlining the point of a complex analysis. I give two examples. When Patricia Crone, writing in *Nativist Prophets of Early Islamic Iran*, explains the contrast between the effects of conversion to Islam in the Arab empire and those of conversion to Christianity in the French and British empires, the comparison becomes shorthand for explaining the difference between imamate and nation-state. When Peter Brown, in *Through the Eye of a Needle*, discusses the paradoxical implications of "detachment" in late antique Christianity, he uses the parallel to Chinese Buddhist ideas to suggest that in both cases detachment provided escape from and justification for the social and religious use of wealth. See Patricia Crone, *The Nativist Prophets of Early Islamic Iran: Rural Revolt and Local Zoroastrianism* (Cambridge: Cambridge University Press, 2012), pp. 16, 170; Peter Brown, *Through the Eye of a Needle: Wealth, the Fall of Rome, and the Making of Christianity in the West, 350–550 AD* (Princeton, NJ: Princeton University Press, 2012), pp. 462–63, 523.

7. On this, see Elliott, *History in the Making*, pp. 172–75. For an example of historical work that responds to the models of economists without succumbing to them, see Jessica L. Goldberg's treatment of Avner Greif in *Trade and Institutions in the Medieval Mediterranean: The Geniza Merchants and Their Business World* (Cambridge: Cambridge University Press, 2012).

8. See Robert N. Bellah, *Religion in Human Evolution: From the Paleolithic to the Axial Age* (Cambridge, MA: Harvard University Press, 2011); Robert N. Bellah and Hans Joas, eds.,

The Axial Age and Its Consequences (Cambridge, MA: Harvard University Press, 2012); and Glen W. Bowersock, "A Different Turning Point for Mankind?" *New York Review of Books* (May 9, 2013), pp. 56–58.

9. For a discussion of this, see Amy Knight Powell, *Depositions: Scenes from the Late Medieval Church and the Modern Museum* (New York: Zone Books, 2012), pp. 10–11. Earlier discussions of the phenomenon of pseudomorphism that put the issue on the table but treat it differently are Erwin Panofsky, *Tomb Sculpture: Four Lectures on Its Changing Aspects from Ancient Egypt to Bernini*, ed. H. W. Janson (New York: Abrams, 1992), pp. 26–27, and Claude Lévi-Strauss, "Split Representation in the Art of Asia and America," in *Structural Anthropology*, trans. Claire Jacobson and Brooke Schoepf (New York: Basic Books, 1963), pp. 245–68. The point of the false similarity, as Powell sees it, is to stimulate the interpreter to ask new questions by decontextualizing the objects. To Panofsky and Lévi-Strauss, the point is to ask why the parallels or analogies occur. In considering this, I was influenced by the contribution of Yve-Alain Bois to the workshop "Postcontextualism" referred to in n. 1 p. 307. Bois's ideas have subsequently appeared in Yve-Alain Bois, "On the Uses and Abuses of Look-Alikes," *October* 154 (Fall 2015), pp. 127–49. Focused on art historical look-alikes rather than religious phenomena, Bois's analysis agrees with my own. At p. 130 he says, "I loathe pseudomorphism—and I find in its failure to provide any explanation for the phenomenon of pseudomorphosis on which it feeds one of the clearest proofs that a purely morphological formalism, as opposed to a structural one, cannot lead anywhere."

10. Cited by Powell, *Depositions*, p. 11, from Gregory Battcock, ed., *Minimal Art: A Critical Anthology* (Berkeley: University of California Press, 1995), p. 163. To Panofsky, pseudomorphosis is a process: "The emergence of a form A, morphologically analogous to, or even identical with, a form B, yet entirely unrelated to it from a genetic point of view." *Tomb Sculpture*, pp. 26–27.

11. Cynthia Hahn, *Strange Beauty: Issues in the Making and Meaning of Reliquaries, 400–circa 1204* (University Park: Pennsylvania State University Press, 2012), pp. 109–10, has some useful remarks on various literary theorists of metaphor. See also James Wood, *The Broken Estate: Essays on Literature and Belief*, with a new introduction (New York: Picador, 2010), pp. 51–52, 109.

12. Fredrickson, *The Comparative Imagination*, p. 13.

13. David Morgan, ed., *Religion and Material Culture: The Matter of Belief* (New York: Routledge, 2010), pp. 1–6. See also Sam Gill, "The Academic Study of Religion," *Journal of the American Academy of Religion* 62.4 (1994), pp. 965–75; Dick Houtman and Birgit Meyer, "Introduction: Material Religion—How Things Matter," in *Things: Religion and the Question of Materiality*, eds. Dick Houtman and Birgit Meyer (New York: Fordham University Press, 2012), p. 3; and Robert A. Orsi, *Between Heaven and Earth: The Religious Worlds People Make and the Scholars Who Study Them* (Princeton, NJ: Princeton University Press, 2005), pp. 2–3.

14. John Stratton Hawley, *The Bhakti Movement—From Where? Since When?* (Delhi: India International Centre, 2009).

15. David Shulman, *Spring, Heat, Rains: A South Indian Diary* (Chicago: University of Chicago Press, 2009), p. 196.

16. Elliott, *History in the Making*, p. 176, comments: "Can apples and oranges usefully be compared? They may be incomparable where matters of taste are concerned, but nevertheless there are obvious points of comparison when it comes to examining their relative nutritional value, or the methods and cost of production. This would give some point to their comparison, whereas there is little to be gained from a comparison of apples and electric light bulbs, even if there may be rough similarities of size, shape and weight." But if one were interested in surfaces and light refraction, one might well compare apples and light bulbs. Moreover, why choose apples and oranges for nutrition or apples and light bulbs for refraction? To say simply that it depends on the question does not seem to go far enough. Wendy Doniger, writing in *The Implied Spider: Politics and Theology in Myth*, rev. ed. (New York: Columbia University Press, 2011), pp. xi–xiii, 29–31, acknowledges this problem when she asserts that all choices for comparison are arbitrary. But even if the comparanda are arbitrary, she argues, one still learns something from the comparison.

17. Of course, the idea of pseudomorphism may get around this problem by proposing, first, that looking like something else may trigger a deeper probing into what the thing is exactly because it is NOT what it looks like and, second, that formal similarities between things that are not the same may also trigger more sophisticated interpretations. Nonetheless the problem of how we know that two things are "like" remains. However convinced one might be by Panofsky's explanation of the different processes by which Punic and medieval tomb sculptures came to be, one might not see as much similarity as he does between the two cases of three-dimensional figures on tombs; see Panofsky, *Tomb Sculptures*, pp. 52, 54.

18. I owe the phrase "the tyranny of morphology" to Christopher Heuer and thank him for it. I thank him also for the opportunity to discuss these issues with his class at Princeton in spring 2013.

19. All three cases are examples of what Kedar calls "soft" comparison, see n. 5.

20. Robert A. Orsi, *The Madonna of 115th Street: Faith and Community in Italian Harlem, 1880–1950*, 3rd ed. (New Haven, CT: Yale University Press, 2010).

21. *Ibid.*, p. 177.

22. Hahn, *Strange Beauty*, pp. 145–47. Online searches produce many other examples of present-day Catholic veneration of female statues, paraded through streets or countryside, decorated by enthusiastic adherents with flowers, jewelry, money, and so forth, and returned again to their niches. The procession of the Madonna delle Grazie through Boston's North End on July 8, 2012, is only one such case of Mary's enthusiastic adherents and her costly adornments. See "Madonna delle Grazie 2012 Procession through Boston's North End [Photos]," http://northendwaterfront.com/2012/07/madonna-delle-grazie-2012-procession-through-bostons-north-end-photos (accessed February 11, 2013). For another example, see "Madonna Della Cava 2012 Feast—Sunday Procession [Photos],"

http://northendwaterfront.com/2012/08/madonna-della-cava-2012-feast-sunday-procession-photos (accessed February 11, 2013). Note that each of these Marys is particular, with her own feast day and personality, yet each is the Virgin Mary with her full power to bring rewards and accept petitions.

23. Rachel Fell McDermott, *Revelry, Rivalry, and Longing for the Goddesses of Bengal: The Fortunes of Hindu Festivals* (New York: Columbia University Press, 2011), pp. 197–99, points out that Puja festivals have traditionally been male-dominated, although the celebrations appeal to both sexes.

24. See McDermott, *Revelry, Rivalry, and Longing*, pp. 1–5, for the process of awakening the goddess.

25. See, among other works, Victor Turner, *The Ritual Process: Structure and Anti-Structure* (Chicago: Aldine Press, 1969), and, with Edith Turner, *Image and Pilgrimage in Christian Culture: Anthropological Perspectives* (New York: Columbia University Press, 1978). For an example of such interpretation, see Joseph Sciorra, "'We Go Where the Italians Live': Religious Processions as Ethnic and Territorial Markers in a Multi-ethnic Brooklyn Neighborhood," in *Gods of the City: Religion and the American Urban Landscape*, ed. Robert A. Orsi (Bloomington: Indiana University Press, 1999), pp. 310–40.

26. One must be careful not to push analytical categories too hard in asking "Who is there?" Some of the participants in Catholic festivals would say that Mary herself is present; others would insist that this Mary is their particular Mary and that other places have other Marys. For similar Hindu reactions, see n. 30.

27. Orsi, *Madonna of 115th Street*, p. xvi, and Caroline Walker Bynum, *Christian Materiality: An Essay on Religion in Late Medieval Europe* (New York: Zone Books, 2011), pp. 208–15.

28. For example, Hahn, *Strange Beauty*, pp. 145–47. See the introduction to this volume, pp. 43–44.

29. For bibliography, see chapter 3, nn. 2–3. See also Alain Dierkens, Gil Bartholeyns, and Thomas Golsenne, eds., *La performance des images* (Brussels: Éditions de l'Université de Bruxelles, 2010).

30. Joanne Punzo Waghorne, "The Hindu Gods in a Split-Level World: The Sri Siva-Vishnu Temple in Suburban Washington, DC.," in Orsi, *Gods and the City*, p. 128. See also the introduction, n. 48. For a thoughtful and nuanced critique of this way of looking at images, see Joseph Leo Koerner, *The Reformation of the Image* (Chicago: University of Chicago Press, 2004), pp. 94–102; see also n. 59 below.

31. McDermott, *Revelry, Rivalry, and Longing*, p. 4, says that priests invite the goddess to leave before the images are immersed. But her description on p. 5 of women bidding farewell to the goddess and offering her sweets before she goes to the river suggests that it is not clear whether she really departs.

32. Shulman, *Spring, Heat, Rains*, p. 78; see also pp. 93, 97.

33. Linda Hess, "An Open-Air Ramayana: Ramlila, the Audience Experience," in *The*

Life of Hinduism, eds. John Stratton Hawley and Vasudha Narayanan (Berkeley: University of California Press, 2006), pp. 115–39, quotation at p. 131. This understanding of the natural world may be very much like the Western medieval assumption that everything is in some sense alive. (See the introduction, pp. 38–39.) But it is important to note that such continuity of life down a kind of chain of being does not in Western Christianity include God. See n. 35 below, where the reflection of creation in the Trinity is through the humanity of Christ.

34. Thomas of Celano, Second Life of Francis, in *Legendae S. Francisci Assisiensis saeculis XIII et XIV conscriptae*, Analecta franciscana, sive Chronica aliaque varia documenta ad historiam Fratrum Minorum spectantia 10, fascicule 2 (Quarrachi: Collegium S. Bonaventurae, 1926), p. 244.

35. Mechtild of Hackeborn, *Sanctae Mechtildis virginis ordinis sancti Benedicti Liber specialis gratiae*, bk. 4, ch. 3, in *Revelationes Gertrudianae ac Mechtildianae*, eds. Monks of Solesmes, vol. 2 (Paris: Oudin, 1877), p. 260. And see chapter 3, pp. 146–47, for further discussion of this passage. On late medieval views of nature, see also Sara Ritchey, *Holy Matter: Changing Perceptions of the Material World in Late Medieval Christianity* (Ithaca, NY: Cornell University Press, 2014).

36. It is worth noting, as J. S. Hawley has pointed out to me, that in Hinduism, *vasudhā* is one of the names of Earth, and that she has a goddess-like status. Another relevant term is *bhūdevī*, where the first syllable means "earth" all by itself and the second two make clear earth's divine status by labelling her "goddess." See n. 75, where I note that some scholars see Durga as lodged more in plants than in images.

37. Richard H. Davis, *Lives of Indian Images* (Princeton, NJ: Princeton University Press, 1997), p. 39.

38. On the tree of Jesse, see https://en.wikipedia.org/wiki/Tree_of_Jesse (accessed September 25, 2019).

39. R. L. Fantz, "Pattern Vision in Newborn Infants," *Science* 140.3564 (1963), pp. 296–97.

40. For examples of such discussion, see Leys, "The Turn to Affect"; and James Laidlaw, "A Well-Disposed Social Anthropologist's Problems with the 'Cognitive Science of Religion,'" in *Religion, Anthropology, and Cognitive Science*, eds. Harvey Whitehouse and James Laidlaw (Durham, NC: Carolina Academic Press, 2007), pp. 211–46.

41. To some art historians, the pseudomorph's capacity to connect the disparate and to mislead is critically useful. See Powell, *Depositions*, pp. 10–11; Panofsky, *Tomb Sculpture*, pp. 26–27, 52, 54; Bois, "On the Uses and Abuses"; Bynum, "Interrogating 'Likeness'"; and my discussion of the issue in nn. 9–10.

42. This is in fact the kind of analysis both Panofsky, *Tomb Sculpture*, and Lévi-Strauss, "Split Representation," argued for.

43. For more analysis of side wound devotion and further references, see Bynum, *Christian Materiality*, pp. 93–101, 195–208.

44. Flora Lewis, "The Wound in Christ's Side and the Instruments of the Passion: Gendered Experience and Response," in *Women and the Book: Assessing the Visual Experience*, eds. Lesley Smith and Jane H. M. Taylor (London: The British Library, 1996), pp. 204–29, esp. pp. 212–17; Karma Lochrie, "Mystical Acts, Queer Tendencies," in *Constructing Medieval Sexuality*, eds. Karma Lochrie, Peggy McCracken, and James A. Schultz (Minneapolis: University of Minnesota Press, 1997), pp. 180–200; Caroline Walker Bynum, "Violence Occluded: The Wound in Christ's Side in Late Medieval Devotion," in *Feud, Violence and Practice: Essays in Medieval Studies in Honor of Stephen D. White*, eds. Tracey Billado and Belle Tuten (Aldershot, UK: Ashgate, 2010), pp. 95–116; Martha Easton, "The Wound of Christ, the Mouth of Hell: Appropriations and Inversions of Female Anatomy in the Later Middle Ages," in *Tributes to Jonathan J. G. Alexander: The Making and Meaning of Illuminated Medieval and Renaissance Manuscripts, Art and Architecture*, eds. Susan L'Engle and Gerald B. Guest (London/Turnhout: Harvey Miller, 2006), pp. 395–414; Silke Tammen, "Blick und Wunde — Blick und Form: Zur Deutungsproblematik der Seitenwunde Christi in der spätmittelalterlichen Buchmalerei," in *Bild und Körper im Mittelalter*, eds. Kristin Marek, Raphaèle Preisinger, Marius Rimmele, and Katrin Kärcher (Munich: Wilhelm Fink, 2006), pp. 85–114; and Amy Hollywood, "'That Glorious Slit': Irigaray and the Medieval Devotion to Christ's Side Wound," in *Luce Irigaray and Premodern Culture*, eds. Theresa Krier and Elizabeth D. Harvey (London: Routledge, 2004), pp. 105–25. I find the interpretations of Lochrie and Hollywood quite possible readings and would indeed argue that they depend more on the fluidity of symbols I pointed out in the 1980s in *Jesus as Mother: Studies in the Spirituality of the High Middle Ages* (Berkeley: University of California Press, 1982), pp. 110–262, than they quite admit. Nevertheless, I think one must separate more than they do the multiple valences and interpretations suggested by the medieval texts themselves (which implications extend, as Tammen convincingly argues, to exploration of the nature of sight as penetration) from modern psychoanalytic readings, however powerful.

45. Silke Tammen, "Blick und Wunde — Blick und Form," p. 90.

46. On the mandorla, see Burton Callicott, "Mandorlas, Halos, and Rings of Fire," *Quest* 88.4 (July–August 2000), pp. 124–27.

47. On birthing girdles, see the introduction, n. 8, and on feminine and maternal images of Christ, see Bynum, *Jesus as Mother*, pp. 110–262.

48. *A Talkyng of the Loue of God: Edited from MS. Vernon (Bodleian 3938) and Collated with MS. Simeon (Brit. Mus. Add. 22283)*. . . , ed. and trans. M. Salvina Westra (The Hague: Martinus Nijhoff, 1950), p. 61.

49. *The Prickynge of Love*, ch. 1, ed. Harold Kane, 2 vols., *Salzburg Studies in English Literature. Elizabethan and Renaisassance Studies* 92.10 (Salzburg: Institut für Anglistik und Amerikanistik, Universität Salzburg, 1983), vol. 1, pp. 9–14.

50. On these badges, see Jos Koldeweij, "'Shameless and Naked Images': Obscene Badges as Parodies of Popular Devotion," in *Art and Architecture of Late Medieval Pilgrimage*

in Northern Europe and the British Isles, eds. Sarah Blick and Rita Tekippe (Leiden: Brill, 2005), vol. 1, pp. 493–519, and vol. 2, figs. 237–56; Malcolm Jones, *The Secret Middle Ages: Discovering the Real Medieval World* (Phoenix Mill, UK: Sutton, 2002), pp. 248–73; and Ann Marie Rasmussen, *Wandering Genitalia: Sexuality and the Body in German Culture between the Late Middle Ages and Early Modernity* (London: King's College London Centre for Antique and Medieval Studies, 2009). Koldeweij asserts (vol. 1, p. 499) that such obscene badges "turn up in an archeological context with astonishing frequency and in mind-boggling variety," although he cites no numbers. Jones stresses (p. 249) that the badges were "mass-produced in the cheapest of materials." Most have been found in the drowned villages of the Schelde estuary. Jones, *The Secret Middle Ages*, pp. 248–51, sees the images as apotropaic rather than parodic.

51. Élisabeth Taburet-Delahaye et al., eds., *Thermes et hôtel de Cluny, Musée National du Moyen Âge: Oeuvres nouvelles 1995–2005* (Paris: Réunion des Musées Nationaux, 2006), p. 58, fig. 28. See also Madeline H. Caviness, "A Son's Gaze on Noah: Case or Cause of Viriliphobia?" in *Comportamenti e immaginario della sessualità nell'alto medioevo*, Settimane di studio della Fondazione Centro Italiano di Studi sul'Alto Medioevo 53, March 31–April 5, 2005 (Spoleto: Presso la Sede della Fondazione, 2006), pp. 981–1026, esp. fig. 20. The Rotterdam badge is reproduced in Joseph Leo Koerner, "Bosch's Equipment," in *Things That Talk: Object Lessons from Art and Science*, ed. Lorraine Daston (New York: Zone Books, 2004), p. 35, fig. 1.5; in Koldeweij, "'Shameless and Naked Images'"; in Jones, *Secret Middle Ages*, p. 255, fig. 12.2; and in Rasmussen, *Wandering Genitalia*, fig. 10.

52. For the image, see Bynum, *Christian Materiality*, p. 97, fig. 31.

53. I pursue the point about parts and whole in *Christian Materiality*, pp. 195–216, and give a few more images of wound as sexualized body part.

54. Davis, *Lives of Indian Images*, pp. 20–21.

55. See Wendy Doniger, *The Hindus: An Alternative History* (New York: Penguin Press, 2009), p. 22, for an image of the Gudimallam Linga, and p. 259 for discussion; see also Wendy Doniger, "God's Body, or, the *Lingam* Made Flesh: Conflicts over the Representation of Shiva," in *On Hinduism* (New Delhi: Aleph Book Company, 2013), pp. 192–206. For other images, see https://en.wikipedia.org/wiki/Lingam (accessed September 28, 2013).

56. An *Encyclopedia Britannica* article online in 2013 states: "[T]he lingam is distinctively aniconic. . . . Whatever phallic symbolism might have been attached to such structures was largely absent after the Gupta period (early 4th to late 6th century CE)." See https://www.britannica.com/topic/lingam (accessed February 11, 2013). There are, however, lingas from later periods that will appear to many viewers to have phallic features. See, for example, the linga in figure 5.10. On the controversy over interpretation of the linga, see Doniger, "God's Body," in *On Hinduism*, pp. 192–206.

57. Doniger, *The Hindus*, p. 385.

58. I realize that each of these terms and hence of the complexities of the approaches

to which they refer could be the subject of a separate study. But much of the literature on presence simply starts by asking about it; so I do not undertake to define terms such as "phenomenological" or "structural" or "religious" here. The difference between choosing look-alikes and choosing things that in some way bring the Other into relation with the ordinary is, for my purposes in this chapter, sufficiently clear. For some further considerations, see Beate Pongratz-Leisten, "A New Agenda for the Study of the Rise of Monotheism," in *Reconsidering the Concept of Revolutionary Monotheism*, ed. Beate Pongratz-Leisten (Winona Lake, IN: Eisenbrauns, 2011), pp. 21–22; Alfred Gell, *Art and Agency: An Anthropological Theory* (Oxford: Oxford University Press, 1998); and Bynum, "Interrogating 'Likeness'."

59. See, for example, Glenn Peers, "Object Relations: Theorizing the Late Antique Viewer," in *The Oxford Handbook of Late Antiquity*, ed. Scott Fitzgerald Johnson (Oxford: Oxford University Press, 2012), pp. 770–93; Josh Ellenbogen and Aaron Tugendhaft, eds., *Idol Anxiety* (Stanford, CA: Stanford University, 2011), pp. 1–2; and David Freedberg, *The Power of Images: Studies in the History and Theory of Response* (Chicago: University of Chicago Press, 1989).

60. Freedberg, *Power of Images*, p. 84.

61. On "distributive agency," see Pongratz-Leisten, "New Agenda." On "representation," see Gell, *Art and Agency*. See also the introduction, pp. 43–44.

62. On the eye-opening ceremony, see Davis, *Lives of Indian Images*, pp. 33–37; Stephen P. Huyler, "The Experience: Approaching God," in Hawley and Narayanan, eds., *The Life of Hinduism*, pp. 33–41; and Doniger, *The Hindus*, p. 352. Mouth-washing is also paradigmatic in some accounts. See Ellenbogen and Tugendhaft, eds., *Idol Anxiety*, pp. 1–2; and Freedberg, *The Power of Images*, pp. 82–84.

63. Davis, *Lives of Indian Images*, p. 39; Hess, "An Open-Air Ramayana," pp. 128–29; Huyler, "Experience," p. 36; and McDermott, *Revelry, Rivalry, and Longing*, pp. 1–5, 103–109.

64. See the introduction, pp. 38 and 45; chapter 3, pp. 133–35, and Bynum, "Interrogating 'Likeness'."

65. On the complexity of how Catholic Christians (and by implication adherents in other religions) view images, see Koerner, *Reformation of the Image*, pp. 94–102.

66. See chapter 3, pp. 130–35.

67. See the introduction, nn. 7, 45, 46, and 70; Robert Javelet, *Image et ressemblance au 12e siècle, de saint Anselme à Alain de Lille* (Paris: Letouzey et Ané, 1967); and Brigitte Miriam Bedos-Rezak, *When Ego Was Imago: Signs of Identity in the Middle Ages* (Leiden: Brill, 2011).

68. Julia Smith has stressed how often relics in the early Middle Ages were not body parts or even materials that had touched bodies but other sorts of noniconic material that was holy (for example, stones or earth from the Holy Land). See Julia M. H. Smith, "Portable Christianity: Relics in the Medieval West (c. 700–1200)," *Proceedings of the British Academy* 181 (2012), pp. 143–67. For bibliography on relics, see the introduction, n. 4. On

sacramentals, the classic work is Adolph Franz, *Die kirchlichen Benediktionen im Mittelalter* (Freiburg: Herder, 1909).

69. Relics raise a different set of issues, although related ones. Christian relics are not divine but they do reveal the power of God in the saints. Their power is what C. S. Peirce would call indexical (they are physically related to a saint by being a piece of his/her body or by having touched a place of holiness) more than iconic or symbolic. They can often be understood as "consecrated"—not so much made holy as recognized to be holy—by the process of translation from cemetery to altar in the early Middle Ages or, after circa 1200, by the saint's canonization. But many cannot be understood as consecrated so much as found and employed. In this they are like found or self-manifesting Hindu objects: see nn. 74, 77, and 83.

70. One might pursue further a comparison of the way divine presence in Christianity and Hinduism relates to food. Although the Christian Eucharist is visually food, when it metamorphoses miraculously to assert itself as God's presence it sometimes becomes flesh. The Hindu image (whether anthropomorphic or not) is visually the god, but in miracle it sometimes becomes or exudes food, such as honey or milk; it is also itself fed or anointed with milk and butter. See Richard H. Davis, ed., *Images, Miracles, and Authority in Asian Religious Traditions* (Boulder, CO: Westview Press, 1998), esp. p. 18.

71. See Bynum, *Christian Materiality*, figs. 41 and 42, and figure 3.2 in this book. For accounts that attribute such appearances to Jewish host desecration, see https://en.wikipedia.org/wiki/Host_desecration (accessed September 25, 2019); Miri Rubin, *Gentile Tales: The Narrative Assault on Late Medieval Jews* (New Haven, CT: Yale University Press, 1999); and Miri Rubin, "Desecration of the Host: The Birth of an Accusation," *Studies in Church History* 29 (1992), pp. 169–85. On host miracles generally, see Caroline Walker Bynum, *Wonderful Blood: Theology and Practice in Late Medieval Northern Germany and Beyond* (Philadelphia: University of Pennsylvania Press, 2007).

72. On these points, see chapter 3, pp. 141–42; Caroline Walker Bynum, "The Animation and Agency of Holy Food: Bread and Wine as Material Divine in the European Middle Ages," in *The Materiality of Divine Agency in Cross-Cultural Perspective*, eds. Beate Pongratz-Leisten and Karen Sonik (Berlin: de Gruyter, 2015), pp. 70–89. On the miraculous corporal at Walldürn, see Bynum, *Christian Materiality*, pp. 109–11, and "Eucharistic Miracle of Walldürn," http://www.therealpresence.org/eucharst/mir/english_pdf/Walldurn.pdf (accessed May 1, 2013).

73. Stewart Guthrie, "A Cognitive Theory of Religion," *Current Anthropology* 21.2 (1980), pp. 181–94; Stewart Guthrie, *Faces in the Clouds: A New Theory of Religion* (Oxford: Oxford University Press, 1993), esp. pp. 103–12; Justin L. Barrett and Frank C. Keil, "Conceptualizing a Nonnatural Entity; Anthropomorphism in God Concepts," *Cognitive Psychology* 31 (1996), pp. 219–47; Jerome Groopman, "Medical Dispatch: Robots That Care," *The New Yorker* (November 2, 2009), pp. 66–77. On such explanations, see the perceptive critique by

Laidlaw, "A Well-Disposed Social Anthropologist's Problems." Guthrie, who sees anthropomorphism as the origin of religion, tends to argue in a circle. Defining religion as that which relates to gods or spirits, he excludes, by definition, experiences and phenomena that are not anthropomorphic. This definition is a problem especially for Buddhism. See also Justin L. Barrett and Rebekah A. Richert, "Anthropomorphism or Preparedness? Exploring Children's God Concepts," *Review of Religious Research* 44.3 (2003), pp. 300–12, which suggests that children can conceive of God in both anthropomorphic and non-anthropomorphic ways.

74. In fact, non-anthropomorphic objects are important loci of the divine in Hinduism and, significantly enough, these sacral "found" or "self-manifesting" objects do not necessarily have to be consecrated. See Davis, *Lives of Indian Images*, pp. 19–21, 137–40, and Hess, "Open-Air Ramayana," p. 131.

75. McDermott, *Revelry, Rivalry, and Longing*, pp. 104–105.

76. Davis, *Lives of Indian Images*, pp. 34–35; McDermott, *Revelry, Rivalry, and Longing*, pp. 1–5, 103–109.

77. See Davis, *Images, Miracles, and Authority*, esp. Robert L. Brown, "Expected Miracles: The Unsurprisingly Miraculous Nature of Buddhist Images and Relics," pp. 23–36. See also n. 32 on Paidi Talli.

78. Freedberg, *The Power of Images*, pp. 89–91.

79. See Auguste Molien, "Bénédiction," vol. 2 (1937), cols. 349–74, and Pierre Bayard, "Consécration," vol. 4 (1949), cols. 248–67, both in *Dictionnaire de droit canonique* (Paris: Letouzey et Ané, 1935–1965).

80. Joseph A. Jungmann, *The Mass of the Roman Rite: Its Origins and Development* (*Missarum Sollemnia*), trans. Francis A. Brunner and Charles K. Riepe, revised and abridged edition in one volume (New York: Benziger Brothers, 1951), pp. 330–37.

81. Jacqueline E. Jung, "The Unifying Role of the Choir Screen in Gothic Churches," *The Art Bulletin* 82 (2000), pp. 622–57.

82. Édouard Dumoutet, *Le désir de voir l'hostie et les origines de la dévotion au Saint-Sacrement* (Paris: Beauchesne, 1926).

83. Hence, Christian miracles are more like the "expected miracles" Robert Brown talks about (see n. 77) than students of Christianity usually recognize.

84. On the story of the fissure in the Gero crucifix healed by the insertion of a Eucharistic host, see Bynum, *Christian Materiality*, p. 328 n. 137; for the broken hand of the Christ Child kept as a relic, see Barbara Newman, "The Visionary Texts and Visual Worlds of Religious Women," in *Crown and Veil: Female Monasticism from the Fifth to the Fifteenth Centuries*, eds. Jeffrey F. Hamburger and Susan Marti, trans. Dietlinde Hamburger (New York: Columbia University Press, 2008), p. 164.

85. It is worth noting also that Christian missionaries to the New World considered Native American rites that annihilated goods to be disturbingly pagan rituals. See Paula

Findlen, introduction to *Early Modern Things: Objects and Their Histories, 1500–1800*, ed. P. Findlen (London and New York: Routledge, 2013), p. 8.

86. On the assumption of concomitance as a way of thinking, see the introduction, n. 29, and Bynum, *Christian Materiality*, pp. 213–16.

87. Smith, "Portable Christianity."

88. See Bynum, *Wonderful Blood*, pp. 66 and 140–41 for examples. See chapter 4, pp. 152–60, for examples that have lasted into modern times.

89. See https://en.wikipedia.org/wiki/Piscina (accessed September 28, 2013). On ablutions generally, see Jungmann, *Mass of the Roman Rite*, pp. 522–27.

90. The anxiety that some Hindus feel currently over the linga as phallic (see Doniger, "God's Body," pp. 204–206) might appear a reflection, or importation, of Western distaste for the organic. But it seems to me to reflect less a general fear that the organic might be inappropriate for the sacred than an importation of a Western obsession with the sexual/scatological such as is reflected in the objections to Chris Ofili's *The Holy Virgin Mary*. See Carol Vogel, "An Artist's Gallery of Ideas: Chris Ofili's Watercolors," *New York Times*, May 5, 2005.

91. Wood, *Broken Estate*, p. 51. Wood is characterizing Melville's use of metaphor. I extrapolate from what he says. I say more about this in the introduction, p. 27.

92. Pseudo-Dionysius (or Denis) the Areopagite, *La hiérarchie céleste*, eds. René Roques, Günter Heil, and Maurice de Gandillac, *Sources chrétiennes* 58 (Paris: Éditions du Cerf, 1958), ch. 2, sections 3–4 (140C–141D), pp. 78–81. See the introduction, p. 48. I thank Cynthia Hahn, *Strange Beauty*, pp. 109–10, for calling my attention to this passage.

CHAPTER SIX: FOOTPRINTS

1. This essay first appeared as "Footprints: The Xenophilia of a European Medievalist," *Common Knowledge* 24.2 (2018), pp. 291–311, and was a contribution to a four-part symposium on xenophilia conceived and edited by Jeffrey Perl. It has been extensively rewritten and a long section on iconography has been added. I would like to thank Brigitte Bedos-Rezak, John Stratton Hawley, Susan R. Kramer, Guenther Roth, Francesca Trivellato, and Stephen D. White for reading the original essay and making helpful comments. I thank Anthony S. Kaufmann of Abaris Books and Emogene Cataldo for assistance with the plates used in the original article. I also thank Karen Margolis and Eleanor Goerss, who have sent me pictures of footprints from all over Europe. Some of my initial ideas about footprints were presented at the conference "Trace(s)/Spur(en)" held at the Freie Universität Berlin from June 29 to July 1, 2016, as part of the program of the Sonderforschungsbereich "Episteme in Bewegung." Later ideas were presented at the conference "Fake Friends: A Symposium on Art History and Comparison," held at the Institute of Contemporary Art, Philadelphia, and Princeton University, Princeton, on November 29–30, 2018. Readers interested in my description of changes in the field of European medieval studies over

the past fifty years can consult the earlier version of this essay in *Common Knowledge* 24.2.

2. Arthur Ransome, *Swallows and Amazons* (London: Jonathan Cape, 1930). The book is a classic of children's literature and remains popular. There are radio, TV, and film versions and many reprints.

3. Walter Benjamin conceptualized "trace" as the opposite of "aura." See his classic article "The Work of Art in the Age of Its Technological Reproducibility" (1936) and Miriam Bratu Hansen, "Benjamin's Aura," *Critical Inquiry* 34 (2008), pp. 336–75. Jacques Derrida used the term "trace" for the simulacrum of a presence that invariably refers beyond itself. See Jacques Derrida, *Of Grammatology*, trans. Gayatri Chakravorty Spivak (Baltimore: Johns Hopkins University Press, 1976), p. 61, and Spivak, "Translator's Preface," p. xvii. I have been much influenced by the research and conceptualizations of Brigitte Bedos-Rezak on medieval seals, traces, and identity. I cite here only two examples: "L'empreinte: Trace et tracé d'une médiation (1050–2300)," in *Matérialité et immatérialité dans l'église au Moyen Âge, Actes du colloque internationale de Bucarest, 23–24 October 2010*, under the direction of S. D. Daussy et al. (Bucharest: Éditions de l'Université de Bucarest, 2012), pp. 127–41, and Brigitte Miriam Bedos-Rezak, *When Ego Was Imago: Signs of Identity in the Middle Ages* (Leiden: Brill, 2011).

4. The classic citation for a sense of God's footprints (*vestigia*) in creation is Bonaventure, *The Journey of the Mind to God*, trans. Philotheus Boehner, ed. Stephen F. Brown (Indianapolis: Hackett, 1993). On the medieval and early modern idea of traces of God in the natural world, see Friedrich Ohly, *Zur Signaturenlehre der frühen Neuzeit : Bemerkungen zur mittelalterlichen Vorgeschichte und zur Eigenart einer epochalen Denkform in Wissenschaft, Literatur und Kunst*, eds. Uwe Ruberg und Dietmar Peil (Stuttgart: Hirzel, 1999). For an interpretation of the significance of footprints as relics, see Anthony Cutler, "The Relics of Scholarship: On the Production, Reproduction, and Interpretation of Hallowed Remains in Late Antiquity, Byzantium, Early Islam, and the Medieval West," in *Saints and Sacred Matter: The Cult of Relics in Byzantium and Beyond*, eds. Cynthia Hahn and Holger A. Klein (Washington, DC: Dumbarton Oaks Research Library and Collection, 2015), pp. 309–45, esp. pp. 315–22.

5. By writing about the topic of the *Common Knowledge* symposium, which is *philia* or desire, I do not mean to deny that there are horrors in the medieval past that we try to understand in order not only to avoid but also to deplore them. Nor do I deny that desire for the medieval past can descend (and often has descended) into romanticizing or fetishizing unattractive aspects of European history. For discussion of recent efforts by scholars to oppose the misuse of medieval ideas and objects to support unfortunate and harmful attitudes in the present, see "What's New about the Medieval?" in Caroline Walker Bynum, *The Resurrection of the Body in Western Christianity*, 200–1336, expanded edition (New York: Columbia University Press, 2017), pp. xxvi–xxviii. I should also recognize here that it is possible to "desire" what one abhors. Indeed, much has been written in the past two decades about the ugly, the disgusting, the violent, and the frightful in the Middle Ages,

but that is not my topic here. See, for example, William Ian Miller, *The Anatomy of Disgust* (Cambridge, MA: Harvard University Press, 1997); Alexandra Cuffel, *Gendering Disgust in Medieval Religious Polemic* (Notre Dame, IN: University of Notre Dame Press, 2007); and Umberto Eco, *On Ugliness*, trans. Alastair McEwen (New York: Rizzoli, 2007).

6. See chapter 5, where I argue that we should seek beneath (or in spite of) similarity of shape or morphology in order to find a deeper religious—or one might say ontological, or psychological, or functional—significance.

7. Janet Bord, *Footprints in Stone: The Significance of Foot- and Hand-prints and Other Imprints Left by Early Men, Giants, Heroes, Devils, Saints, Animals, Ghosts, Witches, Fairies and Monsters* (Loughborough, UK: Heart of Albion Press, 2004).

8. *Ibid.*, pp. 36, 50, 89, and 196.

9. Jacob N. Kinnard, *Places in Motion: The Fluid Identities of Temples, Images, and Pilgrims* (New York: Oxford University Press, 2014), ch. 3.

10. Bord, *Footprints in Stone*, pp. 41–43, and Lenz Kriss-Rettenbeck, *Bilder und Zeichen religiösen Volksglaubens* (Munich: Georg D. W. Callwey, 1963), pp. 40–41 and 69 and plates 82 and 215. Copies of the footprints on the Mount of Olives came to be understood by Christian pilgrims as carrying actual indulgences for remission of sin and were sometimes inscribed with such promises. Thus such copies did convey information about devotion and even salvation.

11. Bord, *Footprints in Stone*, p. 41.

12. *Ibid.*, and *Eternal Presence: Handprints and Footprints in Buddhist Art*, museum catalogue, guest curator Kathryn H. Selig Brown (Katonah, NY: Katonah Museum of Art, 2004), plate 1, p. 34. But see n. 39 in this chapter for the ways in which the footprints of the Buddha and those of Christ are in a sense the god.

13. Anthony Cutler, "The Relics of Scholarship." Whereas Cutler treats footprints across cultures as primarily proofs of having made pilgrimage or performed shrine veneration, I treat them primarily as objects that themselves convey sacrality or power. Neither of us would deny either function.

14. On the Church of Domine Quo Vadis, see https://en.wikipedia.org/wiki/Church_of_Domine_Quo_Vadis (accessed September 27, 2019). On Monte Sant'Angelo sul Gargano, where the archangel Michael supposedly appeared, see John Charles Arnold, "Arcadia Becomes Jerusalem: Angelic Caverns and Shrine Conversion at Monte Gargano," *Speculum* 75 (July 2000), pp. 567–88.

15. Many accounts of apparitions and visions and of the relics they point to do not tell us whether the appearance was a dream, a vision, or a physical encounter. In Caroline Walker Bynum, *Christian Materiality: An Essay on Religion in Late Medieval Europe* (New York: Zone Books, 2011), pp. 22, 108–12, and 292 n. 26, I have discussed how objects are often left behind by figures in apparitions as proof that they appeared. For example, the cloak on which the image of the Virgin of Guadalupe was found became more important in subsequent

cult (in part, of course, because of the reproducibility of the image) than the place of her appearance or even the person of the recipient.

16. See chapter 2, n. 41. Medieval exegetes read the head of Christ as symbolizing his divinity and the feet his humanity; see Robert Deshman, "Another Look at the Disappearing Christ: Corporeal and Spiritual Vision in Early Medieval Images," *The Art Bulletin* 79.3 (1997), pp. 518–46, at pp. 528–30. For Christ washing the feet of the apostles, see Matthew 26:14–39; Luke 22:24–27; John 13:1–17.

17. Kinnard, *Places in Motion*, pp. 56–96; Paul Brian Thomas, "The Riddle of Ishtar's Shoes: The Religious Significance of the Footprints at 'Ain Dara from a Comparative Perspective," *Journal of Religious History* 32.3 (2008), pp. 303–19.

18. David Freedberg, *The Power of Images: Studies in the History and Theory of Response* (Chicago: University of Chicago Press, 1989), p. 91.

19. See chapter 4, p. 49. Earth has a contradictory valence in medieval Christianity as welcoming and threatening, a place of rest and a place of violent dissolution. Both decay and failure to decay thus have positive and negative meanings, as do acceptance and rejection of persons by the earth. On this contradiction, see Bynum, *Resurrection of the Body*, p. 206 n. 20.

20. The prints of Ishtar's shoes at 'Ain Dara and of the Jewish wife's feet at Sternberg may imply a similar conception of the earth as, at least in these cases, polluting and/or dangerous but the conceptions of the organic and the physical implied by their contexts do not seem to be the same. See Thomas, "The Riddle of Ishtar's Shoes," and chapter 4.

21. See nn. 3–4.

22. Eusebius, *Life of Constantine*, bk 3, c. 28, trans. and commentary by Averil Cameron and Stuart G. Hall (Oxford: Oxford University Press, 1999), p. 133. In bk 3, c. 33, p. 135, Eusebius calls it "a tomb full of agelong memory, comprising the trophies of the great Saviour's defeat of death, a tomb of divine presence." Cyril of Jerusalem, in the *Catecheses* (Lenten Lectures), number 14, c. 22, speaks of the "rock of the Sepulcher" and "the stone which was rolled back" as testimony to the Resurrection. See *The Works of Saint Cyril of Jerusalem*, trans. Leo P. McCauley and Anthony A. Stephenson, 2 vols. (Washington, DC: The Catholic University of America Press, 1970), vol. 2, pp. 46–47.

23. On God's footprints in creation, see Bonaventure, *The Journey of the Mind to God*. Hildegard of Bingen's understanding of *viriditas* is also a locus classicus for the sense of God in creation; see Gabriele Lautenschläger, "'Viriditas': Ein Begriff und seine Bedeutung," in *Hildegard von Bingen: Prophetin durch die Zeiten. Zum 900. Geburtstag*, eds. Edeltraud Forster and the Nuns of Eibingen (Freiburg: Herder, 1997), pp. 224–37. For Calvin, see John Calvin, *Institutes of the Christian Religion*, 2 vols., ed. John T. McNeill, trans. Ford Lewis Battles (Philadelphia: Westminster Press, 1977), bk 1, cc. 1–12, vol. 1, pp. 35–66. See *ibid.*, p. 66 n. 42, for debate among scholars about whether Calvin's idea of seeing God in nature amounts to a natural theology. On Christian conceptions of traces in nature, see Ohly, *Zur Signaturenlehre*.

24. Andrea Worm, "Steine und Fussspuren Christi auf dem Ölberg: Zu zwei ungewöhnlichen Motiven bei Darstellungen der Himmelfahrt Christi," *Zeitschrift für Kunstgeschichte* 66.3 (2003), pp. 297–320, at p. 298.

25. Insofar as I have been able to discover, depictions of the footprints are mostly from northern Europe. See the results of a Google search for "ascension of Christ + medieval images," https://www.google.com/search?q=ascension+of+Christ+%2B+medieval+images&client=firefox-b-1&tbm=isch&tbo=u&source=univ&sa=X&ved=2ahUKEwjB5au2yPzfAhWuc98KHZ6MAuQQsAR6BAgEEAE&biw=1600&bih=764 (accessed September 27, 2019). Worm notes only German examples of manuscript depictions of the stone of the Ascension with footprints. There are also examples of representations of footprints in manuscripts from England and the Low Countries and, as I discuss in nn. 66–72, copies of the *Speculum humanae salvationis* from a number of places show the footprints combined with the disappearing Christ. For an English example of footprints left on what appears to be a hill, see the bench-end in Launcells Church, Cornwall, reproduced in Bord, *Footprints in Stone*, p. 37. Kriss-Rettenbeck, *Bilder und Zeichen*, pp. 40–41, refers to a wide diffusion in early modern Europe of "measures" of the footprints left behind at the Ascension. See n. 43.

26. For more on the disappearing Christ, see nn. 59–61.

27. For Paulinus's letter, see Paulinus of Nola, Epistle 31, paragraph 4, in J.-P. Migne ed., *Patrologia latina*, vol. 61, cols. 325–30; here col. 328; "Mirum vero inter haec quod in basilica Ascensionis locus ille tantum de quo in nube susceptus *ascendit*, *captivam* in sua carne *ducens captivitatem nostram*, ita sacratus divinis vestigiis dicitur, ut numquam tegi marmore aut paviri receperit, semper excussis solo respuente, quae manus adornandi studio tentavit apponere. Itaque in toto basilicae spatio solus in sui cespitis specie virens permanet; et impressam divinorum pedum venerationem calcati Deo pulveris perspicua simul et attigua venerantibus arena conservat, ut vere dici possit: *adoravimus ubi steterunt pedes ejus*." And see Worm, "Steine und Fussspuren," pp. 307–308 nn. 25–26.

28. Sulpicius Severus, *Chronica*, bk 2, sect. 33, *La chronique de Sulpice Sévère: Texte critique, traduction et commentaire*, ed. André Lavertujon, 2 vols. (Paris: Hachette, 1899), vol. 2, pp. 75–76. "Quin etiam calcati Deo pulveris adeo perenne documentum est, ut vestigia impressa cernantur, et cum cottidie confluentium fides certatim Domino calcata diripat, damnum tamen arena non sentiat, et eandem adhuc sui speciem, velut impressis signata vestigiis, terra custodit."

29. Jacobus de Voragine, *The Golden Legend: Readings on the Saints*, trans. William Granger Ryan, 2 vols. (Princeton, NJ: Princeton University Press, 1993), vol. 1, p.292. Note the stress on proof. Considering why Christ waited forty days to ascend, James says: "The first [reason] was to provide sure evidence of his resurrection from the dead."

30. See John Wilkinson, *Jerusalem Pilgrims before the Crusades* (Oxford: Oxbow Books, 2002), pp. 180–81, and Worm, "Steine und Fussspuren," p. 308. For Adamnan's account, see *Itinera Hierosolymitana. Saec. IV–VIII*, ed. Paulus Geyer (Vienna, 1898), pp. 220–97, at p. 247.

Bede's *De locis sanctis*, which was widely disseminated, is based on Adamnan. For early pilgrim accounts of footprints of Christ venerated in other sites in Jerusalem, see Denys Pringle, *The Churches of the Crusader Kingdom of Jerusalem: A Corpus*, vol. 3, *The City of Jerusalem* (Cambridge: Cambridge University Press, 2007), p. 401 (for the account of Saewulf, 1103–4) and p. 404 (for that of John of Würzburg, c. 1165). The footprints Saewulf refers to are possibly those earlier attributed to Abraham, Isaac, and/or Mohammed.

31. "In eodem igitur loco, ut sanctus refert Arculfus, sedulus eiusdem frequentator, aerea grandis per circuitum rota desuper explanata collocata est, cuius altitudo usque ad cervicem haberi monstratur mensurata. In cuius medietate non parva patet pertusura, per quam desuper apertam vestigia pedum Domini plane et lucide impressa in pulvere demonstrantur. Illa quoque in rota ab occidentali parte quasi quaedam semper patet porta, ut per eam intrantes facile adire locum sacrati pulveris possint et per apertam desuper eiusdem rotae foramen de sacro pulvere porrectis manibus particulas sumant." *Itinera Hierosolymitana*, p. 247.

32. Pringle, *Churches*, vol. 3, p. 73.

33. John Wilkinson with Joyce Hill and W. F. Ryan, *Jerusalem Pilgrimage 1099–1185* (London: The Hakluyt Society, 1988), pp. 221–22. Abbot Daniel, a Russian pilgrim in 1106–1108, refers to a stone where "the most pure feet of our Lord" stood, but he does not mention footprints. See Pringle, *Churches*, vol. 3, p. 73. The reference by the Icelandic pilgrim to Michael's church is a mistake for the Church of the Ascension. Wilkinson suggests that the association may be because of the church at Monte Gargano in Italy, where there is allegedly a footprint of Michael the archangel. Worm, "Steine und Fussspuren," p. 311, hypothesizes, quite plausibly, that after the loss of the sand footprints, pilgrims marked a stone in order to remember the spot, and that stone became a "touch relic."

34. Belard of Ascoli in the mid-twelfth century says there is a print of the left foot in stone but only the toes and part of the sole are visible; an account in 1187 refers to prints of both feet. Pringle, *Churches*, vol. 3, p. 73.

35. For a full account of the history of the church, see Pringle, *Churches*, vol. 3, pp. 72–88. For Burchard and Nicolas of Poggibonsi, see *ibid.*, p. 750. Francesco Quaresmi, in the early seventeenth century, says that the remaining footprint is the left one (pp. 76–77). At about the same time, Bernardino Amico reports that the second footprint has been removed (p. 77). See also https://en.wikipedia.org/wiki/Chapel_of_the_Ascension,_Jerusalem (accessed June 8, 2016).

36. Pringle, *Churches*, vol. 3, p. 82, says the stone with footprints on display today is 0.5 × 0.74 m. There is debate about the original architecture and vaulting of the aedicule or chapel containing the stone, but it seems to have been at the center of the Crusader Church of the Ascension, of which only remains survive today.

37. See n. 16. For the association of the Magdalen with the feet of Christ, see Deshman, "Another Look at the Disappearing Christ," p. 537. In the widely read *Meditations on the Life of Christ*, the Magdalen is said to kiss the feet of Christ at the deposition. Contributing

to this iconography, of course, is the conflation of several Marys of Scripture, so that the Magdalen was thought to have anointed Christ's feet with expensive ointment (Matthew 26:6–13; Mark 14:3–9; Luke 7:36–50; John 12:1–8). See also Katherine Ludwig Jansen, *The Making of the Magdalen: Preaching and Popular Devotion in the Later Middle Ages* (Princeton, NJ: Princeton University Press, 2000).

38. For the *Noli me tangere*, see John 20:17. We should also note that the feet of medieval devotional figures were especially stroked and adored, some until they were almost worn away. On the worn feet of devotional objects, see Bynum, *Christian Materiality*, fig. 1, p. 23. Contact with Christ's feet, and Christ's action in touching the feet of others, serves not only as a sign of Christ's human nature and of humility but also as the promise of reversal—"the last shall be first" (Matthew 19:30 and 20:16; Mark 10:31; Luke 13:30)—that is a core aspect of medieval Christian belief. On inversion of language and therefore of values as a New Testament literary technique widely used by medieval spiritual writers, see Caroline Walker Bynum, *Jesus as Mother: Studies in the Spirituality of the High Middle Ages* (Berkeley: University of California Press, 1982), pp. 127–28.

39. It is worth noting that Buddhist ideas of relics and footprints are remarkably like Christian ones, despite that fact that the theologies of salvation in the two religions are very different. Handprints and footprints in Buddhism act as do Christian relics and measures; they convey presence, heal, and *are* in some sense the Buddha or bodhisattva they image. See K. Brown, *Eternal Presence.*

40. See "Antonini Placentini Itinerarium," sect. 23, in *Itinera Hierosolymitana*, p. 175; "In ipsa basilica est sedis, ubi Pilatus sedit. . . . Petra autem quadrangulis . . . in qua leuatus est Dominis . . . ubi etiam uestigia illius remanserunt. Pedem pulchrum, modicum, subtilem. . . . Nam de petra illa, ubi stetit, fiunt virtutes multae; tollentes de ipsa uestigia pedum mensuram, ligantes pro singulis languoribus et sanantur." See also Wilkinson, *Jerusalem Pilgrims before the Crusades*, p. 141; Worm, "Steine und Fussspuren," p. 312 n. 48, and Bord, *Footprints in Stone*, pp. 38–39. On the Icelandic pilgrim, see n. 33.

41. "Antonini Placentini Itinerarium," sect. 22, *Itinera Hierosolymitana*, p. 174: "In ipsa ecclesia est columna, ubi flagellatus est Dominus. In qua columna tale est signum: dum eam amplexasset, pectus eius inhaesit in ipsa marmore et manus ambas apparent et digiti et palmae in ipsa petra, ita ut pro singulis languoribus mensura tollatur exinde; et circa collum habent et sanantur." Also Worm, "Steine und Fussspuren," p. 312 n. 48.

42. Kriss-Rettenbeck, *Bilder und Zeichen*, p. 40; Nina Gockerell, "Pilgerandenken aus Jerusalem," in *Dona Ethnologica Monacensia: Leopold Kretzenbacher zum 70. Geburtstag*, eds. Helge Gerndt, Klaus Roth, and Georg R. Schroubek (Munich: Bayerisches Nationalmuseum Institut für deutsche urgleichende Volkskunde, 1983), pp. 163–79, at p. 171; and Worm, "Steine und Fussspuren," p. 320 n. 69. See n. 10 in this chapter. I cannot here go into the important question of how far the nature of the object changes when it becomes the written record of an indulgence or the record of a shrine visit. If it becomes

more a record than a relic, does it still carry presence in the way I have analyzed here?

43. Kriss-Rettenbeck, *Bilder und Zeichen*, plate 215, discussed on p. 120. See also pp. 40–41. For examples of other measures that are aniconic or nonrepresentational, see pp. 68, 137–38. The footprint discussed by Kriss-Rettenbeck is also reproduced in Bord, *Footprints in Stone*, p. 38; for a measure of the Virgin Mary's sandal, see *ibid.*, p. 74.

44. Gregory of Tours, *Glory of the Martyrs*, c. 27, trans. Raymond van Dam (Liverpool: Liverpool University Press, 1988), pp. 45–46.

45. See Adolf Jacoby, "Heilige Längenmasse: Eine Untersuchung zur Geschichte der Amulette," *Schweizerisches Archiv für Volkskunde* 29.1 (1929), pp. 1–17, and 29.4 (1929), pp. 181–216, at pp. 1–3. This is a seventeenth-century text that, however, echoes many earlier ones.

46. Kriss-Rettenbeck, *Bilder und Zeichen*, p. 41. See n. 49 on birthing girdles.

47. David Areford, "The Passion Measured: A Late-Medieval Diagram of the Body of Christ," in *The Broken Body: Passion Devotion in Late-Medieval Culture*, eds. A. A. MacDonald, H. N. B. Ridderbos, and R. M. Schlusemann (Groningen: Egbert Forsten, 1998).

48. The translations of the scroll texts are Areford's, from "The Passion Measured," pp. 223 and 225. For other examples of measures, see Kriss-Rettenbeck, *Bilder und Zeichen*, pp. 40–42, 115, and plates 82–85, and see Gockerell, "Pilgerandenken aus Jerusalem," pp. 165–66, for measures of places in the Holy Land, such as the Holy Sepulcher.

49. The length of the body or the length or circumference of a body part (sometimes the girth of a pregnant woman's belly) was measured with a cord, which then became the wick of a candle made to the measure. See Adolph Franz, *Die kirchlichen Benediktionen im Mittelalter*, 2 vols. (Freiburg: Herder, 1909), vol. 2, pp. 456–57. For examples, see John Shinners, ed., *Medieval Popular Religion, 1000–1500: A Reader* (Peterborough, ON: Broadview Press, 1997), pp. 161, 165, 259–60, and Carl S. Watkins, *History and the Supernatural in Medieval England* (Cambridge: Cambridge University Press, 2007), p. 123. We also find cases where length acquires what we would call iconic similarity and conveys presence. See my discussion in the introduction (pp. 36–38) of the birthing girdle inscribed with the side wound of Christ found in Wellcome MS 632, studied by Mary Morse, "Seeing and Hearing: Margery Kempe and the mise-en-page," *Studia Mystica* 20 (1999), pp. 15–42.

50. Such presences via measure raise interesting issues for art historians about how iconicity and similitude relate to representation, about the relationship of "aura" and "reproduction," about how useful the frequently employed icon/index distinction is, and indeed about what "representation" means. See the introduction, pp. 36–57.

51. I rely here on Renana Bartal, Neta Bodner, and Bianca Kühnel, eds., *Natural Materials of the Holy Land and the Visual Translation of Place, 500–1500* (London: Routledge, 2017), especially the introduction, pp. xxiii–xxxiii, and the chapters by Ora Limor, "Natural Materials in Early Pilgrimage Texts," pp. 3–18 (see esp. p. 8), and Lucy Donkin, "Earth from Elsewhere: Burial in *Terra Sancta* beyond the Holy Land," pp. 109–26. For Sulpicius Severus, see *Chronica*, bk 2, sect. 33, *La chronique de Sulpice Sévère*, ed. André Lavertujon, vol. 2, pp. 75–76.

52. Augustine, *The City of God*, trans. Marcus Dods (New York: Random House, 1950), bk. xxii.8, p. 824. The first three references in this paragraph are taken from Ora Limor, "Natural Materials," p. 7.

53. Gregory of Tours, *Glory of the Martyrs*, trans. R. Van Dam, ch. 6, p. 27. Gregory adds, "Faith believes that everything that the sacred body touched is sacred."

54. Donkin, "Earth from Elsewhere." It is not clear exactly how far Akeldama (or Rome) could be transported. Taken to Ireland or Germany, the soil apparently lost some of its regurgitating or decomposing power. For the related question of whether the holy is diluted by addition of material, see Bynum, *Christian Materiality*, pp. 160–62. See also n. 19.

55. Worm, "Steine und Fussspuren," pp. 310–11 n. 41. Worm also lists two other examples of references to stone relics. Noting that the bits and pieces medieval Christians revered as "relics" were often *not* body parts is an important revision in recent medieval studies. Julia M. H. Smith, "Portable Christianity: Relics in the Medieval West (c. 700–1200)," *Proceedings of the British Academy* 181 (2012), pp. 143–67.

56. The power of material to carry the holy is sometimes referred to as "the contagion of holiness" or the "devotional logic of presence." Elsewhere I have called it "the concomitant habit of mind." See Bord, *Footprints in Stone*, pp. 6–7; Robert A. Orsi, *The Madonna of 115th Street: Faith and Community in Italian Harlem, 1880—1950*, 3rd ed. (New Haven, CT: Yale University Press, 2010), p. xvi; Bynum, *Christian Materiality*, pp. 208–16. Such concomitant thinking has not disappeared from the secular West; see, for example, the practice of burying the ashes left after cremation as if they are the whole body. In Thomas Laqueur's recent study of the long history of burial practices, he describes transporting earth in which "there might have been a homeopathetically small number of inorganic molecules that had once been in my father" to add to the soil of his grandfather's grave in Hamburg. The oddly scientizing description of the bits ("homeopathetically," "inorganic," "molecules") juxtaposed to the act Laqueur actually performed shows both discomfort with and continuation of age-old assumptions about body and matter, parts and wholes. See Thomas W. Laqueur, *The Work of the Dead: A Cultural History of Mortal Remains* (Princeton, NJ: Princeton University Press, 2015), p. 26.

57. See nn. 8–19.

58. I cannot address this larger topic here, although I have discussed it in *Christian Materiality*, pp. 273–80, as it relates to differences between Eastern and Western Christianity and between Christianity, Judaism, and Islam in how relics convey presence. All three of the religions that emerged in the ancient Near East had something like reverence for the burial places of holy figures, a strong emphasis on the practice of pilgrimage to places of holy burial or holy events, and some sense that material objects associated with such places could carry power and presence from it. But even across these three traditions, place and object do not have the same valence and importance. It seems clear that holy place is more important in Islam and Judaism, holy object in Christianity, if one means

this in the specific and careful sense I develop in *Christian Materiality*. Some Muslims claim that the footprint of Mohammed is found in the Topkapı Palace in Istanbul and in the Dome of the Rock in Jerusalem, but these prints are not understood to have either the significance or the power of acting at a distance that Jesus's footprint from the Mount of Olives allegedly has.

59. Robert Deshman, "Another Look at the Disappearing Christ," p. 530 n. 76, cites the tenth-century Blickling homily that emphasized that Christ's miraculously indestructible footprints were "the spot where [he] last stood in the body here in the world, before he ascended into the heavens in his human nature."

60. See Meyer Schapiro, "The Image of the Disappearing Christ: The Ascension in English Art around the Year 1000," *Gazette des Beaux-Arts*, ser. 6, XXIII (1943), pp. 133–52, reprinted in Schapiro, *Selected Papers*, vol. 3, *Late Antique, Early Christian, and Medieval Art* (New York: George Braziller, 1979), pp. 267–87, and Deshman, "Another Look at the Disappearing Christ." Schapiro sees the disappearing Christ as involving a fundamentally new conception of perspective; Deshman disagrees and sees the motif as a literal illustration of the account in Acts 1:9–11. Schapiro and Deshman agree, however, that these images position the viewer with the apostles standing below.

61. See n. 25; Deshman, "Another Look at the Disappearing Christ," pp. 532–37.

62. On saints cuddling Christ's feet and medieval people adoring the feet of devotional statues, see n. 38. On the feet as signifying Christ's humanity, see nn. 16 and 59. Deshman, "Another Look at the Disappearing Christ," p. 532, describes the disappearing Christ as a paradox of presence and absence.

63. Worm, "Steine und Fussspuren," p. 313, associates the appearance of depictions of the stone of the Ascension with the circulation in Germany of pilgrim accounts from about 1100 that mention it. She also mentions the spread of accounts of Mohammed's footprints at the Dome of the Rock as a possible influence on depictions of footprints (p. 312 n. 49).

64. Gertrud Schiller, *Ikonographie der christlichen Kunst*, 4 vols. (Gütersloh: Mohn, 1966–80), vol. 3, pp. 140–64; Peter Murray and Linda Murray, *The Oxford Companion to Christian Art and Architecture* (Oxford: Oxford University Press, 1996), entry on "Ascension," pp. 34–35; and Worm, "Steine und Fussspuren," pp. 313–19.

65. Here I depart a bit from both Schapiro and Deshman (see nn. 59–62), who emphasize mainly the viewing position of the apostles. I think it also matters to note *what* they see, and in many of these images what they see is not so much the departing feet or the left-behind trace as the gap in between.

66. For another example, see Jeffrey F. Hamburger and Nigel Palmer, with a Conservation Report by Ulrike Bürger, *The Prayer Book of Ursula Begerin*, 2 vols. (Dietikon-Zurich: Urs Graf Verlag, 2015), vol. 1, pp. 340–42, and vol. 2, p. 153.

67. *The Mirror*, which paired the life of Christ with Old Testament prototypes and included the Hours of the Passion and the Seven Sorrows and Seven Joys of Mary, was

almost as popular as the Bible and the *Golden Legend*. More than 20 incunabula editions and 190 illuminated manuscripts (some only fragments) survive. For a summary of the *Speculum humanae salvationis* (the *Mirror*), chapter by chapter, see https://iconographic.warburg.sas.ac.uk/vpc/VPC_search/Speculum_summary.html (accessed August 2, 2018). There are many print versions and translations available. See, for example, Jean Miélot (active fifteenth century), *Speculum Humanae Salvationis: Text Critique* (Mulhouse: E. Meininger, 1907-1909). I am extremely grateful to Eleanor Goerss for suggesting that I look at the *Mirror* for images of footprints.

68. Five have a full figure, and in one, Christ is missing entirely, represented only by his footprints. The assembled viewers are the apostles, often including Mary; and in about a quarter of the images, angels stand on either side of the assembled group.

69. I count one with wounds on both feet and footprints, two with wounds in footprints, and four with wounds in Jesus's departing feet. The emphasis in this text is not on blood veneration or suffering but rather on departure with presence left behind. The message is clearly, as the text says, that the joys of heaven will far surpass the sufferings of earth.

70. On the *arma Christi*, as well as these Marian images, see the introduction at n. 22. I emphasize there that what surround Mary are objects, things; it is objects that carry and depict for us the viewers the significance of her crucial experience and emotion. For the images of chapter 44 of the *Mirror*, see the Warburg Institute Iconographic Database, https://iconographic.warburg.sas.ac.uk/vpc/VPC_search/subcats.php?cat_1=14&cat_2=812&cat_3=2903&cat_4=5439&cat_5=13111&cat_6=9889&cat_7=3248&cat_8=1094 (accessed August 3, 2018).

71. It is clear that the little hill with the footprints does signify the Ascension. Therefore it is not strictly accurate to say that what is grouped around her figure are the instruments of the Passion.

72. Mary's grief at being left behind at the Ascension is, in chapter 44 of the *Mirror*, paired with a Pietà. See figure 6.18 for an example.

73. Because of the schematic way in which figures were sometimes depicted in this period—especially figures in profile—it is impossible to be totally accurate about where an artist intends the gaze of a depicted figure to be directed. Therefore, one must be careful not to overinterpret the gaze within the picture.

74. Any scholar who has struggled with deciphering a manuscript or interpreting what a damaged object unearthed from the past represents will readily admit that evidence acts on (both tortures and inspires) those who study it.

75. On the kind of power certain medieval objects unfortunately have in the current political scene, see Bynum, "What's New About the Medieval?" pp. xxvi–xxviii. See also p. 273 n. 84 and n. 5 in this chapter. What I say here about how the footprint always evokes an Other it can never simply replicate suggests that neither current use of objects from the past for political purposes nor simple castigation of them is a wise or appropriate response.

Index

Image Credits

Frontispiece © Kloster Wienhausen.

I.1. © Kurpfälzisches Museum der Stadt Heidelberg.
I.2. Metropolitan Museum of Art. Open access.
I.3a. Princeton Art Museum.
I.3b. Domschatzverwaltung, Halberstadt, Landesamt für Denkmalpflege und Archäologie Sachsen-Anhalt; photographer Juraj Lipták.
I.3c. Princeton Art Museum.
I.3d. Creative Commons. Open access.
I.4. © Vatican Museums.
I.5. Alamy Stock Photo; photographer John Morrison.
I.6. Metropolitan Museum of Art. Open access.
I.7. Trustees of the National Gallery, London.
I.8. Blanton Museum of Art.
I.9. © Museum Ulm; photographer Ingeborg Schmatz.
I.10. Alamy Stock Photo; photographer Gonzalo Azumendi.
I.11. Bayerische Staatsbibliothek, Munich.
I.12. Creative Commons. Open access.
I.13. Clive Moon.
I.14. Department of Special Collections, Stanford University Librairies. Open access.
I.15. Nadine Mai.
I.16. British Library/Granger.
I.17. Manuscripts Division, Department of Special Collections, Princeton University Library.

1.1–2. Metropolitan Museum of Art. Open access.
1.3. © GDKE/Rheinisches Landesmuseum Trier; photographer Th. Zühmer.
1.4. Hetjens-Museum, Düsseldorf.
1.5a. Museum Catharijneconvent; photographer Ruben de Heer.
1.5b. Museum May van den Bergh; photographer Hugo Maertens.

1.6. KIK-IRPA, Bruxelles.
1.7. Metropolitan Museum of Art. Open access.
1.8. © Rheinisches Bildarchiv, rba_c007015.
1.9. © Hohe Domkirche Köln, Dombauhütte, Cologne; photography Matz und Schenk.
1.10. Peter Miranski.
1.11–12. Metropolitan Museum of Art. Open access.
1.13. © Bayerisches Nationalmusuem, Munich; photographer Karl-Michael Vetters, Nr. D151806.
1.14. Digitized text Universiteitsbibliotheek Gent 900000178752. Open access.
1.15. Staatliches Museum, Schwerin/Art Resource, NY; photographer Hugo Maertens.
1.16a–b. Museum August Kestner, Hannover; photographer Christian Tepper.
1.17. © Kloster Wienhausen.

2.1. © Kloster Wienhausen.
2.2a. Hirmer Verlag with permission of Adelhausen Stiftung, Freiburg i. Br., photo archives.
2.2b. Jürgen Matschie, Bautzen; used by permission of the abbess of Marienstern.
2.3. © Domschatz Essen; photographer Christian Diehl.
2.4. © Kloster Wienhausen.
2.5. © Kloster Wienhausen; photographer Ulrich Loeper.
2.6. Brepols Publisher, Turnhout, Belgium.
2.7. Migstock/Alamy Stock Photo.
2.8. Creative Commons; photographer Stephen Dwyer. Open access.
2.9. © Abegg-Stiftung; photographer Christoph von Viràg.
2.10a–b. © Kloster Wienhausen; photographer Ulrich Loeper.
2.11. Marienstern monastery; scan by Eva Schlotheuber.
2.12a–b. © Städel Museum—ARTOTHEK.

3.1. © The Trustees of the British Museum. All rights reserved.
3.2–3.3. Creative Commons. Open access.

4.1–4.4. Caroline Walker Bynum.

5.1. Office du tourisme des Saintes-Maries-de-la-Mer.
5.2. © Matt Conti.
5.3. Universal Images Group North America LLC/Alamy Stock Photo.
5.4. Alamy Stock Photo; photographer Tuul and Bruno Morandi.
5.5. Alamy Stock Photo; photographer Suman Bhaumik.
5.6. British Library/Bridgeman Images.
5.7. Metropolitan Museum of Art. Open access.
5.8. Creative Commons. Open access.
5.9. © RMN-Grand Palais/Art Resource, NY.
5.10. Metropolitan Museum of Art. Open access.
5.11. Creative Commons; photographer Gangadhar Tambe. Open access.
5.12. Creative Commons. Open access.
5.13. Creative Commons; photographer Ilya Mauter. Open access.

6.1. Creative Commons. Open access.
6.2. Yale University Art Gallery. Open access.
6.3. British Library/Granger.
6.4a–b. Abaris Books.
6.5. © Metropolitan Museum of Art/Art Resource, NY.
6.6. © Dommuseum Hildesheim.
6.7. Burgerbibliothek, Bern.
6.8. Callwey Verlag.
6.9. National Gallery of Art, Washington DC. Open access.
6.10. Universitätsbibliothek, Basel.
6.11. National Gallery of Art, Washington DC. Open access.
6.12. © The Trustees of the British Museum. All rights reserved.
6.13–14. Warburg Institute Iconographic Database.
6.15. Bibliothèque royale de Belgique, Brussels.
6.16. Bibliothèque nationale de France, Paris.
6.17. Warburg Institute Iconographic Database.
6.18. Bibliothèque nationale de France, Paris.

Zone Books series design by Bruce Mau
Typesetting by Meighan Gale
Image placement and production by Julie Fry
Printed and bound by Maple Press